Political Criticism

Political Criticism

IAN SHAPIRO

University of California Press

BERKELEY   LOS ANGELES   OXFORD

University of California Press
Berkeley and Los Angeles, California

University of California Press, Ltd.
Oxford, England

First Paperback Printing 1992

Library of Congress Cataloging-in-Publication Data

Shapiro, Ian.
    Political criticism / Ian Shapiro.
      p. cm.
    Includes bibliographical references.
    ISBN 0-520-08032-7
    1. Political science—History—20th century. 2. Political
science—Philosophy. 3. Natural law. I. Title.
JA83.S476   1990
320'.01'1—dc20   89–27229
                                       CIP

Printed in the United States of America
1 2 3 4 5 6 7 8 9

For Xan and Yani

All men by nature desire to know.

Aristotle, *Metaphysics*

We no longer accept the values of a given period as absolute, and the realization that norms and values are historically and socially determined can henceforth never escape us. The ontological emphasis is now transferred to another set of problems. Its purpose will be to distinguish the true from the untrue, the genuine from the spurious among the norms, modes of thought, and patterns of behaviour that exist alongside of one another in a given historical period. The danger of "false consciousness" nowadays is not that it cannot grasp an absolute unchanging reality, but rather that it obstructs comprehension of a reality which is the outcome of constant reorganization of the mental processes which make up our worlds. . . . The attempt to escape ideological and utopian distortions is, in the last analysis, a quest for reality.

Karl Mannheim, *Ideology and Utopia*

The intellectual no longer has to play the role of an adviser. The project, tactics and goals to be adopted are a matter for those who do the fighting. What the intellectual can do is provide the instruments of analysis.

Michel Foucault, *Power/Knowledge*

Contents

Acknowledgments

It is a mark of true intellectual comradeship to help another make as well as possible an argument with which one is out of sympathy. In the course of writing this book I have been a fortunate beneficiary of this rare assistance from Christopher Lasch, Robert Fogelin, and Rogers Smith. Each has read large parts of the manuscript in various drafts, each has helped me to make the argument better and saved me from myself in more ways than I care to think about, and each will—for different reasons—still find much in the final version with which to argue. Without their continuing criticism, advice, and encouragement the present product would be immeasurably worse.

An earlier draft of the first three chapters was presented to the annual meeting of the American Political Science Association in 1985, where it benefited from the insightful comments of Nancy Rosenblum and William Galston. Chapter 5 derived comparable edification at the hands of the Boston chapter of the Conference for the Study of Political Thought in 1986, where the suggestions of Susan Okin and Josh Cohen were particularly helpful. An invitation to speak at the Columbia University American politics seminar in the same year provided useful stimulus in developing the main arguments of chapter 6; these were tried out once more at the conference on Liberalism and the Moral Life sponsored by the Conference for the Study of Political Thought in New York in the spring of 1988. Josh Cohen once again supplied helpful critical suggestions, as did Richard Ashcraft. The main argument of the last two chapters was presented at seminars at the Department of Political Science at Stanford University and at the Center for Advanced Study in the Behavioral Sciences in Palo Alto, where useful comments were received from Michael Dummett, Peter Evans, John Ferejohn, Norman Schofield, and Hans Weiler.

Colleagues at Yale University have been unwitting coauthors in more ways than they will, I hope, ever know. At faculty seminars they read and discussed various incarnations of much of the manuscript, never failing to come up with awkward questions and useful suggestions. In a host of less formal circumstances as well, discussions with many at Yale have been invaluable. Notably helpful have been exchanges with Bruce Ackerman, David Apter, Lea Brilmayer, Shelly Burtt, Jules Coleman, Bob Dahl, Joseph Hamburger, Victoria Hattam, Ed Lindblom, David Mayhew, David Plotke, Douglas Rae, Adolph Reed, Jr., James Scott, George Shulman, Stephen Skowronek, Steven Smith, Georgia Warnke, and Alexander Wendt. My good friends Jeffrey Isaac and John Kane also read substantial parts of the manuscript and made incisive suggestions at many points, as did the late Robert Cover. I would like to thank, without in any way implicating, all of the above.

The research assistance of Debra Morris and Laura Scalia is gratefully acknowledged, as is the editorial help of Kathleen Much, the secretarial assistance of Mary Whitney and Leslie Lindzey, and Carol Baxter's help with computers. At different times while working on this book I have received financial assistance from the Griswold Fund and the Social Science Faculty Research Fund at Yale, the John Simon Guggenheim Memorial Foundation, and the Center for Advanced Study in the Behavioral Sciences. Part of my support at the center was paid for by National Science Foundation grant number BNS87-00864. I am grateful for this support. Richard Holway, Amy Klatzkin, and William McClung of the University of California Press also deserve thanks for their skillful assistance in guiding the manuscript into print.

Finally I must thank Judy. With equanimity and good humor she tolerated the usual catalog of frustrations and inconveniences of being married to a writer. In addition, she put large parts of her own life on hold, embarked on a transcontinental drive to a strange city towing a trailer and a pair of one-year-olds, and devoted a year to the lion's share of child rearing. This supplied me with the leisure to complete this book in the magnificent environment at the Center for Advanced Study. Other spouses and other writers should be so fortunate.

Part One

Terms of the Problem

1 The Turn Away from Neo-Kantian Political Theory

Bernard Williams has conjectured that the impulse toward ambitious normative theorizing about politics is often generated by a sense of political urgency. In his view this at least partly explains why the regularly pronounced obituaries of political philosophy are invariably undone by events: fears that existing institutions face powerful threats and that prevailing practices are undergoing far-reaching changes create fertile soil for speculation about the fundamentals of politics and fuel the need to engage in it.[1]

On its face Williams's speculation helps account for the renaissance in political theory that began in the late 1960s, when John Rawls initiated a revival of the social contract tradition that had long been thought hopelessly defunct, dependent as it was on archaic assumptions about natural law and presocial man. Indeed, it was not only social contract theory that seemed of little more than antiquarian interest by the 1950s: most of what had historically been seen as political philosophy had fallen out of favor in the dominant intellectual culture.[2] In an oft-quoted introduction to the first volume of *Philosophy, Politics and Society*, Peter Laslett announced the death of political philosophy with a dramatic flourish in 1956; by this he meant the death of all normative theorizing about politics. The main alternatives to the natural rights tradition in Western political thought had been Marxism and utilitarianism, both of which were now widely believed to confront insuperable difficulties. The twentieth-century his-

---

1. For Williams's discussion, which I take out of context and embellish a little here, see Williams (1980: 57).
2. As one who has been unable to make any systematic sense of the difference in meaning between *political theory* and *political philosophy*, I use these terms interchangeably throughout.

tory of Marxism had rendered it both decreasingly plausible as an intellectual system and increasingly unattractive as a political program, whereas utilitarianism—with its moral instrumentalism and historical association with legal positivism—had fared little better in an intellectual world traumatized by Nazism and fascism and struggling to come to grips with postwar totalitarianism and the not-so-liberal-or-democratic liberal democracies. Metatheory and other forms of conceptual and linguistic analysis seemed to have won the day in universities partly by default; the last thing anyone would have predicted was the veritable explosion of first-order political theorizing ushered in by Rawls's work.[3]

Yet if first-order moral and political theory no longer seemed possible by the 1950s, there were few who seriously believed them to be unnecessary. The West might have recovered from the ravages of two world wars and the specter of fascism, and Americans might be experiencing a strong economic resurgence. But new threats loomed ominously. The postwar reality of nuclear weapons and cold war decisively laid to rest any utilitarian faith that might still have lingered in the idea that technical advances could in the fullness of time be expected to make moral problems obsolete. The Nuremburg trials held after the Second World War invoked the idea of "human rights" and "crimes against humanity" to justify the conviction of Nazi officials for their obedience to the positive legal system of the Third Reich, as had the Israelis to justify the abduction, trial, and conviction of Adolph Eichmann in 1961.[4] Just what the moral basis of these ideas was, however, was unclear. Moral theorists like R. M. Hare, who tried to generate the Kantian idea of universalizability from his metaethics, conceded that it could not deal with such "fanatics."[5] Yet the idea that the Nazis were a special case—troublesome for any moral theory and therefore safely ignored—was less than an answer to the problem of generating and justifying critical standards. As the 1960s wore on, Americans began to discover how alien and oppressive they were perceived to be in much of the world, and the term *war crimes* began to take on new and disconcertingly more parochial connotations as a result of the Vietnam war. At the same time, urban unrest and enduring poverty at home made the blessings of postwar liberal democracy, now undeniably dependent on

3. The dynamics at work in the retreat to metaethics can be seen in Stevenson's discussion of Hume's naturalism in *Ethics and Language*. See Stevenson (1944: 263, 275, 328, 332–36ff.). In 1952, R. M. Hare neatly summed up the now orthodox view that the business of moral philosophy is the clarification of moral terms by declaring ethics to be "the logical study of the language of morals" (Hare 1952: v). Toulmin (1953) also illustrates this genre.

4. For a useful, if controversial, account see Arendt (1963).

5. See Hare (1963: 106, 110, 112, 153, 159–85, 192–200, 219–22).

the continuing health of the capitalist order, seem mixed at best. In this period of growing unease about American legitimacy, when political and moral philosophers appeared to have argued themselves more or less dumb, it seemed to many intellectuals that some basic rethinking of the moral foundations of politics was inescapable. Rawls's work appeared to supply the tools to do just this: he seemed to rekindle the possibility of philosophically respectable, yet critical, thinking about the fundamentals of political association. Here was a philosophy that might fill the void between the moral demands of the time and the deafening silence about them that had been emanating from the academy for decades.[6]

A Theory of Justice immediately became an object of controversy. It was attacked, defended, admired, denounced, reformulated, imitated, and inevitably canonized as a by-product of the attention it received.[7] Like it or hate it, Rawls's work transformed the intellectual landscape in such a way that it could not be ignored. His ingenious contribution was to replace traditional natural law theory with a version of Kant's ethics as the moral basis for the social contract and to displace its conventional assumptions about presocial man with his argument from the "original position," a thought experiment about the political and economic institutions people might be brought to agree on when kept in ignorance of certain key facts about the actual social world and their places in it.

Rawls argued that there was a unique solution to this problem: people would choose his "general conception" of distributive justice over the alternative possibilities under the relevant conditions specified in the thought experiment. Rawls's general conception requires the equal distribution of all social goods unless an unequal distribution operates to the benefit of all, social goods having been broadly defined to include "liberties and opportunities, income and wealth, and the social bases of self-respect."[8] More specific principles were then derived from this general conception with the help of gradually revealed additional information

6. I do not mean to suggest that Rawls's was the only intellectual response to the perceived crisis in American legitimacy to gain currency during the 1960s. After decades of relative obscurity, Marcuse and Habermas became well-known intellectual figures almost overnight in 1968, and books like Robert Paul Wolff's *In Defense of Anarchism,* published in 1970 and clearly motivated by a sense of crisis in legitimacy spawned by the events of the 1960s, enjoyed considerable attention.

7. Although Rawls's book was not published until 1971, it had begun to have its impact before this. Parts of its central argument had been published in journals in the late 1950s and 1960s. See, for example, Rawls (1962: 132–57). Much of the manuscript of *A Theory of Justice* had been widely circulated during the 1960s.

8. For the general conception of distributive justice, see Rawls (1971: 62), and for the account of primary goods (ibid.: 62, 90–95).

about the actual world inhabited by protagonists making the choice, although new information could never be employed to alter the general conception itself. In this way Rawls came up with his two principles of justice (one dealing with liberties and the basic structure of political institutions, one dealing with the distribution of opportunities, income, and wealth), with rules for resolving conflicts among subordinate principles and with an account of the basic structure of governmental institutions. The method seemed to render it possible to design an entire institutional system and political economy as a result of impartial reasoning imposed by the "veil of ignorance."[9] If the reasoning was sound, if Rawls's conception or something like it was the choice that rational people must make under the relevant conditions of ignorance, it would generate not only a standard that was universalizable in Kant's sense (and therefore consistent with respecting the autonomy of all) but a yardstick for the principled evaluation of existing institutions and practices.[10]

Many who were not persuaded by every aspect of Rawls's argument were nonetheless impressed by this possibility. In 1974 Robert Nozick published *Anarchy, State and Utopia* in which he argued—also from the standpoint of hypothetical social contract theory—that the unique institutional result of voluntary individual choices in a prepolitical world would be the night watchman state of classical liberal theory, "limited to the functions of protecting all its citizens against violence, theft, and fraud, and the enforcement of contracts." Every other possible state (including Rawls's), he argued, engaged in forcible redistributions of wealth and therefore the coercion of some; none was therefore compatible with Kant's requirement that the autonomy of all be respected.[11] Before Nozick wrote, Robert Paul Wolff had already employed Nozick-like reasoning to argue that if Kant's concept of autonomy meant requiring unanimity (which he thought it did), then no political institution could ever be legitimate. Every state coerces at least some of its members some of the time, he noted, and as a result Kant's ethics impose on us a moral obligation to

9. For Rawls's account of the two principles of justice and their derivation, see (ibid.: 54–117), of their lexical rankings (ibid.: 41–45, 61–83) and of the device of the veil of ignorance (ibid.: 12, 19, 136–42).

10. I do not claim to have done full justice to the complexities of Rawls's arguments here or to those of the other neo-Kantians in the summary account that follows. For that the reader is referred to my more extensive discussion in Shapiro (1986: 151–306).

11. The quotation appears in Nozick (1974: 26). For Nozick's derivation of the minimal state as the unique solution to a choice of basic political institutions that can meet the requirement of unanimity, see (ibid.: 10–146); for his critique of Rawls, see (ibid.: 183–231).

reject them all and to become philosophical anarchists.[12] Without appealing directly to Kant, Bruce Ackerman took Rawls's procedural insight to a new extreme by turning the choice problem into one in which people arriving at an uninhabited planet on a spaceship must decide how their new society is to be run. Ackerman devised a set of procedural constraints on their hypothetical constitutional deliberations designed to rule out the imperialism of any particular person's conception of the good and tried to show that argument engaged in within these constraints would generate support for a determinate system of recognizably liberal institutions. In a similar vein Ronald Dworkin tried to reason about the fundamentals of distributive justice by reference to how a group of shipwrecked survivors on a deserted island might allocate resources. He argued that the survivors would divide up all resources by auction and then devise a scheme to compensate people for enduring inequalities of resources by speculating about the cost of insuring against being afflicted by them *ex ante*. Various other reworkings of the basic logic of Rawlsian theory were also attempted.[13]

Rawls's argument thus became a catalyst for a remarkable explosion of academic theorizing about the moral foundations of politics.[14] Four more volumes of *Philosophy, Politics and Society* had followed the first, effectively revealing Laslett's declaration to be premature at best. Special issues of academic journals began to be devoted to political theory in general and to Rawls in particular.[15] New journals like *Political Theory, History of Political Thought, Democracy,* and *Philosophy and Public Affairs* appeared. Teaching positions in political philosophy began to open up in political science and philosophy departments and even in law schools, and undergraduate courses in political theory became among the most heavily subscribed.[16] By the early 1980s all the signs of a vital, interesting, and contentious revival of the discipline of first-order political theory were in place.

12. See Wolff (1970), especially chapters 1 and 2.

13. For Ackerman's defense of his procedural constraints, see Ackerman (1980: 3–30), and for Dworkin's account see Dworkin (1981a: 185–246 and 1981b: 283–345). For another example of the reworking of the method and substance of Rawls's argument, see Rae (1975: 630–47 and 1979: 134–54). For useful summaries of, and contributions to, much of this literature, see Daniels (1975), Fishkin (1979), and Mueller (1979: 227–49).

14. One indication of the extent of Rawls's influence is an annotated bibliography that appeared in 1982 listing 2,511 entries of discussions by and about Rawls. See Wellbank et al. (1982).

15. See, for one of the earliest examples, the special issue of the *American Political Science Review* 69, no. 2, published in 1975.

16. For a useful account of Rawls's impact on jurisprudence, see Parker (1979: 269–95).

If we take Williams's speculation on trust as part of a causal account of the Rawlsian revolution, two further observations naturally follow that set the terms of the problem that concerns me here. The first is that any sense of political urgency that afflicted the intelligentsia of the Anglo-American world in the late 1960s and early 1970s has endured. Although the Reagan era seemed for a time to be heralding a new age of optimism, by the mid-1980s its fervor was mainly spent on superficial symbolism, and the underlying political and social problems of the postwar era began to reassert themselves. Public discussion focused once again on a litany of seemingly intractable problems: social dislocations caused by the requirements of modern industrial production, growing political demands and economic competition from the Third World, regional wars perpetually threatening to escalate into global conflict, potentially catastrophic changes in the environment wrought by the imperatives of modern technological production, manifest corruption and concomitant declining legitimacy in the political process and the financial system, and accumulating evidence of major rifts in the social fabric wrought by the interconnected problems of a growing urban underclass, rampant crime and drug use, and apparently intractable fiscal problems for the maintenance of the welfare state. Many of these problems seemed to reinforce one another, producing a growing sense of social and political unease. Despite little agreement on a precise diagnosis or cure, few in the early 1990s would dispute the claim that the United States and the Western world face social, economic, and political problems at least as serious as any since the Second World War.[17]

Yet if our collective sense of political urgency has deepened (my second observation), a widespread and deep-rooted dissatisfaction has also emerged with the style and content of theorizing that characterized the neo-Kantian revolution of Rawls, his followers, and even many of his critics. Perhaps as a symptom of this dissatisfaction, the sense in which there is a Rawlsian "genre" of political theory is now much in dispute, as is the degree to which his work is, or is any longer, or needs to be, committed to any of Kant's moral arguments, issues that have not been clarified as Rawls himself has substantially altered the various formulations of his argument over the years. Yet in the eyes of many of its critics at least, there is an identifiable style of political theory that gets labeled "neo-Kantian" in the literature, albeit with some mutual injustice to Kant and to those contemporary writers who are identified with him. This genre of work is held by many to be seriously inadequate in at least four respects.

17. For my own account, see Shapiro and Kane (1983: 5–39).

There is great skepticism, first, concerning the neo-Kantians' much-debated aspiration toward a moral neutralism: their search for principles of justice or social organization that can be justified as neutral among different persons, conceptions of the good, and even institutional modes of political organization.[18] Sometimes this skepticism rests on arguments that Rawls's "thin theory" of the good is considerably thicker than he is willing to grant. Sometimes it rests on criticism of Nozickian claims that the Pareto-superior trades of the market constitute the only distributive mechanism that does not involve coercion and paternalistic "moral balancing acts" by the state. Sometimes it rests on arguments that Ackerman's "neutrality" requirement is not neutral among competing conceptions of the good, as he claims. Whatever the particular formulation of the anti-neutrality claim, there is a growing sense not only that all these particular attempts fail but that the whole idea of moral neutrality as a virtue of social institutions is chimerical. It is argued that the Enlightenment aspiration "to provide neutral, impersonal tradition-independent standards of rational judgment" (MacIntyre 1988: 395) must be abandoned. People doubt that neutrality is feasible or desirable.[19]

Second, there is widespread disaffection with the neo-Kantians' failure to offer a satisfying account of political community. The characteristic tendency of the neo-Kantians analytically to separate the self from its cultural affiliations and purposes, in order to include the latter among the objects of moral and political deliberation, is thought deeply to distort social reality while loading the dice in favor of familiar atomistic liberal outcomes. Most systematically elaborated by Michael Sandel, this concern has been raised innumerable times and is an obvious (and acknowledged) source of the renewed interest in Aristotelianism that we find in the writings of William Galston and Alasdair MacIntyre, of Michael Walzer's attempt to give substantive content to the ideal of a liberal community, and of the growing interest in Hegelian political philosophy.[20] Argu-

18. The limiting case of this is perhaps Rawls's (1971: 265–74) claim that his principles of justice are neutral between capitalist and socialist economic institutions. For a heroic attempt to render this argument plausible, see DiQuattro (1983: 53–78). For criticism, see Shapiro (1986: 266–70).

19. For a cogent formulation of this argument see Galston (1983: 621–29). See also Kane (1982), Cohen (1978: 246–62; 1986: 108–35), and, specifically on Ackerman's neutrality principle, Thigpen and Downing (1983: 585–99).

20. Sandel (1982; 1984a: 81–96), Galston (1980), MacIntyre (1984), Walzer (1983a). On the resurgence of Hegel studies in Anglo-American political theory, see Taylor (1979), Charvet (1981), Smith (1987: 99–126; 1989), and Rapaczynski (1987). For other examples of the revival of interest in community see Newell (1984: 775–84), Beer (1984: 361–86), Kateb (1984: 331–60), Hirsch (1986: 151–305), and Yack (1985: 92–112).

ments for the so-called priority of right have been shown many times to rest on implicit conceptions of what constitutes a good political community. As a result people want to confront this question openly and argue over it, not use original positions, adumbrated versions of Locke's state of nature, and spaceships to smuggle undefended assumptions about the good community into premises that are then held to render them unnecessary.

There is disaffection, third, with the neo-Kantians' search for substantive principles of social organization that are deontological in form. Sometimes this disaffection surfaces as skepticism toward pure proceduralism, toward the idea that some set of putatively rational procedures for choosing substantive principles can be specified independently of the content of those principles. Sometimes it emerges in the form of arguments that it is to misuse Kant to suppose that the categorical imperative can generate any substantive principles of political organization. Sometimes it is expressed as plain incredulity at the project of trying to specify principles of politics independently of empirical and historical considerations. In these and other formulations there is a growing sense of the futile irrelevance of the variants of "ideal theory." The whole project of working out principles in the abstract and then descending to the "second-best" situations of the actual world to see how they measure up is thought to be unworkable and misguided.[21]

People are concerned, last, with the ideological dimensions of the neo-Kantian arguments. The appeals to moral consensus behind their various doctrines of hypothetical consent all too easily become "thinly disguised ideology or a rhetorically effective exposition of individual prejudice" (Galston 1980: ix). These arguments hide so many (invariably controversial) substantive commitments in sophisticated attributions to some stylized consensus that they are readily vulnerable to the charge that they do little more than peddle the values those substantive commitments serve. To those not predisposed to those values, this seems pernicious at least: the arguments massage the prejudices of those who agree with them in advance while confirming the opposition of those who do not. For all their internal sophistication and complexity, the arguments of the neo-Kantians fail to come to terms with this charge. We are left with a sediment of enduring skepticism about whether they can generate principled standards for critical engagement with the political problems of everyday life.[22]

If my double observation—that the sense of political urgency that

---

21. For further discussion of this, see Shapiro (1986: 281–82, 295–97).
22. This is argued for at length in (ibid.: 273–305).

fueled the neo-Kantian revolution has deepened while many of us have lost faith in its products—is correct, a further question arises: can there be an alternative political theory and, if so, what will it be like? This is my question. And it is a big one, because if there is a wide consensus on the inadequacies of the neo-Kantians, there is an equally wide dissensus on what to do instead. In the next five chapters I analyze the critical reaction to the neo-Kantians by examining representative works from some of the main directions in which political theorists who are running from Rawls are heading: toward a renewed concern with issues of convention and cultural interpretation and toward a revitalized attention to the history of ideas by theorists who do not see themselves exclusively as historians. The writers I examine differ greatly from one another both over what they take the problems of politics to be and over how those problems should be dealt with. Nevertheless, they share a basic antipathy toward the style and content of the political thinking spawned by the rationalist philosophies of the seventeenth and eighteenth centuries, which were appealed to and approached a new zenith in the neo-Kantian revival of the 1970s. The arguments examined here also differ greatly from one another in their merits, generating useful building blocks but also warnings of pitfalls to be avoided in the construction of an alternative conception of political theory.

I begin with a consideration of the conventionalist arguments of Richard Rorty and Michael Walzer. In chapter 2 I argue that despite the plausibility of Rorty's case against neo-Kantian foundationalism, his pragmatist appeal requires a realist foundational commitment if what is attractive in it is to be rendered plausible. Rorty's failure to see this allows him to commit himself to a conventionalist view of politics that is neither justifiable nor attractive because it makes principled critical argument all but impossible. I show that Rorty's explicit claims about politics do not follow from his conventionalism; instead they result from his privileging of a particular mix of elitist liberal and not-so-liberal political prejudices, in support of which strategy neither argument nor evidence is ever adduced. The absence of social consensus on the desirability of Rorty's values feeds into my more general claim that appeals to consensus alone never generate satisfying standards for critical argument in politics. Even in rare cases where there is consensus, I argue, there are often good reasons for being suspicious of it.

In chapter 3 I argue that Walzer's interpretivist view is superior to Rorty's because it is grounded in a plausible theory of the dynamics of ideological conflict and because Walzer recognizes that much politics results from disagreement about the basic definitions of social goods. But I argue that Walzer fails to link this descriptive account to his normative argument in a compelling way and that as a result this argument must in the end be rejected. Although Walzer's general account of social criticism is plausibly defended against competing conceptions of the enterprise of political theory, his particular account of connected criticism runs into serious difficulties if it is conceived of as anything more than a set of strategic injunctions for making criticism effective. Even on this narrowly strategic interpretation, I argue, there will be circumstances in which Walzer's view should be resisted. Thus although Walzer makes a powerful general case for the desirability of particularism in moral and political argument, his particular particularist account fails to persuade. At the end of chapter 3 we are left with the difficulty that conventionalist appeals in moral and political argument are indeterminate and the acknowledged need for some as yet unsupplied device for furnishing social criticism with principled critical bite.

Next I explore variants of the claim that critical bite in the analysis of social practices is best supplied by looking at them historically. To commit to this claim is a common move for those who both sense the indeterminacy of mere contextualism and remain skeptical of the viability of neo-Kantian theoretical projects; turning to history seems to hold out the hope of generating critical standards without falling into what is taken to be the mire of abstract deontological argument. Yet the appeal to history is often more of a conversation stopper than an argument. What makes an approach genuinely historical is by no means obvious and is perhaps now more vigorously contested than it has been for several decades. My heuristic strategy involves dividing such arguments into three main sorts: those that appeal to the authority of the past and of who are held to be its most important theorists (discussed via an analysis of Allan Bloom's account of the tradition of political theory in chapter 4), those that appeal to the history of ideas in a causal and genetic sense as a way of comprehending—and in some formulations liberating ourselves from—dominant contemporary modes of thought and action (dealt with through a discussion of Alasdair MacIntyre's views in chapter 5), and those that appeal to history as a source of alternative political beliefs and practices (dealt with by reference to J. G. A. Pocock's account of the civic republican tradition in chapter 6). Each of these views of politics is ultimately rejected and with them the claim that there is something unique to historical analysis that can generate critical bite in the analysis of contemporary politics. Yet my discussions of Bloom, MacIntyre, and Pocock reveal particular arguments and insights of which account must be taken in the construction of an alternative view.

Bloom's claim that the tradition of political theory can generate authoritative standards that conventionalist (and other contemporary) views lack is revealed to be false. His depiction of the tradition is both unpersuasive in its own terms and sufficiently broad that it generates problems of indeterminacy that parallel those of conventionalist appeals. Although I endorse Bloom's claim that political philosophy should be geared to discovery of the truth, I reject the distinction between esoteric and exoteric meanings that he takes from Leo Strauss and with it the claim that appeals to the truth—being the preserve of an intellectual elite—have no place in politics. This eventually leads me to argue that although there are frequently tensions between rationalist programs in politics and the discovery of the truth as Bloom asserts, these tensions have quite different political implications than he supposes.

MacIntyre and Pocock describe views of politics that are both traceable (by different lineages) to Aristotle and presented as alternatives to what is seen as a more or less hegemonic liberal political paradigm. Although I show that both views confront serious inadequacies when viewed as normative political theory, my analysis of them opens the way to defense and advocacy of a different neo-Aristotelian view. I argue that MacIntyre's claim that the Aristotelian tradition provides a coherent moral scheme that would permit us to settle the sorts of disputes that typically divide us is implausible, as is his argument that turning to the history of Aristotelianism can by itself generate viable critical standards for political argument. I also reject MacIntyre's causal-historical thesis as unpersuasive at best and argue that his prescriptive proposals are both hopelessly utopian and at variance with the spirit of his Aristotelian account of social practices.

The civic republican tradition described by Pocock is also found wanting as a source of critical standards for contemporary political argument. I argue that Pocock's claim that it presents us with an alternative paradigm to the liberal one cannot be sustained, and I show that little in the way of a distinctive politics can credibly be argued to flow from it. As matters of both history and theory, the republican worldview can be shown to be compatible with virtually every politics from far left to far right and with polities as different as ancient city-states, feudal regimes, and modern territorial states. I argue that the few distinctive political commitments that can be shown to flow from the republican view are morally unattractive in today's world and that they should be rejected. The civic republican reading of Aristotelianism avoids the utopianism of MacIntyre's rendition of it, but at the price of turning Aristotelianism into an instrumentalist politics, thinly cloaked in the language of civic virtue.

The reading of Aristotelianism I defend in the final chapters falls between these extremes. I suggest that an Aristotelian conception of human nature—suitably modified by what we know today about the world, human beings, and the nature of knowledge—is superior to the going alternatives and credible as a basis for political argument. As a prelude to this in chapter 7 I reconsider the four common complaints against the neo-Kantians mentioned earlier in this chapter in light of the intervening analysis.

I find that many specific contentions of the anti-Kantians are valid and that the sense of unease with the neo-Kantian project that often motivates those contentions is well founded. But I reject the general repudiation of foundational theory into which their arguments are frequently swept. If the anti-Kantians are to avoid difficulties comparable to the ones they attack, I argue, commitment to a variant of philosophical realism is inescapable. As it is, many self-styled antifoundationalists commit the fallacy of identifying one bad kind of foundational argument with all attempts to provide adequate foundations for our beliefs. Because we cannot find a secure basis for all knowledge in deductive introspection or transcendental argument, so the argument goes, we should abandon the enterprise. I argue that this makes about as much sense as saying that because there is no single type of foundation on which all buildings, whatever their size, function, and location, can be built to last forever, we should henceforth build all buildings with no foundations at all. They would, then, of course, all quickly fall over. This comparison alerts us to the straw quality of many of the arguments that confront one another in the debates between foundationalists and contextualists. Much metatheoretical huffing and puffing on both sides amounts to the opposition to one another of gross concepts: misleading abstractions that appear attractive only while attention is focused on the evident defects of the contrary misleading abstraction.

The comparison with physical foundations is also useful because it alerts us to the fact that although everything might in some ultimate sense be contingent (as people like Richard Rorty continually remind us),[23] this may be a quite trivial truth. That no building will endure forever tells us nothing about the relative merits of different kinds of construction. Yet I argue that questions of this latter order, in the realm of the relatively enduring, should occupy our attention. The antifoundational claim diverts attention from them by provoking, and getting mired in, artificial debates about questions that have little significance for political theory.

23. See, for instance, Rorty (1986a, 1986b, and 1986c).

In chapter 8 I lay out my own view, which I call *critical naturalism*, contrast it with the principal alternative contenders, and explain some of its consequences for political and social theory. My view is rooted in a realist conception of knowledge and science that presumes the world to consist of causal mechanisms that human beings can reasonably aspire to understand. Because philosophical realism is a foundational view about the nature and reliability of scientific knowledge, the critical naturalist account does not follow deductively from it. Rather the commitment to philosophical realism makes possible a defense of critical naturalism and places some constraints on the kind of defense that can be sustained. But the defense itself rests on corrigible empirical claims about human nature, interests, and the causal structure of human interaction for which arguments and evidence must be independently adduced. In the service of advancing toward this latter goal, I adopt a philosophical psychology—much modified—from Aristotle, argue for its plausibility and attractiveness, and defend it against the main competing views of the human condition available to political theorists today. My view is argued to be more credible than MacIntyre's utopian Aristotelianism, but it does not collapse into the morally unattractive instrumentalism characteristic of the civic humanist view.

In the final chapter I sketch some central moral and political implications of my account of critical naturalism, defending the claim that there is a basic human interest in acting authentically, that is, in knowing and acting on the truth. I argue further that this interest in authentic action is likely to be best served by a commitment to a democratic political ethos of a particular sort, if for reasons different from those generally advanced in defense of democratic practices. I discuss the consequences of this ethos for arguments about the basic structure of political institutions, although no particular institutional arrangements are defended here. I conclude with a discussion of the implications of critical naturalism for the conduct of political theory, defending a view of the enterprise as principled social criticism geared toward the promotion of authentic action. I explain the advantages of this view over Walzer's account of connected criticism, and I discuss some of its implications for the conduct of political argument. These are claims to be more fully developed elsewhere, but I have tried to supply more than a promissory note so that the reader can get a sense of the agenda opened up by what is basically a ground-clearing book.

A word on argumentative style. In this book I analyze and compare various arguments as part of a discursive attempt to incorporate what is useful in each into an alternative view. The author of any such work confronts a basic choice between either characterizing arguments in general terms and discussing them without worrying much about attributing them to anyone in particular, or intensively discussing the views of particular authors that he takes to be representative of the arguments with which he is concerned. Volume one of Roberto Unger's *Politics* and Alasdair MacIntyre's *After Virtue* embody the first approach; Jürgen Habermas's *The Philosophical Discourse of Modernity* and Michael Sandel's use of Rawls as the central target for a critique of modern liberalism exemplify the second. Both methods have their advantages and attendant dangers: the first allows one to cover a great deal of ground, but it often provokes charges that no one actually holds the view in question so that critical discussion of it exhibits a straw or artificial quality. The second approach invites more intensive analytical discussion of particular views, but it frequently triggers the response that other formulations are more powerful than the one discussed or that the author examined was concerned with a narrow class of problems and that one cannot, therefore, legitimately generalize much from a discussion of those views. I have adopted the second method of analysis, although in deference to the spirit of the first all the authors I have chosen to discuss have substantially influenced debates about politics in the past decade—in some cases, perhaps, when they would rather not have done so.[24] It is out of my critical examinations of these views that I build my own argument. As to how successful this discursive method is, I urge the reader to take it on trust and let the pudding prove itself proverbially.

24. Pocock does not conceive of his account of civic republicanism as prescriptive political theory. Just how his historical narrative has become part of the contemporary debate is taken up in chapter 6.

Part Two

Placing Conventions in
Political Argument

2 Liberalism and Postmodernism

"Success comes to political ideas," one group of theorists tells us, "not when they are justified in seminar and speech, but at the moment of their application to life and society." These authors begin their analysis of equality with an elaboration of the logical grammar of everyday conceptions of it "by analyzing the meanings of equality as they appear in actual efforts to promote it." Our attention is directed not to the complexities that arise "*within* the abstract idea of equality but in its confrontation with the world" (Rae et al. 1981: 1–4).[1] Another writer warns us that although justice and equality "can conceivably be worked out as philosophical artifacts. . . . a just or an egalitarian society cannot be. If such a society isn't already here—hidden, as it were, in our concepts and categories—we will never know it concretely or realize it in fact" (Walzer 1983a: xiv). These authors are looking for a fundamentally different starting point for political thinking than that presupposed in the deontological tradition. In contrast to its abstract idealism, its quest for general principles to which a recalcitrant world must somehow be made to measure up (or scolded for failing so to do), they hold that we should work instead from the ground up: understand the conventional beliefs that make up existing political culture as a precondition for normative discussion of any kind.[2] The motivations behind, and purposes of, such projects vary con-

---

1. Unless otherwise indicated, all italics in quotations follow the original, as in this case. Parentheses in quotations also follow the original; my insertions are in square brackets.
2. It might be argued that Rawls's conception of reflective equilibrium is intended to serve a purpose of this kind and that I am consequently overstating the difference between him and his critics on this point. Thus Timmons (1987: 595) depicts Rawls's view as antifoundationalist because it rests on a "coherence view of ethical justification" called "wide reflective equilibrium," and Rorty (1988: 257–

siderably, but they share a general skepticism toward disembodied moral theorizing and a conviction that our (perhaps insatiable) impulse toward thinking in general terms must somehow be grounded in and harnessed by conventional political discourse if it is to generate a political theory that avoids the weaknesses characteristic of the deontological tradition.

One of the most persistent and articulate defenders of the view that American liberalism should abandon its search for Kantian foundations, indeed that it should jettison all preoccupation with foundational questions, is Richard Rorty. Although he grounds his analysis partly in an appeal to the pragmatist writings of Quine and Dewey, he links it more centrally to recent postmodernist arguments against the idea of philosophical justification as such.

I. Rorty's View: Exposition

In a series of papers written during the past decade, Rorty has sought to work out the political implications of his account of the malaise of contemporary philosophy he offered in *Philosophy and the Mirror of Nature* in 1979. His goal has been to describe a politics he thinks we should embrace once we wholeheartedly reject foundationalist philosophical aspirations. He advances two main lines of argument, negative and positive, to establish this, both of which are connected to his analysis of the philosophical muddles of the Enlightenment on which he thinks the neo-Kantian project rests. We must follow him, therefore, in his journey from philosophical diagnosis to political prescription if we are to see both the force and the limitations of his argument.

(i) The Negative Argument

In its stripped-down form, the negative argument is that general theoretical systems do not work and that consequently general moral and political arguments must fail too. The kinds of difficulties that have, for example, been identified in Rawls's attempts to present his principles as "procedural expressions of the categorical imperative" or as a kind of "Kantian constructivism" will attend all such attempts at general moral systems derived from metatheories or "metanarratives" about knowledge and/or existence. The trouble with Kantians like Rawls and Ronald Dworkin, from Rorty's perspective, is that they "want to keep an ahistorical morality-

---

82) has recently recanted his earlier disagreements with Rawls, whom he now portrays as rejecting the Kantian project in an Hegelian spirit not only in his more recent writings but in *A Theory of Justice* as well. These arguments are taken up and rejected below.

prudence distinction as a buttress for the institutions and practices of the surviving democracies" (Rorty 1983: 583).[3] Whether these metanarratives are geared to an endorsement of the liberal status quo, to conservative criticism of it, or to the emancipatory criticism sought after by Habermas, they will fail because there are no metanarratives, there is no consistent and increasingly general structure to our moral (and other) discourse, potentially or in fact. Only the Kantian expectations with which we have all been imbued lead us to expect that there should be (Rorty 1984a: 15–16; 1984b: 32–34).

Although different postmodernist writers ("Posties" as Rorty endearingly dubs them)[4] see their projects differently, they share a deep distrust of all metanarratives and a concomitant rejection of the modernist preoccupation with discovering and justifying the "right" one from first principles. Rorty's view rests on a more radical version of the hermeneutical claim than the arguments of Habermas, Karl-Otto Apel, and Peter Winch, all of whom see the interpretive component as distinguishing the human from the natural sciences. In contrast he wants to model all knowledge on Thomas Kuhn's conception of the natural sciences as "theory-laden," to argue that there is no scientific model of true justified belief that the human sciences should emulate for fear of being declared unscientific.[5] All knowledge must be understood in hermeneutical terms, and explanations in the natural sciences are in this sense continuous with all forms of explanation. We have to accept that there are no criteria external to our beliefs to which appeal can be made to justify those beliefs. For the pragmatist "knowledge," like "truth," is inevitably internal to our system of beliefs; use of either term indicates "simply a compliment paid to the beliefs which we think so well justified that, for the moment, further justification is not needed" (Rorty 1984a: 5). It is not a matter of finding the right deductive system or the right general principles: there are no second-order principles to be found. Moral and political belief, like all belief, is not like that. The supposition that it is rests on confusions that have bedeviled Western philosophy at least since Descartes and is closely

3. It is not clear that Rorty would continue to stand by all aspects of this assessment of Rawls, as is discussed below.

4. Rorty uses this term in his review of Habermas's *Der Philosophische Diskurs der Moderne* in the *London Review of Books*, September 3, 1987, pp. 11–12.

5. See Kuhn (1962). Kuhn deals primarily with the natural sciences, treating the social sciences as "preparadigmatic," and it is therefore ironic that philosophers and social theorists have been primarily interested in his views from the standpoint of the human sciences. See, for example, Lakatos and Musgrave (1970). For a useful account of the differences among Rorty, Gadamer, Apel, Habermas, and Taylor on the natural versus the human sciences, see Warnke (1987: 141–51).

connected to the Enlightenment preoccupation with the chimerical search for certainty, the search for unassailable foundations for what we take to be our knowledge—both of ourselves and of the external world.

In Rorty's view, to think of knowledge as presenting a "problem" about which we ought to have a "theory" is fundamentally misconceived.[6] Our "obsession" with foundational questions is traceable to the seventeenth-century predisposition toward representational theories of knowledge, which derive initially from Descartes's "invention" of the mind, his "co-alescence of beliefs and sensations into Lockean ideas" that provided a field of inquiry seemingly more fundamental than that which had concerned the Ancients, a field "within which certainty, as opposed to mere opinion, was possible." This project was "eventually . . . christened epistemology" when Kant "put philosophy" on the "secure path" of a science by "putting outer space inside inner space (the space of the constituting activity of the transcendental ego)," which enabled him to claim "Cartesian certainty about the inner for the laws of what had previously been the outer." Kant thus turned the study of the foundations of knowledge into a "non-empirical" project, a matter for "armchair reflection, independent of phys-iological discoveries and capable of producing necessary truths"; turned philosophy into the queen of the sciences; and "reconciled the Cartesian claim that we can have certainty only about our ideas with the fact that we already had certainty. . . . about what seemed not to be ideas" (Rorty 1979: 136–64). As Rorty sums up his history of modern philosophy,

> Once upon a time we felt a need to worship something that lay beyond the visible world. Beginning in the sev-enteenth century, we tried to substitute a love of truth for a love of God, treating the world described by science as quasi-divinity. Beginning at the end of the eighteenth century, we tried to substitute a love of ourselves for a love of scientific truth, a worship of our own deep spiritual or poetic nature, treated as one more quasi-divinity. (Rorty 1986a: 6)

In Rorty's view this preoccupation with foundationalism structures the dominant paradigm of post–seventeenth-century Western philosophical thought, and if his critique parallels Hegel's critique of epistemology, as William Connolly (1983: 124–34) has suggested, the question arises as to what the paradigm should be replaced with, since Hegel's teleology and objective idealism are not available to Rorty. Rorty's basic solution to this conundrum is that epistemology should not be replaced, it should simply be given up. We must abandon the preoccupation with whether truth is

6. The remainder of this paragraph is drawn from Shapiro (1982: 550–51).

grounded in the mind or in the world, with language operating as a kind of mediator. We must simply dispense with "the picture of language as a third thing intervening between self and reality" and the idea that if only we could get straight on how the mechanism of intervention operates we would have an unassailable epistemology. We must accept, with Donald Davidson, that there is no point of privileged insight or apodictic certainty. "To say that one's previous language was inappropriate for dealing with some segment of the world (for example, the starry heavens above, or the raging passions within) is just to say that one is now, having learned a new language, able to handle that segment more easily." For,

> as long as we think that "the world" names something which we ought to respect as well as cope with, something which is person-like in that it has a preferred description of itself, we shall insist that any philosophical account of truth save the "intuition" that truth is "out there." This intuition amounts to the vague sense that it would be hubris on our part to abandon the traditional language of "respect for fact" and "objectivity"—that it would be risky and blasphemous not to see the scientist (or the philosopher, or the poet, or *somebody*) as having a priestly function, as putting us in touch with a realm which transcends the human. (Rorty 1986a: 5, 6)

To advance the claim that we should abandon epistemology as it has traditionally been understood, Rorty distinguishes "systematic" from "edifying" philosophy—which distinction is intended to correspond to Kuhn's opposition of "normal" to "revolutionary" science. Systematic philosophers operate within a paradigm according to the rules of truth and reference that it dictates. Edifying philosophers, in contrast, reject such rules and are not concerned with truth at all. For such philosophers (in the present century this means Wittgenstein, Heidegger, and Dewey), the point of philosophy "is to keep the conversation going rather than to find objective truth. Such truth . . . is the normal result of normal discourse" (Rorty 1979: 5, 10–11, 376–89). As a necessary precondition for edification in Rorty's sense, we must accept and embrace the radical contingency of ourselves, our languages, and our communities. Again following Davidson he argues that we need "to get to the point where we no longer worship anything, where we treat nothing as a quasi-divinity, where we treat everything—our language, our conscience, our community—as products of time and chance" (Rorty 1986a: 6). Much underlaboring in philosophy and the human sciences over the past century has made this a realistic possibility:

Contemporary intellectuals have given up the Enlightenment assumption that religion, myth, and tradition can be
opposed to something ahistorical, something common to
all human beings qua human. Anthropologists and historians of science have blurred the distinction between innate
rationality and the products of acculturation. Philosophers such as Heidegger and Gadamer have given us ways
of seeing human beings as historical all the way through.
Other philosophers, such as Quine and Davidson, have
blurred the distinctions between permanent truths of reason and temporary truths of fact. Psychoanalysis has
blurred the distinctions between conscience and the emotions of love, hate, and fear, and thus the distinction between morality and prudence. The result is to erase the
picture of the self common to Greek metaphysics, Christian theology and Enlightenment rationalism: the picture
of an ahistorical natural center, the locus of human dig-
nity, surrounded by an adventitious and inessential periphery. (Rorty 1988: 258)

It is Freudian psychoanalysis, above all, that gives us the capacity to
grasp our absolute contingency. The "common-sense Freudianism of contemporary culture" makes it possible to see our consciences as one of the
random experiments of nature, "to identify conscience with guilt over re-
pressed infantile sexual impulses—repressions which are the products of
countless contingencies that never enter experience." In short, Freud
"makes moral deliberation just as finely-grained . . . as prudential calculation has always been" and thereby "helps break down the distinction
between moral guilt and practical inadvisability, blurring the prudence-
morality distinction into invisibility" (Rorty 1986b: 12). Once we conceive of and accept ourselves as contingent experiments in this way, we can
be liberated from the compulsion to think that morality, like knowledge,
must rest on apodictic foundations, discoverable by "the correct" scientific
philosophy, and open ourselves to the possibilities of edification.

Whether or not Rorty thinks everyone has the capacity to take up edifying philosophy is not clear, but in many places he writes as if this were
so. His essential claim is that once we come to see that the dominant mode
of post–seventeenth-century thinking, with its central commitment to the
search for apodictic certainty, is a "normal" discourse, we can give it up.
Once we come to understand the Cartesian and Lockean confusions that
generated this way of thinking, we will see that not only is it "optional"
but so is epistemology, "and so is philosophy as it has understood itself
since the middle of the last century." Once we realize this we can replace
philosophy with hermeneutics and be satisfied with interpretive dis-

course that "keeps the conversation going." We need to study the history of ideas to get to this point, but its basic purpose is therapeutic: "Just as the patient needs to relive his past to answer his questions, so philosophy needs to relive its past in order to answer *its* questions" (Rorty 1979: 136, 33).

Yet most of us have not learned this lesson. In modern secular culture the priest has been replaced by the scientist, who is now "seen as the person who keeps humanity in touch with something beyond itself," and philosophers and moral theorists "must either pretend to imitate science or find some way of obtaining 'cognitive status' without the necessity of discovering facts" (Rorty 1984c: 1). Rorty thinks that our scientific ideal rests on a misconception of the natural sciences (as we saw), and he believes that any attempt to find an archimedean point for ethics—either in the transcendental structure of logic or reason or in some naturalistic theory of human essence—is doomed to failure via familiar objections. We only believe that there are such points to be found because of our muddled idealization of the natural sciences. By seeking out apodictic foundations for our moral and political beliefs, we actually threaten them because the (inevitable) failure to deliver makes those beliefs appear vulnerable in ways in which they are not. We must stop operating with insatiable criteria for the legitimation of beliefs.

(ii) The Positive Argument

Rorty draws on the linguistic behaviorism of Davidson and Wittgenstein and the pragmatism of Quine and especially Dewey to make his positive argument. In place of truth as correspondence to an external reality and rationality as logical consistency, he defines truth in terms of social consensus and "solidarity" and rationality as "civility"—the result of conversational agreement in an uncoerced culture. Our beliefs do not exist in neat hierarchical systems that are well justified when confirmed by experience mediated through the methods of science or logic; rather, we are constantly reweaving them to adapt ourselves to the evolving culture that we partly constitute and that partly constitutes us. In contrast to Rawls's chooser in the original position "who can distinguish her *self* from her talents and interests," Rorty wants to say, with Gilbert Ryle, that there is no self of this kind. The moral chooser is "a network of beliefs, desires, and emotions with nothing behind it—no substrata behind the attributes." As he elaborates,

> For purposes of moral and political deliberation and conversation, a person just *is* that network, as for purposes of ballistics she is a point-mass, or for purposes of chemistry a linkage of molecules. She is a network that is constantly

reweaving itself in the usual Quinean manner—that is to say, not by reference to general criteria (e.g., "rules of meaning" or "moral principles") but in the hit-or-miss way in which cells readjust themselves to meet the pressures of the environment. On a Quinean view, rational behavior is just adaptive behavior of a sort which roughly parallels the behavior, in similar circumstances, of the other members of some relevant community. Irrationality, in both physics and ethics, is a matter of behavior that leads one to abandon, or be stripped of, membership in some such community. (Rorty 1983: 586)

What is this "usual Quinean manner" by which we reweave our beliefs? In contrast to the empiricist view of beliefs as deriving from sense data that in turn correspond to particulars in the world, Quine outlined the following:

The totality of our so-called knowledge or beliefs, from the most casual matters of geography and history to the profoundest laws of atomic physics or even of pure mathematics and logic, is a man-made fabric which impinges on experience only along the edges. . . . [It] is like a field or force whose boundary conditions are experience. A conflict with experience at the periphery occasions readjustments in the interior of the field. Truth values have to be redistributed over some of our statements. Reevaluation of some statements entails reevaluation of others, because of their logical interconnections—the logical laws being in turn simply certain further statements of the system, certain further elements of the field. Having reevaluated one statement we must reevaluate some others, which may be statements logically connected with the first or may be statements of logical connections themselves. But the total field is so underdetermined by its boundary conditions, experience, that there is much latitude of choice as to what statements to reevaluate in the light of any single contrary experience. No particular experiences are linked with any particular statements in the interior of the field, except indirectly through considerations of equilibrium affecting the field as a whole. (Quine 1953: 42–43)

For Quine there is, then, no simple correspondence between language and experience (although there is a more complex adaptive relationship) and no analytic/synthetic distinction. Beliefs that are commonly thought to be analytic are those toward the center of the "field" on which a great many others depend; our "natural tendency to disturb the total system as little as possible" leads us always to focus revisions on specific statements (often but not necessarily empirical) as close to the edge of the system as possible (ibid.: 44).

Four aspects of this account are worth noticing. First, Quine's analogy captures the intrinsically messy nature of people's beliefs and of the relations among those beliefs. In contrast to a predominant whiggish tendency to expect beliefs to exist in neat, tidy structures of ascending levels of generality, this view captures their fluid nature and the much looser notion of consistency with which people actually operate. Second, Quine's account captures the complexly interlocked character of more and less general beliefs that requires us to go to the more general to understand the less general without making large and implausible claims about the transcendental validity of some list of "key" terms or categories. Third, the field analogy makes it clear that from this point of view there is no categorial distinction between theoretical principles and empirical beliefs, which intuitively conforms to the self-sealing way in which ideologies preserve themselves. Consider how monetarists found a construction of "facts" to support the view that Reagan's policies worked while Keynesians found one to show that they failed and how Marxists can produce constructions of them to show that there *is* a long-term declining tendency in the rate of profit while neoclassical economists can hold that "the facts" disconfirm this. Quine's analogy captures the verity that empirical beliefs need not necessarily be less "basic" than theoretical ones: some empirical beliefs will be closer to the center of a field and less amenable to revision than some theoretical beliefs, and the desire to hold onto particular empirical beliefs may generate complex theoretical modifications. Last, Quine's account is sensitive to the fact that many parts of a system of beliefs can be implicit or unconscious, at least until they meet with recalcitrant experiences or need to accommodate other adaptive changes. Even in these cases agents may be more or less conscious of the ways in which they modify their beliefs. People can "consistently" hold mutually inconsistent beliefs as long as these inconsistencies are not seen to be mutually threatening. This is why writers in the pragmatist tradition shy away from the term "consistency," speak in equilibrating and evolutionary metaphors, invoke notions of "coherence," and see people as adapting their beliefs in order to remain "sane" (Rorty 1984c: 3).[7]

7. The preceding three paragraphs are drawn with some modifications from Shapiro (1986: 11–13).

A key component of Rorty's postmodernism is a distrust not only of
Kantian metanarratives but of all metanarratives, indeed of the very idea
of second-order justification for beliefs.[8] Because every metanarrative ultimately fails to deliver, Rorty thinks it essential that our political institutions should not be thought to depend on any particular one. Merely to
buy into the expectation that our institutions are in need of philosophical
legitimation is to be co-opted by the foundationalist outlook. We must
come to see that there is no sense "in which liberal democracy 'needs'
philosophical justification at all." For Rorty, "although it may need philosophical articulation, it does not need philosophical backup" (Rorty 1988:
260). Rorty thus distances himself from many recent communitarian critics of neo-Kantian liberalism such as Robert Bellah, MacIntyre, Sandel,
Charles Taylor, and the early Unger. These authors in some measure share
Horkheimer's and Adorno's view "that liberal institutions and culture
either should not or cannot survive the collapse of the philosophical justification that the Enlightenment provided for them." But although the new
communitarians correctly reject "the individualistic rationalism of the Enlightenment and the idea of 'rights,'" in Rorty's view they are wrong to
"see this rejection as throwing doubt on the institutions and culture of the
surviving democratic states" (Rorty 1988: 259). Sandel in particular is
guilty of dressing up Kantian expectations in anti-Kantian philosophical
garb. He argues that Rawls's conception of the self rests on an "incomplete" deontological vision, the implication being that it must be "comple-
mented" by a view of the self as "radically situated." Yet he fails, in Rorty's view, to see not only that there is no such thing as a philosophically
complete vision of the self but that Rawls does not want one anyhow. In a
recanting of his earlier criticisms of Rawls, Rorty now describes him as a
"Deweyan naturalist" and allies their causes under the pragmatist flag
(Rorty 1988: 267–68).

Rawls, Rorty now argues, has been misunderstood by many of his critics—including Rorty himself—who failed to see that his principles of justice are "political, not metaphysical."[9] Rather than resting on a particular
foundational argument, they are intended to be compatible with competing philosophical views. One of Rawls's repeated analogies is to the prin-

8. Thus Rorty follows Lyotard in characterizing the *postmodern* stance as one
that is "incredulous toward metanarratives." The term *modern* is understood to
"designate any science that legitimates itself with reference to a metadiscourse of
this kind (i.e., 'a discourse of legitimation with respect to its own status, a discourse called philosophy') making an explicit appeal to some grand narrative, such
as the dialectics of the Spirit, the hermeneutics of meaning, the emancipation of
the rational or working subject, or the creation of wealth" (Rorty 1984b: 32).

9. For Rawls's most extended treatment of this point, see Rawls (1985).

ciple of religious toleration, and just as Jefferson did not base his commitment to such tolerance on the interpretation of a particular passage of scripture, so Rorty reads Rawls to be saying that "for purposes of social theory, we can put aside such topics as an ahistorical human nature, the nature of selfhood, the motive of moral behavior, and the meaning of human life. We treat these as irrelevant to politics as Jefferson thought questions about the Trinity and about Transsubstantiation" (Rorty 1988: 261–62). Because we cannot settle these questions definitively, we must make our political theory independent of them, an attitude that is "thoroughly historicist and antiuniversalist. Rawls can wholeheartedly agree with Hegel and Dewey against Kant and say that the Enlightenment attempt to free oneself from tradition and history, to appeal to 'Nature' or 'Reason,' was self-deceptive" (ibid.: 262, footnotes omitted). It is therefore misleading to think of Rawls's view as "rights-based" instead of "goal-based" (as Dworkin does for example), for "the notion of 'basis' is not in point" (ibid.: 263). All Rawls need assume is that in designing political institutions we must be tolerant of different philosophical views. "Like many other figures of the Enlightenment, Jefferson assumed that a moral faculty common to the typical theist and the typical atheist suffices for civic virtue." Analogously, Rawls "shows us how liberal democracy can get along without philosophical presuppositions." The idea of reflective equilibrium on which his entire argument rests is, after all, an historicist appeal to the "overlapping consensus" in our culture, the consensus that, as Rawls said in a recent paper, "includes all the opposing philosophical and religious doctrines likely to persist and gain adherents in a more or less just constitutional democratic society" (ibid.: 257, 261, 262; Rawls 1985: 225–26).

Illuminating as this account is about Rorty's views, it is not remotely plausible as a reading of Rawls, early or late. Methodologically it ignores Rawls's explicit definition of his project in Kantian terms, his claim that the principles of justice are intended to be "procedural expressions of the categorical imperative," his admonition that we "should strive for a kind of moral geometry with all the rigor which this name connotes," that the eventual goal (which he does not claim yet to have reached) ought to be to produce a theory of justice that is "strictly deductive," and his explicit philosophical defense of the priority of the right over the good on the basis of his distinction between deontological and teleological theories and his own "thin theory" of the good. Rorty's account substantively ignores Rawls's claim that the principles of justice are applicable wherever "the circumstances of justice" (of which the most important is "moderate scarcity") obtain, that they are "neutral" between capitalist and socialist forms of economic organization, and that conceptions of the good that are inconsistent with them are irrational.[10] It is true that Rawls has more recently emphasized the argument from reflective equilibrium (though he continues to refer to his position even in the Dewey lectures as "Kantian constructivism"); and that even in *A Theory of Justice* he wanted to establish that prevailing values in our culture could generate his principles as well as could his "Kantian interpretation"—two ways of walking up the same hill. Yet he has never repudiated the Kantian argument because without it the argument from the original position would be utterly without point. If Rawls's principles are to be persuasively defended, such defense must be independent of the theoretical device of the original position. This can be seen by reference to his account of fairness, where he argues that the fair way to divide a cake is to require the cutter to take the last slice (Rawls 1971: 85). But this assumes that the division that would result *is* a fair division. If those among whom the cake was being divided included a diabetic and someone who had not eaten for three days, we might be disinclined to say that an equal division was presumptively fair. In the same vein, even if it is true (which many critics will not allow) that if we cast ourselves into a state of "reflective equilibrium" we will agree that Rawls's principles would be chosen by the inhabitants of the original position,[11] this entails nothing about their being acceptable as principles in the absence of independent argument.[12] It is precisely because he is aware of this that Rawls feels the need to give his alternative Kantian construction of his argument, on which the defense of his principles must stand or fall.[13]

If the attempt to appropriate Rawls is unpersuasive,[14] we are left with Rorty's claim that it makes no sense to ask questions in justification of liberal democracy. Such a view confers a privileged status on the beliefs that happen to prevail in a culture at any given time, and Rorty wants heartily to embrace this ethnocentricity. He rejects the view (popularized by Bernard Gallie and others) that contemporary cultures consist of competing, mutually antagonistic paradigms,[15] holding instead to the "holistic" view of a continuum of disagreement. Thus although Tasmanian abo-

10. Rawls (1971: 17–22, 251–57, 121, 24–30, 274, 265–74, 395–404). For extended discussion, see Shapiro (1986: 151–305).

11. For my account of why Rawls's liberties would not necessarily be accorded the priority Rawls ascribes to them and why the difference principle would not be chosen at all, see Shapiro (1986: 218–34).

12. On this see Gewirth (1982: 44).

13. See Rawls (1971: 251–57, 1980: 515–72). For elaboration of this point, see Shapiro (1986: 204–70).

14. For additional criticism of this attempt, see Bernstein (1987: 538–63).

15. See Gallie (1955: 167–98; 1956: 116–33).

rigines and British colonists had trouble communicating, he argues that "this trouble was different only in extent from the difficulties in communication experienced by Gladstone and Disraeli" (Rorty 1984a: 8).[16] If I imagine myself to have been parachuted into an alien culture and trying to communicate with one of the strange inhabitants who "presumably finds me equally strange," I will begin by formulating a theory about her behavior, as will she about mine.

> If we ever succeed in communicating easily and happily, it will be because her guesses about what I am going to do next . . . and my own expectations about what I will do or say under certain circumstances, come more or less to coincide, and because the converse is also true. She and I are coping with each other as we might cope with mangoes or boa constrictors—we are trying not to be taken by surprise. To say that we come to speak the same language is to say, as Davidson puts it, that "we tend to converge on passing theories." (Rorty 1986a: 5)

The extent to which such convergence is possible in particular cases is an empirical question, but Rorty thinks there is much more common ground among most of us than the metaphor of competing conceptual frameworks implies. This is why he thinks morality can, and must, ultimately rest on appeals to existing consensus. He has little doubt that for us the political content of this consensus is liberalism with Rawlsish stripes, minus its Kantian foundations. This is why he designates his view as ethnocentric, even though he believes there are no necessary bars to intercultural communication. Although "traditional Kantian liberals like Rawls draw back from pragmatism" out of a misplaced fear of "relativism" and "lonely provincialism," the former is a red herring (we all share common values) and the latter a virtue (there is no sounder basis for morality) (Rorty 1984a: 12–13).

If Rorty thinks we should embrace existing liberal institutions while junking the neo-Kantian metanarratives liberals typically invoke to justify them, he is equally skeptical of the realist metanarratives employed by Marxists and others to criticize liberal institutions. They, too, have no privileged knowledge of an archimedean point or of true human essence beyond appearances. Indeed their criticisms only appear plausible if we

16. More generally, see Rorty (1982: 3–17). There is a tension between this claim and Rorty's view that we must give up the modernist discourse of metanarratives in favor of the postmodernist liberation from foundational questions. This and other difficulties with his so-called ethnocentricity are taken up below.

harbor Kantian metaexpectations to begin with.[17] We need to realize that "there is nothing wrong with liberal democracy, nor with the philosophers who have tried to enlarge its scope." Things only come adrift when we "attempt to see their efforts as failures to achieve something they were not trying to achieve—a demonstration of the 'objective' superiority of our way of life over all other alternatives." There is "nothing wrong with the hopes of the Enlightenment, the hopes which created the Western democracies. The value of the ideals of the Enlightenment is, for us pragmatists, just the value of some of the institutions and practices which they have created" (Rorty 1984a: 16).

Internal to this argument is an evident tension which Rorty has recently acknowledged. For if the institutions that Enlightenment thinkers were determined to create are sound, can we be confident that the philosophical defenses adduced in their support are at best irrelevant window dressing and at worst actively subversive of them? He addresses this by arguing that although "the vocabulary of Enlightenment rationalism" revolving around notions of "truth, rationality and moral obligation" was "essential to the beginnings of liberal democracy," it has become "an impediment to the progress of democratic societies." Writers like Isaiah Berlin, Dewey, Michael Oakeshott, and Rawls are appealed to as having realized this, all in one way or another having defended liberal democracy while "dropping Enlightenment rationalism." Unlike Sandel and the other communitarian critics of liberalism, these writers see no point in seeking justifications of our institutions. They have helped "undermine the idea of a transhistorical 'absolutely valid' set of concepts which would serve as 'philosophical foundations' for liberalism." Yet each of them thought of this undermining as a way of strengthening liberal institutions. Oakeshott's account of morality as a learned language, a "practice in terms of which to think" rather than a set of axioms for action; Berlin's negative freedom; Rawls's agnosticism about ends; and Dewey's pragmatic adaptions reveal that "all four would grant that a circular justification of our practices, a justification which makes one feature of our culture look good by citing still another, or comparing our culture invidiously with others by reference to our own standards, is the only sort of justification we are going to get." For Rorty these writers represent "the self-cancelling and self-fulfilling triumph of the Enlightenment. Their pragmatism is antithetical to Enlightenment rationalism, but was itself made possible only by Enlightenment rationalism, and now serves as the vocabulary of a ma-

17. For Rorty's rejection of technical and intuitive realisms, see Rorty (1982: xxi–xxxvii, 12–15).

ture Enlightenment liberalism" (Rorty 1986c: 10, 13). Liberal democracy is no longer in need of justification, although "apologetic" for it continues to be useful.

> To offer an apologetic for our current institutions and practices is not to offer a justification of them, nor is it to defend them against their enemies. Rather, it is to suggest ways of speaking which are better suited to them than the ways which are left over from older institutions and practices. To engage in apologetics is more like refurnishing a house than like propping it up or placing barricades around it. (Ibid.: 10)

II. Rorty's View: Three Difficulties

I will subsequently argue that Rorty's account contains some useful insights that we need to take into consideration. But his view is inadequate and question begging in three major respects that must be dealt with before we can recast and appropriate what remains. These inadequacies concern his argument against metanarratives, his misleading opposition of solidarity to objectivity, and his assumptions about community membership and identification.

(i) The Rejection of Metanarratives Metanarrative

It is, first, false that the pragmatist view rests on a rejection of all metanarratives. Although Rorty is fond of asserting that pragmatists contend that knowledge is not something about which we can have a theory (a view I have debunked elsewhere),[18] the Quinean view that he endorses and employs involves assumptions both about the nature of the world and about our knowledge of it. Taking the second of these first, Quine's equilibrating metaphors, talk of our natural tendency to disrupt our systems of beliefs as little as possible, and Rorty's corresponding claim that we adapt to remain sane all assume a natural conservatism to our beliefs, conservatism in the Peelian sense of changing what we must to conserve what we can. Beyond this the pragmatist view rests on a negative dialectical account of the relationship between knowledge and experience. In place of the covering-law model of knowledge that bids us to seek ever more general explanatory formulations, here we see knowledge as evolving in negative terms, ruling things out, discarding what cannot be retained, rejecting things. We can know what we cannot accept, but that is all. In morals and politics this implies that we can rule out practices as unacceptable but not

18. Shapiro (1982: 550–53). See also chapter 8, section I below.

that we can consistently articulate some general theory of what is acceptable. Our system of beliefs is too underdetermined for that. Recent work
on the idea of intergenerational justice, for instance, reveals that some of
our familiar notions of right break down, or generate insuperable problems, once we start to apply them to future generations.[19] On the moral
analogue of the covering-law model, we should regard this, if true, as
grounds for revising our notion of what counts as having a right.[20] If,
however, we invent and modify concepts reactively in particular contexts
for particular functional purposes "in the hit-or-miss way in which cells
readjust themselves," we should not expect them to have perfectly general
application. This is not to say that the notion of an unborn person's rights
can make no sense to us but that we have no general theory to accommodate it because we have no general theory. We may notice, for instance,
that ordinarily our concept of a right presupposes the capacity for intentional agency by the bearer of that right, which is not present (at least
unambiguously) in potential persons, fetuses, some catatonic mental patients, and persons in irreversible comatose states. But on the pragmatist
view we would see no necessary reason to revise our everyday usage
merely on these grounds. We might be much more likely to treat the term
right as what Wittgenstein referred to as a family resemblance concept;
accept that there must be some tensions and line-drawing about its applications and leave it at that.[21] We would see no reason to be more ontologically demanding of our moral discourse. Morality and prudence, as Rorty
says, flow into one another.

Plausible as such an account might be, there is no denying that it rests
on a particular metanarrative. Rorty might maintain that he is not in the
business of discussing these issues, but this is question begging. To say
that we can operate with inconsistent beliefs so long as those inconsistencies are not perceived to be mutually threatening may be a much weaker
ontological requirement than conventional notions of consistency, but if it
is to be anything more than a descriptive account of how people's beliefs

19. My example, not Rorty's. For discussions of some of the difficulties involved, see Sikora and Barry (1978).

20. For a good illustration of this style of moral argument at work, see Fishkin
(1982). Fishkin argues that the familiar notions of obligation to others with which
we operate in our individual morality break down when confronted with large
numbers of others and that consequently these notions are in need of drastic refor-
mulation (1982: 46–47, 70–79, 153).

21. Wittgenstein noticed that there is a class of generic terms like *game,* which
we all understand perfectly well, although there is probably no single defining
characteristic that all games share. See Wittgenstein (1953: 31–34). For a useful
discussion, see Bambrough (1966: 186–204).

operate and evolve (which Rorty's and Quine's interchangeable uses of *knowledge* and *belief* imply), then it is a criterion.

In addition to this metanarrative about knowledge, Rorty's view rests on second-order metaphysical assumptions. It is true that pragmatists reject correspondence theories of truth, but in the Quinean formulation to which Rorty appeals there is some relationship between language and experience. Quine explicitly supposes this in his field metaphor when he speaks of recalcitrant experiences generating adjustments at the "edges" of our fields of beliefs and of experience as constituting the "boundary conditions" of those fields, causing modifications within them. Rorty adopts a different metaphor when he talks of revising beliefs in terms of replacing planks in a boat at sea,[22] but this assumes things about water and its properties vis-à-vis boats, about the imperatives for remaining afloat, and so on. Experience may be relatively underdetermining in that there might be a variety of viable conceptual modifications for coping with a particular experience and making sense of it, but this still presumes, as does the whole evolutionary metaphor, that there is an external world that operates (at least partly) independently of our beliefs about it and indeed that it partly shapes those beliefs. In short this view rests on an implicit version of the realism that Rorty claims to reject.[23] If this is so we need to try to account for the nature of that world and why we interact with it in the ways that we do, however difficult this might be. A biologist trying to explain the adaptive behavior of an organism by studying only what it did while totally ignoring its environment would not get at all far. Yet this is what Rorty's claim to be beyond metanarratives reduces to. He engages in metanarrative by assertion and assumption, and the results, we will see shortly, are less than convincing. Note for now the tension in his account between maintaining, on the one hand, opposition to every explanation of our beliefs that appeals to some external explanatory realm as a "reductionist" search for foundations and appealing, on the other, to a linguistic behaviorism that many would regard as a paradigm case reductionist view.[24] To declare that he is a "non-reductive behaviorist" about mind (Rorty 1986a: 5) is oxymoronically to restate the tension rather than resolve it, for his thesis amounts exactly to reducing every explanation (whether moral, aesthetic, causal, rational, psychological, or other) of every belief and action to his adaptive behavioral model. The logic of his argument for collapsing morality into prudence collapses everything else

22. See Rorty (1982: 15).
23. See Rorty (1982: xxi–xxxvii, 3–17; 1984a: 3–4).
24. For criticism of Wittgenstein's linguistic behaviorism for just this reason, see Chihara and Fodor (1966: 384–419).

into it as well. To avoid this problem, he needs to explain how his appeal to a single basic explanatory realm is not reductionist, something he never attempts to do.

(ii) The Misleading Opposition of Solidarity to Objectivity

There is a radical internalism to Rorty's appeal to convention, and in attending to it we begin to see the concrete implications of his particular metanarrative. His denial that we can know anything about a culture beyond its self-understanding (leaving aside, for now, just what that consists in) rests on an opposition between "solidarity" and "objectivity," between appeals to community versus appeals to some extrinsic standards, as the two alternative (implied: mutually exclusive) bases for knowledge and action (Rorty 1984a: 1–5). In another formulation of this he conceives of the moral universe as divided between *Kantians* (those who believe that there is a "supercommunity" that everyone identifies with and that generates "an ahistorical distinction between the demands of morality and those of prudence") and *Hegelians* (those who reject this contention, holding instead that humanity "is a biological rather than a moral notion" and that there is "no appeal beyond the relative merits of various actual or proposed communities to impartial criteria which will help us weigh those merits") (Rorty 1983: 583–84). But these simplistic oppositions obscure more than they reveal about actual moral and political debate and are not consistent with Rorty's unacknowledged foundational commitments.

We saw that Rorty's contention that the pragmatist partisan of solidarity "does not have a theory of truth" (Rorty 1984a: 5) is false, that his evolutionary language presumes a realist account of why individuals and communities adapt and evolve in the ways they do. Conceiving of humanity in biological and adaptive terms implies that the driving determinant of whether or not a belief will be fostered is its conduciveness to survival; a contingent fact will be whether or not this issues in solidarity toward any particular community or set of communities. As Colin Turnbull's study *The Mountain People* indicates, there will be circumstances where only antisocial behavior conduces to survival and where prevailing communal standards break down. Consider the example of religious belief. If we press the biological metaphors of which Rorty is so fond, we should be inclined to say that beliefs in objective theocratic standards will abound in a community when such beliefs are conducive to its survival and that they will be replaced by a scientistic ethos, or a subjectivist one, if and when the latter becomes more expedient for the survival of the community (or—more accurately—of dominant elements within it). The interesting question is not whether the scientist has replaced the priest, but why. It is surely an unavoidable question for someone who wants to argue, as Rorty does, that we expect too much from science, for there are likely to be good (functional) reasons why we do. Whether there is some straightforward explanation in terms of the success of the natural sciences or a more complex ideological explanation to the effect that these beliefs help legitimate dominant institutions and power structures, the explanation must be materially relevant to the claim Rorty wants to make. What drives pragmatist logic is not the imperatives of solidarity but those of survival; any connection that solidarity has to this is purely incidental in Rorty's logic. Were he to acknowledge this, he would realize that his account requires him to explain dominant beliefs in a culture causally because their evolutionary functions might be different from their subjective forms as beliefs. In contemporary America people marry for a variety of subjective reasons, but whether they intend it or not, or understand it or not, they thereby reproduce the social structure of the nuclear family. If we take Rorty's evolutionary pragmatism seriously, there is no reason to take *any* beliefs in a culture at face value. Rather we should constantly be on the lookout for their various functions—ideological, sociological, psychological, and biological—and, as the example of marriage suggests, there will often be exceedingly complex relations between the subjective form that a particular belief takes and its various functional causal roles.

The implications of this for Rorty's argument are substantial, for it is difficult to see how he can base his position on a simple appeal to consensus. The entire discussion of solidarity and "rationality as civility" assumes that in the Western democracies there is genuinely free discussion and that this forms the basis of political life. When he tells us that "notions like 'unforced agreement' and 'free and open encounter'—descriptions of social situations—can take the place in our moral lives of notions like 'the world,' 'the will of God,' 'the moral law,' 'what our beliefs are trying to represent accurately,' and 'what makes our beliefs true,'" (Rorty 1984c: 11), he is asking us to accept that there is unforced agreement and free and open encounter and that this is the causal basis of our social lives. Rorty tells us that the pragmatist holds the view that "there is nothing to be said about either truth or rationality apart from descriptions of the familiar procedures of justification which a given society—ours—uses in one or another area of inquiry." In contemporary American culture this is said to be a process of "cooperative human inquiry" based on "rationality as civility" (ibid.: 5).

Another way of getting at the naiveté of this view is to see that Rorty's account of "mature" apologetics for liberal democracy and negative freedom rests on something very like a combination of Daniel Bell's (1960) "end of ideology" thesis and the philosophical neutralism of the neo-Kantians. Rorty is appreciative, as we saw, of Rawls's effort to "stay on the surface, philosophically speaking," to devise a conception of justice that is indifferent among competing philosophical conceptions of the good, modeled on the liberal doctrine of religious toleration. In defending this, he argues, we appeal to "a moral faculty common to the typical theist and the typical atheist," not to any particular religious argument, so that we can be "as indifferent to philosophical disagreements about the nature of the self as Jefferson was to theological differences about the nature of God." Because liberal democracy is philosophically agnostic in this way, it does not require "extrapolitical grounding," it "can get along without philosophical presuppositions." Views "about man's nature and purpose" can be "detached from politics" so that "questions about the point of human existence or the meaning of human life" will be "reserved for private life," for we must learn to put "democratic politics first, and philosophy second." Whereas it is "appropriate to speak of gustatory or sexual [or religious?] preferences, for these do not matter to anybody but yourself," it is misleading "to speak of a 'preference' for liberal democracy." Rather we must say that its opponents are simply mad; "they are crazy because the limits of sanity are set by what *we* can take seriously" (Rorty 1988: 262, 257, 263, 264, 261, 263, 269, 263–64, 266–67).

If Rorty does not want to say, with Hegel, that we have reached the end of history, he does appear to think that he has a solution to the problem of the ordinary consciousness's inability to penetrate the "real" truth of things: we must design political institutions without reference to philosophical views. If this were possible, it might be desirable, but as the proponents of "procedural democracy" and the neo-Kantians discovered in different ways to their cost some time ago, it is not. To take one example from the argument that Rorty so keenly embraces, Rawls's primary goods are those things about which it is alleged there is consensus on their desirability: whatever our particular conception of the good turns out to be, we will all want more rather than less of liberties and opportunities, of income and wealth, and of "the social bases for self-respect." These are alleged to be goods without reference to any particular philosophical system;[25] any individual conception of the good that is inconsistent with these primary goods, in the lexical order stated, is declared to be irrational.

Yet many of us would say that it is undesirable to build institutions on

25. See Rawls (1971: 90–95, 395–99).

the assumption that more rather than less income and wealth is always better or that no liberty, however minor, should ever be sacrificed for improvements in economic well-being, however major.[26] Certainly the view rests on a particular contestable philosophical conception of human nature, and it is not enough to say that someone who did not want these goods could give them away because that person may conceive of them as bads, actively harmful to an individual or a society (surely the ascetic would conceive of income and wealth this way). Alternatively we might think different primary goods are more important.[27] Likewise with Rorty's discussion of religious toleration: it is false that his variant of the doctrine does not rest on a particular theological view. By declaring religion to be a private affair, Rorty is embracing a Lutheran view of the relationship between man and God in terms of which the individual conscience is supreme and in which there is no recognized secular authority for settling religious differences. This was Locke's view too, but of course Locke's case assumes a particular account of the scriptures derived from the theory of biblical exegesis articulated in the *First Treatise*. There Locke argued that although there would inevitably be ambiguities in scriptural interpretation, these could only be settled by the individual's direct reading of the text, unmediated by competing secular authorities.[28] Many American Jews and Catholics, not to mention fundamentalist Christians, find this view anathema.[29] As the abortion debate over the past two decades reveals all too clearly, the idea that it is possible to divorce public policy from competing philosophical conceptions of human nature, to make it neutral among them, is not plausible. The history of ideas is littered with the intellectual corpses of those who have proclaimed that there is finally enough social consensus to have genuinely neutral government or that there is finally enough disillusionment with all ideologies to make neutrality possible. The crusading conservatism of the New Right of the 1980s is but the most recent disconfirming instance.

26. For extended discussion of this and related questions in Rawls, see Shapiro (1986: 204–70).

27. For a more elaborate discussion of the thickness of Rawls's thin theory of the good and of his account of toleration, see Shapiro (1986: 213, 283–84, 222–24).

28. For elaboration, see Ashcraft (1987: 60–96).

29. Rorty comes close to conceding this when he admits that "it is not clear how to argue for the claim that human beings ought to be liberals rather than fanatics without being driven back on a theory of human nature, on philosophy." But his response manifestly fails to meet the challenge: "Accommodation and tolerance must stop short of a willingness to work within any vocabulary that one's interlocutor wishes to use, to take seriously any topic that he puts forward for discussion" (Rorty 1988: 268).

Not only is the idea of morally neutral politics chimerical, but the idea of privacy Rorty invokes is also deeply problematical. Almost a century of debate (of which Rorty appears unaware) on Mill's harm principle has established that the boundary between public and private spheres necessary for the negative libertarian view is exceedingly difficult to draw and is invariably charged ideologically. This is because a standard way in which power is effectively exercised is by declaring the realm of its operation to be private, as feminists are the first to point out with respect to the family.[30] Rorty's own example of toleration is, indeed, a case in point. Although this toleration brought about a radical expansion of religious freedom in seventeenth-century England, the negative libertarian view on which it rests—as freedom above all from politics—was later pressed into the service of quite different causes. Today that negative libertarian view is one of the main ideas that legitimates the minimal state and delegitimates attempts by government to ameliorate the external effects of capitalist competition on the grounds that the market is part of the private sphere.[31] Apart from the descriptive inaccuracies, then, Rorty's uncritical embracing of neutrality and negative liberty rests on a whiggishly benign view of power relations that is too sanguine for our circumstances.[32] Rorty's genial conservatism with respect to everyday beliefs preserves the dominant interests in our culture behind philosophical window dressing about the end of philosophy and false proclamations about the neutrality of our public institutions. Thus although he acknowledges that cultures can "protect themselves by institutionalizing knowledge-claims, and making people suffer who do not hold certain beliefs," this protection takes the form of "bureaucrats and policemen, not of 'rules of language' or 'criteria of rationality'" (Rorty 1984c: 5–6). Rorty does not need to posit any "ideal speech situation" (as Habermas does) because his benign view assumes it exists here and now in contemporary America—a heaven on earth.

30. For a useful account of the debate on Mill's harm principle, see Feinberg (1973).

31. I discuss this question extensively in Shapiro (1986: 71–72, 77–79, 167–69, 186–87, 191–92, 195, 198–202, 211, 213, 232–33, 283, 303; 1987: 999–1047; 1989b).

32. In a recent essay, Rorty pointed to the affinities between Dewey and Foucault, arguing that they are "trying to do the same thing," although "Dewey seems to me to have done it better, simply because his vocabulary allows room for unjustifiable hope, and an ungroundable but vital sense of human solidarity" (Rorty 1987b: 258). The last part of this bizarre claim seems to undermine the first, and even if there are affinities between Dewey and Foucault, it is hard to see any between Foucault and Rorty, given the absence of any attention to the power dimensions of language—indeed the explicit denial that there are any—in Rorty's analysis (Rorty 1984c: 5–6).

Rorty is sensitive to the charge that not every community has valued his "American" ideals. "Dewey was accused," he tells us, "of blowing up the optimism and flexibility of a parochial and jejune way of life (the American) into a philosophical system. So he did, but his reply was that *any* philosophical system is going to be an attempt to express the ideals of *some* community's way of life" (Rorty 1984c: 12). This may be so, but Rorty seems unaware of the massive ideological leap involved in moving from it to the claim that the liberal ideals of "unforced agreement" and "free and open encounter" are instantiated in American political life. One need not go all the way with theories of repressive tolerance to wonder whether the senses in which the capitalist democracies ensure freedom of speech are not limited, whether the voluntary transactions in the market-place of ideas are not instrumental in reproducing relations of domination and control as their economic analogues often do, and whether the range of issues that gets onto the public agenda is not critically determined by powerful interests that are able to ensure that the "mobilization of bias" functions to their advantage.[33]

Rorty would doubtless respond that all such claims ultimately rest on just one more metanarrative, but this is a bad argument for two reasons. First, as we have seen, the claim that he escapes metanarrative of this sort is bogus. Second, it is one thing to claim that we have a theory of how capitalist democracies "really" work, a theory that demonstrates all sub-jective beliefs to be epiphenomenal and shows them to be irrelevant to the functioning of the system (except insofar as they facilitate that process), and quite another to suspect that the world of subjective appearances does not begin to tell the whole story of how the social world functions and is reproduced. Most of us may well have grown skeptical of Marx's mecha-nistic formulations, and we have all become too sensitive to the socially constitutive functions of language ever to be able to ignore beliefs as merely epiphenomenal. None of this, however, amounts to a good reason for taking at face value received beliefs within a culture as accurate de-scriptions of it. There is no better a priori reason to accept *that* metaphys-ical commitment on faith than there is to accept the vulgarist economic determinism, unless we want to replace one implausible reductionism with another. The primacy Rorty ascribes to received beliefs in a culture generates a mindless, if genial, political conservatism.

The difficulties attending this view can be summed up by noting that one person's consensus is another's hegemony. Why characterize the ab-sence of manifest conflict about political values as a genuine consensus

---

33. See Bachrach and Baratz (1962: 947–52; 1963: 632–42), Lukes (1974), and Lindblom (1977: 201–21).

rooted in a social structure that is fundamentally open and tolerant? When students of comparative politics confront high levels of this behavior in cultures that they have independent reasons for thinking are based on relations of hierarchy and domination (as in Mexico), they turn to a concept like hegemony for an explanation. When they discern relatively few of the conflicts they expect in contemporary capitalist countries, they turn to concepts like liberal corporatism to explain the ideological incorporation of the working classes.[34] Controversial as such explanations often are, there is no a priori reason for thinking them less likely to be true than to assume, with neither argument nor evidence, that agreement is indicative of fundamental social consensus.

The truth is that we know little about the complex mechanisms by which the social world is produced and reproduced, and it is highly unlikely that there is any general explanation of the role played by subjective beliefs in that process. Some social relationships, such as friendship, can be called wholly and internally belief-dependent in that they rest entirely on the beliefs of the agents about the relationship. Our ceasing to believe that we are one another's friends can be sufficient to terminate that relationship. But it is wrong to think that all, or even most, socially and politically significant relationships are of this logical form. Marital relationships are belief-dependent, but not internally so in the same way as relations of friendship: my wife cannot terminate our marriage merely by ceasing to believe she is my wife. Such relationships are parasitic on the beliefs of others, and on institutionalized forms, in ways that relations of friendship are not. Parent-child relations differ again because of the introduction of a biological component, and if we consider the social position of a Jew in Nazi Germany we must discern an interaction between beliefs of various relevant agents and physical-biological characteristics. Wage-labor relations in a market system are different again: they lack a biological basis, but there is a structural coercive element. These differ yet again from relations of slavery, where structural coercion is manifest and dominant rather than latent. In these various situations the socially constitutive functions of the beliefs of agents differ from one another, yet they are all familiar parts of social reality.[35] That we lack any single account of the

34. See Stepan (1978: 3–113) and Panitch (1977: 61–90).
35. For useful discussions of the complex and frequently opaque relationships between agents' perceptions of social relationships and their actual structure, see Connolly (1981: 63–89), Edelman (1985: 10–19), and Elshtain (1985: 20–26). These authors recognize both that language plays important constitutive roles in political life and that the ways in which agents use it are not typically transparent to them, that it may serve important legitimating functions of which they are only dimly aware. For my account in relation to J. L. Austin's "linguistic phenomenol-

social world that describes and explains them is no reason to ignore them. We can know that the social world is dense and that social and political relationships are reproduced at a variety of interrelated (and more and less opaque) levels, without for a minute supposing that we have a general explanation (or that there is a general explanation waiting to be discovered). All we need assume is that society is reproduced by a variety of causal mechanisms, some of which we understand well, some of which we misunderstand, some of which we understand partly, some of which we dimly perceive, and some of which escape us entirely. To assume that the social world is in all important particulars as it appears to social agents is more a matter of sticking one's head in the sand than of rejecting metanarratives.

Rorty is setting up a misleading dichotomy if he thinks that by questioning the extent to which capitalist democracies rest on "rational civility" and "unforced agreement," whatever people believe, we are opting for one more metanarrative that we have no way of sustaining. It would be closer to the spirit of Dewey's pragmatism to take this possibility seriously and see how it squares with other things we think we know or suspect about American culture than to decide by fiat and circular argument that our politics is based on agreement because we (or some of us) agree that it is. In this respect Rorty's argument is more explicitly relativist than those of most other antifoundationalists because of his unwavering confidence that there is no reason for "throwing doubt on the institutions and culture of the surviving democratic states" (Rorty 1988: 259) and therefore no reason to ask questions concerning their justification. He wants to go further than contextualists like Don Herzog (1985: 15–17)—who seeks a contextual view of justification in political theory—by saying that we should not be interested in justification at all.

It is indeed ironic that Rorty, with all his reliance on adaptive metaphors, seriously advocates that we accept the institutions of the post-Enlightenment as fundamentally sound while rejecting the philosophy that (he claims) spawned them, as though there were no important connection between the two. In *Philosophy and the Mirror of Nature* he argued that we have all been operating with a Cartesian epistemology that is not false (he has no criteria for truth and falsity at this level) but optional. His therapeutic metaphor implies that studying the history of ideas is like engaging in psychotherapy: once we understand how Des-

---

ogy" and the uses of it made by Quentin Skinner and others, see Shapiro (1982: 554–63) and chapter 8, section I (i) below.

cartes, Locke, and Kant developed the view of scientific knowledge with which they have saddled us, we will be free of it just like any neurosis. This is an implausible view of how ideas and ideologies evolve. Just because we refuse to accept the transcendental validity of what Rorty conceives of as the Cartesian/Lockean/Kantian worldview,[36] it does not follow that it can simply be dismissed. There are good material and historical reasons why this way of thinking became rooted in the West in the seventeenth century and even more deeply embedded in the centuries that followed.[37] To portray this way of thinking as optional in the same breath as one claims to reject Cartesian epistemology invites the charge that Rorty has not come to terms with this voluntarist theory of beliefs being tied to Descartes's epistemology.[38] It would surely be more plausible to suppose (at least as a point of departure) that the powerful felt need in contemporary culture to articulate intersubjective normative standards is anthropologically significant, that there are politically interesting reasons why people try to attack and defend existing institutions in these terms. It may be less, as Rorty supposes, that we all regard liberal institutions as sound (seeking only for the right justification of them) and more that we fear they are not. That liberal writers are so preoccupied with problematic notions of natural and human right, with concepts of justice beyond positive legal rules, suggests a sensitivity to the shaky foundations and often morally questionable effects of our political institutions and a recognition that these might permit—even generate—kinds of domination and exploitation that make them morally ambiguous at best. We only seek to justify things when there are reasons for doubting their justness—no one wonders whether traffic regulations or the game of Trivial Pursuit can be justified from first principles. By Rorty's own logic we should be interested in our Kantian drives and why we have them, in what it is about the institutions to which we try to apply them that makes us want to apply them, and in what institutional legitimating functions they perform.

Rorty seems dimly aware of this when he remarks that although most American intellectuals in Dewey's day thought of America as a "shining historical example," after the Vietnam War many of them could no longer identify with the national community in the same way. Some became "marginalized" as a result, whereas others "attempted to rehabilitate

36. Rorty's account of the rise of foundationalism relies so heavily on caricature that one is bound to wonder, with Bernstein (1987: 559), "if there ever was a 'foundationalist'—at least one who fits the description of what Rorty calls 'foundationalism.'"

37. For my own account of these reasons see Shapiro (1986).

38. For further discussion of the relationship, see Shapiro (1986: 101, 105, 144–45, 196, 235, 245, 276, 277, 281, 283, 284, 302, 304).

Kantian notions in order to say, with Chomsky, that the War not merely betrayed America's hopes and interests and self-image, but was immoral, one which we had no right to engage in in the first place." Dewey, Rorty tells us approvingly, "would have thought such attempts at further self-castigation pointless"; although they may have served short-term cathartic purposes, "their long-run effect has been to separate the intellectuals from the moral consensus of the nation rather than to alter that consensus" (Rorty 1983: 588).

All this assumes that fighting the war was a bad thing and that the only issue is finding the most efficacious language in which to condemn it. Yet there are those, not insignificant in number or influence, who believe that America betrayed its "hopes and interests and self-image" not by fighting the war but by failing to fight it successfully. Indeed, a powerful case could be made that it is Rorty who is out of touch with the "moral consensus of the nation" if he believes that the language of good and evil, virtue and corruption, right and wrong, and ultimate justifiability do not play a powerful role in the ways in which Americans conceive of and evaluate their public realm.

Critics like Bernstein (1987: 538–63) have repeatedly taken Rorty to task for his imperialistic use of the term *we* to declare his values to be the core of the moral consensus of the nation, and Rorty, who regards himself as a social democrat, has been perturbed by the suggestion that his genial relativism might be a form of political conservatism in disguise. To defuse such claims, he has recently set out a "political credo," which, he alleges, provides common ground not only between him and Bernstein, but also among Rawls, Habermas, Berlin, Bellah, Bell, Irving Howe, Sidney Hook, John Dunn, Charles Taylor, "and lots of other people who might not mind describing themselves as 'social democrats'" (Rorty 1987a: 567). Even if some of them might dissent from one or another aspect of it, taken as a whole it sums up their shared political platform. The eight-point credo is as follows:

(1) Given the failures of central government planning, we can no longer make "nationalization of the means of production" a central element in our definition of "socialism." Instead, we have to use some such definition of "socialism" as Habermas's: "overcoming the . . . rise to dominance of cognitive-instrumental [interests]." (Alternatively, perhaps: "overcoming the greed and selfishness which are still built into the motivational patterns impressed on our children, and into the institutions within which they will have to live.") We have to find a definition that commits us to both greater equality and a change in moral climate, without committing us to any particular economic

setup. Nobody so far has invented an economic setup that satisfactorily balances decency and efficiency, but at the moment the most hopeful alternative seems to be governmentally controlled capitalism plus welfare-statism (Holland, Sweden, Ireland). There is nothing sacred about either the free market or about central planning; the proper balance between the two is a matter of experimental tinkering.

(2) The world is currently divided into a rich, relatively free, reasonably democratic, notably selfish and greedy, and very short-sighted First World; a Second World run by ruthless and cynical oligarchies; a starving, desperate Third World.

(3) Within the First World, the social democratic scenario of steady reform along increasingly egalitarian lines (lines that would lead to the eventual realization of Rawls's two principles of justice) has been stalled for decades, largely because the political right within the First World (made up of the people who have no interest in increasing equality) has diverted public attention, money, and energy to combating Soviet imperialism.

(4) Soviet imperialism is indeed a threat. Granted, for example, that SDI is just a gimmick to make Reagan's rich friends richer at the cost of the poor, there is still a need for military defenses against the Soviets. There is still considerable reason to think that a NATO-free Western Europe would, sooner or later, come under the same kind of Moscow-dominated governments as now rule Eastern Europe, with the same loss of democratic freedoms. Again, granted that a lot of American intervention in the Third World has been for the sake of protecting investments (or supporting oligarchs who hired the right Washington lobbyists), it remains quite likely that Third World governments manned by graduates of Patrice Lumumba University will end up as the same kind of ruthless oligarchies that we find in contemporary Rumania and Vietnam—with the same forcible suppression of reform from below.

(5) Not only is Soviet imperialism a threat, but time seems to be on the Soviet side. Since the days when Lyndon Johnson gradually gave up on the Alliance for Progress, there has been no serious attempt by the First World to support the kind of social democratic revolutions in the Third World that might provide alternatives to takeovers by the ex-students of Lumumba U. In the absence of such an attempt, it seems likely that the next century will see a steady extension of Moscow's empire throughout the Southern hemisphere—a gradual absorption of the Third World by the Second. Where else, after all, can revolutionary movements in the Third World turn?

(6) So we social democrats have to maneuver on (at least) two fronts—against enemies at home in the interest of, for example, the people in

the urban ghettos and rural slums of the First and Third Worlds, and against Soviet imperialism in the interest of the human race. The struggle against the latter threat has as little to do with "the struggle between socialism vs. capitalism" as the present institutions of the Second World have to do with socialism (in Habermas's sense of the term).

(7) So no single set of slogans is going to help. There is no way to consolidate our enemies in any interesting "theoretical" way. The shadowy millionaires manipulating Reagan (people who are happy to see democratic politics turned into sham battles between telegenic puppets), the nomenklatura in Moscow, the Broederbond in South Africa, and the ayatollahs in Iran are so many gangs of thugs concerned to hold onto the power and wealth they have managed to grab. They use the other gangs for mutual reinforcement in the way in which, in 1984, the governments of Eurasia, Oceania, and Eastasia use each other. Unfortunately, however, much of what each gang says about its rivals is all too true.

(8) Still, this does not mean that "there is no significant difference" between the First and Second Worlds. We have hope, and they (unless Gorbachev astonishes us all) do not. We have freedom of the press, an independent judiciary, and universities in which teachers continually urge students to combat (in Bernstein's words) "the forces and tendencies at work (e.g., class conflict, social division, patriarchy, racism) which are compatible with liberal political practices but nevertheless foster real inequality and limit effective political freedom." Such fragile, flawed, institutions, the creation of the last 300 years, are humanity's most precious achievements. It is impossible to imagine, in their absence, anything like approximation to, or continuing conformity with, Rawls's two principles of justice. It is quite possible that all such institutions may vanish by the year 2100 (as an isolated First World gradually collapses). There will then (given the powers that modern technology makes available to thugs) be nothing to prevent the future being, as Orwell said, "a boot stamping down on a human face, forever." Nothing is more important than the preservation of these liberal institutions. (Rorty 1987a: 565–67, footnotes omitted)

This author tried out Rorty's in some ways refreshingly candid statement of political assumptions on twenty-two Yale University juniors and seniors in a political theory seminar in the spring of 1988. Asked to evaluate it as a whole and explicitly to assume that disagreement with one or another aspect of it should not necessarily disqualify the credo as a whole, two thought it "just stupid," nine found it attractive in varying degrees, and eleven rejected it out of hand (one as "horrendous," five as "dangerous," three as "naive," and two as "dishonest"). Whether or not they were attracted to it appeared unrelated to whether or not they considered themselves to be social democrats; of the nine who were positive about it, five described themselves as social democrats while four rejected that description. Of the thirteen who opposed it, six described themselves as social democrats while the remaining seven said that they were not. As these conflicting responses (from a self-selected sample of political theory students in a notoriously liberal university) indicate, Rorty's claim that self-described social democrats agree on the main thrust of his credo is not credible, and it becomes even less so when we recall that he has invoked theorists as progressive in their politics as Dewey, as liberal as Berlin, and as conservative as Oakeshott in support of his defense of liberal institutions.

Rorty's credo confronts the further difficulty that it is not self-evidently true (as he appears to suppose). Elements of the credo may well be defensible, though I would argue that Rorty greatly overestimates both the power of the Soviets and the benevolence of liberal institutions while underestimating the moral diversity of political institutions in the Second and Third Worlds to an astonishing degree, and that he is wedded to an outmoded cold war–dominated view of superpower geopolitical relations. The latter seems so out of touch with the realities of the contemporary world that not only does it undermine the possibilities for progressive change—with its alarmist suggestion that our institutions are so wonderful, but fragile, that we had better not fiddle with them—but it blinds us to the greatest threats to social democratic institutions at home and abroad, most notably religious fundamentalism. I do not pretend to have established any of these claims here; indeed it seems to me that they are among the sorts of questions we should be arguing about. The point here is rather that Rorty wants to treat his geopolitical views as assumptions, as self-evident to all right-thinking people, which manifestly they are not.

More serious theoretically, Rorty's account of his credo, which rests on a view that many people's political beliefs are distorted for ideological reasons, that only the particular strand of American culture he embraces is genuinely American, undermines his appeal to consensus. What he takes to be the social democratic scenario is assumed to be self-evidently American, whereas the actions of "enemies" on the right, or of the "thugs" in the Reagan administration, are ideologically motivated, diverting public attention from what would otherwise be the manifest desirability of Rorty's political agenda. He seems to think he can simply appeal to Americans to be faithful to their own traditions, yet these are many and conflicting. They include *Dred Scott* as well as the Fourteenth Amendment, *Plessy v.*

Ferguson as well as *Brown*, aggressive militarism as well as commitments to peaceful coexistence, McCarthyism as well as the First Amendment, willful union-busting courts as well as the Wagner Act, would-be dismantlers of the welfare state as well as its defenders, the New Right with its crusading moral agenda as well as the genial liberal intellectual establishment that Rorty seems to think definitively American. He lurches between a blind appeal to consensus, on the one hand, where everyone is asserted to agree on all moral and political essentials, to a remarkable (and undefended) account of ideology, on the other. In terms of the latter, his geopolitical assumptions are presented as self-evident truths, so that those who do not share them must either be elites—thugs who divert public attention for ulterior purposes—or those whose attention has presumably been diverted. In either case Rorty feels no compulsion to defend any of the substantive positions he adopts with either reasons or evidence. It turns out that Rorty has his priests after all, that small group (smaller than he realizes) of liberal intellectuals who, though they are too philosophically sophisticated to claim to know any philosophical truths, nonetheless hold the key to the political universe. Their politics need be defended with neither argument nor evidence, merely delivered with resounding conviction—even impatience—from the philosopher's armchair.

It is one thing to be skeptical of the ultimate utility of the competing-paradigms metaphor of political discourse and to argue that there is much common ground of vocabulary and commitment—common ground that makes political argument possible—and quite another to suppose that there are intuitively self-evident right answers to substantive questions on the public agenda. Likewise, we may want, with Rorty, to reject Kantian appeals to order as a basis for our critical judgments, but to do that we need to find a way that leaves open the possibility of meaningful political argument.

Rorty's solidarity/objectivity dichotomy leaves him no basis for distinguishing various strands of American culture, for promoting some of its tendencies and rejecting others. Why should the intellectuals, in his Vietnam example, have tried to alter what Rorty took to be "the moral consensus of the nation"? Why should they not have argued instead for a more aggressively fought war? For Rorty to address such questions at all, he would have to formulate arguments about what *is* in the interests of the American national community, or significant parts of it, whatever others (even possibly a majority) in that community believe. It seems to me beyond question that such arguments would appeal both to solidarity and to objectivity, both to what people believed and articulated their aspirations to be and to an analysis of what was really going on; that is, Rorty would need an account of the geopolitical realities surrounding the Vietnam War and an account of why one of the available ways of dealing with these realities was superior to the others. His credo reveals all too clearly his geopolitical assumptions, and if he adduced some arguments in support of them, he might actually persuade someone that he is right. Rorty is afraid of walking down this path because it seems to lead toward a realist meta-narrative, but he is already committed to it; it is just hidden by the misleading solidarity/objectivity dichotomy.

The pragmatist view does provide a basis for attacking these questions while at the same time revealing why they are so difficult to settle and why general a priori moral theories will never advance their solution. But to see this we have to bite the realist bullet and realize that we must make some claims about the objective interests of individuals and communities without presuming to supply yet another general theory that explains everything about man, morality, history, and knowledge. In the final chapters of this book I suggest that this can be done if we look closely at the implications of the Quinean account. For now, notice that the pragmatist view makes it inevitable that these issues arise and unavoidable that we try to deal with them. If we stick to Rorty's account we evade all substantive issues or settle them by assumption, thereby becoming subject to exactly the same difficulty that the neo-Kantians face: we convince those who agreed with us before we began at the price of confirming the opposition of those who did not.[39] We can embrace Rorty's rejection of the competing-paradigms metaphor, as well as his claim only to be speaking ethnocentrically about American culture (leaving aside the complex international dependencies in today's world that inevitably give such claims a disingenuous air) and still find ourselves with no tools for dealing with substantive political disagreements.

(iii) Cross-cutting Community Identification and Membership

Rorty's discussion of solidarity fails to take into account that societies consist of (and are parts of) a great many cross-cutting communities whose needs and interests frequently differ and conflict. Like many liberal writers reacting against Rawls's inadequate account of the good community, Rorty assumes (without argument) that the basic relevant moral community is the national community, although his discussion of this issue is often maddeningly vague. From the Gladstone/Tasmanians example we

39. For my account of how this happens with the neo-Kantians, see Shapiro (1986: 151–305).

see that at times Rorty conceives of his cultural holism on a global scale, but most of his appeals are to the American national community and certainly take no account of the difficulties generated when it has refused membership (or full membership) to certain groups historically or failed to acknowledge obligations that members of other national and international communities believe we owe them.

Rorty does admit that not everyone identifies with the same communities in the same ways. In a discussion of the social responsibilities of intellectuals, he notes that it is pointless to castigate intellectuals for irresponsibility toward a community of which they do not think themselves members—"otherwise runaway slaves and tunnelers under the Berlin Wall would be irresponsible" (Rorty 1983: 583). He goes on to argue that such castigation can make sense only if we hold a Kantian belief in a "supercommunity" and that this cannot be sustained. But he never returns to the politically central questions of why particular communities rather than others exist, why some people identify with them while others do not, why communities allow some to be members and reject others, whether there are causally significant community memberships in people's lives—such as economic class—of which they might be only dimly aware (Rorty treats membership and subjective identification as synonymous but offers no reasons for this massive conflation), or whether people's various community affiliations might not be in fundamental conflict with one another. All he says that is remotely relevant to these issues is that "most moral dilemmas are . . . reflections of the fact that most of us identify with a number of different communities and are equally reluctant to marginalize ourselves in relation to any of them. This diversity of identifications increases with education, just as the number of communities with which a person may identify increases with civilization." In Rorty's view there is no criterion to which to appeal to resolve moral dilemmas precisely for this reason: "Nations or churches or movements are . . . shining historical examples not because they reflect rays emanating from a higher source, but because of contrast-effects—comparisons with other, worse communities." All moral force derives from one (actual or imagined) community identification or another; "nothing else has *any* moral force" (Rorty 1983: 587, 586).

This is question begging in two ways. First, if a person has conflicting commitments to two communities, it is not clear how she can see that one is better through contrast-effects without appealing to some standard independent of the two relevant communities. Otherwise each will presumably appear inferior from the point of view of the other. This is true independently of whether the standards people employ, implicitly or explicitly,

are parts of general moral systems, the imperatives of survival, or anything else; all Rorty has a basis for saying is that contrast-effects will reveal that their injunctions for action are different. But the Catholic Democrat trying to decide whether to support Mondale-Ferraro after the
admonitions of Archbishop O'Connor concerning abortion knows *that*:
she is looking to resolve the question, and this requires critical judgments
about the relevant communities. She may ultimately make those judgments with her feet or on some other basis, but the idea of deciding that
one of the injunctions is better presumes the possibility of such critical
judgments. In this and many other cases it is no good to appeal exclusively
to the adaptive metaphors. From that point of view, and as the example
indicates, several options may be feasible: the issue is to choose among
them. Even when this problem does not arise, the adaptive metaphor assumes that there are criteria beyond contrast-effects deriving from the
survival needs of the relevant organism. It is presumably those needs that
make one choice appear better than another, that make effects contrast.
But if this is so the true appeal is to the needs of the organism, not to the
contrast-effects, and there is a moral force other than various felt community identifications, namely, an implicit naturalist theory of needs.
Rorty ignores these issues.

Second, he begs the question of why particular communities exist with
the particular cross-cutting identifications they embody, mainly because
he keeps the discussion at so high a level of abstraction. His only specific
remark—that differentiation of community identification increases with
education and civilization—is hopeless. A brilliant and popular physicist
who has always been accepted into and rewarded by a community, easily
rising to positions of security and prestige within it, may feel many fewer
conflicting community identifications than a high school dropout who
went to Vietnam, invested in an understanding of national community
identification that turned out not to be socially valued on his return, resulting in involuntary marginalization and no settled community identification. The well-adjusted family man of good education and respectable
standing may be much less conflicted than the closet homosexual of limited education who finds he belongs to communities that he does not like
and is rejected by those to whose membership ranks he aspires. The half-
Jewish child may be rejected by Jewish communities if her mother is not
Jewish while simultaneously stigmatized as a Jewess in an anti-Semitic
culture, resulting in tremendously complex conflicting identifications,
whatever her level of education.

Anyone who hopes to come to terms with these problems must begin
by deciding which are the relevant communities. These will often differ

for the political theorist, the sociologist, the anthropologist, and the psychologist, and their identification will seldom, if ever, be uncontroversial. Explanatory and historical work will have to be done on these communities: why do they exist, what purposes do they serve, who are their members, and how did they come to be such? What are the implications for other communities? Is it inevitable that they exist and function in the ways that they do or might they be altered in various ways—if so, what are the realistic options and what are their implications? Rorty, like Sandel (whose argument on this point he endorses)[40] and other communitarian liberals retreating from Rawls, continually berates us with the discovery that substantive moral judgments about politics require the acceptance of some notion of the good community as their basis, and as a consequence there is a growing debate over community versus no community in liberal theory. But this is just a beguiling opposition of gross concepts. Of course substantive judgments about how communities ought to be organized and governed assume accounts of how they are formed and reproduced, of what their goals and purposes must be, and of how they should limit community action—both internally, with respect to the individual actions of members, and externally, with respect to the needs and activities of other communities. We can no more make substantive judgments about politics without reference to a notion of a good community than we can make substantive judgments about food without reference to a notion of the purposes of eating. The question is never whether community but what sort.

III. Conclusion

To sum up, Rorty's pragmatism does not rest on a rejection of metanarratives; it presumes, though it does not defend, a realist account of adaptive human behavior. Furthermore, the unthinking appeal to consensus behind the solidarity/objectivity dichotomy is deeply problematical, and it reintroduces the patent implausibility and related ideological difficulties that many of us hoped to be leaving behind with the neo-Kantian tradition. Whether it is in Rorty's concealed commitments to the end of ideology and neutralism implicit in his appeals to consensus or in his more recent attempts to declare without evidence or argument that there must be a consensus among right-thinking people for his political program, both are unconvincing on their own terms and read more like ideological rationalization than critical argument. Finally, his discussion of the communities that form the basis of his account is so general that it evades virtually all

40. See Rorty (1983: 586).

substantive political concerns. His account of conflicting community identification in terms of education and civilization is riddled with difficulties,
and no other substantive criteria are offered.

Yet it would be a mistake to think that the pragmatist view has nothing
to offer. The pragmatists' failure to solve the problems of how to make
moral choices in many circumstances does not negate their account of the
intrinsically messy character of our beliefs or the utility of the much
weaker notions of consistency suggested by their adaptive metaphors and
their rejection of universalist Kantian expectations. Likewise, the difficulties attending Rorty's uncritical acceptance of what he takes to be received
beliefs, and his failure to take account of the many intricate ways in which
the cognitive realm is connected to other levels of action and experience,
do not obviate the importance of recognizing that the ways in which
people understand their social circumstances play important parts in creating and reproducing those circumstances, even if this is difficult to generalize about and it is only one of a variety of causally relevant factors.
Last, the weakness of Rorty's general account of community identification
and membership should not prevent our recognizing that substantive
moral and political judgments invariably do rest on and invoke various
(actual or imagined) community identifications and that an understanding
of these will often be central to a critical evaluation of those judgments.
In short, the reasons Rorty supplies for rejecting the aspirations of the
neo-Kantians and for being centrally concerned with conventional political language are good reasons. What we need is a better way of looking at
conventional political language that takes account of its constitutive functions while simultaneously making possible and plausible critical judgments about it.

3   Political Theory as Connected Social Criticism

If a contextually bounded political theory is to be convincingly described, an idea of immanent criticism must be unpacked that is grounded in the internal logic of conventional argument while somehow looking beyond it. However difficult, the goal must be to combine the roles of participant and anthropologist in our political culture and thus try to get a critical purchase on our practices that can then be used to generate adequate standards for normative argument about them. This is the project attempted in *Spheres of Justice, Interpretation and Social Criticism* and other recent writings by Michael Walzer.[1]

I. Walzer's View: Exposition

Walzer does not so much want to propose a theory as to explore and expose difficulties in the ways we characteristically think and act within our terms of reference. He wants people to look critically at their own practices, or, better, he wants to chronicle and extend patterns of critical argument that already exist. Social criticism, he tells us, "is less the practical offspring of scientific knowledge than the educated cousin of common complaint." It is developed "naturally, as it were, by elaborating on existing moralities and telling stories about a society more just than, though never entirely different from, our own" (Walzer 1987: 65). Social criticism is an immanent activity:

1. Walzer's arguments are applied by example in *The Company of Critics*, published as this book was going to press. Although I have added some references to it, I do not discuss it in detail, preferring to rely on his explicitly theoretical statements of his view. This view is not altered or modified in the new account.

> "Social" has a pronominal and reflexive function, rather like "self" in "self-criticism," which names subject and object at the same time. No doubt, societies do not criticize themselves; social critics are individuals, but they are also, most of the time, members, speaking in public to other members who join in the speaking and whose speech constitutes a collective reflection upon the conditions of collective life. (Ibid.: 35)

(i) Dominance, Hegemony, and the Inevitability of Social Criticism

For Walzer the need for social criticism is a function of relations of social domination and control and more particularly of the social conflict engendered by such relations. "Most societies," he argues, "are organized on what we might think of as a social version of the gold standard; one good or one set of goods is dominant and determinative of value in all the spheres of distribution." A good becomes dominant, for Walzer, when the fact of owning it confers on the owner "command [of] a wide range of other goods," so that these latter goods become used in ways that are not "limited by their intrinsic meanings." Although dominance can sometimes result from monopoly ownership of an essential good, more typically it is "the work of many hands, mixing reality and symbol." Dominance has historically been based on various social characteristics: physical strength, familial reputation, religious or political office, landed wealth, capital, and technical knowledge (Walzer 1983a: 10–11). It is the presence of dominance that makes social criticism both possible and necessary:

> Social criticism must be understood as one of the more important by-products of a larger activity—let us call it the activity of cultural elaboration and affirmation. This is the work of priests and prophets; teachers and sages; storytellers, poets, historians, and writers generally. As soon as these sorts of people exist, the possibility of criticism exists. It is not that they constitute a permanently subversive "new class," or that they are the carriers of an "adversary culture." They carry the common culture; as Marx argues, they do (among other things) the intellectual work of the ruling class. But so long as they do *intellectual* work, they open the way for the adversary proceeding of social criticism. (Walzer 1987: 40)

Walzer elaborates this in terms of Gramsci's theory of hegemony. What makes criticism a permanent possibility for Walzer is that "every ruling class is compelled to present itself as a universal class." Every dominant ideology exhibits a "double embodiment" deriving from the need to universalize hegemonic claims:

> Trapped in the class struggle, seeking whatever victories are available, the rulers nevertheless claim to stand above the struggle, guardians of the common interest, their goal not victory but transcendence. This self-presentation of the rulers is elaborated by the intellectuals. Their work is apologetic, but the apology is of a sort that gives hostages to future social critics. It sets standards that the rulers will not live up to, cannot live up to, given their particularist ambitions. One might say that these standards themselves embody ruling class interests, but they do so only within a universalist disguise. And they also embody lower-class interests, else the disguise would not be convincing. Ideology strains toward universality as a condition of its success. (Ibid.: 40–41)

This double embodiment in the dominant ideology of beliefs of both ruling and ruled makes criticism possible and inevitable. The "fact of hegemony," as Walzer quotes Gramsci, ensures "that one takes into account the interests and tendencies of the groups over which hegemony will be exercised" and requires "that the hegemonic groups will make some sacrifices of a corporate nature." Because of these sacrifices ruling ideas "internalize contradictions, and so criticism always has a starting point inside the dominant culture." So, for example, if we consider how the idea of equality enshrined in bourgeois ideology becomes hostage to radical criticism, we can see how "upper-class ideology carries within itself dangerous possibilities." Considered in Marxist terms

> as the credo of the triumphant middle classes, equality has a distinctly limited meaning. Its reference, among French revolutionaries, say, is to equality before the law, the career open to talents, and so on. It describes (and also conceals) the conditions of the competitive race for wealth and office. Radical critics delight in "exposing" its limits: it guarantees to all men and women, as Anatole France wrote, an equal right to sleep under the bridges of Paris. But the word has larger meanings—it would be less useful if it did not—subordinated within but never eliminated from the ruling ideology. These larger meanings are, to use a Gramscian term, "concessionary" in character; with them or through them the middle classes gesture toward lower-class aspiration. (Ibid.: 41–43)

These gestures are not insincere; if they were "social criticism would have less bite than it does have." But the gestures can nonetheless be invoked by the social critic who "exploits the larger meanings of equality, which are more mocked than mirrored in everyday experience." The resources for social criticism, then, "are always available, because of what a moral world is, because of what we do when we construct it" (ibid.: 43, 46).

To stress that this is not a functionalist view, Walzer points out that "the capacity for criticism always extends beyond the 'needs' of the social structure itself and its dominant groups." Although the moral and the social worlds are more or less coherent, "they are never more than more or less coherent. Morality is always potentially subversive of class and power." This is why "we live anxiously with our ideologies; they are strained and awkward; they do not ring true, and we wait for some angry or indignant neighbor or friend or former friend, the private version of a social critic, to tell us so." Like ancient prophets such as Amos—who exemplifies the social critic at his best for Walzer—effective social critics' work is always immanent. It rests on "the identification of public pronouncements and respectable opinion as hypocritical, the attack upon actual behavior and institutional arrangements, the search for core values (to which hypocrisy is always a clue), the demand for an everyday life in accordance with the core" (ibid.: 21–22, 47, 87). No social good ever achieves perfect dominance, then, and herein lies the basis of social criticism. Because "dominance is always incomplete and monopoly imperfect, the rule of every ruling class is unstable." It is "continually challenged by other groups in the name of alternative patterns of conversion"—conversion, that is, of the resources available to the dominant interest into the basic unit of social value (Walzer 1983a: 11).

It is unfortunate that Dworkin and other critics of Walzer, who fault him for not attempting to supply a consistent general defense of his theory, have paid no attention to this account of immanent criticism of dominant ideologies because it is clearly integral to his project.[2] An ideology, for Walzer, is a claim to monopolize a dominant good "when worked up for public purposes." Struggles among conflicting ideologies take a "paradigmatic form" in which, Walzer tells us, "I have sought the guiding thread of my own argument." What is this paradigmatic form? Some group—"class, caste, strata, estate, alliance, or social formation"—comes to control a dominant good and to convert it "more or less systematically" until it pervades society.

2. See Dworkin's "To Each His Own," a review of *Spheres of Justice* that appeared in the *New York Review of Books* on April 14, 1983, and a reply by Dworkin to Walzer's response that appeared on July 21, 1983.

So wealth is seized by the strong, honor by the wellborn, office by the well educated. Perhaps the ideology that justifies the seizure is widely believed to be true. But resentment and resistance are (almost) as pervasive as belief. There are always some people, and after a time there are a great many, who think the seizure is not justice but usurpation. The ruling group does not possess, or does not uniquely possess, the qualities it claims; the conversion process violates the common understanding of the goods at stake. Social conflict is intermittent, or it is endemic; at some point, counterclaims are put forward. (Walzer 1983a: 12)

This process has no logical conclusion or outcome; for Walzer there is no dynamic teleology to immanent criticism as there is for Hegel, no process by which social arrangements become progressively more adequate as a result of historical changes. "One group wins, and then a different one; or coalitions are worked out, and supremacy is uneasily shared. There is no final victory, nor should there be" (ibid). To think that there could be is to expect too much from moral and political argument. Critical interpretations can do no more than "set the terms of moral argument"; the argument itself goes on forever, with "only temporary stopping points, moments of judgment" (Walzer 1987: 49). Everyday moral argument takes the form of story telling, and this is preferable to attempts at scientific ethics that will settle things for all time,

better even though there is no last story that, once told, would leave all future storytellers without employment. I understand that this indeterminacy prompts, not without reason, a certain philosophical apprehension. And from this there follows the whole elaborate apparatus of detachment and objectivity, whose purpose is not to facilitate criticism but to guarantee its correctness. The truth is that there is no guarantee, any more than there is a guarantor. Nor is there a society, waiting to be discovered or invented, that would not require our critical stories. (Ibid.: 65–66)

The picture is almost Foucaultian: relations of domination constantly replace and supersede one another but are never abolished.[3] Social conflict over patterns of conversion is endless, and particular arguments about dis-

---

3. This is not to say that Walzer subscribes to Foucault's localist analysis of power, which he has explicitly rejected (1983b: 481–89). Aspects of his discussion of Foucault are taken up below.

tributive justice might best be thought of as provisional solutions from the points of view of particular social groups.

Why take this view of political theory as social criticism? Walzer's defense turns on comparing it with the principal alternatives, the paths of "discovery" and "invention." Those who opt for the path of discovery assume that "morality is a creation; but [that] we are not its creators." Most religious morality and conventional natural law theory are of this kind, but so is much secular political philosophy. Plato, Marx, and the utilitarians were all philosophers of discovery in Walzer's sense. The injunctions of arguments that rest on appeals to discovery are invariably at odds with reality, and herein lies the source of their critical edge. Discovery is "critical from the beginning, for it would hardly be a revelation if God commanded us to do and not do what we were already doing and not doing." Accounts of natural law or natural rights "rarely ring true as descriptions of a new moral world." Indeed, discoverers like Bentham, who evidently believe that they have discovered some eternal facts about the human condition, are often so startled by the degree to which apparent implications of their discoveries depart from the everyday experience that they fiddle with their arguments to yield arguments "closer to what we all think" (Walzer 1987: 4, 19, 6–7). The second possibility, the path of invention, rests on the assumption "that there is no pre-existent design, no divine or natural blueprint to guide us." Not surprisingly, those who have walked this path—Descartes is the paradigm example—begin with questions of method, with a "design of a design procedure." Central to the path of invention is agreement. The work of Descartes's legislator "is very risky unless he is a representative figure, somehow embodying the range of opinions and interests that are in play around him," and it is not surprising in contractarian political theory that inventors from Hobbes to Rawls are concerned with the creation of institutions that can win the assent of all. Assuming the death of God and the meaninglessness of nature, there is no alternative appeal; the task for inventors is to conjure up the moral world "that would have existed if a moral world had existed without their inventing it." It is just because this morality commands assent that we can use it as a standard "against which we can measure any person's life, any society's practices." Morality by invention derives its critical force "from the process by which it was created. If we accept it, it is because we have participated, or can imagine ourselves having participated, in its invention" (ibid.: 10, 12–13).

To exhibit the superiority of the path of interpretation over both these alternatives, Walzer argues that they collapse into it. He advances the metaphor of the three branches of government. Discovery "resembles the work of the executive: to find, proclaim, and then enforce the law." Invention "is legislative from the beginning." It involves the creation of that which is to be enforced. Interpretation, by contrast, is "the proper work of the judicial branch"; its goal is to get at the meanings of authoritative values, to interpret them in light of existing practice (ibid.: 18–19). Walzer's purpose in invoking the analogy is to establish what it obscures as well as what it reveals. Just as we know that the acts of executive and legislative branches involve interpretation, so too in moral philosophy, whatever path we think we walk, we end up walking his third. Discoverers in moral philosophy can only really discover what they already know. "I do not mean to deny the reality of the experience of stepping back, though I doubt that we can ever step back all the way to nowhere." Just as the great majority of legislation involves modification and codification of existing precedent, so the path of invention at least "runs close" to that of interpretation (ibid.: 6–7, 19). As Walzer elaborates,

> The claim of interpretation is simply this: that neither discovery nor invention is necessary because we already possess what they pretend to provide. Morality, unlike politics, does not require executive authority or systematic legislation. We do not have to discover the moral world because we have always lived there. We do not have to invent it because it has already been invented—though not in accordance with any philosophical method. No design procedure has governed its design, and the result no doubt is disorganized and uncertain. It is also very dense: the moral world has a lived-in quality, like a home occupied by a single family over many generations, with unplanned additions here and there, and all the available space filled with memory-laden objects and artifacts. The whole thing, taken as a whole, lends itself less to abstract modeling than to thick description. Moral argument in such a setting is interpretive in character, closely resembling the work of a lawyer or judge who struggles to find meaning in a morass of conflicting laws and precedents. (Ibid.: 19–20)

Walzer does not go all the way with the claim that discovery and invention are simply forms of disguised interpretation, but he argues that "the more novel these are, the less likely they are to make for strong or even plausible arguments." Unless they generate results that conform to our everyday moral intuitions—which are "the product of time, accident, external force, political compromise, fallible and particularist intentions"—they are unlikely to be taken seriously (ibid.: 21, 20).

Even if the paths of discovery and invention turn out to be negotiable,

Walzer wants to argue that they are unattractive. Discovery can at best reveal minimal moral standards that are unlikely to shed much new light. "Consider [Thomas] Nagel's discovery of an objective moral principle," Walzer tells us, "that we should not be indifferent to the suffering of other people. I acknowledge the principle but miss the excitement of revelation. I knew that already." [4] The minimal code may command universal assent, so that "though it might require explanation, [it] would presumably not require conversion." But by the same token it will not issue in concrete injunctions for action or solve actual moral dilemmas as they arise in particular circumstances without the addition of contextually based moral argument. So we can think of the prophet Jonah as a "minimalist critic": although he issued some general injunctions for moral behavior, "we do not really know what sorts of changes he required in the life of Nineveh." Amos, by contrast, expressed his injunctions in terms the Israelites themselves embraced, so although we may be able to extract a minimal injunction from his teaching—such as "do not oppress the poor"—his power and authority "derives from his ability to say what oppression means, how it is experienced, in this time and place, and to explain how it is connected with other features of a shared social life" (Walzer 1987: 45, 89–91).

Invention may be more radically alienating than discovery because in setting up the goal of constructing an all-purpose morality, its proponents rule out those particular and parochial aspects of our lives that fashion our morality. It is "as if we were to take a hotel room or an accommodation apartment or a safe house as the ideal model of a human home." Although it may be that if deprived of a home and required to design rooms that any of us might live in "we would probably come up with something like, but not quite so culturally specific as, the Hilton Hotel," it would not be satisfying. Even if it were comfortable for all or it catered effectively to the needs of the most disadvantaged, Walzer argues in allusion to Rawls's principles of justice, "we might still long for the homes we knew we once had but could no longer remember. We would not be morally bound to live in the hotel we had designed." There is something about being at home that is essential to our sense of well-being; even in Kafka's journal hotel rooms are preferred because he feels more at home in them. Even in this case, there is "no other way to convey the sense of being in one's own place except to say 'at home'" (ibid.: 14, 15).

4. Walzer (1987: 6, footnote omitted). As he elaborates, "What is involved in discoveries of this sort is something like a dis-incorporation of moral principles, so that we can see them, not for the first time but freshly, stripped of encrusted interests and prejudices. Seen in this way, the principles may well look objective; we 'know' them in much the same way as religious men and women know the divine law. They are, so to speak, *there*, waiting to be enforced. But they are only there because they are really here, features of ordinary life."

Despite his use of Gramsci's account of hegemony and the terminology of class conflict, Marxism as a philosophical system offers little from Walzer's point of view. Its explanatory theory is an instance of the path of discovery; its socialist utopia perhaps more properly described as invention. Yet its treatment of everyday beliefs as epiphenomenal writes off the vast majority of what moral argument is really about; indeed, revolutionary Marxists do not engage in social criticism at all. They are more interested in conquest than conversion:

> Marxists never undertook the sort of reinterpretation of bourgeois ideas that might have produced Gramsci's "new ideological and theoretical complex." The reason for this failure lies in their view of the class struggle as an actual war in which their task, as intellectuals, was simply to support the workers. . . . Marxists are not properly called critics of bourgeois society, for the point of their politics is not to criticize but to overthrow the bourgeoisie. They are critics of the workers instead, insofar as the workers are ideological prisoners and so fail to fulfill their historical role as the agents of overthrow. (Ibid.: 52, 56–57)

Marxism's great mistake is that, to the extent that it acknowledges a commonality of values, it treats this as a failure to be explained in terms of false consciousness and in so doing "misses a critical opportunity to describe socialism in socially validated and comprehensible terms." Yet the only alternative for Marxists "is not to describe it at all" because discovering or inventing socialist principles anew "does not seem to have been a practical possibility. Why should the workers stake their lives for *that?* Marx would have done better to take seriously his own metaphorical account of the new society growing in the womb of the old" (ibid.: 57).

Yet Walzer does not want to go all the way with the ordinary language philosophers who take people's conceptions of their ideals and actions at face value; he wants to show that often, perhaps even typically, people do not actually believe in or do what they claim to believe or do. They do not consistently apply the principles they think they live by, and as a result the moral world generated by their actions fails to measure up to the one they describe or advocate. Like Hume, then, Walzer appeals to convention[5] but is not a *conventionalist.* Walzer distances himself from Oakeshott's view of interpretation, which involves the mere "pursuit of

---

5. Thus he explicitly follows Hume's account of the emergence of a norm against theft, "which 'arises gradually, and acquires force by a slow progression and by our repeated experience of the inconvenience of violating it'" (Walzer 1987: 24, footnote omitted).

intimations" inherent in our traditions of behavior. For Walzer, although Oakeshott is right to insist that there is no "mistake-proof apparatus" that can be appealed to to tell us which intimations are most worth preserving, Oakeshott fails to see that "cultures are open to the possibility of contradiction (between principles and practices) as well as to what Oakeshott calls 'incoherence' (among everyday practices)," which makes critical political argument both possible and necessary. Interpretation, then, "does not commit us to a positivist reading of the actually existing morality" (ibid.: 29). We are all interpreters of the morality we share, and we are bound to explore and argue over the tensions that get generated within this morality and between it and our everyday practices.

(ii) Second-Order Critical Claims

At one level, then, Walzer's discussion of equality and pluralism in *Spheres of Justice* is simply an account of critical thinking. Individuals and groups adversely affected by the dominance and monopoly of particular goods appeal to the "abolitionist" idea of equality and make the "pluralist" claim that the patterns of convertibility currently prevailing in the interests of dominant groups involve the illicit extension of the distributive principle attending a particular good to spheres beyond those entailed by its meaning. As a descriptive thesis about how at least one major kind of political argument proceeds, Walzer's account seems both insightful and plausible. Dominant groups frequently twist and manipulate socially accepted meanings to achieve dominance and monopoly, as Walzer describes. He is surely right that these attempts to manipulate meanings can never be complete because of the many-sided nature of political terms such as equality, freedom, right, and justice. Hanna Pitkin made this clear in her response to the claim that acknowledging the Wittgensteinian equation of meaning with use need not generate historicism and relativism, as many have charged.[6] Using a term like *justice*, says Pitkin, in a whole mesh of interrelated and overlapping ways limits the political manipulability of the term and its cognates and always leaves open the possibility of critical evaluation of a particular substantive use. We do (or fail to do) justice to meals as well as to criminals, to an author's intentions as well as to a corrupt politician, to our convictions as well as to our students, and this whole network of overlapping meanings cannot simply be detached from a single particular substantive use for an ulterior purpose. The Orwellian specter of a Newspeak ideology in which WAR IS PEACE and FREEDOM IS SLAVERY seems shocking to us because the degree of hegemonic

6. See Pitkin (1972: 175–76). For a recent formulation of the conservative relativism charge, see Bloor (1983).

control this suggests (which was not total even in that case) would require a revolution in accepted meanings and uses so complete that the very possibility of critical appraisal of what appear to us now as deviant uses would be foreclosed. But limiting cases are limiting cases, and their very existence indicates that our normal expectations and experiences are different. In practice hegemony is never complete and acquiescence in relations of domination by the dominated is intrinsically vulnerable to immanent attack. In this connection it should be noted that Walzer sees his embracing of prevailing valuations of social goods as a starting point for immanent critical argument, not as the conclusion to a Burkean endorsement of the status quo. This is neatly summed up in the context of his rejection of the Marxist tactic of refusing to acknowledge the importance of the pluralist ideal in liberal societies when he says that "the point is not to reject separation [of spheres] as Marx did but to endorse and extend it, to enlist liberal artfulness in the service of socialism" (Walzer 1984a: 318).

Walzer describes himself as deliberately standing "in the cave, in the city, on the ground" and denies that he is searching for an "ideal map or a master plan." Instead he has sought the "guiding thread" of his argument in the struggles of particular ideologies in conflict (Walzer 1983a: xiv, 26, 12). Yet he does want to offer his own substantive account, which moves beyond a description of the dynamics of ideological conflict in at least two ways. The more general of these concerns the proposition that in advocating pluralism and equality he is doing no more than advocating critical argument. Because he seems to think that patterns of domination and the "convertibility" they bring with them never disappear but are simply replaced by different ones, he might, at first blush, be read as having sympathies for oppressed groups and encouraging them to attack prevailing patterns of domination and the convertibility of dominant goods. The consistent position underlying this claim would be sympathy for the underdog without a substantive positive position beyond this. This reading of Walzer would make it an act of bad faith for the social critic to accept *any* prevailing distribution of social goods because of the convertibility it brings with it. The only viable standpoint is a perpetually critical attitude toward existing distributive practices, whatever these might be.

Yet this characterization misses the fact that Walzer does not call, as Marx did, for relentless criticism of all existing institutions. Indeed, it is integral to Walzer's conception of effective social criticism that the critic retain a basic moral and emotional connectedness to the community whose practices he criticizes. This is what Walzer finds admirable in Camus's attitude toward the *pied noir* community during the Algerian war, in contrast to such French intellectuals as Jean-Paul Sartre and Simone de

Beauvoir, who "established their detachment and denounced the local barbarians" but refused to see atrocities on the other side. They separated
themselves, ideologically and emotionally, from the *pied noir* community
by blind and unconditional support for the FLN against the French. So
although de Beauvoir knew about the brutality of the FLN's internal wars,
she "chose not to write about it; she seems never to have given a thought
to the likely fate of the *pied noir* community after an FLN victory." She
defined the FLN as representing liberation in an "ideologically flattened
world" and thus achieved critical distance at the price of something close
to hypocrisy. Her severing of herself from the French nation with de
Gaulle's return to power in 1958 amounted to a denial of her identity
(Walzer 1984b: 426–27). Sartre took a similar view, believing that the
intellectual must adopt the role of "permanent critic." The danger with
this posture is that the intellectual who cuts loose all parochial ties may
find himself "with no concrete and substantive values at all." In that case
"universality turns out to be an empty category for deconditioned men
and women, and so their commitment to the movement of the oppressed
is (as Sartre at one point says it should be) 'unconditional.'" Walzer is thus
unsurprised that once Sartre committed himself to the Algerian national-
ists, "he seemed incapable of a critical word about their principles or policies. Henceforth he aimed his ideas, as a soldier with more justification
might aim his gun, in only one direction" (Walzer 1987: 57–58). Camus,
by contrast, is admirable for Walzer because he refused to do this. Camus
belonged to a community that (from the Marxist point of view he largely
accepted) was "historically in the wrong," but although he criticized the
French he would not renounce his own community and detach himself
from it. He accepted who he was. "I believe in justice, but I will defend
my mother before justice," Camus said, a proposition that Walzer adapts
and incorporates by saying that a conception of justice that has no place
for love is unacceptable. "Camus had no use for philosophers who loved
humanity and disdained the men and women among whom they lived."
Thus he asks how a solution to the problems of Algeria "that ignored
Camus's mother, or the interests of the *pied noir* community generally,
could possibly be just. Men and women don't lose their rights even if they
are 'historically in the wrong.'"

Here Walzer is making more than the familiar point that it is moral
cowardice, not moral courage, to run away from a difficult situation and
criticize it from a safe distance (although he clearly wants to say that); he
also wants to say that justifiable social criticism must have an affective
component, that we must have connections with, and commitments to,
the communities whose practices we criticize. "Even 'true intellectuals'

have parents, friends, familiar places, warm memories," he notes. "Perfect solitude, like existential heroism, is a romantic idea" (Walzer 1984b: 428–30). Because we all have powerful emotional commitments of this kind, a view of critical thinking that ignores—or pours scorn on—them cannot be acceptable.[7] In *Interpretation and Social Criticism* Walzer modifies this view slightly, recognizing that criticism may require a degree of critical distance. "It is not clear, though, how much distance critical distance is," and he continues to resist the "conventional view" that treats radical detachment as the critical ideal.[8] Marginal people or "members of subject classes or oppressed minorities, or even outcasts and pariahs" might be good critics. But none of these is unconnected. Indeed, the conventional view is at fault precisely for requiring that even the marginal critic be "detached from his own marginality."

> In the conventional view, the critic is not really a marginal figure; he is—he has made himself into—an outsider, a spectator, a "total stranger," a man from Mars. He derives a kind of critical authority from the distance he establishes. We might compare him to an imperial judge in a backward colony. He stands outside, in some privileged place, where he has access to "advanced" or universal principles; and he applies these principles with an impersonal (intellectual) rigor. He has no other interest in the colony except to bring it to the bar of justice. (Walzer 1987: 36, 37, 38)

The detached critic is often thought to be heroic, "for it is a hard business . . . to wrench oneself loose, either emotionally or intellectually. To walk 'alone . . . and in the dark' [as Descartes sought to do] is bound to be frightening." Yet Walzer is less than impressed by this heroism; whereas the detached critic may pay a price in terms of lost "comfort and solidar-

7. Walzer is thus unimpressed by Foucault's refusal to identify with any interest or community as its intellectual spokesman, with his much flaunted political detachment. "[O]ne cannot even be downcast, angry, grim, indignant, sullen or embittered *with reason* unless one inhabits *some* social setting and adopts, however tentatively, its codes and categories" or, much more difficult, unless one tries to create alternative codes and categories. Foucault refuses to do either, and his relentlessly critical stance is, for Walzer, uninteresting even if it is intelligible. See Walzer (1983b: 490).

8. "I do not mean to banish the dispassionate stranger or the estranged native. They have their place in the critical story, but only alongside and in the shadow of someone quite different and more familiar: the local judge, the connected critic, who earns his authority, or fails to do so, by arguing with his fellows—who, angrily and insistently, sometimes at considerable personal risk . . . objects, protests, and remonstrates. This critic is one of us" (Walzer 1987: 38–39).

ity," it is more than compensated for once detachment is achieved. Disentangled from the complexities and commitments of everyday life in society, criticism becomes both easy and costless (ibid.: 36–37).

The standard view of critical distance, then, rests on the homely but misguided analogy that we are more likely to find fault with others than with ourselves. This leads us to turn our own people into "the others"—to treat them as strangers or make ourselves strangers to them.

> The trouble with the analogy is that such easy fault-finding is never very effective. It can be brutal enough, but it doesn't touch the conscience of the people to whom it is addressed. The task of the social critic is precisely to touch the conscience. Hence heretics, prophets, insurgent intellectuals, rebels—Camus's kind of rebels—are insiders all: they know the texts and the tender places of their own culture. Criticism is a more intimate activity than the standard view allows. (Walzer 1984b: 432)

The attractiveness of the model of detached criticism derives from the expectation that if we can only get the critical standards right, "the argument can be won once and for all. Hence that heroic figure, the perfectly disinterested spectator, imagined as a kind of all-purpose, general-service social critic." The claim of detached criticism rests on a divided view of the self. Self one is "still involved, committed, parochial, angry," while the second is "detached, dispassionate, impartial," and quietly watching the first. Self two is thought in the conventional view to be superior, his criticism "more reliable and objective, more likely to tell us the moral truth about the world in which the critic and all the rest of us live. Self three would be better still." Yet why would self two be interested in criticism at all? Would such a detached critic not rather adopt the role of "radical skeptic or a mere spectator or a playful interventionist, like the Greek gods"? If self two abandons the moral beliefs and motivations of self one, he cannot "experience those beliefs and motivations in the same way, once he has evacuated the moral world within which they have their immediate reality and distanced himself from the person for whom they are real." Radical detachment involves "drowning out" the values "that arise from the critic's own life in his own time and place." Although this detachment can certainly result in mandates for radical social and political change, it is "more likely to be a conversion or a conquest," the "total replacement of the society from which the critic has detached himself with some (imagined or actual) other." Walzer does not go so far as to exclude all such criticism by definition, but he sees it most often as morally unattractive, not a form of objectivity that we should admire (Walzer 1987: 50, 49–50, 51, 52).

Strategically, no one in the relevant community minds what the unconnected critic says because of his lack of connectedness. "The detached and disinterested moralist goes on and on, and we don't care." His opinions do not matter, but those of the connected critic do because the latter accepts us. Our notions of self-esteem, and our sense of collective legitimacy, are bound up with that acceptance because the critic is an identifying, constitutive component of our community. The critic must speak to those who accept, respect, and even rely on him if he is to speak effectively. He must pull them by their own convictions to the position he advocates; to do this, he must retain their acceptance and respect. There must be bonds of mutuality, intellectual and emotional; there must be "commitment to particularity" for social criticism to work. "It's not that one severs the threads [with one's community] in order to become a critic, but that the force of one's criticism leads one to think about severing the threads." Yet this temptation must be resisted "for the social critic must have standing among his fellow citizens. He exploits his connections, as it were, not his disconnections." If an identifying social critic so despairs of his own community's actions as to be reduced to silence—as Camus eventually was by the irretrievable deterioration of the Algerian conflict—this speaks more powerfully than the self-righteous outpourings of the unconnected critic. "The silence of the connected social critic is a grim sign—a sign of defeat, a sign of endings. Though he may not be wrong to be silent, we long to hear his voice" (Walzer 1984b: 432, 426, 432).

Commitment to particularity, then, is at the heart of good social criticism. Again Walzer finds an analogy to judging helpful on this point, although what he has in mind might be more accurately described as common law making. The question presented to courts, he notes, invariably refers "to a particular body of laws or to a particular constitutional text, and there is no way to answer the question except by giving an account of the laws or the text." Neither the accumulated body of law nor the statutory texts have "the simplicity and precision of a yardstick against which we might measure the different actions urged by the contending parties. Deprived of a yardstick, we rely on exegesis, commentary, and historical precedent, a tradition of argument and interpretation" (Walzer 1987: 22). Although every given interpretation will turn out to be contentious, we must accept that just as there is no alternative in legal argument, so too there is none in moral argument. In debates about equality and affirmative action, for example, many of us take it for granted that the question "what is the right thing to do?" is the correct question.

> The general question about the right thing to do is quickly
> turned into some more specific question—about the ca-
> reer open to talents, let's say, and then about equal oppor-
> tunity, affirmative action and quotas. These . . . require
> us to argue about what a career is, what sorts of talents
> we ought to recognize, whether equal opportunity is a
> "right," and if it is, what social policies it mandates. These
> questions are pursued within a tradition of moral dis-
> course—indeed they only arise within that tradition—
> and they are pursued by interpreting the terms of that dis-
> course. The argument is about ourselves; the meaning of
> our way of life is what is at issue. The general question we
> finally answer is not quite the one we asked at first. It has
> a crucial addition: what is the right thing *for us* to do?
> (Ibid.: 23, footnote omitted)

(iii) First-Order Critical Claims

How does this account of Walzer's view of critical thinking enable us to
understand his concrete political claims? The relationship between these
two levels of argument is difficult to pin down, partly because of an ambiguity in Walzer's uses of the concepts of pluralism and equality in *Spheres
of Justice*. The ambiguity is between the uses already described—to indicate the mechanisms by which systems of domination and the convertibility of dominant goods are regularly challenged and displaced (equality as
abolitionist politics and pluralism as the means for advocating separation
of control of a particular good from another)—and the substantive, characteristically liberal commitments to doctrines of pluralism and equality.
Advocating pluralism and equality as a method of attacking any and all
systems of domination and control on the grounds that this method best
takes account of the typical nature of political conflict differs from engaging in substantive criticism of prevailing doctrines of pluralism and equality in contemporary liberal culture, and Walzer clearly wants to engage in
the second activity as well as the first. He wants to apply his pluralist and
egalitarian method of social criticism to the doctrines of pluralism and
equality as they work themselves out in contemporary liberal practices to
show that the latter function to legitimate practices of domination and the
convertibility of dominant goods.

For Walzer, that liberals have characteristically failed to oppose various
kinds of domination and the convertibility of dominant goods—despite
their professed commitments to substantive doctrines of pluralism and
equality—tends to be "less importantly a failure of nerve than a failure of
perception." He has no conspiracy theory of liberal ideology; liberal writ-

ers "literally did not 'see' individual wealth and corporate power," for example "as social forces, with a political weight, as it were, different from their market value." For this reason they genuinely thought they had done enough to secure liberty by creating a market, opposing state intervention, and setting entrepreneurs free; they did not perceive either the extent to which such institutions would require an active state for their effective maintenance or the possibilities for the corruption of other social spheres (notably politics) inherent in the evolution of the market system (Walzer 1984a: 322). Walzer wants to show liberals that they "have not been serious enough about their own art" of separating spheres of social and political activity (ibid.: 320).

Walzer's essential claim, then, is that if we take seriously prevalent conceptions of pluralism and equality within their own terms, they generate conclusions that many liberals would find unacceptably radical, resting as they do on substantive accounts of the good and of the good community. The immanent logic of these accounts requires practices that are frequently at variance with contemporary liberal practices. "Complex equality" requires determining the meanings of the goods that prevail in different spheres of social interaction and then shoring up the boundaries among them. Equality, for Walzer, "is a complex relation of persons, mediated by the goods we make, share, and divide among ourselves," not "an identity of possessions." It requires "a diversity of distributive criteria that mirrors the diversity of social goods" (Walzer 1983a: 18). Contemporary liberal culture is hypocritical in that the dominance of certain spheres by distributive criteria alien to them contravenes its professed pluralist foundations. It is not that Walzer has a general theory that pluralism is good and dominance is bad; his point is that these are the official values of liberal culture. Part of what pluralism means is acknowledging the existence of a plurality of goods and practices making up the social world, goods and practices that are neither reducible to one another nor intrinsically better or worse than one another. The social differentiation that prevails in modern Western culture (a comparatively recent development) is basic to the conventional liberal outlook. Thus the "old, preliberal map [of society] showed a largely undifferentiated land mass"; what we today refer to as pluralism assumes a society divided into spheres of activity undertaken by different groups for different purposes, a society based, as Walzer puts it, on the "art of separation" (Walzer 1984a: 315). That we characteristically refer to the use of money to obtain political influence as *bribery* indicates how we value it—we regard it as an illegitimate extension of money into the political sphere (Walzer 1983a: 100). The critic who turns around and says, "Aha! There is a suppressed major premise behind such a claim holding that bribery is bad" is missing the point. No one doubts that bribery is bad; if they did they would not describe it as bribery. There may be many substantive disagreements about whether a particular action counts as bribery, about whether Abscam-style entrapment mitigates bribery, and so on, but the very existence of such controversies indicates a wide consensus on the evaluative-descriptive content (to use a term of Quentin Skinner's [1973: 298–304]) of the term itself. Similar points could be made concerning Walzer's use of such terms as *dominance, monopoly, tyranny,* and *justice,* the key elements of his critical analysis. His point is that if we look critically at liberal culture in terms of its official values, we will come up with conclusions that have a uniquely decisive moral force in liberal culture. Where our practices fail to measure up they will be revealed as endorsing hypocrisy and pretense. Again Walzer has no general moral theory to which he turns to be told that hypocrisy is bad; his point is that if you reveal people to be hypocritical they will see their own actions as reprehensible. Think again of Pitkin's point about the limits to the manipulability of the term *justice*. The Abscam bribee will (apart from the issue of positive legal sanctions) try endlessly to explain why he was not really accepting a bribe, for in many other contexts he must attack bribery, and he does not want to be revealed as a hypocrite.

This sort of evidence is important for Walzer. The ubiquitous practice of social criticism underlines the extent to which morality has to do with justification in the eyes of others. "Men and women are driven to build and inhabit moral worlds by a moral motive: a passion for justification," Walzer argues. Although this passion might once have been satiated by an appeal to religious or other extrinsic standards, in a secular age the appeal has to be other people.

> It is not only rulers who want to be justified in the eyes of their subjects; each of us wants to be justified in the eyes of all the others. . . . We try to justify ourselves, but we cannot justify ourselves by ourselves, and so morality takes shape as a conversation with particular other people, our relatives, friends, and neighbors. . . . Because we know the people, we can, we have to, give these arguments some specificity: they are more like "love thy neighbor" (with a suitable gloss on all three words) than "don't be indifferent to the suffering of others." They are worked out with reference to an actual, not merely a speculative, moral discourse: not one person but many people talking. (Walzer 1987: 46–47)

Perhaps the clearest illustration of Walzer's method of immanent criticism at work on the substantive egalitarian and pluralist commitments of liberal ideology can be found in his defense of industrial democracy as the economic analogue of religious democracy implied by the liberal principle of religious toleration. His basic argument is that liberalism requires abolition of the power exercised outside the market by the possessors of wealth within the market for the same reasons as it required the disestablishment of the church. He notes that pluralism worked against "state churches and church states" not only by disestablishing the churches themselves but also by divesting them of their enormous secular wealth and power; that historically this was justified not only by Lutheran appeals to private conscience but also in the name of congregational self-government; and that while this is not the only possible institutional arrangement once church and state are separate, it is "the cultural form best adapted to and most likely to reinforce the separation" liberalism requires. Analogously, the pluralist art of separation must work against "both state capitalism and the capitalist state" (Walzer 1984a: 322).

Just as religious disestablishment would have been a fiction had the church not been divested of its instruments of public power, the market system today, although nominally private, is not effectively walled into this space; in fact, there is a "ready convertibility of wealth into power, privilege and position." The de facto private governments thus created must be socialized just as established churches were; the goal must be "the confinement of the market to its proper space" (ibid.: 322–23). This is why religious democracy must find its parallel in an industrial democracy with two main features: there must be room for the new entrepreneur ("just as there is room for the evangelist and the 'gathered' church") and there should not be room for economic power to shape public policy ("any more than for the high ecclesiastical authority that routinely calls upon the 'secular arm'"). Political power requires protection "not only against foreign conquest but also against domestic seizure." The liberal state must be made by liberals to live up to liberal proclamations of its neutrality with respect to different private lives, and "the idea of privacy presupposes the equal value, at least so far as the authorities are concerned, of all private lives." This can be true only if the state cannot be hostage to private economic power (ibid.: 323, 326, 320).

For Walzer it makes no sense to consider abolishing so enduring a characteristic of our current circumstances as the market system or to reject outright so central an aspect of contemporary culture as the market ideology. To do this would cost too much credibility. Rather the market's critic must turn the market on itself and show that the liberal ideal of freedom from domination that the market system is supposed to preserve requires a degree of socialization of capital and industrial democracy. For if capital takes control of the state and is convertible into power in other spheres, it must ultimately threaten everything from academic freedom to the system of meritocratic advancement that even capitalism requires for its continued well-being.

The logic of Walzer's analysis is reminiscent of Marx's (1974: 76–87) discussion of the fetishism of commodities. Just as Marx argued that this fetishism arises when what is actually a social relation among producers appears as a material relation among things and that people's failure to perceive the socially interdependent character of production hides from them the reality that they do not own what they make (as liberal ideology on its surface requires), so Walzer wants to reject the social primacy of the market for comparable reasons. Individual rights and the requirements of individual consent, although essential to the market system, make for a "bad sociology. They do not provide either a rich or a realistic understanding of social cohesion; nor do they make sense of the lives individuals actually live, and the rights they actually enjoy, within the framework of on-going institutions" (ibid.: 324).

Walzer and Marx differ, of course, in their explanations of the convertibility of capital into a mechanism of broad social and political power, and Marx would doubtless voice skepticism at the claim that it is possible to have a well-functioning market system appropriately walled in from other decisive areas of social and political life: for him the logical imperatives of capitalist production and accumulation made this impossible. Although it may be a sound criticism of Walzer to say that he needs to tell us more about how the appropriately walled in market is going to function (not least because of the lack of historical illustrations), how capital formation is going to occur, how wages will be set, and so on, it can be argued that he is pushing in the most viable direction. Marx never supplied a convincing theoretical account of how an efficient allocation of resources and production would occur without a market system, and in those industrial countries that have tried to do without it in the name of communism, the inefficiencies are both chronic and legion. Moreover these systems have not come close to reducing domination in Walzer's sense. Marx's whimsical and utopian dictatorship of the proletariat was transformed as it traveled into practice on the wings of Lenin's vanguard theory, and the reality has been dictatorship to the proletariat by the vanguard party. There has been no withering away of communist states, as Walzer notes in his critique of Foucault's exclusive concentration on the local exercise of power (Walzer 1983b: 487–88). Ironically perhaps, Foucault is guilty of a pluralist ignorance (or ignoring) of the decisive coercive power of the centralized state in the modern world, something that Walzer thinks undeniably central to all systems of political power and domination, not least those that prevail in the Soviet bloc countries.[9] The sources of domination differ under communism, but it is not credible to deny their existence; for this reason communist systems cannot be argued to be even provisional solutions from the standpoint of the dominated classes under liberal capitalism. It cannot therefore be surprising that Walzer does not explore this revolutionary possibility as a viable option for the capitalist democracies. Whether his critique of communist practices would make any sense from the standpoint of a social critic living in a so-called socialist country would be a different question, one Walzer has not explicitly addressed. But one would have to anticipate that it would not—that Walzer would expect social criticism in such circumstances to focus on the discrepancies between socialist ideology and practice, not between socialist practice and liberal ideology.[10]

II. Walzer's View: Three Difficulties

Walzer's argument contains much that is attractive, even compelling. Yet it confronts difficulties relating to its assumptions about the nature of political conflict and the content of social criticism, and his account of connected criticism must ultimately be rejected. Powerful as it is as a set of strategic considerations for the effective conduct of social criticism in certain circumstances, it fails as an account of political theory as social criticism.

(i) Intra- and Intercultural Political Conflict

Unlike Rorty, Walzer does confront the problem of conflicting values within and among cultures. He distinguishes two kinds of moral disagreements: those "within a cultural tradition" where people "interpret meanings in somewhat different ways or . . . take different positions on bound-

9. "[Foucault] provides no principled distinction, so far as I can see, between the Gulag and the carceral archipelagos. . . . Nor does he provide a genealogy of the Gulag and, what is probably more important, his account of the carceral archipelago contains no hint of how or why our own society stops short of the Gulag. . . . [He] believes that discipline is necessary for this particular society—capitalist, modern or whatever; he abhors all its forms, every sort of confinement and control, and so for him liberalism is nothing more than discipline concealed. For neither Hobbes nor Foucault does the constitution or the law or even the actual workings of the political system make any difference. . . . In fact, I think these things make all the difference" (1983b: 487).

10. This is certainly suggested by Walzer's analysis of Breyten Breytenbach in *The Company of Critics*, where Walzer argues that even apartheid is amenable to connected criticism. See Walzer (1988: 210–24).

ary disputes and on overlapping or entangled goods" (such as in arguments about quotas and affirmative action in contemporary America) and those disagreements that derive from "radically different cultural traditions, as in many third world states today."[11]

This distinction is not without its difficulties, however. For one thing, it is not obviously a characteristic of *Third World* as distinct from First World states, as witness the example of Northern Ireland. Walzer might readily concede this as an exceptional case, but consider a more typical one: the 1984 miners' strike in Britain that centered on the issue of whether comparatively inefficient pits should be closed even though such closure would mean certain destruction of various mining communities. Certainly some disputed the claim that the pits were unsalvageable from the standpoint of economic efficiency, but many accepted that their continued operation would involve a state subsidy (at least in terms of opportunity-cost pricing) but maintained that members of the mining communities were justified in expecting and requiring that the government not close down the pits. Some might say that this is a paradigm case of Walzer's "overlapping and entangled goods" in a society committed to both utilitarian efficiency and the value of preserving local communities and their unique traditions. But certainly not all the relevant actors in this dispute conceived of it this way. Some saw it as a battle to wrest decisive control of British industry from the unions and return to Parliament the authority to decide on the management of the public sector, a battle between Margaret Thatcher's government and the unions over "who governs Britain." Some, like Arthur Scargill, saw the conflict as an opportunity to transform the underlying socioeconomic structure into one in which a social wage trumps considerations of utilitarian efficiency. Others, such as many miners and their families, had no commitment to any such programmatic agenda; they simply attached supreme importance to their jobs and communities, without particularly caring about the broader socioeconomic consequences of preserving them. It might be argued that they had no business taking that attitude because they existed in and depended on the national economy in a multitude of ways, but to make an argument of this form is to accept a globalizing logic that most liberals, as well as Walzer I suspect, would want to avoid. In any case it seems antithetical to the idea of taking conventional beliefs as a basis for political argument to declare some subclass of them illegitimate. Walzer's more likely response would be that we need to show these particular protagonists that their view of things entails paying attention to other issues (con-

11. *New York Review of Books,* July 21, 1983, p. 44.

vincing parochial miners that it is in their interest, that in the long run it will do less damage to their communities—or do damage to fewer of those communities—if serious account is taken of the imperatives for the health of the British coal industry as a whole). Taking Walzer's claim that political argument proceeds in terms of "internal principles," we can imagine trying to pull these parochial miners by their own convictions to a less parochial view.

One difficulty with this line of reasoning is that it assumes that the conflict is not zero-sum, that there is in principle a solution that speaks both to the needs of efficiency and to those of the local communities such that the miners can be pulled by their convictions into accepting a different construction of the situation. Walzer's distinction between two kinds of disagreements takes too little account of the many conflicts within the advanced capitalist countries where there is a range of possible solutions (*outcomes* might be a better term) that benefit different groups differently and no obvious "best" solution. Ultimately in such conflicts there are winners and losers—winners at the expense of losers—and some subcultures, groups, and communities survive, reproduce themselves, and thrive at the expense of others. This is consistent with Walzer's descriptive thesis about the nature of ideological conflict but not obviously so with any particular solution or outcome to a conflict that Walzer or anyone else might want to advocate. To say that justice must take account of the interests of all the parties (as Walzer argued with respect to the *pied noir* community in Algeria) does not tell us how that account is to be taken or indeed whether there is a solution that speaks adequately to the interests of all the relevant parties. Walzer's distinction between First and Third World countries as paradigmatic of disagreements within and between cultural traditions assumes that in First World countries there could be solutions to distributive disagreements that could speak, in principle, to the interests of all and that we could all be brought to agree both on what the appropriate division within a sphere should be and on the correct lines of demarcation among spheres. Even when allocation of a good within a sphere is not a zero-sum problem, we may be unable to agree on how a surplus is to be divided. Once we acknowledge this, the possibility has to be taken seriously that sides will have to be taken that may entail disconnecting from a particular dominant group and refusing to acknowledge the legitimacy of its claims.[12] Anything less may simply perpetuate the distributive status quo

12. In Shapiro (1989b) I argue that a degree of illegitimacy attaches to every possible distribution of goods and power and indeed that this fact generates a unique justification for democratic decision making over the allocation of all social goods. This issue is taken up more generally in chapter 9, section II.

because the dominant group may refuse to make a significant movement. A certain amount of what Walzer refers to as "ideological flattening" doubtless occurs in all such circumstances, but this can surely be construed as necessary for maintaining links with the community one genuinely values. The price of maintaining Walzerian connectedness to one's community may be disconnecting from communities that threaten it.

Joseph Frank (1985: 105–7) makes an analogous point when he notes that it is quite possible to agree with Walzer's analysis of the merits and demerits of the respective positions of Sartre and Camus on the Algerian war but reverse the characterizations of disconnection and connection. Sartre's primary reference group was the French intelligentsia, "predominantly left-wing and in favor of the anti-colonial uprising; [he] was not risking anything he valued by going along with *them*. On the contrary, he was very eager to keep their favor." Camus, by contrast, "lived and wrote in the same 'world' and functioned in a very similar 'champ intellectuel' [as Sartre]; but his response was considerably different." Although he did not renounce the French intellectuals, his position alienated them, and in this regard it was Camus who became disconnected. Frank goes further, arguing that Camus's refusal to take the side of the *pied noir* community unconditionally alienated him from it as well; thus the price of his "genuine independence" of mind was forcible disconnection from all.

To this Walzer might respond that in cases where political or distributive conflict is zero-sum, there is simply no just solution to it,[13] but what some of us find difficult to accept is that this is not the typical case, particularly in recent years in the advanced capitalist democracies. During the 1970s, when everyone was writing about liberal corporatism and the inevitability of a negotiated social-democratic consensus among business, government, and labor, the alternative view might have been convincing. But in an era when the governments of the New Right on both sides of the Atlantic have flatly rejected this consensus, are busily dismantling the welfare state, and are successfully engaging in open warfare with organized labor in ways that most social scientists once thought impossible, this view seems altogether too benign for our circumstances. At the very least it cannot be accepted without argument that most significant distributive conflict in advanced capitalist countries is intracultural in Walzer's sense.[14]

13. In the case of Algeria, Walzer hints (1984b: 430) that partition might have been a solution, but the examples on record—Poland, India, Northern Ireland, Cyprus, and the West Bank—are neither individually nor collectively encouraging.

14. For my own views on these developments as they relate to macroeconomic policy-making, see Shapiro and Kane (1983: 5–39).

Walzer is aware of this difficulty. In his dispute with Dworkin over the provision of medical care in the United States, he acknowledges that different distributive principles are embraced by different people but continues to argue that "justice demands" a more egalitarian distribution of medical care in our society "because of what medical care means to us." Of this argument Walzer says,

> The argument is historical, sociological, contingent. Dworkin wants an entirely different kind of argument, so that one might say at the end, flatly, that a rich society that leaves medical care to the market "would not be a just society." I am in fact disinclined to say that just like that, for it may be the case that the wealth of some particular society ought to be spent on the cure of souls, not of bodies, or on defense, or drama, or education. I don't see how these priorities can be philosophically determined. But that is not to rule out radical criticism, for the actual distribution of salvation, security, and culture is likely to be distorted, has historically been distorted, by wealthy and powerful elites, and it is one of the tasks of moral philosophy (and of social theory too) to explain and condemn the distortions.[15]

But what precisely is being claimed here? What is this notion of distortion that makes social criticism possible and necessary? The claim that the solution to such conflicts cannot be "philosophically determined" is reminiscent of Marx's critique of German idealism summed up in the *Theses on Feuerbach*, but for Marx the rejection of philosophical solutions to questions of social justice in societies based on class conflict and domination entailed a programmatic concern with the actual structure and dynamics of that conflict and domination that both explained it and provided a basis for radical criticism of it. Marx had no qualms about articulating a theory of objective human interests in terms of which social relationships could be criticized. The real question for Walzer, who wants to avoid such commitments, is how to make sense of a notion of distortion without such a theory.[16]

Two issues present themselves in this regard. The first, which will

15. *New York Review of Books*, July 21, 1983, p. 44.
16. Walzer offers one tantalizing hint that he does have such a theory when he remarks that the stance of the social critic is natural: "We know that we do not live up to the standards that might justify us. And if we ever forget that knowledge, the social critic appears to remind us. His critical interpretation is the 'natural' one, given what morality is. Like Shaw's Englishman, the social critic 'does everything on principle.' But he is a serious, not a comic, figure because his principles are ones we share" (Walzer 1987: 48).

trouble many others more than it does this author, is whether Walzer can talk in terms of the distortions in a culture without having some implicit account of what an undistorted culture would be like.[17] To this there are three arguments in Walzer's defense. First, he can argue by reference to his account of the general dynamics of ideological conflict that in any culture there will invariably be distortions to be attacked and criticized because of the convertibility of dominant goods. There will always be those who benefit from prevailing patterns of convertibility at others' expense; these others will challenge dominance via arguments that the meanings of the relevant goods themselves do not justify prevailing distributive practices. Second, with regard to his analysis of the substantive doctrines of pluralism and equality in contemporary America, we have already seen that Walzer can give substantive content to immanent criticism by arguing that liberal practices violate liberal ideology in this specific sense: the liberal doctrines of pluralism and equality entail a state that enforces the autonomy of spheres of social action in some neutral way that is belied by liberal practices. This is not to say that philosophical accounts of neutral states are internally consistent or coherent but that there is this component in the dominant ideology: that life in liberal culture is undistorted, or at least that something is wrong if it is not. Whether or not the notion of an undistorted culture makes theoretical sense and whether or not such a culture could arise in practice, given the dynamics of ideological evolution that Walzer describes, basic assumptions about the lack of distortion in the official values of liberal culture can supply resources for attacking such structures of domination and convertibility as can be shown to exist. Again Marx's discussion of the fetishism of commodities comes to mind: that the bourgeois ideal of neutral exchange is belied by the practices conducted in its name. Whether there could be a system of exchange where analogous things did not happen is another matter.

Third, it is simply not true in general that the concept of distortion when applied as a descriptive term about social practices presupposes some account of an undistorted culture. To assume the converse is to take too little account of the negative and reactive ways in which we evaluate and try to alter social practices. We are constantly made aware, as we stumble through life, of what is inadequate, unworkable, unsatisfying, and unfair in vast areas of individual and social existence without necessarily hav-

17. This is implied in Dworkin's charge that Walzer, in *Spheres of Justice*, "tacitly assumes that there are only a limited number of spheres of justice whose essential principles have been established in advance and must therefore remain the same for all societies." See the *New York Review of Books*, April 14, 1983, p. 6.

ing at our disposal well-formulated notions of adequacy, workableness, satisfaction, and fairness. Here the evolutionary metaphors discussed in relation to Quine and Rorty in the last chapter are worth calling to mind. Organisms adapt and change in essentially negative terms, shying away from practices that threaten. When one strategy does not work they try another. They try to deal with the inadequacies of their circumstances by altering them. But none of this entails that adequate circumstances exist from the point of view of a particular organism or that if they do it will know and pursue them. Someone may well be able to diagnose a situation as inadequate to her needs and/or aspirations without knowing what, if anything, would be adequate. Think of how many unhappily married people experience precisely that predicament. Walzer's uses of the idea of social distortion resulting from mechanisms of domination and the con-vertibility of dominant goods might be thought of in such terms.[18] A set of distributive practices that confers power on some at the expense of oth-ers, despite official proclamations to the contrary, can seem unsatisfactory to the dominated (and no doubt to some of the dominant—if only for the reason supplied in Hegel's *Phenomenology*), even if they have no idea of what would be satisfactory distributive practices in general or whether these could be achieved in principle or in fact. There is a negative and adaptive evolutionary component to all biologically based life, and human life is no exception. It has a backward-looking and evasive quality that constantly confronts us with distortions and inadequacies, with what is unacceptable and no good in our lives, with the failures of individuals and of social mechanisms to survive and thrive. These facts frequently gener-ate the desire for general theories of good, adequate, and undistorted so-cial arrangements, but this does not for a moment entail that these can be articulated or attained even if they can be described.

It can plausibly be argued, then, that for these reasons Walzer's com-ments about social criticism being directed at prevailing cultural distor-tions need not require or presuppose a general theory of an undistorted culture. In linguistic terms, Walzer's critical account of prevailing linguis-tic norms need not presuppose any Habermasian theory of ideal speech situations and communicative competence. However, a second matter re-mains to be addressed. This concerns the substantive accounts of domina-tion and convertibility on which the practice of immanent criticism de-pends. In each of the three sets of reasons just supplied to defend Walzer's account of social criticism against the charge—leveled by Dworkin—that

18. This is not to say that Walzer would accept this as a characterization of his view.

there is an implicit preordained general theory behind Walzer's account, assumptions were made about actual practices and their conformity, or lack of it, to those required by prevailing ideological norms. If prevailing practices are to be criticized for this reason, however, such criticism will depend on an account of the practices themselves. We need to know what is going on in a given situation, who the dominators and the dominated are (seldom an uncontroversial question—the example of the French in Algeria is atypical in this regard because none of the protagonists wanted to argue that the French were not "historically in the wrong"), what the realistic alternatives are, and how they would benefit and harm different groups differently. Walzer is right to point out that these are not philosophical questions, and in denying this it seems writers like Dworkin are simply expecting too much from philosophical theories. But in making this claim Walzer is implicitly acknowledging the vast empirical tasks that confront the social critic. He cannot simply assume that the capitalist countries have reached the point where all significant distributive conflict is intracultural, for this assumes away some of the most contentious and controversial, but nonetheless central, cases.

(ii) The Content of Social Criticism

Leaving aside questions about the empirical nature of distributive conflict, a lacuna in Walzer's account of the moral content of social criticism has to be addressed. His substantive accounts of complex equality and pluralism are intended to provide the basis for a critique of prevailing practices in terms of the official values of liberal culture, and his discussion of industrial democracy was presented as a paradigm case of this immanent criticism at work. But the same question arises that arose in relation to Rorty: are liberal values as Walzer describes them the dominant values in American culture? Are they the official values such that his social critique will serve the function that he says social criticism must; will he touch the consciences of those he seeks to influence? There seems a case to be made that Walzer's account is a partial depiction of dominant American values and that there are other powerful influences—republican, nationalist, and antisocialist, for example—which limit American commitment to liberal and pluralist values in practice and which call into question whether most American consciences would be touched, for instance, by Walzer's parallels between disestablishment of the church and industrial democracy.

There are available to Walzer two responses to this charge that were not available to Rorty. The first is that Walzer can concede this point without making his whole analysis vulnerable because he is not holding that we live in a culture that is in its fundamental structure pluralist and egalitarian; his account of the dynamics of ideological conflict leaves room for the view that actual social practices deviate widely from official values. He thus carries a much less heavy burden than Rorty, for whom liberalism is supposed accurately to characterize both the dominant ideology and the actual social structure, so that it is unnecessary even to consider that there might be systematic divergences between the two. Indeed, as we saw, for Rorty we cannot even formulate questions about this relationship without venturing from the Garden of Eden and corrupting ourselves with metanarrative. For Walzer the socially constitutive character of beliefs means that ideology and practice are inevitably and intimately related, but the relationship between the two is not taken for granted and treated as transparent. On the contrary Walzer supplies us with good reasons for expecting there to be tensions between ideology and practice, tensions that are the raison d'être of social criticism and that can be exploited by the social critic.

Yet the question remains, what will Walzer say to the moralizing conservative republican with his interventionist social agenda who rejects liberal constructions of the principle of toleration out of hand, probably believes that we would be living in a better world had the church not been disestablished, and is openly hostile to the proposition that the state has no business interfering with a range of activities that have traditionally been regarded by liberals as part of the private sphere? One suspects that Walzer's response would be to challenge the extent to which such antiliberal notions have an exclusive hold on even the most doctrinaire members of the New Right. After all, their interventionist social agenda is typically accompanied by an extreme laissez-faire attitude in matters economic, and a liberal critic could at least hope to find some ideological opening by pressing for an explanation of this disjunction: finding some point at which the opponent does adhere to more traditional liberal notions and working at the boundaries of his convictions. So Walzer would not need to deny that many Americans have powerful commitments to different and conflicting moral and political values; all he would need to show is that the commitment to liberal principles is powerful enough that at some point most protagonists will want to hold onto them in some form. Then there is an opening for critical argument.

Things, however, are more complex. Although Walzer has written that the task of social criticism is to "touch the conscience," he has a more ambitious concrete agenda than just that. He wants to advocate substantive political courses of action beyond noting and rubbing our noses in the ways in which we violate our own professed principles. In *Spheres of Jus-*

tice and elsewhere he advocates concrete positions on questions ranging from the allocation of medical care, the purposes of education, and the use of quotas as remedial devices to the necessity for limiting the social and political power of money. Indeed, most of *Spheres of Justice* is devoted to arguing for a particular division of social goods along with particular distributive principles. But the question still remains: why is one set of distributive principles to be adopted over others that are also arguably consistent with conventional meanings? Why should we accept Walzer's contention, for example, that the purpose of the sphere of education is to prepare children for democratic citizenship, rather than for enlightenment or excellence (Walzer 1983a: 197–226)? Surely the latter values are at least as strongly represented as the former in our political culture. Put differently, we can accept Walzer's claim that for justice or equality to be realized they must be implied in our conventional behavior, that if a just society "isn't already here—hidden, as it were, in our concepts and categories—we will never know it concretely or realize it in fact" (ibid.: xiv), and still believe that many possible, perhaps mutually contradictory, distributive practices are hidden in our concepts and categories. To say that *ought* entails *can* is only partly to finesse the fact/value problem: it delimits what we can advocate to the realm of the possible, but within that realm it does not tell us what to advocate. Unless we want to embrace some Hegelian notion that there is a unique logical next step in social evolution somehow implied in the last (which Walzer surely does not), why pick one substantive position over the available alternatives? Why should we, in the industrial sphere, "enlist liberal artfulness in the service of socialism" (Walzer 1984a: 318), rather than one of the other possible causes in which it might be enlisted? Unless we want to take the view that there is only one possible way for market economies to evolve, only one set of practices consistent with liberal premises (in which case there would not be much point in advocating anything), we need to know why what Walzer advocates is better, to be preferred. On this point Walzer has not responded adequately to Dworkin's critique, even if he is right that Dworkin's solution fails too. Choices present themselves in political life that are unavoidable and inevitably controversial. Several of the things we might do about the distribution of medical care, several of the policies we might consider for abolishing racism can be argued to be consistent with the meanings of the relevant moral and political vocabularies. Different interpretations of the meanings will benefit different groups differently, and in advancing one position over others the social critic is making a choice, however implicitly.

In short, Walzer's claim that his own method of argument is superior to the "view from nowhere," which latter can at best generate a "minimal code" that will not resolve concrete moral and political dilemmas, breaks down. His own view is vulnerable in just the same way. It is indeterminate not only in the sense he explicitly embraces—that we should not expect solutions to moral dilemmas to be permanent—but also in the stronger sense that it will not even generate provisional solutions or "temporary stopping points" (Walzer 1987: 49) in moral and political disputes. To appeal to conventional meanings in a world where these are inevitably competing and conflicting will not resolve moral arguments without some additional premises that will allow for adjudication among those conflicting meanings. In short, the commitment to connected criticism does not tell the critic what to say.

(iii) The Situation of the Critic

Two difficulties arise concerning Walzer's discussion of the necessity for the social critic's being connected to the community she criticizes. Remember that Walzer reformulated Camus's remark about being a supporter of justice but not at the cost of his mother's life by saying that a conception of justice that has no room for love is inadequate *as a conception of justice*. For Walzer, our conception of justice must have room in it for our affective commitments, our feelings for "parents, friends, familiar places, warm memories," and social criticism that ignores or openly scoffs at these seems both cowardly and irrelevant. We must be who we are. Even if the community to which the critic belongs is "historically in the wrong," she should not simply repudiate it and deny the legitimacy of its members' claims.

This argument can be interpreted two ways, one tactical and one normative. The tactical interpretation is that if a social critic wants to convince the relevant community of her claim, she must accept that community and be known to accept it authentically. If a critic's respect for her community is valued by her group, this gives her moral leverage. A difficulty with this argument is that if her fellows know that her commitment is unconditional, how can she have any leverage with them? Surely the authentic emotional commitment to a group can be effective only if the group values that commitment, perhaps in some way depends on it, and if there is some realistic possibility that the commitment might be withdrawn. If people who are reluctant to change their ways know that when the chips are down they can count on her support, it is hard to see how her position is tactically strong. If they know she will never decide they have gone too far, they may not take account of her views at all. One only has to think of Israel's willful disregard of much American opinion about its policies in the West Bank between 1987 and 1989. Our children may legit-imately expect unconditional commitment from us until they are able to take responsibility for their own actions, but no one else, and certainly no political cause, merits the critical abdication it requires. In Walzer's terms, the critic should exploit her connections, not her disconnections, but con-nections cannot be exploited to much advantage if there is no realistic pos-sibility of disconnection.

This aside, the tactical interpretation of Walzer's claim assumes a par-ticular view of political change and conflict that, as I suggest in section II(i) above, might well be atypical. If we think of situations of irreconcil-able conflict or if we think that most significant distributive conflicts are zero-sum or that there is no uncontroversial way to allocate a surplus, it may be a hopeless tactical proposition to say that the effective route to change is immanent criticism of the dominant or ascendant group. Taking account of the dominant group's interests by definition may mean refusing to take account of some other groups' interests, and in these circumstances the critic will have to make her choice. This will in general be true when conflicting groups have staked out mutually exclusive claims to any finite resource. To hold onto the view that our conception of justice must under no circumstances lead us to renounce our emotional ties and bonds may reduce, in this situation, to the proposition that our conception of justice is nothing more than those ties and bonds.

Whether or not these issues can be resolved, they do not capture all of what Walzer wants to say about the affective relationship between the so-cial critic and the community to which she belongs. It is clear from his discussions of Sartre, de Beauvoir, and Foucault that Walzer thinks there is something reprehensible about disconnected social criticism, in addition to its being ineffective. He clearly wants to resurrect Camus for the dem-ocratic left and to establish that he was courageous in a way that Sartre and de Beauvoir were not. They took the easy way out by disconnecting from the *pied noir* community and taking an "ideologically flattened" view of the situation.[19] Yet there is a deep difficulty here for Walzer if he is simultaneously appealing to our affective commitments and making critical judgments about the behavior of Sartre, de Beauvoir, or anyone else. Affective commitments are nothing if they are not authentic; we can go along with a position we do not like because we are convinced that it is justified, that good reasons can be given for it, or that someone we care about wants it. But we cannot feel a commitment on these grounds; we

19. Indeed, one might go further and say that for Sartre, at least, it was—within his own terms—a hypocritical act of existential "bad faith" to pin his hopes for liberation in Algeria unconditionally on the FLN.

cannot decide to retain an emotional bond that we do not feel. When de Beauvoir declared, following the referendum endorsing de Gaulle's return to power in 1958, that she was no longer a member of the French people, that the results of the referendum "severed the last threads linking me to my country,"[20] she was describing how she no longer could feel connected. It seems pointless to say that she ought to have felt differently: she felt that way because of who she was. When Sartre saw as his primary bond the French left, rather than any other group with a stake in the Algerian conflict, that was what he felt because of who he was. Or when Walzer complains that Lenin was a bad social critic for "looking at Russia from a great distance and merely disliking" what he saw (Walzer 1987: 63), he is implicitly expecting that Lenin could have been someone other than who he was, which is in tension with the appeal to affective commitments. Had Camus disliked his mother, perhaps his attitude to the *pied noir* community might have been different, and had he felt no particular tie to them how could we criticize him for this while appealing to affective commitments as the basis for social criticism? In sum, once we appeal to affective connectedness as the basis for social criticism, it seems that valid social criticism is always a unique expression of the particular affective history of the individual social critic. The bonds, or lack of them, the emotional ambivalences, these things all reflect and constitute the social critic's specific history and nature. If we take seriously Walzer's injunction to be ourselves, then all social criticism is necessarily radically individual. One might even argue that this view of social criticism tells us more about the social critic, and about her emotional and psychological propensities and affiliations, than about the practices or structures she attacks. Indeed, we might be tempted to think of her criticism more as autobiography than as what is traditionally thought of as argument, so decisively is it tied to her unique experiences and identity.

III. Conclusion

The weaknesses of Walzer's account, then, are that it fails to supply us with a satisfying picture of the nature of political disagreement and that it evades the issue of the critic's own normative agenda and how that relates to choice among conflicting possibilities in a given situation. In addition, Walzer's account of the affective basis for social criticism raises difficulties for the tactical and normative cases he wants to advance. Indeed, when followed to its logical conclusion, his account seems to threaten our capacity to evaluate social criticism as argument (rather than autobiography) at

20. Quoted in Walzer (1984b: 426).

all. In chapter 9 I develop an alternative view of social criticism to Walzer's, which I describe as *principled criticism*. It rests on agreement with Walzer about the disutility of ex cathedra moral argument, but I argue for a different way of giving it up. Note, for now, that Walzer conflates the distinction between universality and particularity in moral argument with the unrelated distinction between the emotional connectedness or disconnectedness of the social critic. It is possible to be a particularist with respect to the first of these distinctions, to believe that general moral and social theories should be eschewed because they invariably fail and are pernicious in a variety of ways, but to hold at the same time that the feelings and motivations of the social critic are irrelevant to the moral content of her social criticism. I will argue that this latter is the superior view.

Part Three

Contemporary Political Theory
and the History of Ideas

4 The Tradition of Political Theory as Political Instruction

One of the most trenchant critics of political theory in its contemporary manifestations is Allan Bloom. In *The Closing of the American Mind*, published in 1987 to wide critical acclaim, Bloom synthesized arguments he has been advancing for some years into a relentless critique of modernity as illuminated by the problems of American universities. He is committed to counterposing to contemporary political theory a particular view of the tradition of political philosophy that, he believes, contains forgotten insights about politics and human nature, insights that are essential to understanding our contemporary problems. Bloom's view of the tradition is derived from the teaching and writing of Leo Strauss, and his arguments can be understood only in the context of that commitment. But Bloom's mode of argument and its characteristic insights and difficulties are of more general interest and come into central focus whenever the authority of a canon of texts is appealed to as a source of critical standards for evaluating conventional political and cultural practices.

To include a discussion of so radical an anticonventionalist and antihistoricist as Bloom in an analysis of appeals to context and history in contemporary political theory might seem odd, but to take this view would be to miss noteworthy dimensions of his argument. Certainly Bloom, with his avowedly premodern moral and political predilections, would reject out of hand the postmodern inclination to abandon concern with foundational questions. Indeed, he would likely see this suggestion as but one more instance of the nihilism inherent in the modernist project. But as I explain below, his analysis of that project is intended to render problematical the Enlightenment aspiration of grounding politics on reason in a way that is instructively compared with Rorty's. In at least some of its formulations, Bloom's historical argument is an attempt to show that the Enlightenment project was deeply misguided and to explain why it issues in our time in arguments like Rawls's. Bloom shares a radical antimodernism with the postmodernists, then, even if he draws different conclusions from it.

I. Bloom's View: Exposition

Bloom's attack on contemporary political theory is rooted in what he sees as its failure to come to terms with the crisis of modern culture. Just what that crisis consists in will concern us shortly; note for now that in the intellectual world it is reflected in, and to a degree caused by, a thorough ignorance of the Western tradition of political philosophy. This ignorance leads contemporary theorists to miss the fundamental insights of the masters who make up that tradition and to lose sight of the fundamental problems of political philosophy. Both of these deficiencies are, for Bloom, epitomized in Rawls's *A Theory of Justice*, which takes for granted a fundamental premise of moral and political equality. Rawls's book "begins by dismissing discussion of its egalitarian premise. It is only an analysis of what an egalitarian society should be, if you accept that equality is just" (Bloom 1980: 120; *see also* Bloom 1975a: 654–57).

(i) The Crisis of Modernity

The precise nature of Bloom's alleged crisis of modernity is difficult to pin down, although it centers on the breakdown of extrinsic conceptions of the good following the Enlightenment, the rise of historical consciousness, and a view of the decline of Western culture identified most famously by Leo Strauss in *Natural Right and History*. Strauss conceived of "three waves of modernity," which Bloom describes as "modern natural right, prepared by Machiavelli and developed by Bacon, Hobbes, Spinoza, Descartes, and Locke; the crisis of modern natural right and the emergence of history, begun by Rousseau and elaborated by Kant and Hegel; [and] radical historicism, begun by Nietzsche and culminating in Heidegger." Each of these waves "began with a Greek inspiration, but these returns were only partial and ended in a radicalization of modernity" (Bloom 1974a: 384).

In *The Closing of the American Mind*, Bloom elaborates on this account. His basic distinction between ancients and moderns is that the former were convinced that political institutions could not be based on reason, while the latter thought that they could. For the ancients contemplation was seen as the highest form of life, and those who engaged in it must first and foremost ensure that prevailing political conditions allow it to be engaged in. The difficulty, as Socrates discovered, is that the philosopher's commitment to truth makes him seem politically dangerous to most people because it leads him to question the opinions on which their institutions rest. The ancient philosophers therefore allied themselves to "the gentlemen" who did not fully understand the philosopher but could "glimpse something noble in him," those who voted for Socrates's acquittal for example. Because there was no hope of philosophers actually leading society, Bloom, following Strauss, holds that in *The Republic* Plato was actually intent on demonstrating the impossibility of an ideal city rather than advocating one[1]—the philosophers must humor the gentlemen to get their support, "making themselves useful to them, never quite revealing themselves to them, strengthening their gentleness and openness." The gentlemen exhibit this openness because "they have money and hence leisure and can appreciate the beautiful and useless" and because "they despise necessity." The ancient philosophers capitalized on this, realizing that philosophy's best response to the ever-present possibility of a hostile civil society was "an educational endeavor, rather more poetic or rhetorical than philosophic, the purpose of which is to temper the passions of gentlemen's souls." The ancient philosophers were "to a man proponents of aristocratic politics, but not for the reasons intellectual historians are wont to ascribe to them." They believed in principle that reason should rule and that only philosophers can be fully devoted to reason. But this was "just a theoretical argument" because philosophers can never rule; thus the ancient philosophers "were aristocratic in the vulgar sense, favoring the power of those possessing old wealth, because such men are more likely to grasp the nobility of philosophy as an end itself, if not to understand it" (Bloom 1987: 275–77, 279, 281, 284).

The moderns appeared to reject this logic for the more ambitious view that reason could be made to reign in politics. The Enlightenment thinkers "understood themselves to be making a most daring innovation: according to Machiavelli, modern philosophy was to be politically effective." Philosophy, he announced, "can be used to conquer fortune," and it was this expectation that grounded the Cartesian and Hobbesian scientific projects of the seventeenth century, issuing in the doctrines of the social contract

---

1. This is perhaps the most problematical of all Strauss's interpretive claims—endorsed by Bloom in his translation of *The Republic* as well as *The Closing of the American Mind*—because it undercuts the claim that the ancients were in basic agreement on this question. Aristotle clearly interpreted Plato to be arguing what he appeared to be arguing (and disagreed with it) rather than the opposite, which Strauss and Bloom attribute to him. See Miles F. Burnyeat (1985: 30–36) and Nussbaum (1987: 20–26). For an extended critique of Bloom's and Strauss's readings of Plato, see Klosko (1986: 275–93).

that decisively shaped the modern West. These doctrines rested on a notion of individual natural rights that are "nothing other than the fundamental passions, experienced by all men, to which the new science appeals
and which it emancipates from the constraints imposed on them by specious reasoning and the fear of divine punishment" (ibid.: 263, 286, 287).

The most basic and universal source of human motivation was understood to be the fear of death; thus the life-preserving passions "act as the
premises of moral and political reasoning." It was in attempting to base
politics on them that Machiavelli "blamed the old writers for building
imaginary principalities and republics that neglect how men actually live
in favor of how they ought to live." He argued instead that princes and
philosophers alike should "accommodate themselves to the dominant
passions." As a result of embracing this injunction, the philosophers
"switched parties from the aristocratic to the democratic." They now assumed that the people, "who were by definition uneducated and the seat
of prejudice," could be educated if we changed our expectations about education and came to see it not as "experience of things beautiful" but rather
as "enlightened self-interest" (ibid.: 287–88, 285–86, 288).

Yet the Enlightenment philosophers "had no illusions about democracy" and knew they were "substituting one kind of misunderstanding for
another" because they did not believe that there could be a unity of theory
and practice. They were "as much philosophers as were the ancients" because they "were perfectly conscious of what separates them from all
other men." This gulf, they knew, could not be bridged. Their new posture
toward politics was more daring because of the expectations it could en-
gender from politics. From the Enlightenment onward the issue, Bloom
tells us, is this: "Does a society based on reason necessarily make un-
reasonable demands on reason, or does it approach more closely to reason
and submit to the ministrations of the reasonable?" The danger, once
"politics has been theoreticized and philosophy politicized," is that "there
is no theory and no practice" and that the "distinction between the eternal
and the temporal" is overcome. This result of the Enlightenment may not
have been inevitable and "goes counter to the intentions of the Enlight-
eners," but it decisively shaped the politics of modernity (ibid.: 289,
290–91).

> Modernity is largely of these philosophers' making, and
> our self-awareness depends on understanding what they
> wanted to do and what they did do, grasping thus why our
> situation is different from all other situations. . . .
> Whether it is called liberal democracy or bourgeois soci-
> ety, whether the regime of the rights of man or that of

> acquisitiveness, whether technology is used in a positive or a negative sense, everyone knows that these terms describe the central aspects of our world. They are demonstrably the results of the thought of a small group of men with deep insight into the nature of things, who collaborated in an enterprise the success of which is almost beyond belief. (Ibid.: 292, 293)

In Bloom's view the Enlightenment view of science and the rights-based theory of contract were the heart of the American constitutional experiment. The United States "is one of the highest and most extreme achievements of the rational quest for the good life according to nature." We are a people founded on "rational principles of natural right," the core commitment of which is "uniting the good with one's own" (ibid.: 39).

Bloom's sense of crisis has a more immediate dimension rooted in developments since the 1960s and particularly in what he takes to be the triumph of egalitarian ideals, initially in the student movement and more generally as its generation achieved positions of power in dominant institutions. The "old view" of the American melting pot implied that "class, race, religion, national origin or culture all disappear or become dim when bathed in the light of natural rights, which give men common interests and make them truly brothers," but the 1960s were fundamentally about rejecting this notion. That era generated an "openness" that "pays no attention to natural rights or the historical origins of our regime, which are now thought to have been essentially flawed and regressive." The "movement away from rights to openness" promoted a kind of "cultural relativism." Democracy and liberalism were detached from their natural rights foundation, and students were taught "that the only danger confronting us is being closed to the emergent, the new, the manifestations of progress." John Rawls's argument that all are equally worthy of self-esteem "is almost a parody of this tendency, writing hundreds of pages to persuade men, and proposing a scheme of government that would force them, not to despise anyone" (ibid.: 27, 28–29, 30).

For the founders, minorities were "in general bad things, mostly identical to factions, selfish groups who have no concern as such for the common good," but today they are given a legitimate, even special, status. The new openness was "designed to provide a respectable place for these 'groups' or 'minorities'—to wrest respect from those who were not disposed to give it—and to weaken the sense of superiority of the dominant majority." Yet, Bloom argues, the dominant majority "gave the country a dominant culture with its traditions, its literature, its tastes, its special claim to know and supervise the language, and its Protestant religions."

Thus although the early civil rights movement operated within the dominant traditions of American politics and could thereby charge whites "not only with the most monstrous injustices but also with contradicting their own most sacred principles," by the late 1960s separatists like the black power movement were rejecting the principles of the American regime and the melting pot ethos as racist and demanding black identity, not universal rights (ibid.: 31, 32–33).

Since the 1960s an "egalitarian effervescence" has permeated establishment institutions, turning the movement for equality of opportunity into a relentless drive for substantive equality. The triumph of this "McCarthyism of the Left" has meant that "a whole range of thought about the alternatives for man has vanished." Indeed, for Bloom the 1960s were far more damaging to American universities than the 1950s, when McCarthyism—which was so patently antiacademic—gave universities a "sense of community, defined by a common enemy" that has since been lost. By contrast the 1960s were the American Weimar, defined by the ethos that commitment is "profounder than science, passion than reason, history than nature, the young than the old." The 1960s were "an exercise in egalitarian self-satisfaction that wiped out the elements of the university curriculum that did not flatter our peculiar passions or tastes of the moment." This led to the destruction of the European traditions on which so much of the curriculum had been based, so that the "longing for Europe has been all but extinguished in the young." We are doomed to an egalitarian mire, and its influence penetrates so deeply that the prospects for change are minuscule (Bloom 1974b: 63–64; 1987: 324, 314, 320, 145).

The 1960s should, however, be understood as the culmination of a long decline. For at least half a century the "unity, grandeur and attendant folklore of the founding heritage" has been under attack. Carl Becker's economic analysis of the Declaration of Independence, Dewey's pragmatism, and "Marxist debunking of the Charles Beard variety" all treated the past "as radically imperfect and regarded our history as irrelevant or as a hindrance to rational analysis of our present." These works are geared toward "trying to demonstrate that there was no public spirit, only private concern for property, in the Founding Fathers, thus weakening our convictions of the truth or superiority of American principles and our heroes." The New Left is yet another instance of this delegitimation, for "the radicals in the civil rights movement succeeded in promoting a popular conviction that the Founding was, and the American principles are, racist" (Bloom 1987: 55–57).

Although the current generation of students is bored, docile, and narrowly instrumentalist, it is the unwitting inheritor of the actions of its predecessors. Students now take for granted the routinized, unthinking egalitarianism that has made it impossible for universities to pursue genuinely educational ends. The liberal arts are now the "decaying rump of the university," the social sciences are governed by the search for ever more deterministic explanations of human action, and philosophy, understood as the search for objective standards of truth and justice, "is not only not practiced, its very possibility is denied." No wonder our students are led "by force or interest": we teach them nothing else, and we fail to inspire them even to consider other possibilities (Bloom 1974b: 65, 63).

Central to the more general diagnosis of the crisis of the West to which Bloom subscribes is the rise of *historicism, relativism, nihilism*, and *subjectivism*, terms that have more frequently been strung together as poignant symbols of contemporary evil than analyzed or even distinguished from one another by Strauss and his followers, a deficiency for which they have, with some justice, been criticized.[2] But the main claim appears to be that the very possibility of objective judgments about the good is foreclosed in contemporary culture and by its dominant intellectual spokesmen, that "the modern historical consciousness has engendered a general skepticism about the truth of all 'world views,' except for that one of which it is itself a product" (Bloom 1968: viii). The very possibility of political philosophy—understood as the search for objectively valid moral judgments—"is doubted, nay denied, by the most powerful movements of contemporary thought. And that crisis is identical with the crisis of the West, because the crisis of the West is a crisis of belief—belief in the justice of our principles" (Bloom 1980: 113–14).

The tenor of much of Bloom's writing suggests that this problem may be beyond resolution, for he believes that the only hope lies in a return to the study of the texts of the tradition we have forgotten. Our thought and politics "have become inextricably bound up with the universities," yet we are ignorant of the intellectual developments that have played so large a part in the creation of our circumstances. "To return to the reasons behind our language and weigh them against the reasons for other language would in itself liberate us"; as a result Bloom sees his appeal to tradition as providing "the outline of an archeology of our souls as they are" (Bloom 1987: 382, 239). Returning to the texts of tradition may enable us to break out of the "circle of subjectivism" in which contemporary culture is trapped (Bloom 1980: 127; 1975a: 662).

2. Thus Bloom's declaration: "Science's latest attempts to grasp the human situation—cultural relativism, historicism, the fact-value distinction—are the suicide of science. Culture, hence closedness, reigns supreme" (Bloom 1987: 38–39). See also Strauss (1953: 1–80).

(ii) Philosophical Prescriptions

The peculiar horror of modern tyranny has been its alliance with "perverted philosophy," Bloom remarks in reference to the fates of the writings of Rousseau and Nietzsche. Rousseau did not cause the Reign of Terror or Nietzsche the Nazis, "but there was something in what they said and the way they said it which made it possible for them to be misinterpreted in certain politically relevant ways." Because Strauss had a "respect for speech and its power," he exercised self-restraint (ibid.: 387, 388–89). Yet it is not simply the self-restrained and disinterested pursuit of truth that impresses Bloom but that this pursuit is conducted via the study of the greats making up the tradition of political philosophy.

Central to his conception is the view that the writings of the greats are part of a single tradition defined by common preoccupations. "Throughout the whole tradition, religious and philosophic," he tells us, "man had two concerns, the care of his body and the care of his soul, expressed in the opposition between desire and virtue. In principle he was supposed to long to be all virtue, to break free from the chains of bodily desire." It was in reaction against this central preoccupation that the moderns defined their concerns. Machiavelli "turned things upside down" by arguing that happiness could be achieved in this life (which the ancients had denied), and building on this, Hobbes "blazed the trail to the self, which has grown into the highway of a ubiquitous psychology without the psyche (soul)." This move informed Locke's philosophy and Rousseau's critique of the early contract theorists; the "psychology of the self" became and remained the central problem of political philosophy (Bloom 1987: 174, 175, 178–79). Although the moderns rejected the assumption of the ancients that philosophy and politics could never be combined, even this rejection indicates a basic "unity of the tradition." The Enlightenment was "an attempt to give political status to what Socrates represents." The modern attacks on academic institutions "made first by Rousseau and then by Nietzsche are attacks on Socratic rationalism made in a Socratic spirit. The history of Western thought and learning can be encapsulated in the fate of Socrates, beginning with Plato defending him, passing through the Enlightenment institutionalizing him, and ending with Nietzsche accusing on him" (ibid.: 267–68).

Perhaps Strauss's greatest achievement, for Bloom, was that he "addressed himself to the whole tradition." He "liberated himself" from the misleading glosses of contemporary commentators "and could understand writers as they understood themselves. He talked with them as one would talk with a wise and subtle contemporary about the nature of things." The proof that Strauss had achieved this understanding of the tradition is his "late writings read in conjunction with those writings about which he wrote." Although they are difficult for us to grasp, they are simple in form and expression because they penetrate to fundamentals, and although this simplicity earned him something of a reputation for innocence, he rather enjoyed the label because it "meant that he had in some measure succeeded in recovering the surface of things" (Bloom 1974a: 384–85).

(iii) Practical Prescriptions

An irreducible sense of political despair permeates Bloom's diagnosis. Neither *The Closing of the American Mind* nor any of Bloom's other writings contain any practical injunctions beyond a plea for the reading of old books, and Bloom's despairing tone often implies that we may well be beyond salvation. Although a liberal education is intended to open the young to the possibilities from the past, our students cannot hear its message. "As long as they have the Walkman they cannot hear what the great tradition has to say." Yet, "after its prolonged use, when they take it off, they find they are deaf" (Bloom 1987: 81).

The general purpose of appealing to the tradition is to get us to see that what we take for granted can and should be questioned, as it was in the past, and that the possibility of a neoclassical politics in the contemporary world should not be discounted. There is an apparent tension between this appeal to the tradition—on its face remarkably un-Greek—and Bloom's affirmation of classical Greek values. Strauss's view on this subject is a matter of some dispute among both followers and critics, but it seems clear that although the ultimate goal may be to practice Platonic philosophy—unbounded by tradition—to discover and contemplate the truth about the nature of things, we must first return to the tradition that modern thinkers in the wake of Machiavelli have abandoned. This is why, for Strauss, philosophy and history are inseparable.[3]

From the standpoint of practical prescriptions, however, this view has to be qualified in two respects, both deriving from most people having neither the intellectual capacity nor the education to tread this difficult path. The first concerns one of Strauss's most contentious claims: that because only a tiny minority of philosophers can grasp philosophical truth, it is hopeless to try to found politics on reason. A reverence for tradition should be instilled in the rest of us not because "the tradition" can provide rational philosophical foundations for political institutions—

---

3. See Gunnell (1978: 122–34; 1985: 339–61), Drury (1985: 315–37), and Tarcov (1983: 5–29).

ultimately it cannot—but because society must inevitably rest on *some* opinion.

> Philosophy or science, the highest activity of man, is the attempt to replace opinion about "all things" by knowledge of "all things"; but opinion is the element of society; philosophy or science is therefore the attempt to dissolve the element in which society breathes, and thus it endangers society. Hence philosophy or science must remain the preserve of a small minority, and philosophers or scientists must respect the opinions on which society rests. (Strauss 1959: 221–22)

This reasoning generated Strauss's distinction between esoteric and exoteric writing. When communicating with one another, philosophers should (and do) employ various literary devices to obscure their meanings, lest what they say undermine the opinion on which society rests. They "will distinguish between the true teaching as the esoteric teaching and the socially useful teaching as the exoteric teaching; whereas the exoteric teaching is meant to be easily accessible to every reader, the esoteric teaching discloses itself only to very careful and well-trained readers after long and concentrated study" (ibid.: 222). It is always disguised by what Bloom (1987: 279) refers to as the "gentle art of deception."

Even when modern philosophers allied themselves with the claims of democracy, "they were substituting one kind of misunderstanding for another." Despite their claims to be founding politics on a rational fear of death, the moderns knew "that the rational, calculating, economic man seeks immortality just as irrationally as, or even more so than, the man who hopes for eternal fame or for another life." For this reason the great modern philosophers were "as much philosophers as were the ancients." They knew "that their connection with other men would always be mediated by unreason" (ibid.: 289–90).

There is a tension, then, between revealing the truth and the requirements of society. For Strauss, because social science reveals and stresses the "arbitrary character of the basic assumptions underlying any given society," he thought it politically dangerous: "if I know that the principles of liberal democracy are not intrinsically superior to the principles of communism or fascism, I am incapable of wholehearted commitment to liberal democracy" (Strauss 1959: 222). Despite Strauss and his followers' railings against the relativism of modernity, there is thus a significant sense in which they are indifferent to the nature of the regime, as long as it is not hostile to philosophy. Notwithstanding all the talk about objective values in the tradition, then, the exoteric message is conceived of instrumentally and is, ironically, basically conventionalist in nature, even if part of what makes the exoteric message effective requires denying that this is the case.

It is less than clear what the exoteric message should be when it is believed that a society is in foundational crisis. This unclarity is reflected within the Straussian movement in disagreements over whether and how to become involved in day-to-day politics and whether to affirm or attack the principles of liberal democracy. Some, like Nathan Tarcov, hold that Strauss's argument was not that liberal democracy is itself pernicious but that it has been undermined. It is not "modern liberalism but loss of confidence in it [that] constitutes the crisis." In this view Strauss's purpose "is not to undercut liberalism practically but to find a theoretical solution to the problem posed by its having already been undercut" (Tarcov 1983: 9). If this is so, exoteric teaching should, presumably, be geared toward restoring confidence in liberal democratic institutions. Bloom's view is at once more radical and more conservative. He thinks that instilling the values that he perceives to be central to the tradition offers the only possible escape from the ever-increasing excesses of liberal democracy and the seemingly relentless drive toward substantive equality.

Bloom is aware that most people, even most intellectuals, do not study what he conceives the tradition to be. His work with Harry Jaffa on Shakespeare was in part motivated by this realization, for although "the most striking fact about contemporary university students is that there is no longer any canon of books which forms their taste and their imagination," Shakespeare's plays and poetry continue to be read and might in principle be used as a source of public morality. In the past Shakespeare has provided that common understanding; he was recognized as a great author and constantly returned to as a source of meaning and value. Marlborough, for instance, said that he "had formed his understanding of English history from Shakespeare alone." Although a revival of such reverence is unlikely, "Shakespeare could still be the source of education and provide the necessary lessons concerning human virtue and the proper aspirations of a noble life," for he "is respected in our tradition, and he is of our language" (Bloom and Jaffa 1964: 1–2).[4]

---

4. To perform this role, however, Shakespeare must be rescued from the new post-Romantic critics, who deny that poets had intentions that we can discover or teachings that are pertinent to our circumstances. Shakespeare needs to be read naively because "he shows most vividly and comprehensively the fate of tyrants, the character of good rulers, the relations of friends, and the duties of citizens, [and so] can move the souls of his readers, and they recognize that they understand life better because they have read him; he hence becomes a constant guide and companion" (Bloom and Jaffa 1964: 2–3).

II. Bloom's View: Four Difficulties

Later in this book we will see that Bloom's suspicion that no system of political institutions can in the end be shown to rest on rational foundations merits serious attention, as does his claim that the central task of political philosophy is to discover and articulate the truth. But these insights do not have the implications that Bloom would have us believe they do, and they must be extracted from four unpersuasive aspects of his analysis. These aspects concern Bloom's diagnosis of our circumstances, his identification and description of the tradition, his assumptions about interpretation, and his prescriptions.

(i) Diagnosis

If the difficulties we confronted in Rorty's discussion of postmodernism in chapter 2 revolved around his uncritical endorsement of the prevailing institutions in contemporary American culture, with Bloom we confront an opposite problem: his attitude toward every manifestation of modernity is so unrelentingly negative that it, too, precludes any useful critical argument. Like Rorty's postmodernism, Bloom's antimodernism leaves us without any satisfying critical purchase on contemporary political reality or argument. Why is this?

The first reason is that Bloom does not offer a single diagnosis. He oscillates between the claim with which he begins *The Closing of the American Mind*—that departures from the natural rights philosophy of the founding fathers have fatally undermined liberal democracy—and the claim that the founding principles were themselves flawed and contained the seeds of their own destruction. Bloom tells us first that the melting pot ideal and its eschewal of factions was a great strength of the founders and that the rejection of "integrationism" as "just an ideology for whites and Uncle Toms" was thus the most damaging aspect of the 1960s because it created a separatist ideology that has now been institutionalized in the practice of affirmative action. We are told that Locke's ideas were abused at Cornell and elsewhere in the 1960s; "under pressure from students the Founding was understood to be racist, and the very instrument that condemned slavery and racism was broken." After that, "the theory of the rights of man was no longer studied or really believed," and as a result "its practice also suffered" (Bloom 1987: 31, 94–96, 318–19, 335).

Yet in many places Bloom insists that the Lockean principles, on which he takes the American regime to have been based, have always been flawed. In this mood Bloom endorses Tocqueville's dictum that "in democratic societies, each citizen is habitually busy with the contemplation of a very petty object, which is himself," and argues that although this preoccupation with self has intensified in recent years, it is the manifestation of an "inevitable individualism, endemic to our regime." Whereas he previously complained that the separatist ethos of black power and affirmative action was destructive because it was inimical to the basic Lockean principle of equal natural rights, Bloom subsequently regrets the destruction of ethnic difference. Although an Italian immigrant in 1920 lived a life that "was by necessity and choice Italian, and he lived with Italians," Bloom bemoans the egalitarianism that mandates that the immigrant's grandson at Harvard will be friends with individuals he likes independent of their ethnicity. His "sexual attractions, and hence his marriage, will not be influenced by his national origin or even by his traditional Catholicism." On this telling the principles of the regime are themselves flawed. Thus Bloom endorses Nietzsche's argument that modern democracy (rather than its perversion) is at fault, that its "rationalism and its egalitarianism are the contrary of creativity" (ibid.: 66, 86, 88, 97, 143).

Bloom's oscillations between these two diagnoses seem to explain his schizoid attitude toward American values. He complains bitterly in many places that we have lost pride in our ethnocentricity and argues repeatedly that this loss is contributing to the fragmentation of American culture. Yet elsewhere his account oozes with antipathy for all things American; in these formulations the problem appears to be that we have lost touch with European culture. The Europeans are said to produce children with "a vastly more sophisticated knowledge of the human heart than we are accustomed to." We are repeatedly told that we lack cultural depth, as is shown by the fact that it is "possible to become an American in a day"; we are incapable of the "collective consciousness" to which a "high work of art" like Wagner's *Gesamtkunstwerk* is directed (ibid.: 47, 53, 54, 97).

A second defect in Bloom's diagnosis concerns the sheer generality of his attack on all Enlightenment and post-Enlightenment thought, institutions, practices, ideals, and conflicts. His assault on modernity is conducted from such a great height, with so little reference to its constituting detail, that it is irrelevant to the concerns of almost all contemporary political agents. To some extent this is unavoidable for Bloom because his thesis is that most people live in an ideological frame of reference that prevents their even perceiving the genuine questions of politics. To the charge that he fails to speak to their concerns, then, is the natural response that they have the wrong concerns, that they assume away all the interesting and important questions, and that it would be to abdicate the basic purpose of political philosophy as Bloom sees it to forsake his terrain for theirs.[5]

5. It is amusingly ironic that a book with this message has climbed the nonfiction bestseller lists and catapulted its author to national prominence.

One suspects that Bloom does not particularly care whether his arguments have a lasting impact, indeed he might even consider such success a sure sign of their imminent corruption. Just as he finds reticence to publish impressive in others, so in his own work he may be more at home raging against modernity than seeking to influence it. Discrediting existing institutions from the standpoint of an ill-depicted but earnestly desired premodern past becomes an end in itself; there is no other point to Bloom's political commentary. In this regard he is more precisely termed reactionary than conservative, for the essence of conservatism lies in that which Burke and Tocqueville shared with Peel: the view that change and innovation should be countenanced to the extent needed to preserve existing institutions and practices with as much integrity as possible. It is a pragmatic and adaptive doctrine, sensitive to the demands of changing circumstances and conditions. For Bloom, by contrast, there seems to be nothing in the existing array of institutions and practices worth preserving: they are all objects of his alternating rage and scorn.

A third defect in Bloom's diagnosis derives from his implausible, if implicit, causal idealism. Despite the metaphorical talk about the waves of modernity, there is a notable lack of any identifiable causal argument in Bloom's account of our decline or in Strauss's discussion from which Bloom borrows. We are told that the modern Western systems of government are "surely a result" of the Enlightenment, that "modernity is largely of these philosophers' making" (ibid.: 291, 293), without being told how this happened. It is unclear whether the rise of historical consciousness, the emergence of "modern natural right," the three waves of modernity, or the growth of contemporary "relativism" and "nihilism" are the causes of changes in contemporary culture (in which case one wonders how) or the results of some other causal processes (in which case one wonders what these were).

Even the nature of the alleged changes is difficult to pin down. Although at the outset of *The Closing of the American Mind* Bloom denies that he intends to say that "things were wonderful in the past" or that "any comparison with the past [is] to be used as grounds for congratulating or blaming ourselves" (Bloom 1987: 22), almost every subsequent page effectively refutes this claim. "Parents do not have the legal or moral authority they had in the Old World," he laments in his remarks on the family. The decline of the family has resulted "in nothing less than parents' loss of control over their children's moral education at a time when no one else is seriously concerned with it." Our loss of faith in the Bible and all equivalent moral texts has led to a "gradual stilling of the old political and religious echoes in the souls of the young." In the educational developments of the last half-century there has been a "fudging of the distinction between liberal and technical education." Our students have "lost the practice of and the taste for reading"; they are so ignorant that we are "long past the age when a whole tradition could be stored up in all students" because the "old teachers who loved Shakespeare or Austen or Donne, and whose only reward for teaching was the perpetuation of their taste, have all but disappeared." In the world of music we are told that the "romanticism that had dominated serious music since Beethoven appealed to refinements—perhaps overrefinements—of sentiments that are hardly to be found in the contemporary world."

Today, by contrast, we are asked to picture a thirteen-year-old doing his homework, wearing a Walkman, or watching MTV. He is nothing more than a "pubescent child whose body throbs with orgasmic rhythms; whose feelings are made articulate in hymns to the joys of onanism or the killing of parents. . . . In short, life is made into a nonstop, commercially prepackaged masturbational fantasy." We are told repeatedly that our civilization is "weak and exhausted," that we have become deaf to what "the great tradition has to say," that our families and communities and traditions "have been rationalized and have lost their compelling force," that the human political impulse has been "so attenuated by modernity that it is hardly experienced," and that "the administrative state . . . has replaced politics." Harvard, Yale, and Princeton are "not what they used to be—the last resorts of aristocratic sentiment within the democracy" (ibid.: 58, 59, 61, 62, 64–65, 70, 75, 76, 79, 81, 85, 89). And so on.

For Bloom to introduce these claims (a small subset of his idealizations of the past) with the denial that he intends any moralizing about the present is disingenuous. To the extent that it is possible to pin him down, he seems to be an idealist in the classical sense, that is, he believes that ideas shape institutions, that corrupt ideas corrupt institutions, and that the only potential for liberation from corrupt institutions lies in returning to uncorrupted ideas. It is characteristic of idealist appeals of this kind that the Golden Age is more a point of theoretical reference than any historical society, or even set of beliefs about society, that can be depicted in a systematic way, let alone substantiated with even illustrative evidence. Yet this fact is scarcely an argument for acceptance of those appeals. In Bloom's case, the failure to supply even the rudiments of a defensible causal account of the decline that he insists has occurred means that he is unlikely to persuade anyone who is even mildly skeptical of his thesis.

(ii) Parochialism in Identifying the Tradition

Whereas Marxists identify the texts canonized in traditions as making up or reflecting a dominant ideology, for Bloom they are the key to liberating us from it, not in the sense that we can come to perceive a hold they had on us of which we were previously unaware but rather in that they contain forgotten truths that we need to relearn. But what is the tradition to which we must open ourselves? As Bloom himself frames the dilemma, "Who are these men to whom such reverent attention should be paid?" How do we find out who they are, especially when Bloom is arguing "that we are in large measure ignorant about what we need to know" (Bloom 1980: 123)?

Bloom supplies two answers. The first, which he admits to be less than entirely adequate given the nature of his complaints against prevailing consensual values, is to appeal to (an unidentified) consensus: "One can begin from the general agreement about who the great philosophers were, especially the farther away they are in time," when fads have "dissipated" (ibid.). Yet it is difficult to see how this constitutes even a beginning for two reasons. First, if the ignorance of professional academics and establishment intellectuals concerning the fundamental problems of political theory is so complete and if their misreadings and misuses of the texts of the tradition are so pervasive, then it is difficult to imagine why their agreement concerning which texts constitute the tradition should be of any significance. It is dubious, second, that there is a consensus about the nature of the tradition over time and space, and it is at the very least true that when different establishments attribute canonical importance to certain writers, it is often for widely different reasons, as anyone who has worked in more than one philosophical tradition knows.[6]

Even within a single intellectual culture there are great variations over time and space. Hobbes, for instance, so pivotal in the Western tradition as perceived by political theorists, is a comparatively minor figure from the philosopher's standpoint, and the converse is true of Berkeley. Many others are discipline centric in this way: Tocqueville and Leibniz, Burke and Descartes, Montesquieu and Carnap. What then is the tradition? Even within a single academic establishment canonized figures displace one another as historiographical concerns change. Fads do not dissipate as Bloom suggests; preoccupations come and go that lead us to reread the past in

6. For example, the undergraduate who studies philosophy and political theory in an English university will likely learn that there is a fundamental divide in the Western tradition or even that there are two major Western traditions: naturalist and antinaturalist, the first traceable to Aristotle and the second to Plato. Yet the comparable American undergraduate is much more likely to be taught that the basic division is between ancients and moderns and will learn what Plato and Aristotle allegedly had in common. This difference goes a long way toward explaining the congenital inability of English intellectuals to take Straussian historiography seriously. See, for example, Burnyeat (1985: 30–36).

different ways for different purposes.[7] For instance, the current revival of interest in Bodin is mainly a result of the rediscovery of the state by political scientists; his writings are thought by some to shed light on the modern state's genesis. Does this mean that fads have now dissipated and Bodin is clearly part of the tradition or have we simply developed a different agenda that gives him a renewed relevance? What are we to make of the revival of interest in Tocqueville, whose works had been out of print in English for many years? To appeal to academic consensus as a way of identifying an enduring tradition of thought will not do. The most that could be said is that different figures are often thought to stand for various competing philosophical positions and that as these positions become relevant to contemporary debates their arguments are constantly invoked or attacked. Yet even this claim is questionable and would at least require a good deal of defending because writers like Aristotle, Hobbes, Locke, Rousseau, Hegel, and Marx have, at different times, been pressed into the service of virtually every imaginable political and intellectual cause.[8]

Bloom's "second and sounder criterion" for identifying the tradition derives from "what the thinkers say about one another." The essential claim here is that the greats of the tradition identify one another, that the "men of quality know the men of quality" (ibid.: 123–24).[9] Just how they are supposed to know them and how we are supposed to know that they know them are both exceedingly unclear. At times Bloom appears to think that the answer lies in an identity of views on the fundamental issues of political philosophy, superficial differences notwithstanding.[10] Yet he is aware that it would be absurd to posit general agreement on all fundamental issues of political philosophy among the various people he designates as greats and, indeed, he takes others to task for taking insufficient account of differences among these thinkers.[11] Bloom's claim appears to be that, although they do not agree on answers, what unites them and gives them their coherence as a tradition is their agreement on what the questions

7. For a useful demonstration of how definition of the tradition can change, as a kind of "victor's history," see Kuklick (1984: 125–39).

8. For a useful illustration of this, see Dickenson's (1976: 28–45) discussion of changing interpretations of Locke's views after 1688.

9. See also Bloom (1987: 292) for a discussion of this thesis in connection with Rousseau, who, although he disagreed with the Enlightenment thinkers "in crucial respects," also allegedly knew that they were his "theoretical kin."

10. Thus Bloom is impressed by Tocqueville's debt to Rousseau in his discussion of the role of virtue in egalitarian institutions. Although he does not argue that "Tocqueville is simply the same as Rousseau" he claims that "the more I think about it, the difficulty is more on the side of differentiating them than of assimilating them" (Bloom 1980: 137–39).

11. See, for instance, Bloom (1975b: 573–76).

are. Even when they disagree, the underlying agreement on the terms in which their disagreement is cast is significant. Tocqueville's and Rousseau's alleged disagreements with "Hobbes and Locke" concerning whether civilized life is superior to man's natural state tells us something about the "crucial question" evaded by "modern thought." Hobbes's attack on Aristotle shows us that Aristotle "is the man to attack" (ibid.: 136, 123).

Yet it is difficult for two reasons to see how this kind of disagreement can be regarded as significant. First, Hobbes criticized many besides Aristotle who are not regarded by Bloom as greats: why is Aristotle singled out rather than the medieval scholastics or Coke or the many others that Hobbes explicitly or implicitly attacked? Why does Locke's *First Treatise* not reveal that Filmer is "the man to attack"? Bloom never explains the principles for selecting significant antagonists, which is a serious omission, for the notion that the greats identify one another even when they disagree cannot otherwise be salvaged. This aside, the authors Bloom identifies as making up the tradition do not agree on what the fundamental questions of politics are. To take his own example of Hobbes and Aristotle, it is surely beyond argument that for Hobbes the central issue of politics is power and that the central questions of his political theory deal with its nature, implications, and harnessing. Aristotle, by contrast, is mainly concerned with virtue in political communities, human potential, and a related set of issues that are difficult even to raise in Hobbes's mechanistic and nominalist conception of the world. Such differences may, if accurately described, illustrate that politics was thought about in fundamentally different terms in seventeenth-century England and in classical Greece, but they can indicate preoccupation with the same "permanent questions" only in the most trivial and attenuated sense. If Hobbes and Aristotle agree on the fundamental questions of political philosophy, so does everyone else.

Even among the moderns Bloom's is an exceedingly difficult case to make. Locke and Hegel, Rousseau and Mill can be argued to have had some common preoccupations from some points of view; but they differ so greatly in their views of history, method, human nature, and the purposes of politics that it is nonsense to identify them as constituting a tradition in virtue of their agreement on the permanent questions while professing fidelity to their intentions as the basic exegetical axiom. The same is surely true of the ancients, despite the heroic attempts by Strauss and his followers to minimize their differences and establish the identity of their concerns. We need not go all the way with Burnyeat's claim that Plato and Aristotle had nothing in common to hold that it only makes sense to see them as making up a tradition from one of several possible points of view and to acknowledge that there are others.[12]

There is a deeper circularity to the claim that "the men of quality know the men of quality." If it takes one to know one, how can Bloom be sure of who the greats are and of who they are not? How can he be certain, for instance, that Rawls is not a new member of the tradition, or, put differently, supposing by hypothesis that he is, how could we find out? A case could certainly be made on the basis of all Bloom's exegetical tools, which he so obviously violates in reading Rawls. He accuses Rawls of taking egalitarianism for granted and thereby avoiding the central questions posed in the tradition of political philosophy. Yet a close reading of *A Theory of Justice* reveals a deep ambivalence on the subject of equality, and there is little in Rawls's argument that is necessarily egalitarian. Indeed, highly inegalitarian distributions of income and wealth, including in some circumstances regressive systems of taxation, are all consistent with his distributive maxims. Likewise on subjectivism, which Bloom regards as the bugbear of modern liberalism, Rawls is quite equivocal, and his concept of primary goods is intended to permit some objective or interpersonal moral judgments that ordinal conceptions of utility notoriously foreclose.[13]

One suspects, however, that it is not with the technicalities of the difference principle, reflective equilibrium, or primary goods that Bloom is concerned when he complains that Rawls takes egalitarian premises for granted but with Rawls's attempt to derive principles of justice from a fundamental (unquestioned) assumption of people's moral equality. Yet in this connection two points must be noted. First, such assumptions of moral equality fail, for Bloom, to disqualify Hobbes, Locke, and Kant from membership in what he takes the tradition to be, so why should it, in itself, disqualify Rawls? Second, a more subtle "Bloomian" reading of Rawls might be argued to reveal that he speaks in an egalitarian vernacular because it is impossible to do otherwise in contemporary America but that his esoteric message is that we should find ways to limit the egalitarian consequences of widely accepted egalitarian premises. This is a level of argument, it might be claimed, that "is not immediately accessible on the surface" of *A Theory of Justice*. We can only get at it "by way of ever-deepening reflection" on the book as it "relate[s] to the problems of the world." There is no "short cut to the initiation" into this alleged deeper purpose of Rawls's, for "great books are full of hidden references and quotes which reveal themselves only to initiates" (Bloom 1980: 134–35).

12. See Burnyeat (1985: 30–36) and Klosko (1986: 275–93).
13. See Rawls (1971: 17–83, 90–95, 48–51) and Shapiro (1986: 204–70).

In short, it is impossible to demonstrate whether such an interpretive claim is true or false. There is enough depth and ambiguity to Rawls's discussion of and assumptions about equality and subjectivism to ensure that it is not absurd on its face; once we move from this fact to a set of assertions about hidden agendas and messages available only to initiates, who is Bloom to dispute them? The would-be canonizer of Rawls will simply claim that Bloom is not enough of an initiate to understand Rawls's subtle and complex purposes.

(iii) Tensions Between "Fundamental Intention" and Tradition

The difficulties we have encountered with Bloom's parochial identification of the tradition raise more general questions about the nature of traditions, their significance, and how to study them. Central to Bloom's anti-modernism is his claim that we must not read a text for a particular ideological purpose but that we must try to regain the fundamental intention of its author via intensive textual analysis. Bloom is caught in a double bind, however, because if there is an interesting and illuminating view of the tradition of Western political theory identified by Strauss, it has little to do with the intentions of the authors composing it. Further, if Bloom and Strauss's other followers take Bloom's view of exegesis seriously, they cannot embrace Strauss's conception of the tradition. Let me explain why.

Any text can be studied from at least two points of view, which I have identified elsewhere as internal and external.[14] An *internal reading* is concerned with what the author conceived herself to be doing in writing or at least with what she could in principle be brought to accept as an accurate description of her task. Recovering an author's fundamental intention is an enterprise of internal reading in my sense, leaving aside, for now, what exegetical tools are best suited to this purpose. *External readings* are, by contrast, concerned with received meanings, with what texts are taken to stand for by others, with their ideological functions and their canonization. External meanings typically change with time and are greatly influenced by the contexts in which texts are read and the goals their readers are trying to achieve. The internal meaning of a text does not change, although opinions about what it is may change and may in some cases, perhaps even typically, be incorrect. But whatever we know, or think we know, about the *Second Treatise*, Locke intended whatever it was that he intended when he wrote it.

Traditions can be relevant to both internal and external readings. Locke

14. See Shapiro (1982: 535–78; 1986: 8–11).

may have seen himself as responding to particular problems within the natural law tradition he inherited from Saint Thomas Aquinas, and if he did his intended meaning cannot be grasped without reference to that tradition and his comprehension of it. In addition, however, Locke's text subsequently became part of a number of traditions in political theory and took on different meanings in those different traditional contexts. Locke's concept of consent had a meaning in the context of the religious and constitutional conflicts of seventeenth-century England quite different from its meaning for the American founding fathers, and it has quite another meaning for contemporary libertarians like Robert Nozick. It may be that one (or none) of these is closest to Locke's intended meaning, but each locates Locke's text in an evolving tradition of ideas within which it is thought, or argued, to have significance.

What divides most schools of textual exegesis from one another is that one external reading is alleged to capture the internal meaning of the text and is thereby legitimated as definitive, so that Locke was "really" a bourgeois theorist, or a neo-Thomist, or a proponent of modern natural right. It is unlikely that there is a general system of exegetical rules that will divulge the internal meaning of all texts (different writers employ different styles and techniques in different circumstances for different purposes), but it can be said with some confidence that broadly conceived traditions, extending well into the future from the standpoint of the texts that compose them, are likely to consist mainly of external readings in my sense. The process of canonization could not otherwise occur. The intentions of authors whose texts are subsequently read into traditions are often quite parochial, at least from the point of view of such catchall concepts as "ancients," "moderns," "bourgeois modes of thought," or "the decline of Western civilization" that generally drive traditions.

This does not mean that broadly conceived traditions are not interesting or illuminating or that they do not explain aspects of our thought and action, but that the sorts of abstraction from original historical context necessary to place texts in these sweeping historical constructions will almost inevitably distort an author's intended meaning. Life is too complex, the demands on traditions too unpredictable and diverse, the texts that make them up too ambiguous to expect anything else. Indeed, one might speculate that only writers whose intended arguments are ambiguous enough to be claimed by many sides in intellectual disputes will become canonized. Their persistence in traditions over long periods of time may well indicate the exact opposite of what Bloom contends: they may contain no single determinate meaning or message, or if they do that message will likely be sufficiently flexible that although it places some limits on the range of possible external readings, it does not render a particular external reading definitive.[15]

What is difficult to swallow, then, is that the internal meanings, the fundamental intentions of the authors that Bloom, following Strauss, identifies as making up the tradition, can be linked to one another at the same time as they are placed in his own sweeping account of Western civilization, the fundamental divide between ancients and moderns, the rise of historical consciousness, and the three waves of modernity culminating in Nietzsche's nihilism. Skepticism toward the Straussian exegetical claim is confirmed by the fact that, as interpretations of authors' intended meanings, several of Strauss's readings have been shown to be seriously vulnerable in recent years by the historical work of the new Cambridge historians Quentin Skinner, John Dunn, J. G. A. Pocock (on this side of the Atlantic), and their students.

This group blazed its exegetical trail not by rejecting the idea that the purpose of exegesis is to recover authorial intention but by undermining the notion that this can be done by reading the text, in the phrase of John Plamenatz, "over and over again." Rather the intentions of the author must be decoded from their historical and linguistic contexts in their view; an author's intention cannot be said to have been understood until we understand him as his historical contemporaries did, which requires detailed historical knowledge of the conflicts he was engaged in and the goals he was trying to achieve. Skinner and his associates have also argued that this is the best way to study the history of ideas as the history of ideologies, a more dubious claim.[16] Yet whatever the broader historical significance of the results of their historical research may be, if one accepts that the basic goal is to recover intentions, the findings of the Cambridge historians cannot be ignored by seekers after authorial intention. The Cambridge historians and the Straussians are engaged in this same enterprise: to recover with as much certainty as possible precisely what the author intended.[17]

---

15. For elaboration and defense of this exegetical point, see Shapiro (1986: 8–11).

16. For a critical analysis of it, see Shapiro (1982: 535–78).

17. In Skinner's (1969: 28) words, no agent can be said "to have meant or done something which he could never be brought to accept as a correct description of what he had meant or done." More recently, Skinner and some allies have talked of their view of the history of ideas in the surprisingly Straussish metaphor of a "convocation of resurrected thinkers" who are brought, by various exegetical devices, to an authentic understanding of one another's intentions. The goal of studying the history of ideas is elaborated by reference to an imaginary encyclopedic *Intellectual History of Europe*, which each of those discussed reads and

It is a basic methodological commitment of the Cambridge historians that this kind of recovery of authorial intention is normally possible, that "there are always what have been called 'rational bridgeheads'. . . . which have made conversation possible across chasms" (Rorty, Schneewind, and Skinner 1984: 2). Yet these historians have done more than talk about method; they have undertaken masses of historical research on English, European, and American political thought, no doubt of varying degrees of quality and persuasiveness.[18] In the area of early modern thought, for instance, we now know that Locke's theology was central and indispensable to his theory of rights, that the modern idea of natural right did not emerge with the writings of Machiavelli or Hobbes; rather there were several conflicting views of natural rights in the seventeenth century, parts of competing Ockhamist, Gersonist, and Conciliarist traditions that are traceable to the beginning of the Florentine Renaissance at least. We know that the exclusive natural rights theories of Grotius, Hobbes, and Pufendorf differed fundamentally from Locke's inclusive theory of common property. At the very least those who speak of Hobbes and Locke in one breath as standing for "the doctrine" of modern natural right, or who claim that Locke did not really believe in his theory of natural law, take on a heavy burden of proof in the light of this scholarship.[19]

Strauss was a notable intellectual figure because he developed a distinctive view of our culture and parts of its intellectual heritage, which latter he approached through the canonized tradition of political philosophy as he perceived it. What makes him significant is not whether he was right or wrong about this or that passage in Plato or Locke but that he had a genuinely distinctive point of view. This was, no doubt, bound up with his particular biographical history, in particular the impact that the Holocaust had on him, and his point of view of course informed his approach to the tradition. If this meant that he had a tendency to discover in its texts

---

"endorses the description of himself as, though of course insufficiently detailed, at least reasonably accurate and sympathetic," so that they are able to converse authentically with one another about their disagreements (Rorty, Schneewind, and Skinner 1984: 1–2).

18. The writings of this school on the eighteenth century have proved vulnerable, particularly the attempts by Donald Winch (1980) to reread Adam Smith into the civic humanist tradition. See Harpham (1984: 764–74). Skinner's reading of Machiavelli has also attracted heavy critical fire. See Tarcov (1982: 692–709). I dispute Pocock's readings of Harrington and the neo-Harringtonians in chapter 6.

19. On Locke's view of natural law, see Dunn (1969); on his theory of property, see Tully (1980), who also undertakes a comprehensive analysis of various competing natural law theories of property in Locke's day. On the medieval origins of natural rights theories, see Skinner (1978), especially volume 1, and Tuck (1979).

observations and insights relating to his central preoccupations, we can scarcely be surprised, for it is characteristic of distinctive thinkers. No doubt this predilection will at times produce quirky readings. But such writers are not historians at all, and most historians would likely bore them. Neither do such writers achieve unideological readings; it is often the ideological dimensions of their arguments that make them interesting.

Commentators such as Gunnell, Burnyeat, and Drury are persuasive, then, that Strauss's purposes were at bottom rhetorical and aimed at the problems of the twentieth century as he conceived them, that a good many of his historical claims are seriously vulnerable, and that his corpus should be approached "as an example of political theory as evocation" (Gunnell 1985: 339).[20] For Strauss's construction of the tradition was intimately linked to, and dictated by, his contemporary political concerns. As such Strauss will doubtless be remembered as one of the distinctive social critics of the twentieth century, but those like Bloom and Tarcov (1983: 5–29) who want seriously to defend his particular external reading of the tradition as an historically accurate rendition of the intentions of its authors face what is likely an impossible task.

Leaving aside the issue of Strauss's alleged authentic communication with the canonized authors of the tradition, it seems beyond question that the position of his followers with respect to that tradition is different from his. His followers approach texts not directly, as Strauss claimed that we should and as they claim that he did, but rather indirectly, always mediated by Strauss's interpretations and eager to defend them from what is seen as hostile and ideologically motivated criticism.[21] Bloom is thus happy to acknowledge that his interpretation of Plato is derivative of Strauss's and even interprets this charge as a compliment. Bloom seems almost eager to prostrate himself before Strauss's alleged greatness, apparently unaware of the irony of simultaneously claiming that part of that greatness consisted in rejecting doctrinairism. To say that it is proof that Strauss understood the writings of the greats to read his interpretations of them in conjunction with the texts, without any appeal to external evidence of any

20. See Gunnell (1978: 122–34; 1985: 339–61), Burnyeat (1985: 30–36), and Drury (1985: 315–37).

21. See, for instance, the slew of responses published by the *New York Review of Books* on October 10, 1985, in response to M. F. Burnyeat's review of Strauss's *Studies in Platonic Political Philosophy*. The degree of cultish persecution mania surrounding the Straussian movement is astounding, epitomized for this author by the graduate student who maintained in all seriousness that the *New York Review of Books* had revealed its "anti-Straussian bias" by *publishing* Harry Jaffa's response to Burnyeat on the grounds that it was a weak letter that could be predicted to harm the Straussian cause.

kind, is bizarre at least. Not surprisingly, it is difficult to imagine what, for Bloom, could count (even in principle) as demonstrating an error in any of Strauss's readings at any point in any text.

(iv) Prescriptions

We saw earlier that Bloom's prescriptions are difficult to pin down for two reasons. The first is that in his diagnosis he oscillates between the more conventional (conservative) Straussian claim that we have lost faith in sound liberal-democratic institutions and the more radical (reactionary) position that the institutions themselves have become corrupted and, by implication, need to be replaced. Second, at least at times, Bloom seems to think our problems are beyond resolution. This confusion is further complicated by the fact that his proffered solution—respectful study of the tradition as interpreted by an intellectual elite—differs with respect to that elite and to the rest of society. Modern culture evidently feels the lack of both the esoteric and the exoteric meanings of the tradition.

With respect to the intellectual elite, and assuming the diagnosis to be that we have lost faith in institutions that are fundamentally sound, the main reasons for returning to the tradition seem to be two: to rediscover that the project of founding political institutions on reason is both intellectually impossible and politically dangerous and to interpret the tradition for the rest of us in such a way as to restore our lost faith in our institutions. We have seen that the first of these goals assumes a far greater homogeneity within the tradition of political theory, even as defined by Strauss and his followers, than has ever existed and rests on exegetical maxims that assume what they allegedly establish.

The difficulties become more serious when we move to the impact these prescriptions are intended to have on society at large. First, there are the large assumptions, never acknowledged let alone argued for, that the intelligentsia studying the humanities in universities can have an effect on the world at large and that if they can it will be the effect they intend. Certainly the latter (and, I would argue, the former) is questionable historically. Could Hobbes, a pragmatic conservative, have predicted that his ideas would pervade the liberal tradition centuries after his death? Could he have had even the vaguest idea of what that tradition would be like? Could Marx have had the slightest notion of how his ideas would eventually be used? Bloom seems to assume that only the esoteric message is dangerous and needs to be hidden. But there are many possible exoteric messages, with widely different political and social implications, and the purveyor of those messages can have no more or less confidence in what, if anything, their political impact will be than he can have with respect to the esoteric message. It is surely naive to suppose that values like "the duties of citizens," "the character of good rulers," and "the relations of friends," which Bloom believes can be learned from Shakespeare,[22] cannot be pressed into the service of evil regimes as well as good ones.

In this light we see that there is a deep tension between advocating the doctrine of exoteric teaching and claiming simultaneously that readings of the texts on which this teaching are based are unideological. Depending on one's theory of meaning, a case for ideological neutrality might in principle be made for esoteric meanings, but because the point of the exoteric meaning is precisely to have certain political effects and not to have others, it must be ideological in Bloom's sense by definition. It is surely the doctrine of exoteric meaning that such critics as Gunnell (1978: 122–34; 1985: 339–61), Burnyeat (1985: 30–36), and Drury (1985: 315–37) have in mind when they argue that Strauss had an implicit political agenda. I argue in chapter 9 that political theory should indeed be committed to discovering and articulating the truth rather than advancing any particular ideological program, but we will see there that this view cannot be rendered consistent with any variant of the doctrine of exoteric teaching.

Second, there is the difficulty that Bloom's educational prescriptions bypass the vast majority of the population. Bloom's diagnosis of our vulgarization and his prescriptions for cure are cast entirely within the context of universities and the humanities at that. Even when distinguishing the small intellectual elite equipped to divine the esotericism of the tradition and pass it on from the rest of society, Bloom is thinking of the educated rest, the "gentlemen" or the modern-day equivalents of Marlborough. As far as the great mass of people who will never read Shakespeare (under what Bloom takes to be the corrosive influence of the New Critics or any other way) is concerned, this is surely all beside the point. It never seems to occur to Bloom that he is comparing contemporary mass culture with the elite culture of early modern Europe. Thus when he laments that "a young person walking through the Louvre or the Uffizi" sees only "colors and forms—modern art" because he is ignorant of the biblical, Greek, and Roman stories from antiquity that Raphael, Leonardo, Michelangelo, and Rembrandt took for granted in their audiences, he is surely not thinking of the masses of Renaissance Europe. Likewise when he complains that *Kramer vs. Kramer* "may be up-to-date about divorces and sex roles, but anyone who does not have *Anna Karenina* or *The Red and the Black* as part of his viewing equipment cannot sense what might be lacking," he is again indicting contemporary mass culture for its failure to live up to

22. See Bloom and Jaffa (1964: 2–3).

the artistic standards of a tiny elite in the nineteenth century. Bloom's attack on rock music—which he alleges brought about the death of classical music for the young—rests on the same kind of inappropriate comparison. Bloom concedes that there has been a proliferation of classes in classical music in universities, but insists that this is the exception that proves the rule on the grounds that no more than 5 or 10 percent of the students take them. "Classical music is now a special taste, like Greek language or pre-Columbian archeology, not a common culture of reciprocal communication and psychological shorthand" (Bloom 1987: 63, 64, 69). Yet in an age when hundreds of thousands of students inhabit major universities, if 5 to 10 percent of them take specialized courses in classical music, that is a remarkable number. In the European past to which Bloom appeals, their socioeconomic equivalents would never have thought of higher education, let alone known anything about literature or classical music. Thus we are bound to ask ourselves how much of an indictment of modern culture it is that the contemporary masses, literate at all for the first time in history, fail to live up to the standards of "reciprocal communication and psychological shorthand" that Bloom identifies in the elites of Renaissance and early modern Europe.

Once we deign to go beyond the world of the university to look at mass culture, the claim is preposterous that contemporary America is more vulgar than Elizabethan England. That world of the educated gentleman after which Bloom hankers was the world of a tiny elite, insulated by wealth and power from the vulgarity, poverty, and endemic violence with which the vast majority lived throughout their short and painful lives. Even assuming away all these facts as Bloom does, what is supposed to be the impact of naive readings of the greats by the educated elite on the beliefs, attitudes, aspirations, and values of the rest of society? Bloom seems never to perceive this question, yet it is surely centrally on the agenda if reading the greats by the intellectual elite is going to cure "the crisis of the West" and restore "our" faith in "traditional" values.

This language raises a hornets' nest of further difficulties because many, often conflicting, values can be considered traditional. Just as legal commentators who argue that the Constitution should be interpreted in the light of natural law principles fail to notice that this simply pushes the problem back a step, that there always were widely differing and powerfully conflicting conceptions of natural law, so the appeal to traditional values is likewise question begging. This appeal assumes, without the hint of evidence or even theoretical argument, the existence of a morally homogeneous past in the tradition, in the culture, and in the relations between the two. Just where and when these happy circumstances are supposed to have existed is never stated, and waving an Anglophilic hand across the Atlantic simply will not do. Anyone with the slightest knowledge of English history and culture knows that England was and remains as conflict-ridden as many other societies and that many of the values embodied in English historical practice are less than self-evidently desirable. The English ruling classes have spent not insignificant parts of their history slaughtering populations under their control both inside and outside the British Isles; they invented concentration camps and have often shown scant respect for the values of the societies they sought to dominate. In short, the English history Marlborough learned from Shakespeare was but one of many English histories, most of them less than flattering to the high culture Bloom so earnestly craves.

These difficulties are compounded when we consider Bloom in his reactionary mood and thus assume that the problem is not the loss of confidence in liberal-democratic institutions but the institutions themselves, with their open embrace of subjectivism, their "egalitarian effervescence," and their already accomplished destruction of what he takes the values of the tradition to have been. The notion that changing the attitudes (assuming we knew what to change them to) of a few intellectuals in universities would help solve this problem looks even less promising if this is the root complaint. The claim that intellectuals should be open to traditional values cannot cut much ice until we are told what those values are, why they are worthwhile, and how they might be implemented—at least in principle—in today's world.

III. Conclusion

At the start of this chapter we found ourselves with the problem that, as an alternative to neo-Kantian foundationalism, the arguments of the contextualists generate insufficient critical bite on the practices of contemporary politics. Yet Bloom's analysis suffers from an opposite malaise: it has so much critical bite that it swallows the entire modern world. Like Rorty, Bloom sees the Enlightenment goal of founding politics on reason as a failure with dangerous political ramifications for liberal democracies. But where Rorty thinks we should embrace liberal-democratic institutions while junking the metanarratives traditionally used to justify them, in most moods Bloom appears to think that liberal-democratic institutions are now so corrupted that although we should restore some version of the metanarrative, we should junk the institutions.

Bloom's diagnosis turns out on closer inspection to be two competing diagnoses issuing in contradictory arguments about the viability of the egalitarian basis of American politics concerning whether the basic problem is the universalist egalitarianism built into the American regime from the beginning that people like Rawls invoke or what Bloom takes to be our departure from that ethos since the 1960s. At times he writes as if the second is a logical outgrowth of the first; at other times, as if it is a flat rejection of it. In either case we saw that, like Rorty, Bloom fails to articulate any plausible (even identifiable) causal account of how our circumstances came to be what he takes them to be. Rorty and Bloom are both causal idealists who believe that the ideas of a few Enlightenment thinkers decisively shaped the politics of the modern West, but neither begins to describe, let alone defend, accounts of the causal processes that are supposed to have been involved. As a result it cannot be surprising that as historical anthropology of contemporary politics, both their arguments fail to persuade.

My discussion of Bloom's parochial view of the tradition reveals the dangers of believing that appeals to traditions can by themselves generate satisfying critical evaluations of contemporary moral and political problems. What we see as the tradition itself changes over time and space and is inevitably a subject of argument and debate. Just as my discussion of Walzer revealed the need to come to terms with conflicting interpretations within and among communities, so here I have established the need to come to terms with analogous conflicts within and among traditions. Appealing to tradition qua authority never settles moral and political disputes; traditions are by their nature too internally diverse and admit of too many conflicting interpretations for this to be so. Analysis of this issue led me to explicate the distinction between internal and external analysis in the history of ideas—external analysis being essential to a critical understanding of traditions in political theory—and of their relationship to social and political change. It is Bloom's failure to see this, or to render plausible the particular external account that he offers, that makes his historical argument so unsatisfying.

The weaknesses in Bloom's prescriptive arguments follow directly from those attending his diagnosis. He believes that egalitarianism should be questioned and that studying the tradition will teach people to question it, but he offers no account of what values he favors or of how they might influence contemporary politics or political argument. Bloom's diagnosis amounts to a self-righteous affirming of a fictitious past, and it is conducted from such a great height that it leaves no room for discriminating comparative political judgments about the actual political alternatives in the present, a problem that is reinforced by his conventionalist understanding of the exoteric dimension of the tradition. In the realm of prescription we found that Bloom's account is a mirror image of Rorty's and by that token equally unhelpful. "Reject modernity!" turns out to be as useless a tool of critical argument as "transcend modernity!" We need more discriminating methods of political argument.

Yet there is one enduring insight in Bloom's view, namely, that there is a deep tension between the human desire to know and act on the truth and every rationalist attempt at the design of political institutions. Although Bloom offers neither reasons nor evidence in support of his claim that this tension exists, I argue in the final chapters of this book that there are good reasons for thinking that it does. But I also show that the nature of knowledge in the human sciences is such that the interest in knowing and acting on the truth cannot credibly be restricted to an elite (philosophical, scientific, or any other) and that as a result no variant of the doctrine of exoteric teaching is justifiable. On the contrary, I argue that finding out and publicly articulating the truth must lie at the core of any defensible account of the political theorist's enterprise. This means that the tension between rationalist projects in political theory and the human interest in knowing and acting on the truth has quite different implications from those that Bloom and the Straussians suppose.

5 The History of Ideas
as Therapeutic Diagnosis

Bloom and Strauss's other followers fail to render plausible accounts of the tradition as a vantage point from which the problems of contemporary politics can confidently be engaged, but this by no means exhausts historical approaches. The disillusionment of many at the failure of contemporary theorists either to resolve the internal disputes that litter their journals or to speak in any appropriate way to contemporary political issues has fueled a much more broadly based revival of interest in history and in the history of ideas.[1] One recurring set of concerns that permeates this revival revolves around the notion that the difficulties contemporary political theorists confront must themselves be understood historically. We have already confronted a variant of this claim in chapter 2, but Rorty's historical argument is highly schematic and it does not deal explicitly with the history of *political theory*. The claim that there is something distinctive about the dilemmas of contemporary politics and political theory that can only be resolved historically has been defended most forcefully by Alasdair MacIntyre, and it is to an examination of his arguments that I now turn.[2]

I. MacIntyre's View: Exposition

Like Bloom, MacIntyre contends that the central problems of contemporary politics can be understood only through recovering a lost tradition of

1. See, for one of many possible illustrations, Richard Tuck's assertion that conflicts among various conceptions of individual, natural, and human rights that preoccupy contemporary political theorists can "be solved historically, by an investigation of how the relevant language . . . developed" (Tuck 1979: 1).

2. MacIntyre's most explicit defense of this thesis appears in *After Virtue*, first published in 1981 and revised in 1984, and this work is my central concern here. In addition, I discuss some elaborations of and qualifications to his arguments that appear in *Whose Justice? Which Rationality?*, published in 1988.

political theory. Also like Bloom, MacIntyre believes that the tradition he invokes has been so seriously obscured by changing events and beliefs that most people are ignorant of it. But MacIntyre's diagnosis may initially be distinguished from Bloom's in two main respects. First, where for Bloom there is a radical disjunction—the tradition dictates a set of normative commitments from which all modern politics deviates and should be criticized for that reason—MacIntyre sees us and our politics as products of a tradition. We have corrupted the tradition rather than forgotten it, and as a result the first prerequisite for a clearheaded contemporary politics is the achievement of a historical understanding of the causal processes by which this corruption occurred. Second, MacIntyre's turn to tradition is a product of his disillusioned retreat from Marxism both as a science of contemporary political economy and as the source of a credible programmatic political agenda for the future.[3] His rejection of the science of historical materialism derives partly from a more general disillusionment with predictive social science. Our inability to foresee certain kinds of conceptual innovations, the conditional nature of many of our decisions on events that are yet to occur, the game-theoretic character of much social action that makes it contingent on the interacting and mutually conditional decisions of many agents, and the "pure contingency" of all social events combine to render the search for lawlike generalizations in the social sciences hopeless (MacIntyre 1984: 88–108).[4] Less generally, Marx's analysis

---

3. For a good indication of how far MacIntyre has moved in this regard, compare his antipathy toward Marxism as an explanatory science and as the basis for a political program in *After Virtue*, discussed in the next several paragraphs, with the argument of *Marxism and Christianity*, published in 1968. There his argument is that, whatever the defects of Marxism as a political ideology, Marx humanized Christianity in such a way as to "present a secularized version of the Christian judgment upon, rather than the Christian adaption to, the secular present" and that "the Marxist project remains the only one we have for reestablishing hope as a social virtue" (MacIntyre 1968: 143, 116). With the writing of *Whose Justice?*, MacIntyre appears to have come full circle, identifying himself as an Augustinian Christian (MacIntyre 1988: 10).

4. In MacIntyre's view, social scientists only manage to sustain the legitimating myths of their activities because they tolerate counterexamples to their generalizations in ways that would never be countenanced in the natural sciences, they state their generalizations too imprecisely to generate clear statements about the conditions under which they are supposed to hold, and they manipulate probabilistic generalizations systematically to evade counterexamples and hypotheticals beyond the limits of the original observation that they were adduced to explain. For these reasons they are not, strictly, generalizations at all, and despite their obsessional employment of the nomenclature of the natural sciences, social scientists will never discover predictive generalizations because there are none to be discovered. This is why, MacIntyre believes, in all but the most trivial instances the predictions of economists, demographers, sociologists, and political scientists have proved to be hopelessly wrong (MacIntyre 1984: 93–100, 91–92, 89).

of the dynamics of capitalism was simply wrong in some key respects, in MacIntyre's view. Marx's assumptions about base and superstructure, for instance, missed the fact that people's conceptions of their social allegiances and their senses of justice "are partly constitutive of the lives of social groups, and economic interests are often partially defined in terms of such conceptions and not *vice versa*" (ibid.: 253).

At the level of programmatic politics the central reason for Marxism's bankruptcy is its failure to deliver anything remotely approaching emancipation from capitalism either within its own terms or in those of some imagined future society. "The theory which was to have illuminated the path to human liberation had in fact led into darkness," and the "deeply optimistic" faith behind revolutionary Marxism in all its variants is simply without foundation (ibid.: 261–62). Even in principle Marxism offers no adequate solutions. Its "moral defects and failures arise from the extent to which it, like liberal individualism, embodies the *ethos* of the distinctively modern and modernizing world," and because MacIntyre's aim in *After Virtue* is to argue that we need to reject a large part of that ethos if we are to come up with "a rationally and morally defensible standpoint from which to judge and act," we must be prepared to reject Marxism as a political program (ibid.: ix–x).[5]

(i) Tradition and Narrative in Political Argument

To get at what MacIntyre understands by the tradition of political theory, we must first attend to his distinction between traditions and narratives. Narratives exist within traditions; they are the first-order stories in terms of which we comprehend reality and make the chaos around us intelligible. Although traditions evolve over time, they provide relatively enduring normative structures that make political debate over first-order narratives possible. By way of illustration, MacIntyre might say that even Bloom's wholesale attack on what he takes to be the egalitarianism of modernity could not even be intelligible to us, we could not even disagree with it if we did not share something of a tradition of philosophical commitments with him. The existence of traditions does not preclude argu-

5. "For however thoroughgoing its criticism of capitalist and bourgeois institutions may be, it [Marxism] is committed to asserting that within the society constituted by those institutions, all the human and material preconditions of a better future are being accumulated. Yet if the moral impoverishment of advanced capitalism is what so many Marxists agree that it is, whence are these resources for the future to be derived? It is not surprising that at this point Marxism tends to produce its own versions of the *Übermensch:* Lukács's ideal proletarian, Leninism's ideal revolutionary. When Marxism does not become Weberian social democracy or crude tyranny, it tends to become Nietzschean fantasy" (MacIntyre 1984: 262).

ment and conflict. On the contrary, for MacIntyre, it requires them. Just because a particular narrative interpretation makes partial sense of some realm of human experience via simplifying descriptive explanations, there will always be vulnerabilities and questionable assumptions in their component elements. "If I am a Jew, I have to recognize that the tradition of Judaism is partly constituted by a continuous argument over what it means to be a Jew" (MacIntyre 1977: 456). The narrative task "generally involves participation in conflict" (MacIntyre 1988: 11).

In MacIntyre's view, Kuhn is partly right but partly misleading to describe changes in scientific knowledge in terms of the conceptual incommensurability of contending paradigms.[6] In the evolution of scientific knowledge theories are complex narrative explanations that displace one another but always within broader traditions of understanding.[7] This view of knowledge and its evolution have direct consequences for MacIntyre's politics and political theory. Just as it is mistaken to think, in the philosophy of science, of periods of revolution as opposites of or disjunctions from periods of normal or traditional science, so it is misleading in politics to counterpose revolution to tradition. The "individualist mode" of thinking "deform[s] my present relationships" by cutting me off from that past that has made me what I am. But conservatives like Burke have misled us, for ideological purposes, by reifying traditions and refusing to acknowledge that "when a tradition is in good order it is always partially constituted by an argument about the goods the pursuit of which gives to that tradition its particular point and purpose." A living tradition is "an historically extended, socially embodied argument" (MacIntyre 1984: 221–22).

Why does MacIntyre use the term *narrative?* His aim is to disabuse us of our scientistic fetishes about theories by suggesting that understanding at every level of human experience is reducible to a storytelling form. To elucidate this, MacIntyre appeals to Bruno Bettleheim's account of how children create order out of chaos in the earliest stages of their development. Before the age of six the child's experience is chaotic; as he gradually begins to make some sense of the world outside him, the first type of descriptive explanation to which he can relate is a simple myth or fairy

---

6. This version of the critique of Kuhn is more systematically developed by Toulmin (1970: 39–47), among others.

7. "The criterion for a successful theory is that it enables us to understand its predecessors in a newly intelligible way. It, at one and the same time, enables us to understand precisely why its predecessors have to be rejected or modified and also why, without and before its illumination, past theory could have remained credible. It introduces new standards for evaluating the past. It recasts the narrative which constitutes the continuous reconstruction of the scientific tradition" (MacIntyre 1977: 460).

tale. Fairy tales enable the child "to engage himself with and perceive an order in social reality" (MacIntyre 1977: 456–57). It makes much more sense to a six-year-old child to believe that the world is held up by a giant than it does to entertain the view that it is a spinning globe suspended in space. The child's early explanations prove increasingly inadequate to her experiences, prompting questions and the growth of critical faculties. As she sees the inadequacies of what she had hitherto believed, more complex narratives are constructed to answer the questions that continually press themselves on her. But the form of the narrative myth remains, becoming more complex and explaining new felt experience as well as the reasons for the inadequacies of earlier narratives. "To raise the question of truth [of a particular fairy tale or narrative myth] need not entail rejecting myth or story as the appropriate and perhaps the only appropriate form in which certain truths can be told" (ibid.: 457). MacIntyre wants to say that we never do reject stories as the appropriate form. "Man is in his actions and practice, as well as in his fictions, essentially a story-telling animal." Just as depriving children of their stories leaves them "unscripted, anxious stutterers in their actions as in their words," there is no "way to give us an understanding of any society, including our own, except through the stock of stories which constitute its initial dramatic resources." There is a significant sense, then, in which human beings' only resource is "psychological continuity" grounded in our "narrative concept of selfhood" (MacIntyre 1984: 216–17).

(ii) Diagnosis

MacIntyre wants to attack a particular set of narratives about human beings and their purposes that seems to him to permeate contemporary culture, but he wants simultaneously to argue that the tradition within which these narratives seem intelligible is in serious decay. Narrative and tradition reinforce each other in a mutually damaging symbiosis. Our only hope for avoiding the consequences of this is to recover and reconstitute the tradition in its original integrity, which will in turn enable us to escape the incoherent prison of our own narrative dilemmas (ibid.: 263).

MacIntyre thinks we live in a world dominated by instrumental politics where riches, power, status, and prestige, wholly detached from the pursuit of goods for their own sake, have become external rewards. This is reflected in a "rootless cosmopolitanism" characterized by "the late twentieth-century language of internationalized modernity" where people aspire to be at home anywhere except in "what they regard as the backward, outmoded undeveloped cultures of traditions." We are "in an important way citizens of nowhere." We live fragmented lives, manifested in "divided moral attitudes expressed in inconsistent moral and political principles, in tolerance of different rationalities in different milieus, in protective compartmentalization of the self, and in uses of language that move from fragments of one language-in-use through the idioms of internationalized modernity to fragments of another" (MacIntyre 1988: 32, 388, 397).

MacIntyre aims to render this thesis plausible by describing and explaining its genesis. To get us to take it seriously at the outset, he describes symptoms of the disease. He notes that everyday disputes on such issues as nuclear disarmament, abortion, what, if anything, to do about racial discrimination, and public versus private provision of health care are interminable; they are never resolved and people do not, characteristically, expect them to be resolved. They think it normal for wide areas of disagreement on such questions to prevail; "people now think, talk and act *as if* emotivism were true, no matter what their avowed theoretical standpoint may be." Emotivism is thus "embodied in our culture" (MacIntyre 1984: 22, 253; *see also* 1988: 1–2).

It is an individualist culture, inhabited by "post-Enlightenment" people, who respond to "the failure of the Enlightenment to provide neutral, impersonal tradition-independent standards" of rational argument by concluding that no set of beliefs proposed for acceptance is justifiable. We live in a culture in which "individuals are held to possess their identity and their essential human capacities apart from and prior to their membership in any particular social and political order" (MacIntyre 1988: 395, 210, *see also* 343). Such persons "cannot understand the action of entering into any scheme of belief except as an act of arbitrary will, arbitrary, that is, in that it must lack sufficient supporting reasons." With the development in universities of a conception of scholarly competence based on the fiction that there could be an objective neutrality in terms of which moral questions could be debated, "considerations of belief and allegiance were excluded from view altogether." As a result there is "a deep incompatibility between the standpoint of any rational tradition of enquiry and the dominant modes of contemporary teaching, discussion, and debate, both academic and nonacademic" (ibid.: 396, 399, 400).

Yet emotivism runs much deeper than this for MacIntyre; he offers an almost Foucaultian analysis of its social and political consequences in terms of an obliteration of the distinction between "manipulative and non-manipulative social relationships" (MacIntyre 1984: 23–24). But where Foucault would see such a conflation as endemic to all forms of social organization, varying only in its institutional manifestations, for MacIntyre it is the distinctive feature of emotivist culture, dominated by a fundamental indifference to all ends. Thus although the initial liberal aim was to "provide a political, legal and economic framework in which assent to one and the same set of rationally justifiable principles would enable those who espouse widely different and incompatible conceptions of the good life" to live together in the same society, this has resulted in a "compartmentalized" self for whom no good is supreme and who takes an instrumental attitude towards the satisfaction of his own preferences. "What each individual and each group has to hope for from these rules [of liberal association] is that they should be such as to enable that individual or that group to be as effective as possible in implementing his, her, or their preferences." This instrumental rationality is epitomized for MacIntyre in Rawls's open embrace of an heterogeneous conception of the good with the remark that "although to subordinate all our aims to one end does not strictly speaking violate the principles of rational choice . . . it still strikes us as irrational or more likely as mad." In saying this "Rawls equates the human self with the liberal self" that "moves from sphere to sphere, compartmentalizing its attitudes (MacIntyre 1988: 335–36, 337).[8] The liberal acceptance of irreducibly different and competing conceptions of goods and ends makes the fragmented life of the emotivist self all but inevitable for MacIntyre; in moving into liberal modernity we "move into a world in which the exercise of practical rationality, if it is to occur at all, has to be embodied in contexts of fundamental disagreement and conflict" (ibid.: 325).

Kant distinguished ends from means by arguing that no human relationship can be informed by morality unless it is geared toward respecting others as ends. On MacIntyre's interpretation this at least involves offering to those affected by our actions "good reasons for acting in one way rather than another," leaving it to them "to evaluate those reasons." To respect the other as an end "is to be unwilling to influence another except by reasons which that other . . . judges to be good." This in turn requires an "appeal to impersonal criteria of the validity of which each rational agent must be his or her own judge" (MacIntyre 1984: 23–24). Emotiv-

---

8. This is a misreading of Rawls's account of the good in that Rawls's primary goods are intended to be universal and, in the terminology of political economists, at least in part interpersonally comparable. Rawls wanted to argue that his primary goods were things one would want more of rather than less of, whatever one's particular conception of the good turned out to be. See Rawls (1971: 87, 91–94; 1982: 164–85). The view that MacIntyre here attributes to Rawls—that the "recognition of a range of goods is accompanied by a recognition of a range of compartmentalized spheres within each of which some good is pursued: political, economic, familial, artistic, athletic, scientific" (MacIntyre 1988: 337)—is actually closer to Walzer's view. See chapter 3 above.

ism as an outlook is indifferent, by contrast, to the ways in which we try to influence one another, and indeed to our purposes in so doing.[9] In an emotivist world "the generalizations of the sociology and psychology of persuasion are what I shall need to guide me, not the standards of normative rationality" (ibid.: 24). The quality shared by such distinctive characters of modernity as the aesthete, the bureaucrat, and the therapist is their indifference to social ends. The aesthete is consumption personified, the kind of character who occupies the intellectual milieu with which Henry James concerned himself in *The Portrait of a Lady,* where the use of others for personal gratification was accepted, even encouraged. It was a culture "in which the manipulative mode of moral instrumentalism triumphed." Although James was concerned with a small, circumscribed elite, MacIntyre's claim is that he captured the essence of a much larger tradition of moral commentary reaching back to Kierkegaard and Diderot. "The unifying preoccupation of that tradition is the condition of those who see in the social world nothing but a meeting place for individual wills, each with its own set of attitudes and preferences and who understand that world solely as an arena for the achievement of their own satisfaction, who interpret reality as a series of opportunities for their enjoyment and for whom the last enemy is boredom." The cultural impact of emotivism is exemplified for MacIntyre by the way in which the Bloomsbury group appropriated parts of G. E. Moore's *Principia Ethica* to rationalize their elevation of aesthetic pleasure above all other goods, ignoring the dimensions of his theory that were hostile to emotivism (ibid.: 24, 25, 14–16).

Another facet of emotivist culture is illustrated by contemporary psychotherapy, in particular its indifference towards ends, its preoccupation with technique, with "transforming neurotic symptoms into directed energy, maladjusted individuals into well-adjusted ones." The therapist cannot engage in moral debate about ends from within his therapeutic role, and he thereby reinforces the emotivist tendency to regard them as exogenous. This means centric therapeutic mode of being extends outward from the professional's office; its idiom shapes vast areas of social and religious existence. But the contemporary character who embodies its spirit most powerfully and who gives emotivism its social content of "bureau-

9. Despite this appeal to Kantian autonomy as the basis for this critique of emotivism, it is to Aristotle, not Kant, to whom MacIntyre ultimately turns. Given this, the nature and relevance of this implicit appeal to Kant is unclear, not least because Kant's conception of autonomy has been argued by many to entail a radically subjectivist ethics. See, for instance, Nozick (1974: 32, 228, 337n4, 338n1), Hayek (1976: 166–67), Rawls (1971: 31n, 43n, 251–57, 586; 1980: 515–72), and Shapiro (1986: 161–64, 242–46, 253, 276–84, 296–97).

cratic individualism" is the manager who, once again, "treats ends as given, as outside his scope." His concern "is with technique, with effectiveness in transforming raw materials into final products, unskilled labor into skilled labor, investments into profits" (ibid.: 30). The bureaucratic manager is the embodiment of instrumental reason; his judgments are "in the end criterionless," for his very definition as a manager requires indifference to ends. Emotivism, then, is no defunct philosophical doctrine; many of the social roles we frequently think of as definitive of contemporary culture instantiate it as a social practice.

This state of affairs is perplexing for MacIntyre in that most people's "avowed theoretical standpoints" are not emotivist. People argue about moral questions in terms of all the forms of rational discourse; they argue from premises that they believe to be true to conclusions via chains of allegedly consistent and relevant reasoning. They criticize opponents' proffered premises for alleged lack of accuracy and opponents' reasoning for irrelevance and internal inconsistency. In short, people argue about moral questions in a terminology that would be entirely without point if there were no solutions to moral disagreements. That the moral argument of modernity is thus interminable we have come to accept. It is characteristic of "modern political orders" that they "lack institutionalized forums within which these fundamental disagreements can be systematically explored and charted, let alone there being any attempt made to resolve them." Academic philosophy fares no better because it turns out "by and large to provide means for a more accurate and informed definition of disagreement rather than for progress toward its resolution." Professors of philosophy disagree with one another as much as anyone else about basic moral questions; thus the pursuit of neutrality in university teaching has confronted students with "an apparent inconclusiveness in all argument outside the natural sciences, an inconclusiveness which seems to abandon him or her to his or her prerational preferences" (MacIntyre 1988: 2, 3, 5–6, 400).

MacIntyre sees the paradoxical tension between the simultaneous presence of emotivist practices and the forms of rational moral argument as the central fact about contemporary culture that needs to be understood historically. He thinks that the very existence of this paradox should make us suspicious; it suggests that our inherited moral vocabulary may once have allowed for the resolution of moral disagreements. Hence his dual thesis is that the philosophical tradition we have inherited did once make moral agreement possible and that it has since been eroded so as to generate our current paradoxical circumstances. It is as if a cataclysmic revolution destroyed our normative tradition at some point in the distant past, and all that remains are fragments of it, without the unifying assumptions that gave them their coherence as a tradition.[10]

(iii) Causal Historical Thesis

What happened? What was the tradition we destroyed and how did we destroy it? This is difficult to get at, partly because MacIntyre describes the processes of its disintegration backward. Although his account of the decline of the virtues that made possible the rise of emotivism is traced ultimately to the preclassical Homeric world, his central historical preoccupation is with the Enlightenment. The Enlightenment Project—the central preoccupation of such different writers as Kierkegaard, Kant, Diderot, Hume, and Smith—was that of "justifying morality," of finding an incontrovertible basis for making moral decisions. This project revolved around a view in which "each science, each mode of knowledge and understanding" was seen "as deriving from some set of evident first principles, principles whose evidentness is such that they have no need of further rational support of any kind and whose status as first principles is such that they cannot have further rational support" (ibid.: 47–59; MacIntyre 1988: 225). Although the decline of religious bases for morality played a role in the formulation of the Enlightenment Project, religious justifications (here MacIntyre includes all the major religions)[11] are merely one class of teleological justifications, and thus he sees them as falling within the tradition that he characterizes as Aristotelian.[12]

The Enlightenment Project had to fail because the terms in which it was constructed were anti-Aristotelian in this sense: its proponents combined a search for a justification for morality with a rejection of all teleological conceptions of ethics. Hume's naturalism, Kant's rationalism, and Kierkegaard's "criterionless fundamental choice" define the universe of perceived possible justifications for morality during and since the Enlightenment, and adherents to variants of any one of these views typically establish it by refuting the other two (MacIntyre 1984: 49–50). But MacIntyre's claim is that all three are antiteleological views, and for this reason

10. See MacIntyre's fictional analogy to a comparable destruction of the natural scientific tradition (MacIntyre 1984: 1–5).

11. In the postscript to the second edition of *After Virtue* (ibid.: 278), MacIntyre acknowledges that there may be difficulties with his characterization of all religious and secular teleological arguments in the West as parts of the same tradition. But he gives no indication of how they might be dealt with.

12. MacIntyre offers a more complex historical account of different Western traditions in *Whose Justice?* These differences do not bear on this thesis, as he notes (MacIntyre 1988: x), and are taken up further later in this section and in section II(i) of this chapter.

as modes of justifying morality they must fail. They represent competing narratives in a disintegrating tradition, and because the various protagonists are unaware of this, they cannot resolve their differences. In *Whose Justice? Which Rationality?*, MacIntyre equivocates on this claim. At one point he refers to liberalism as a tradition whose narrative history is yet to be written (MacIntyre 1988: 349), and at several points he portrays our political disagreements as emanating from traditions that speak past one another, rather than emanating from a single tradition that is in decay.[13] Much of his argument in *Whose Justice?* is aimed at showing how these traditions contended with one another historically and how difficult it was to make themselves mutually intelligible to one another.[14] Part of his positive thesis (taken up in detail in section II (iii) below) is that in defending a view of justice and rationality, one must inevitably appeal to one such contending tradition. This might be taken to imply a major departure from the main diagnosis of *After Virtue*, wherein MacIntyre argued that it was the destruction of tradition as such that was at the core of modernity's problems and our inability to resolve moral and political disagreements rather than a modern circumstance in which each person is confronted with "a set of rival intellectual positions, a set of rival traditions embodied more or less imperfectly in contemporary forms of social relationship and a set of rival communities of discourse, each with its own specific modes of speech, argument, and debate, each making a rival claim upon the individual's allegiance" (ibid.: 393). MacIntyre tries to render the two accounts mutually compatible by arguing that all the traditions he describes are inconsistent with contemporary liberalism's rejection of teleology. Modern liberalism is incapable of engaging with any of them and has driven them all from the field. "So-called conservatism and so-called radicalism in . . . contemporary guises are in general mere stalking-horses for liberalism: the contemporary debates within modern political systems are almost exclusively between conservative liberals, liberal liberals, and radical liberals." In these circumstances there is little place "for

---

13. Thus MacIntyre now distinguishes among the Aristotelian tradition, which "emerges from the rhetorical and reflective life of the *polis* and the dialectical teaching of the Academy and the Lyceum"; the Augustinian tradition, which "flourished in the house of religious orders and in the secular communities which provided the environment for such houses both in its earlier, and in its Thomistic, version in universities"; and the "Scottish blend of Calvinist Augustinianism and renaissance Aristotelianism," which "informed the lives of congregations and kirk sessions, of law courts and universities." He also refers to Judaism as a "tradition of enquiry" (ibid.: 349, 10).

14. See, for examples (ibid.: 10, 11, 146, 164, 166–67, 182, 326, 329, 343, 349, 354, 369, 392).

the criticism of the system itself, that is, for putting liberalism in question" (ibid.: 392).

Whereas for Rorty the problem since Descartes has been unrealistic expectations about what can be achieved in ethics (as in all other realms of philosophy) so that we have to abandon our fetish with incontrovertible solutions,[15] MacIntyre thinks definitive answers to moral questions are available in principle and were reached in moral debate at various times in the past when the traditions in terms of which they were rationally debated were intact. The possibility of definitive answers to moral questions was destroyed, albeit inadvertently, by the Enlightenment philosophers' conception of their project. They disassembled the concept of the ethical that they had inherited (via a long and intricate lineage to be sure) from Aristotle[16] and abandoned those components of it relating to human purposes that had made agreement about moral ends possible. The "general form of the moral scheme" analyzed by Aristotle in the *Nicomachean Ethics* was irreducibly teleological because it was defined in terms of "a fundamental contrast between man-as-he-happens-to-be and man-as-he-could-be-if-he-realized-his-essential-nature." Ethics, for Aristotle, was the science that instructs men how to get from the one to the other.

> We thus have a threefold scheme in which human-nature-as-it-happens-to-be (human nature in its untutored state) is initially discrepant and discordant with the precepts of ethics and needs to be transformed by the instruction of practical reason and experience into human-nature-as-it-could-be-if-it-realized-its-*telos*. Each of the three elements of the scheme—the conception of untutored human nature, the conception of the precepts of rational ethics and the conception of human-nature-as-it-could-be-if-it-realized-its-*telos*—requires reference to the other two if its status and function are to be intelligible. (MacIntyre 1984: 52–53)

This scheme, although "complicated and added to," survived more or less intact through various secular and religious metamorphoses until the eighteenth century. In its theistic incarnations, "whether Christian as with Aquinas, or Jewish with Maimonides, or Islamic with Ibn Roschd," its precepts were understood not merely as teleological injunctions but as divine injunctions as well. Although the Aristotelian table of virtues and

15. See chapter 2, section I(i).
16. "The general form of the [Aristolelian] moral scheme . . . in a variety of diverse forms and with numerous rivals came for long periods to dominate the European Middle Ages from the twelfth century onwards, a scheme which included both classical and theistic elements" (MacIntyre 1984: 52).

vices had to be amended so that the concept of sin could be "added to" the classical notion of error, although man's true end can no longer be realized in this world, and although the law of God requires a "new kind of respect and awe," the threefold Aristotelian structure of moral reasoning "remains central to the theistic understanding of evaluative thought and judgment" (ibid.: 53).

The first signs of serious decay in this structure of moral reasoning can be seen in the rise of Jansenist Catholicism and Protestantism, with its new emphasis on the centrality of man's subjectively experienced individual relationship with God. But it was the secular rejection of both Protestant and Catholic theology, reinforced by the scientific and philosophical rejection of Aristotelianism, that was decisive. It entailed a repudiation of all teleological argument and a concomitant rejection of any notion of "man-as-he-could-be-if-he-realized-his-*telos*." With this move the language of morality, the point of which had been to enable man to pass "from his present state to his true end," became fragmented and incoherent (ibid.: 54). It left behind a moral scheme composed of the two remaining elements whose relationship to one another would necessarily become deeply problematical.

> Since the moral injunctions were originally at home in a scheme in which their purpose was to correct, improve and educate that human nature, they are clearly not going to be such as could be deduced from true statements about human nature or justified in some other way by appealing to its characteristics. The injunctions of morality, thus understood, are likely to be ones that human nature, thus understood, has strong tendencies to disobey. Hence the eighteenth-century moral philosophers engaged in what was an inevitably unsuccessful project; for they did indeed attempt to find a rational basis for their moral beliefs in a particular understanding of human nature, while inheriting a set of moral injunctions on the one hand and a conception of human nature on the other which had been expressly designed to be discrepant with each other. . . . They inherited incoherent fragments of a once coherent scheme of thought and action and, since they did not recognize their own peculiar historical and cultural situation, they could not recognize the impossible and quixotic character of their self-appointed task. (Ibid.: 55)

This inevitable failure of the Enlightenment Project of justifying morality laid the foundation for emotivism's Predecessor Culture, summed up by the aesthetic moral flippancy of the Bloomsbury group, and subsequently worked its way into all the major cultural roles of the modern world. It is therefore with a rejection of the Enlightenment Project that we must begin if we are to revive the possibility of the moral life.

(iv) Prescriptions

For MacIntyre the basic choice that confronts us is between Aristotle and Nietzsche: between a return to the tripartite, teleologically based structure with its scheme of Aristotelian virtues and to an ever more egocentric philosophy of the will that underpins bureaucratic individualism. The merits of the choice are, for him, self-evident, for Nietzsche's "great man" turns out "not to be a mode of escape from or an alternative to the conceptual scheme of liberal individualist modernity, but rather one more representative moment of its internal unfolding." Nietzsche is Aristotle's "ultimate antagonist," but in the end his stance "is only one more facet of that very moral culture of which Nietzsche took himself to be an implacable critic" (ibid.: 259).

MacIntyre has prescriptions both for moral theory and for practical politics, but his explicit attention is focused almost exclusively on the former. He recognizes that the metaphysical biology at the heart of Aristotle's account of the *telos* is unavailable to us, that Aristotle's account "presupposes the now-long-vanished context of the social relationships of the ancient city-state," and that where Aristotle saw conflict primarily as something to be "avoided or managed," deep conflicts about what human flourishing consists in occupy a central place in "our cultural history" (ibid.: 163, 162).[17] As a result MacIntyre advances a different and more complicated view than Aristotle's. He adopts what he takes to be the Sophoclean view that tragedy and the conflict it brings with it are not the mere result of flaws in an otherwise heroic character (as both the Aristotelian and Homeric views would have it) but that they are the result of "the conflict of good with good embodied in their encounter prior to and independent of *any* individual characteristics." To this aspect of tragedy Aristotle is necessarily blind in MacIntyre's view, because of his assumptions about natural harmony.[18] This blindness to "the centrality of opposition and conflict in human life conceals from Aristotle also one important source of human learning about . . . [the] practice of the virtues," for it is "through conflict and sometimes only through conflict that we learn what our ends and purposes are" (ibid.: 132, 163–64).

This raises the question of the extent to which MacIntyre's account is

17. See also MacIntyre (1988: 10, 13, 35).
18. For a different reading of Aristotle on conflict, see Yack (1985: 92–112).

Aristotelian, as he is well aware,[19] and to this MacIntyre responds by in-voking his earlier distinction between narrative and tradition and the ar-gument that it is in the nature of traditions that people disagree within them, that since "conflicting answers may be given within the tradition, the narrative task itself generally involves participation in conflict" (MacIntyre 1988: 11). So in his rejection of the account of natural har-mony, for instance, he engages Aristotle within his own terms, attempts to recover what he thinks was the tradition as it appeared to Aristotle, suggests that in his disagreement with Sophocles, Aristotle partly misread him, and implies that had he not done so he would have taken a more central account of conflict and looked more critically at his own Platonic assumptions about unity and harmony (MacIntyre 1984: 162–64). Whether or not MacIntyre is right in these claims, the essential thesis from this standpoint is that the criticism of Aristotle is meant to be im-manent, that he and Aristotle could, in principle, have argued intelligibly about it and, presumably, have resolved their differences. Argument about the nature and relevance of human conflict to the virtues is in this sense internal to the Aristotelian tradition. MacIntyre distinguishes this view from the "illusion" that morality is simply a matter of free choice. Thus "all morality is always to some degree tied to the socially local and partic-ular" so that "the aspirations of the morality of modernity to a universal-ity freed from all particularity is an illusion." The choice between mind-less adherence to tradition and radical freedom is chimerical for him; morality is inevitably, and should self-consciously be, a matter of critical engagement with our inherited traditions. So, for MacIntyre, there is no way to possess the virtues "except as part of a tradition in which we inherit them" (ibid.: 126–27). It is this tradition that is Aristotelian and that "is not to be confused with that narrower tradition of Aristotelianism which consists simply in commentary upon and exegesis of Aristotle's texts." Although the term *classical* is too broad to capture it and *Aristotelian* ultimately too narrow, it is not as difficult to recognize as it is to name; after Aristotle "it always uses the *Nicomachean Ethics* and the *Politics* as key texts, when it can, but it never surrenders itself wholly to Aristotle. For it is a tradition which always sets itself in a relationship of dialogue with Aristotle, rather than in any relationship of simple assent" (ibid.: 165).

Yet the Aristotelian tradition can also be characterized in more positive terms by reference to the alternatives to it, the main one being Stoicism. What is distinctive about Stoicism for MacIntyre is its exclusive focus on

19. See MacIntyre (1984: 163).

law and what may legitimately be prohibited, to the exclusion of considerations of virtue. A community "which envisages its life as directed towards a shared good which provides that community with its common
tasks will need to articulate its moral life in terms *both* of the virtues *and*
of law"; it is therefore not surprising that Stoicism arose with the disappearance of such societies. "Just such a disappearance . . . was involved in
the replacement of the city-state as the form of political life by first the
Macedonian kingdom and later the Roman *imperium*," which meant that
"any intelligible relationship between the virtues and law would disappear" (ibid.: 169–70). Stoicism remains "one of the permanent moral
possibilities within the cultures of the West," and "whenever the virtues
begin to lose their central place, Stoic patterns of thought and action at
once reappear." The crisis of the post-Enlightenment as MacIntyre conceives it was "strikingly anticipated" by Stoicism (ibid.: 170). Because we
live in a neo-Stoic age (albeit extreme), Aristotelianism, the historical alternative to Stoicism, provides the needed perspective, revolving around
the tradition of the virtues, from which to criticize it and within which to
seek alternatives.

MacIntyre's analytic exploration of the concept of virtue begins with
the notion of a practice, by which he means "any coherent and complex
form of socially established cooperative human activity through which
goods internal to that form of activity are realized." Not all human, or
even all social, activities are practices in his sense: ticktacktoe, throwing a
football with skill, bricklaying, and planting turnips are not practices. The
games of football and chess; the inquiries of physics, chemistry, history,
and biology; painting, music, and architecture; the "ancient and medieval" conceptions of the creating and sustaining of human communities,
households, cities, and nations, politics "in the Aristotelian sense"—
these are all practices (ibid.: 187–88). Although these examples suggest
that a degree of cooperative complexity is the main criterion, MacIntyre
specifically refrains from attempting to spell out what makes a practice a
practice (the implications of which will concern us later) and moves on to
distinguish goods that are internal from those that are external to practices. An internal good is bound up with the purpose of the relevant practice, whereas an external good is contingent with respect to that purpose.
This distinction is of course relational and will vary with context, as
MacIntyre recognizes, but in any particular circumstance it should be
clear. There is a difference between winning a game of chess by mastering
the rules and excelling at their sophisticated employment and winning by
cheating. A good is internal to a practice, then, if "in the course of trying
to achieve those standards of excellence which are appropriate to, and par-

tially constitutive of, that form of activity," the participants realize that good, "with the result that human powers to achieve excellence, and human conceptions of the ends and goods involved, are systematically extended" (ibid.: 188, 187).[20]

Virtues are defined for MacIntyre in terms of internal goods. A virtue is *"an acquired human quality the possession and exercise of which tends to enable us to achieve those goods which are internal to practices and the lack of which effectively prevents us from achieving any such goods"* (ibid.: 191). In contrast to utilitarian conceptions of the good, which treat all pleasure as fungible, MacIntyre's conception differentiates among the virtues appropriate to different practices; in this sense these latter are analogous to Walzer's mutually independent spheres of justice, governed by different distributive mechanisms.[21] The parallel may be extended by noting that Walzer's conception of dominance is an analogue of MacIntyre's external goods, because MacIntyre wants to argue that only the goods internal to practices are conducive to the practice of the virtues and hence justifiable. A second difference with utilitarianism becomes clear when MacIntyre elaborates on what it means to participate in a practice. Just because practices are cooperative human activities that (in some form) typically outlive any given class of participants, any discussion of the virtues must take account of two related characteristics of human nature and action. Because we typically become involved in ongoing practices in which there are other participants, we have to accept the existing structure of rules, learn them, and accept the other participants with the purposes they are trying to realize through the relevant practice. We can achieve the goods internal to a practice only

> by subordinating ourselves within the practice in our relationship to other practitioners. We have to learn to recognize what is due to whom; we have to be prepared to

20. In *Whose Justice?* this account of internal and external goods is expanded into a more general distinction between goods of effectiveness and those of excellence. External rewards are characteristic of goods of effectiveness. They are goods that are defined solely in terms of winning, where the only thing that matters is the result and "no consideration counts as a reason except in respect of its actually motivating some person." In the case of such goods "any common good at which cooperation aims is derived from and compounded out of the objects of desire and aspiration which the rival participants brought with them to the bargaining process." Goods of excellence, on the other hand, are always defined internally with respect to the standards internal to an ongoing community practice, and it is on this notion that MacIntyre argues that Aristotle's ethics is built and of which he thinks we have lost sight. Modern societies are dominated by the goods of effectiveness (MacIntyre 1988: 31–32, 45, *see also* 37–38, 43, 69, 88, 108–9, 144).

21. See chapter 3, section I.

> take whatever self-endangering risks are demanded along
> the way; and we have to listen carefully to what we are
> told about our own inadequacies and to reply with the
> same carefulness for the facts. (Ibid.: 191)

Maximizing our own satisfactions and pleasures is always contingent on
the integrity of the relevant practice and, therefore, on the ability of others to satisfy their aspirations through it as well. "Under the normal conditions of life in human societies each person can only hope to be effective
in trying to obtain what he or she wants, whatever it is, if he or she enters
into certain kinds of cooperation with others and if this cooperation enables both him or her and those others generally to have potentially well-
founded expectations of each other" (MacIntyre 1988: 36). A degree of
reciprocity is thus essential to all human interaction, which in turn requires recognizing others' lives as narrative unities with independent purposes, and here we run into a quasi-Kantian element: every entering participant discovers other participants and cannot pursue her own life as a
coherent narrative whole without recognizing that others have the same
aspiration, for successful realization of her individual *telos* requires others' recognition, and even affirmation, of its realization.

Another distinctively antiutilitarian component of MacIntyre's account
is that it makes history and tradition integral to the satisfaction of human
aspirations. First, although we initially discover others in the context of
discrete episodes, because our basic mode of understanding takes a narrative form, "we always move towards placing a particular episode in the
context of a set of narrative histories, histories both of the individuals
concerned and of the settings in which they act and suffer. . . . We render
the actions of others intelligible in this way because action itself has a
basically historical character." Because we live our own lives and make
them intelligible as narratives, "the form of the narrative is appropriate
for understanding the actions of others" (MacIntyre 1984: 211–12). Second, the way in which we learn the rules that govern the practices we
participate in has a necessary historical dimension. To enter a practice is
to join an ongoing activity governed by rules and standards of excellence.
It is "to accept the authority of those standards . . . [and] to subject my
own attitudes, choices, preferences and tastes to the standards which currently and partially define the practice." I have to learn rules and criteria
of evaluation that existed before me, that have histories. Although they
are not immune from my criticism and they change over time, I cannot
criticize them or hope to influence their evolution without understanding
their historical logic and, to a degree, accepting their authority (ibid.:
190). This, then, is an historicized version of the pragmatist thesis dis-

cussed in chapter 2: just as we are constrained by the structure of the boat at sea in repairing it for Rorty's account,[22] here we cannot escape the histories of the practices in which we participate, even when we criticize them; to participate at all is to acknowledge that they have at least the authority of survival and additionally to give to them their future.

Yet MacIntyre's account is not as relativistic as it might seem because he thinks that our various individual practices must be thought of in the broader context of our overriding purposes, both individual and social, for "without an overriding conception of the *telos* of a whole human life, conceived as a unity, our conception of certain individual virtues has to remain partial and incomplete." Unless there is a "*telos* which transcends the limited goods of practices by constituting the good of a whole human life, the good of a human life conceived as a unity, it will *both* be the case that a certain subversive arbitrariness will invade the moral life *and* that we shall be unable to specify the context of the virtues adequately." From this it follows that there are some virtues—those integral to this unifying human purpose—that either dominate the virtues appropriate to subordinate practices or regulate the mechanisms of their attainment. Honesty is such a virtue, for it implies that cheating (the pursuit of external goods)[23] is unjustifiable in any practice and that justice and courage are virtues on a similar regulative footing; they go not to what practices in which we engage but to how we engage in them. There are also substantive[24] virtues that attach to the overriding *telos* of a whole human life, the most important of which is integrity, constancy, or singleness of purpose. This notion can have no application "unless that of a whole life does" (ibid.: 202–3, 191, 203).

When MacIntyre confronts the question of whether there are inherently evil practices, he has two lines of response. To the question of whether torture or masochistic sexuality are such practices, he first replies that they are not practices at all. Recognizing, perhaps, the inherent vulnerability of this logic, he does not rest his argument there but argues in addition that although the virtues "need initially to be defined and explained with reference to the notion of a practice," this in no way entails

22. See chapter 2, section I.
23. MacIntyre does not deny that external goods are goods; on the contrary, he notes such pursuit of goods can dominate an entire culture, as in Hobbes's war of All against All or in Colin Turnbull's account of the Ik in *The Mountain People* (MacIntyre 1984: 196). It is precisely where the tradition of the virtues is eroded that this becomes a possibility. Presumably the culture of bureaucratic individualism institutionalizes, even reifies, the pursuit of external goods on MacIntyre's diagnosis.
24. *Regulative* and *substantive* are my terms in this context, not MacIntyre's.

"approval of all practices in all circumstances." That the virtues "*are* defined not in terms of good or right practices, but [merely] of practices, does not entail or imply that practices as actually carried through at particular times and places do not stand in need of moral criticism." They have to be evaluated in terms of the virtues that flow from the "larger moral context" of the integrated, unified life with its overarching purpose. It is therefore not the existence of practices that is critical but the overriding unity of purpose that gives them their point and in terms of which they are evaluated. "The unity of a virtue in someone's life is intelligible only as a characteristic of a unitary life, a life that can be conceived and evaluated as a whole." It is this conception that is unavailable to the emotivist self, with its differentiated roles and its lack of an idea, even, of what a unified purpose could be. The institutions of contemporary politics seek to manage rather than resolve conflict but this is no more than "civil war carried on by other means" (ibid.: 200, 201, 204, 205, 253).

What is the overarching purpose that could in principle supply to our lives integrity as unified wholes but that is denied to us by all modern politics? In the Aristotelian view it is the attainment of our potential. Because for MacIntyre what is distinctively human is that we understand our reality and ourselves in essentially narrative form, to achieve our potential we must be able to make our lives into good stories. They must have purposes and morals, their various subplots and ancillary themes must be integrated into our broader goals, and above all there must be those broader goals. The better the story we are enabled to make of our lives, the more we will approach that excellence that is characteristically human, but this is systematically frustrated by existing social and political arrangements. Our institutions are dominated by instrumental and manipulative modes of rationality; the ethos of bureaucratic individualism has long since lost sight of the very idea of broader purposes and goals.

Oppositional politics fares little better. Marx's theoretical account is inadequate in its own terms because "he wishes to present the narrative of human social life in a way that will be compatible with a view of the [*sic*] life as law-governed and predictable." But for MacIntyre it is essential to the idea of dramatic narrative, of a distinctively human life, that it be unpredictable (ibid.: 215). Although liberal conceptions of freedom of choice are artificial in their failure to recognize that we choose within the context of our particular practices and the possibilities they present, that "we are never more (and sometimes less) than the co-authors of our own narratives," we are and must aspire to be those coauthors. Marx made the mistake of first supposing that history is law governed and that the nature of those laws could be definitively understood and then reifying the belief in their existence into a short-sighted and mechanistic science of revolution. From this perspective it is small wonder that as Marxists approach power they invariably tend to become Weberians, replicating the alienating institutional structures of bureaucratic individualism that they allegedly seek to overthrow (ibid.: 213, 215–16, 261–62).

For MacIntyre the possibility of creating a world in which the virtues reign has not been foreclosed decisively. Although the present and future look grim, things are not predetermined and we have no choice but to try to recreate the moral life. But creating a society in which the practice of the virtues can flourish is no easy matter, as witness the failure of eighteenth-century republicanism to recreate anything remotely approaching a genuine classical politics. Part of the reason for this was that the eighteenth-century republicans inherited their idiom from Roman rather than Greek sources as transmitted through the Italian republics of the Middle Ages, where a Machiavellian gloss prevailed. But at the institutional level it was at best a partial restoration of the republican tradition because, as the Jacobins learned to their cost, "you cannot hope to reinvent morality on the scale of a whole nation when the very idiom of the morality which you seek to re-invent is alien" to the population (ibid.: 238). In these circumstances we have to begin more modestly:

> What matters at this stage is the construction of local forms of community within which civility and the intellectual and moral life can be sustained through the new dark ages which are already upon us. And if the tradition of the virtues was able to survive the horrors of the last dark ages, we are not entirely without grounds for hope. This time however the barbarians are not waiting beyond the frontiers; they have already been governing us for quite some time. And it is our lack of consciousness of this that constitutes part of our predicament. We are waiting not for a Godot, but for another—doubtless very different—St. Benedict. (Ibid.: 263)

II. MacIntyre's View: Three Difficulties

Serious difficulties attend MacIntyre's discussion of traditions, his diagnostic account of our circumstances, and his prescriptions. Before what is useful in his account can be endorsed and built on, these must be exposed and his bad arguments repudiated.

(i) The Analysis of Traditions

The most serious difficulty confronting MacIntyre's discussion of the Aristotelian tradition is that if the tradition is characterized as broadly as it is by MacIntyre, it cannot begin to do the theoretical work he requires of it. This tradition is broadly characterized in at least three different senses: it differs in important particulars from the tradition both as Aristotle conceived it and from Aristotle's own writings, it explicitly includes conflict and disagreement about its key defining elements, and it encompasses a variety of religious and secular traditions that have been at war with one another for centuries and that are in intense mutual foundational conflict today. The notion that Judaism and Islam are part of the same tradition can certainly be defended at some level, and of course historically they have the same Semitic roots even though it is stretching things for MacIntyre to characterize them as Aristotelian. Yet if a tradition includes conflicting ideologies that have been involved in massive wars with one another throughout most of recorded history and that battle intractably with one another in the Middle East and elsewhere today, how can mere appeal to this same tradition be expected to resolve the kinds of disputes whose lack of resolution so troubles MacIntyre? Disputes about the legitimacy of abortion, the proper funding of medical care, the justifiability of nuclear deterrence, and the desirability of quotas to achieve social change (ibid.: 6–7, 253)—and our inability to resolve them—motivated his inquiry in *After Virtue* to begin with. Yet a tradition defined this broadly cannot seriously be counted on to resolve these questions, and it is hardly surprising therefore that MacIntyre does not even try to show how, on his account, any of them might be settled even in principle.

The same difficulty permeates the analysis in *Whose Justice?* MacIntyre begins with a series of specific questions: "Does justice permit gross inequality of income and ownership? Does justice require compensatory action to remedy inequalities that are the result of past injustice, even if those who pay the costs of such compensation had no part in that injustice? Does justice permit or require the imposition of the death penalty and, if so, for what offences? Is it just to permit legalized abortion? When is it just to go to war?" He then repeats his claim that we cannot resolve such questions because what we are educated into "is not a coherent way of thinking and judging, but one constructed out of an amalgam of social and cultural fragments inherited both from different traditions from which our culture was originally derived (Puritan, Catholic, Jewish) and from different stages in and aspects of the development of modernity" (MacIntyre 1988: 1, 2). Yet nowhere in his analysis does MacIntyre give the slightest indication of how any of the philosophical traditions he discusses would resolve these questions. The focus of his attention is on how different traditions cope with conflict, and his answer in the end to this question is that one simply has to accept one's own tradition. This will depend "on who you are and how you understand yourself." MacIntyre's considered judgment is that it is impossible to answer any first-order questions concerning justice and rationality without embracing a tradition (possibly as a result of a conversion rather than any reasoned process), that "we have to begin speaking as protagonists of one contending party or fall silent." He then implies that an individual will be able to resolve specific moral dilemmas by testing "dialectically the thesis proposed to him or her by each competing tradition." Yet as we have seen, MacIntyre continues to characterize his own traditionalist commitments in the broadest conceptual strokes, and because he has defined traditions as involving conflicting answers to moral and political questions, mere appeal to any tradition is necessarily insufficient to answer the questions with which he begins (ibid.: 396, 393, 399, 401, 398). As with *After Virtue*, it is possible to work through all of *Whose Justice?* and still not have the slightest idea of how MacIntyre thinks we should answer the specific questions about distributive justice (or any others) he raises at the outset, let alone how he would go about arguing for his views within the Aristotelian tradition even if we knew what they were. He concludes that "only by either the circumvention or the subversion of liberal modes of debate can the rationality specific to traditions of enquiry reestablish itself sufficiently to challenge the cultural and political hegemony of liberalism effectively" (ibid.: 401), but he gives no indication what these traditions would tell us to do. Indeed the thrust of his historical analysis suggests that there is always enough disagreement within traditions to ensure that we would not definitively resolve the specific moral dilemmas with which he begins.[25] His analysis not only directs attention away from first-order moral questions to the traditions of discourse in terms of which they are presented, but it undercuts his critique of modernity that revolves around the fact of interminable moral argument.

A second major difficulty concerns MacIntyre's characterization of the tradition he is trying to recover as Aristotelian at the same time as he explicitly rejects so many of Aristotle's arguments. MacIntyre considers his relationship with Aristotle's writings to be one of dialogue and argument, but his disagreements with Aristotle are so major that it is hard to know how to evaluate this claim. His rejection of Aristotle's assumptions about harmony (discussed further below) is but one of many. He acknowledges, without comment, that "to treat Aristotle as part of a tradition, even as its greatest representative, is a very un-Aristotelian thing to do." He notes that Aristotle's dismissal of non-Greeks as incapable of political relationships should "affront us." He rebukes Aristotle for his lack of at-

25. See, for one excellent illustration, MacIntyre (1988: 175–78).

tention to political conflict, he claims that medieval "uses of, extensions of and amendments to" Aristotle marked "a genuine advance in the tradition of moral theory" but that the "medieval stage" was nonetheless in "a strong sense Aristotelian," and he repeatedly rejects Aristotle's metaphysical biology (MacIntyre 1984: 146, 159, 163–64, 180, 196–97). In addition many of Aristotle's other substantive commitments are unattractive to MacIntyre, such as his views on the natures and social functions of women and slaves.[26]

Now there is nothing wrong with endorsing some of Aristotle's arguments and rejecting others as a matter of moral or political theory; in chapter 8 I advocate just such a course. But unlike MacIntyre, I have no particular stake in calling myself an Aristotelian or in establishing that Aristotle could in principle be brought to accept my modifications of his views (I doubt that he could). Nor do I think there is anything in the nature of a tradition's being characterized as *Aristotelian* that matters from the standpoint of analyzing contemporary politics or defending a political or moral theory. Because MacIntyre's critical diagnostic case rests so heavily on the claim that we must recover a *lost* Aristotelian tradition before the problems of modern politics can even be understood, his subsequent willingness to reject so many of Aristotle's core arguments, when push comes to shove, undermines his initial diagnosis. Indeed, it is difficult to pin down just what makes a view Aristotelian for MacIntyre. Much of his analysis seems to point to the claim that what distinguishes Aristotelian from Stoic and all post-Enlightenment moralities derives from Aristotle's commitment to a teleological view of ethics, yet even here MacIntyre is on shaky ground at best.

It is false to assume, as MacIntyre does, that all influential post-Enlightenment moralities are antiteleological. Utilitarianism in its classical variants was a teleological doctrine and was rejected by many for just that reason. It may be true that utilitarianism in most of its twentieth-century mutations has shed the third element of MacIntyre's scheme ("man-as-he-could-be-if-he-realized-his-*telos*") by relying on ordinal rather than cardinal utilities and thereby denying the possibility of paternalistic and interpersonal judgments of utility. But this was not true of classical utilitarianism (its principal defect in the eyes of deontologists like Rawls),[27] and even the neoclassical variants of utilitarianism can be shown implicitly to be teleological. Indeed, the whole dichotomy between deon-

26. See MacIntyre (1988: 104, 105, 121). On Aristotle's treatment of women generally, see Elshtain (1981: 19–54), Okin (1979: 73–96), and Saxonhouse (1986: 403–18).

27. See, for instance, Rawls (1971: 22–27).

tological and teleological moral argument is artificial and misleading; the real argument is never over whether or not *telos* but over which.[28] It may be true that utilitarian conceptions of the human *telos* are unsatisfying to MacIntyre and liberalism's other communitarian critics and that "utilitarianism gave the good a bad name," as Sandel (1982: 174) puts it, but to say this is to acknowledge both that in its major historical variants utilitarianism was a teleological doctrine and that to hold that teleological argument is inescapable in arguments of right and justice is to hold very little.

If the appeal to Aristotle is to advance MacIntyre's purposes, then, there must be more to it than simply endorsing Aristotle's account of the teleological character of moral argument. Here the difficulties become more serious because MacIntyre's account of what has to be rejected from the Aristotelian tradition undermines his account of what he thinks should be retrieved. This is because Aristotle's account of human practices, and the realization of unified human lives through them, requires the assumptions about natural harmony that MacIntyre claims to reject. If Marx's one enduring insight was that conflict is endemic to human social organization, as MacIntyre believes,[29] the whole account of the realization of the virtues through practices becomes vulnerable because the existence of the practices and their relationships to one another will be causally linked to the conflicts and relations of power that prevail in a given society. In this light the modeling of social practices on a game like chess is misleadingly benign, and, as with Rorty's account of communities, many basic political questions are never addressed.[30] There is no discussion of how and why people enter some practices rather than others, no mention of people who may be excluded from various practices against their wishes. Indeed, MacIntyre concedes that the Aristotelian view is inherently indifferent to outsiders and other noncitizens such as women and slaves and that it was criticized historically for just that reason.[31] There is an unwarranted and unstated "invisible hand" assumption that, within a given practice, all participants can excel by learning the rules and adhering to them, whereas once we jettison Aristotle's natural harmony assumptions, it is surely more reasonable to assume, as Pigou did,[32] that individ-

28. For extended defense of this claim, see Shapiro (1986: 4, 19, 213, 251, 286–87) and Shapiro (1989a: 51–76).

29. MacIntyre (1984: 252–3).

30. See chapter 2, sections II(ii) and (iii).

31. See MacIntyre (1988: 107, 121, 146, 147). This issue is taken up at greater length in relation to the civic republican tradition in chapter 6, section II(iii).

32. Pigou (1960: 317). See also Furniss (1978: 399–410) and Blaug (1978: 409–10) for related discussions.

ual actions typically involve externalities—unintended consequences for others that may or may not frustrate their attainment of their own goals within a given practice or related ones.

These omissions mean that a great deal is loaded onto MacIntyre's account of the general context of a unified human life as a mechanism for resolving the conflicting demands of individual practices and for deciding whether some practices are inherently evil. "The virtues find their point and purpose not only in sustaining those relationships necessary if the variety of goods internal to practices are to be achieved and not only in sustaining the form of an individual life . . . but also in sustaining those traditions which provide both practices and individual lives with their necessary historical context." Even when we have to make "tragic choices" among conflicting goods, MacIntyre wants to stress that these choices are different from the dilemmas facing the modern adherents of rival and "incommensurable moral premises" in two respects. Genuinely tragic choices in his sense are distinctive, first, in that "both of the alternative courses of action which confront the individual have to be recognized as leading to some authentic and substantial good" (MacIntyre 1984: 223–24). Second, the tradition of the virtues tells us how best to confront such choices: courageously and honestly, not as cowards and cheats. Yet this schematic notion of the unity of life does not do the theoretical work MacIntyre requires of it.

Ultimately, of course, the idea of a unified life must drive MacIntyre's entire ethics because it provides the archimedean point for the evaluation of the individual practices in terms of which the virtues are intelligible. But once MacIntyre concedes that conflict is endemic to human existence, this notion becomes inadequate. For one thing, it undercuts his critique of modernity as being somehow distinctive in preventing the living of integrated lives. Second, MacIntyre's account deals only with circumstances in which an individual must make a choice among competing goods; it says nothing about the circumstances in which there is serious disagreement over what the purpose of a particular practice is or in which achieving that purpose for one individual means frustrating it for another. Third, the general injunctions deriving from MacIntyre's conception of a unified life tell us little that can be expected to resolve actual moral dilemmas. Consider the actions of Adolf Eichmann as portrayed in Hannah Arendt's (1963) account of his trial in Jerusalem. Eichmann was a willing participant in a series of practices for the deportation and ultimate extermination of European Jews and operated according to the rules created by others who were his superiors in the prevailing legal and political order. He carried out his duties with imagination and creativity and tried to excel at the practice as it was defined. Are we to say, in terms of MacIntyre's scheme, that he was courageous for attempting to excel at this practice or that he was cowardly for not attempting not to? Would it not have been more desirable for him to cheat and be dishonest in these circumstances rather than to try to advance the policies constituting the practice as best he could? For MacIntyre to deny that this activity was a practice is, of course, to beg the question. We need to know *why* not, for if every activity that is harmful to third parties is not a practice, this rules out a great deal, arguably everything. There are massive difficulties generated here concerning who participates in a practice, who is a third party, what claims, if any, third parties might have over the conduct of practices that affect them, and so on.

The difficulties are not restricted to the extreme and grisly case of Nazi war crimes (which, no doubt, are problematical for almost any political theory); many of the debates about immigration in the advanced industrial countries turn on hotly contested accounts of who is affected by the actions of a government and of powerful groups as, in a different way, do arguments about the rightful entitlements of the unemployed and the legitimate claims of marginal countries on the management of the world economy. There is scarcely an area of political argument in which the issues of who is affected, who has the right to be included, who has a right to alter the rules or affect their alteration, or which practices are legitimate are not objects of core dispute. Yet MacIntyre's account speaks to none of these issues, although in fairness it should be acknowledged that this is a difficulty he shares with Aristotle. In Book Two of the *Nicomachean Ethics*, Aristotle offers his account of the virtues and of the doctrine of the mean, in terms of which we are always to avoid excess and deficiency in the pursuit of particular goods. Yet he never supplies an account of why he has chosen that particular list of virtues, and he has thus often been criticized for reifying the dominant values in Athenian culture as *the* virtues, for the elitism inherent in his treatment of women and slaves and in his view that the highest (contemplative) form of life is available only to the few, and for his failure to include among the virtues such qualities as benevolence and philanthropy.[33] In addition, Aristotle departs from the doctrine of the mean with the claim that there are some actions where it

33. See, for instance, Russell (1963: 185–95). MacIntyre himself offered a version of this critique in *A Short History of Ethics*, noting that Aristotle's audience was a "small leisured minority," so that in his account of the virtues we are not faced "with a *telos* for human life as such, but with a *telos* for one kind of life. . . . All Aristotle's conceptual brilliance in the course of the argument declines at the end to an apology for this extraordinarily parochial form of human existence" (MacIntyre 1966: 83).

does not apply "because they have names that directly connote depravity, such as malice, shamelessness and envy, and among actions adultery, theft and murder." These "and more like them" he regards as "evil in themselves" (Aristotle 1977: 100, 102). This argument is intended to deal with exactly the kind of difficulty raised by my earlier discussion of Eichmann, but just as MacIntyre omits to tell us what makes an activity a practice, so Aristotle fails to explain what rules out certain actions as "evil in themselves." The debatable moral status of at least some of those actions makes Aristotle, like MacIntyre, vulnerable to the charge that they are at best an arbitrary list.

Later I argue that although MacIntyre is right to appeal to a generalized version of Aristotle's understanding of practices, we need to take both less and more from Aristotle's view than MacIntyre advocates. We need to take less in the sense that all that is worth holding onto is the *structure* of Aristotle's account of human psychology, not his (or any) particular class- and culture-specific list of virtues and vices. This means that practices we might find repugnant will have to be accepted as fitting the definition and that we even have to face up to and live with the possibility MacIntyre evades: that of entire lives that are as integrated as any other yet still morally deplorable.[34] As I argue in chapter 9, however, we can take more from the Aristotelian view than MacIntyre realizes just because we have to live with this possibility. Once we abandon the notion that unified lives in the Aristotelian sense are, have been, or could be possible and take seriously the likelihood that every possible social ordering of practices works to the disadvantage of some, the Aristotelian defense of hierarchy that MacIntyre endorses also breaks down. No rational ordering of practices is possible, and under conditions of relative ignorance about the future and much else, we have good reason to resist every entrenched ordering of social practices. MacIntyre fails to see that his rejection of Aristotle's theory of natural harmony also renders the account of unified lives vulnerable. As a result he interprets the existence of fragmented lives as a parochial product of modernity and sets up the mutually reinforcing but misleading dichotomies of ancient/modern and unified/fragmented lives. Yet once we see that unified lives in Aristotle's sense are not a possibility even in principle, we are bound to resist such dichotomous thinking: whether and to what extent lives can be more rather than less integrated in different circumstances becomes a matter of degree—a subject for investigation and argument, not for armchair speculation. In chapter 8 I also make the case that although Aristotle and MacIntyre are right to insist

34. See chapter 8, section II(ii).

that in our basic psychologies we are teleological creatures, we turn out to be teleological creatures who are endemically ambivalent about our purposes. Thus there are psychological reasons, as well as reasons that have to do with the logic of social interaction, for being skeptical of the claim that unified lives in Aristotle's sense are possible even in principle.

(ii) Diagnosis

MacIntyre's diagnosis of our current ills and his causal account of how they came to be such must be considered together because of his methodological idealism. Put simply, the claim in *After Virtue* is that the Aristotelian tradition (defined to include all religious and secular teleological moral systems since Aristotle) began to disintegrate with the ascendancy of the Enlightenment. In *Whose Justice?*, MacIntyre modifies this claim, at times distinguishing among several premodern traditions. Yet he continues to insist that they have all become unavailable in the politics of the modern world, so that it is only through the "circumvention or the subversion of liberal modes of debate" that the "cultural and political hegemony of liberalism" can be challenged and the "rationality specific to traditions of enquiry [can] reestablish itself" (MacIntyre 1988: 401).

A tradition, for MacIntyre, "may cease to progress or may degenerate. . . . When a tradition is in good order, when progress is taking place, there is always a certain cumulative element" to it (MacIntyre 1984: 146). This is lacking in the modern world, but it is difficult to see why this should be the case, what causes traditions to be in good or bad order, how judgments about the disintegration of traditions are to be made at all, or what the exact role of philosophical narrative in this process is supposed to have been. MacIntyre's argument is replete with such assertions as "eighteen or nineteen hundred years after Aristotle the modern world came systematically to repudiate the classical view of human nature"; "the medieval vision of the moral life" was "historical in a way that Aristotle's could not be"; the core components of the lost conception of the virtues "derive from different stages in the development of the tradition"; the modern world is contrasted with "the particular ancient and medieval view [of] . . . political community"; and in "the traditional Aristotelian view" egoistic behavior does not exist so the perceived but unattainable need for altruism does not arise (ibid.: 165, 176, 186, 195, 229). But how can "the modern world" repudiate? What is "the classical view" of human nature, "the medieval vision" of moral life, or "the particular ancient and medieval" view of political community? How can MacIntyre speak of "the traditional Aristotelian view" of human nature when the tradition has been so expansively defined over time and space and explicitly been portrayed as evolving over time?[35] If the tradition is reified in this way and construed as an entity that developed and progressed until a certain point in history when it allegedly began to fall to pieces, we are bound to ask questions about the nature of the causal processes involved. What was it about the narratives that the Enlightenment philosophers related that could have had this devastating result? MacIntyre's response—their definitive rejection of teleology—fails to convince even within its own terms, given his admission that the Stoics and many other influential philosophical movements have likewise rejected teleological arguments in circumstances that did not result in the moral annihilation of entire cultures (ibid.: 168–70).

There are more serious methodological difficulties. MacIntyre's extreme philosophical idealism leads him literally to identify developments in the history of philosophy with changes in the social and political world. "The key episodes," he tells us, "in the social history which transformed, fragmented and . . . largely displaced morality—and so created the possibility of the emotivist self with its characteristic form of relationship and modes of utterance—were episodes in the history of philosophy" (ibid.: 36). Earlier he says more fully:

> This transformation of the self and its relationship to its
> roles from more traditional modes of existence into con-

35. It should be noted that despite MacIntyre's distinguishing, in *Whose Justice?*, of traditions that were conflated in *After Virtue,* he continues to characterize his traditionalist commitments in the broadest conceptual strokes. He refers to himself as an Aristotelian, as an "Augustinian Christian," and he concludes with an approving reference to a description of this tradition in which "Aristotle's scheme of thought was developed by Aquinas in a way which enabled him to accommodate Augustinian claims and insights alongside Aristotelian theorizing in a single dialectally constructed enterprise." This results in an Aristotelian tradition that exhibits "resources for its own enlargement, correction, and defense" (ibid.: 396, 10, 401, 402). At many points this tradition is characterized as broadly as in *After Virtue,* to include Islam, which has made a "large contribution to the Aristotelian tradition" as a "sequence of thought which begins from Homer" and provides a "framework on the basis of which and by means of which later thinkers can extend and continue Aristotle's enquiries in ways which are both unpredictably innovative and genuinely Aristotelian." MacIntyre depicts the tradition dialectically, as always remaining open to the possibility of further development that "renders possible the work of a tradition elaborating upon, revising, emending, and even rejecting parts of Aristotle's own work, while still remaining fundamentally Aristotelian." He speaks of Aristotelianism flourishing "within medieval Islamic, Jewish and Christian communities." Aquinas "writes out of a tradition, or rather out of at least two traditions [?], extending each as part of his task of integrating them into a single systematic mode of thought." His account of the virtues is a synthesis of "Pauline and Augustinian with Aristotelian elements." The rejection of teleology continues to be common to "ancient and medieval views of the matter" (ibid.: 11, 99–100, 101, 164, 182, 210).

> temporary emotivist forms *could not have occurred* of
> course if the forms of moral discourse, the language of
> morality, had not also been transformed at the same time.
> *Indeed, it is wrong to separate the history of the self and
> its roles from the history of the language which the self
> specifies* and through which the roles are given expres-
> sion. What we discover is *a single history and not two
> parallel ones.* (Ibid.: 35, italics added)

If this is taken at face value, it is not surprising that there are almost no
explicit causal assertions in MacIntyre's historical account. If the history
of political, social, and economic change is nothing but the history of
changes in "the language of morality" and that history is nothing but the
history of academic philosophy, then mere description of the evolution of
this history is all that we legitimately should expect.[36] This extreme hermeneutic claim is central to MacIntyre's historical account as well as to his
prescriptions (as we will see), for it generates the implication that all we
need to do to change our current circumstances is rethink our philosophical commitments in light of his account of our philosophical decline. He
thus assumes a view of the history of ideas long fashionable in literary
circles, and recently popularized in the history of political theory by
Quentin Skinner and his followers, according to which the historian of
ideas should see the text "not in causal and positivist terms as a precipitate
of its context, but rather in circular and hermeneutic terms as a meaningful item within a wider context of conventions and assumptions" (Skinner
1975: 215–16). But MacIntyre's view is more heavily idealist than even

---

36. In *Whose Justice?*, MacIntyre sums up his view in a somewhat less radically
idealistic fashion: "On the view which has emerged here from the discussion of
tradition-constituted and tradition-constitutive enquiry such thought and enquiry
have a history neither distinct from, nor intelligible apart from, the history of
certain forms of social and practical life, nor are mere dependent variables. Philosophical theories give organized expression to concepts and theories already embodied in forms of practice and types of community. As such they make available
for rational criticism and for further rational development those socially embodied
theories and concepts of which they provide an understanding. Forms of social
institution, organization, and practice are always to a greater or lesser degree socially embodied theories. . . . The reductionism which appears recurrently in the
sociology of knowledge rests upon the mistake of supposing that preconceptual
interests, needs, and the like can operate in sustained forms of social life in independence of theory-informed presuppositions about the place of such interests and
needs in human life" (ibid.: 390). MacIntyre does not discuss the implications of
this milder version of his causal claim for the argument of *After Virtue*. Yet clearly
the claim that philosophical theories give "organized expression" to concepts and
theories that are "already embodied in forms of practice and types of community"
implies that some causal account of those forms of practice and types of community should be forthcoming that is not read off from the philosophical theories.

Skinner's.[37] Where Skinner argues that the intentions of authors must be decoded from the prevailing social and linguistic context—that to understand what Hobbes meant we must find out what his contemporaries understood him to mean—MacIntyre's view is that the broader context of social relationships and transformations must be assumed not merely to have been determined by the writings of philosophers and political theorists (a powerfully idealist claim in itself) but in some (unspecified) sense actually to be those writings.

Now it would be one thing to argue that developments in the history of ideas supply poignant metaphors for developments in the broader social world or that analysis of the arguments of political theorists that have been canonized in a culture, and are held in great esteem in its established institutions, can supply useful insights into the dominant ideology[38] and quite another to make this double identification between changes in social reality and in prevailing linguistic norms and between changes in those linguistic norms and in the writings of philosophers and political theorists. Only Hegel's less than overwhelmingly plausible architectonic of the Absolute Idea working itself out through history (via successively transcendent processes of determinate negation) could conceivably justify such a view. Yet this is surely unavailable to MacIntyre, given his outright rejection of all forms of deterministic historical argument (MacIntyre 1984: 88–108).

Both the conjunctions implied in MacIntyre's massive causal conflation are problematical. First, the uncritical identification of prevailing concepts and categories with social reality rests on the same internal and transparent view of language discussed in connection with Rorty in chapter 2.[39] The defects exposed there—deriving from the opacity of language, the relative autonomy and manipulability of uttered speech and written texts, and the significance of extralinguistic factors in shaping linguistic categories—are likewise applicable here. But where Rorty's view of language was argued to presuppose a version of the realist pragmatism he claimed to reject, MacIntyre's unequivocally Winchean view appears to be that the structure and evolution of language are internally driven and that social reality literally is language. The second conflation—that these concepts and categories *are* the writings of philosophers and political theorists—completes the idealist hermeneutic that enables MacIntyre to think he can

37. For a discussion of the idealist implications of Skinner's view, see Shapiro (1982: 535–78).

38. This latter is the view I defend in Shapiro (1986: 3–11) and more fully in Shapiro (1982: 535–78).

39. See chapter 2, section II(ii).

read off social reality from the writings of these few intellectuals. His praxis seems to be that theory is practice, and even within these terms MacIntyre is less than consistent. The classical Greek texts and especially the writings of Aristotle are taken to mirror a reality that we have lost and should strive to regain, even if difficulties are acknowledged (deriving from the fact that we no longer live in "the context" of the ancient polis). But the qualification itself assumes a good deal. That MacIntyre's is a naive picture of that context (ancient Greece) is undeniable in the face of much historical scholarship, as many of his critics have been quick to point out.[40] His discussion of the ancient and medieval worlds betrays not the slightest interest in the deviations of reality from theory, the ideological uses of philosophical theories, or the impact of social and political conflict on their formulation, which is astonishing for someone with MacIntyre's intellectual history.[41] Uncritical nostalgia for a classical reality, either read off from the works of the ancients or conjured up from an unspecified model of the "communitarian" principles by which undefined "traditional societies" allegedly operated, permeate his diagnosis of our "moral decline." Emotivism's "predecessor cultures" displayed "unity and coherence"; they were cultures in which "philosophy did constitute a central form of social activity, in which its role and function was very unlike that which it has with us." In heroic societies "morality and social structure are in fact one and the same thing." Adkins is cited approvingly for the proposition that, in contrast to Homeric societies that are competitive, despite the presence of conflict in Athenian democracy, it is basically cooperative. In modern societies patriotism can no longer be a virtue "in the way that it once was," for we no longer have a society where government expresses or represents "the moral community of the citizens." No evidence (other than references to classical texts) is ever offered for any of these assertions, but once they are made, MacIntyre thinks himself justified in *explaining* changes in the social structure by reference to developments in philosophy and political theory. It was the "failure of philosophy" to provide what religion could no longer furnish after the Reformation that "was an important cause of philosophy losing its central cultural role and becoming a marginal, narrowly academic subject." Post-

40. See, for instance, Wallach (1983: 233–40). Seminal works on this subject are G. E. M. de Ste. Croix (1981) and Finley (1973). For recent discussion, see the double issue of *History of Political Thought* 6, nos. 1–2 (Summer 1985) devoted to issues raised by de Ste. Croix's work, especially the papers by F. D. Harvey, George Huxley, Roger Just, and Christopher Tuplin.

41. In *Whose Justice?*, MacIntyre modifies his claims about ancient Greece, but the form this modification takes creates as many difficulties as it resolves. See below.

Enlightenment thinkers inherited "incoherent fragments of a once coherent scheme of thought *and action*" (ibid.: 33, 18, 37, 36, 123, 133–34, 254, 50, 55, italics added). The fact/value distinction is "an inescapable truth for philosophers whose culture possesses only the impoverished moral vocabulary *which results from the episodes* [in the history of philosophy] I have recounted" (ibid.: 59, italics added).

At times MacIntyre seems aware of the massive conflations behind these causal assertions, as when he notes that there is controversy over how reliable the Homeric poems or the sagas are as evidence concerning the societies they portrayed. Yet he refuses to confront the implications of these concessions for his argument:

> Happily I need not involve myself with the detail of those arguments [about the reliability of texts as descriptive of their societies]. What matters for my own argument is a relatively indisputable historical fact, namely that such narratives did provide the historical memory, adequate or inadequate, of the societies in which they were finally written down. More than that they provided a moral background to contemporary debate in classical societies, an account of a now transcended or partly-transcended moral order whose beliefs and concepts were still partially influential, but which also provided an illuminating contrast to the present. (Ibid.: 121)

This begs every question it raises. What is "the historical memory" of a "society"? How can a "moral order" have "beliefs" and "concepts"? How does MacIntyre know what the influence of texts was on largely illiterate populations in ancient and medieval Europe and Asia? How can it be thought of as an "indisputable fact"—without any reference to any evidence—that the classical texts shaped actual moral debate in classical societies? How can MacIntyre ask us to believe that the premodern world was so fundamentally communitarian that "protest" and "indignation" are "distinctive modern emotions" (ibid.: 71)?

Here we begin to see that MacIntyre's method is not applied consistently. Once he reaches the Enlightenment, texts are no longer taken at face value as descriptive of their societies but are mediated through a theory of ideology. When he reaches "modernity" reference is made to the ideological functions of moral and political argument. *Then* we discover that "despite the theoretical incoherence" of the mismatch between the "individualism of modernity" and the last vestiges of traditional moral argument, it was not without "ideological usefulness." With the Enlightenment morality becomes "*available* in a quite new way" for ideological manipulation (ibid.: 222, 110). Such assertions raise questions about the interests served by this ideological manipulation, all of which are sidestepped:

> If moral utterance is put to uses at the service of arbitrary will, it is someone's arbitrary will; and the question of *whose* will it is is obviously of both moral and political importance. But to answer that question is not my task here. What I need to show . . . is only how morality has become available for a certain type of use and that it is so used. (Ibid.: 110)

But how can one enterprise be conducted without some at least rudimentary account of the other?[42] Even if we pass over this issue and accept his description of his task, we are left with the problem of his different treatments of ideology in the ancient and modern worlds. Whatever one's theory of ideology turns out to be, it is scarcely credible that the dynamics of it would change so radically that at some point in human history the language of moral argument would suddenly become available for ideological manipulation. What reason could we have for supposing that the nature of social structures and their reproduction would undergo such an inexplicable change? Why is it that the ancient philosophers accurately depicted social reality but that although virtually no philosopher defends emotivism today, MacIntyre's independent analysis leads him to discover it at every turn, structuring all moral and political debate?

To the extent that we find MacIntyre's account of the manipulative uses of moral discourse in the contemporary world plausible, this is provisional and contestable evidence that the language of morality is always used in these ways, at least where relations of political power are to be found. In *After Virtue* it is MacIntyre's unstated but ever-present assumption that there were no power relationships in the premodern world that can make this methodological disjunction seem credible, but of course the assumption only has to be stated for its absurdity to be plain. In *Whose Justice?* he takes a somewhat more credible view: he acknowledges in general terms the presence of conflict in the ancient polis (MacIntyre 1988: 10, 11) and explains such conflict by causal reference to the power structures that prevailed there.[43] In his criticism of Aristotle's treatment of women

42. For a good discussion of the weakness of MacIntyre's implied theory of power, see Wallach (1983: 233–40).

43. Thus he notes that it is always possible "to subordinate goods of the one kind [excellence] to those of the other [effectiveness], and the fundamental conflicts of standpoint in much Greek and especially Athenian life were provided by those who did so. In the actual social orders of city-states not only was recognition

and slaves, he argues that Aristotle's "error" may have arisen "from a kind of fallacious reasoning typical of ideologies of irrational domination" and the failure "to understand how domination of a certain kind is in fact the cause of those characteristics of the dominated that are then invoked to justify unjustified domination." Yet the implications of this have not begun to work their way through the rest of MacIntyre's argument. Although rejecting the view that the polis should involve "irrational domination," he continues to agree with Aristotle that it should be hierarchically structured. Yet MacIntyre conspicuously fails to explain how it is possible to have hierarchy without domination, telling us only that "hierarchy of the best kind of *polis* is one of teaching and of learning" (ibid.: 105, 106). More seriously, once MacIntyre has conceded that the actual world of ancient Greece was characterized by power relations of "irrational domination" and that it was at least part of Aristotle's task to legitimate those relations,[44] then it is not clear what moral force the appeal to the polis or to Aristotle's account should have for us. Yet MacIntyre appears blind to these difficulties, continuing to romanticize both in *Whose Justice?* Thus we are told that "since it is only the institutionalized forms of the *polis* which, not only on Aristotle's view but on that common to educated Greeks, provided such an integrated form of life, Aristotle's account of the good and the best cannot but be an account of the good and the best as it is embodied in a *polis*." Or in his discussion of Aristotle on desert we are told that this concept only has application where there is "some common enterprise to the achievement of whose goals those who are taken to be more deserving have contributed more than those who are taken to be less deserving; and there must be a shared view both of how such contributions are to be measured and of how rewards are to be ranked." Both these conditions, we are told, "are satisfied in the life of the *polis*" (ibid.: 90, 106–7). MacIntyre also continues to romanticize a more loosely specified premodern past as being qualitatively different from "modernity." Thus in the course of his discussion of the sixteenth-century revival of Aristotelianism,[45] he remarks that what led the European educated classes to reject Aristotelianism was "the gradual discovery during

---

accorded to both sets of goods, but it was often enough accorded in a way that left it indeterminate where the fundamental allegiance of those who inhabited that social order lay" (MacIntyre 1988: 35).

44. See, for example (ibid.: 89–90).

45. This discussion is introduced with the remark that the "revival of Aristotelian studies, let alone of Aristotelian modes of thought and action, in the sixteenth-century has so far been the subject of only preliminary historical enquiry" (MacIntyre 1988: 209) that readers of the literature on civic republicanism since the 1960s will find astonishing. See chapter 6.

and after the savage and persistent conflicts of the ages, that no appeal to any agreed conception of *the* good for human beings, either at the level of practice or theory, was now possible." Although "it is no doubt true that for a very long time" such appeals were illusory, it was still possible for Leibniz to "envisage this practical outcome [promotion of the general good] as one of the realistic goals not only of political negotiation but also of a rational theology which should embody a cogent shared conception of the good." When we compare the twentieth-century debates about justice and rationality with their seventeenth- and eighteenth-century predecessors, we find that we have moved from a world in which "the exercise of practical rationality presupposes some kind of social setting" into one in which "the exercise of practical rationality, if it is to occur at all, has to be embodied in social contexts of fundamental disagreement and conflict." Thus MacIntyre continues to maintain that modernity is a new, alienated state in which the "procedures of the public realm" and the "psychology of the liberal individual" reinforce one another in cutting loose our teleological moorings[46] (ibid.: 209–10, 325, 339). Yet as in *After Virtue*, no account is supplied of what the causal mechanisms that brought this about are supposed to have been other than the implied argument throughout that it was changes in the philosophical theories themselves.

If MacIntyre's causal account, once brought to the surface, is less than plausible, his generalized description of our current malaise is likewise vulnerable. Notice that despite his repeated insistence on the importance of understanding our malaise historically, his own account of that malaise is strikingly unhistorical in two important senses. There is, first, the problem generated by his extreme methodological idealism just discussed: that it is not at all clear *how* any of the alleged developments actually occurred historically. How, for instance, did the actions of a small group of fringe intellectuals like the Bloomsbury group, in appropriating parts of G. E. Moore's intuitionism (assuming that they did), in any sense cause or even contribute to the existence of "bureaucratic individualism" in the contemporary world? Supposing MacIntyre could somehow rescue this thesis, there is a second problem of ahistoricity deriving from the breadth of his characterizations of "bureaucratic individualism" and "emotivist culture." In MacIntyre's view these infect establishment institutions and opposition movements throughout the modern world, communist and capitalist.

---

46. "In Aristotelian practical reasoning it is the individual *qua* citizen who reasons; in Thomistic practical reasoning it is the individual *qua* enquirer into his or her good and the good of his or her community; in Humean practical reasoning it is the individual *qua* propertied or unpropertied participant in a society of a particular kind of mutuality and reciprocity; but in the practical reasoning of liberal modernity it is the individual *qua* individual who reasons" (ibid.: 339).

Even if MacIntyre's account, suitably qualified, is part of the explanation of why instrumentalist modes of thinking prevail in England (or in something called "Anglo-American culture" or even "the West"), *by itself* how can it credibly be advanced as an historical account of the institutional structure and political culture of the entire non-Western industrial world? How can it even be part of such an account? To explain the bureaucratic structures that prevail in the Soviet Union and Eastern Europe historically, we would need to trace their political, economic, and cultural histories, come to terms with the conditions under which they were formed and the domestic and international geopolitical environments in which they have since evolved. Only if we built the most crass version imaginable of modernization theory atop a bastardized Hegelian historical teleology and thereby assumed that all of reality was tending to become like MacIntyre's conception of contemporary Anglo-American culture could this be thought to be an historical explanation, leaving aside questions of its credibility. Even the most rudimentary knowledge of Soviet and East European politics should tell us that although bureaucracies play decisive roles in daily political life, they are very different from bureaucracies elsewhere and, specifically, are not characterized by what MacIntyre refers to as "bureaucratic individualism." The notion of the manager, concerned only with means, instrumental efficiency, and conflict management, may illuminate something about our own culture, but communist bureaucracies are obviously teleological in MacIntyre's sense, even if they typically fail to realize their purposes or if MacIntyre does not like those purposes.

Even within what we might understand one another to mean by Western culture, MacIntyre's account is so sweeping and undiscriminating that analogous problems are raised. His depiction of such distinctive characters of modernity as the Rich Aesthete, the Manager, and the Therapist (MacIntyre 1984: 30–35) invites two sorts of response. One wonders, on the one hand, how distinctively these characters represent modernity—both in the sense that there have always been aesthetes and managers in the world, as well as priests and others who have played the roles of contemporary therapists, and in the sense that there are many other characters in today's world who are not instrumentalist in MacIntyre's sense. There are teachers, ministers, public interest organizations of various sorts, political movements, some trade unions, charities, and parents, none of which can be reduced to mere instrumentalist roles and certainly not in the absence of all argument.[47] On the other hand, even if his char-

47. At the end of *Whose Justice?*, MacIntyre concedes that the estranged selves of modernity may be "portrayed in modern literary and philosophical texts more frequently than they are to be met with in everyday life," but he in no way sees

acters are definitive of modern culture in ways other than those just alluded to, it is not obvious that this says anything about emotivist culture and instrumental modes of behavior. How accurate is it to say, for instance, that the contemporary therapist "treats ends as given, as outside his scope; his concern is with . . . technique, with effectiveness in transforming neurotic symptoms into directed energy, maladjusted individuals into well-adjusted ones" (ibid.: 30)? MacIntyre explains this no further, and as with many of his diagnostic observations, one immediately senses that although it contains a kernel of illumination it is wildly overstated. There is certainly a good deal of "fix-it" therapy, indifferent toward ends in MacIntyre's sense, practiced in contemporary America. One popular school of psychotherapy, the so-called logotherapy of Victor Frankel and his followers, is built explicitly on agnosticism toward patients' substantive sources of meaning, seeking only to restore faith in goals that supply life with meaning without independently evaluating the goals themselves.[48] But such claims about agnosticism of ends by therapists do not withstand much scrutiny; the nature of the therapeutic relationship is such that the analyst's evaluation of which sources of meaning are healthy, which neurotic, invariably shapes the therapy.[49] Of course, it has long been a standard critique of Freudian and other traditional schools of psychoanalysis that their implicit pictures of the healthy or normal human mind are in various ways biased by contextual Puritan values and are sexist.[50] The notion that therapists are indifferent toward ends, especially those therapists who believe that they are, is just too simple; it involves uncritically accepting and internalizing the liberal faith in procedurally neutral principles to one more realm of human experience, when in the practice of therapy, as in economics and politics generally, the pursuit of neutrality among ends is not itself neutral.[51] It is a normative stance that supplies de facto endorsement of the values prevailing in a culture. MacIntyre's tendency to tie himself to the claim that purposive values have vanished in contemporary culture (rather than argue that he does not like

---

this as requiring him to alter the diagnosis of modernity or any of the other arguments of *After Virtue* (ibid.: 397, x, 343, 395–403).

48. See Frankl (1959: 119–57) and (1978).

49. Even Frankl has more recently made this explicit by arguing that there is a "spiritual unconscious" and an irreducible religious component to the will for meaning in everyone (Frankl 1975: 60–74).

50. See, for example, Horney (1937: I, 13–29, 168–82; 1967: 24–26, 62–63) and Chesler (1972: 19, 58–62, 67–113).

51. MacIntyre himself argues repeatedly that neutrality is impossible to achieve (MacIntyre 1988: 3–4, 144, 166, 395).

the purposive values that predominate), together with his lack of a theory of power and ideology (which would force critical attention to the nature of and purposes served by prevailing values), generates this misleadingly simple view. Analogous responses are invited by his treatments of the Manager and the Rich Aesthete. The latter clearly has commitments and evaluative purposes, however distasteful and morally flippant they may be argued to be, whereas the former's pursuit of efficient outcomes replicates some values and power structures and inhibits the formation of others. MacIntyre's analysis of modern instrumentalism would, perhaps, have penetrated more deeply and illuminated more had he begun by treating it as an ideology and tried to discern its function.

(iii) Prescriptions

The two most serious difficulties with MacIntyre's prescriptions are that his own view of ethics suggests that they are unwise and unworkable and that they do not address the malady he has diagnosed. MacIntyre's neo-Aristotelian view of ethics was grounded in the concept of a practice, a complex cooperative human activity governed by rules that change over time but that, from the point of view of any given individual, existed before her arrival and will typically survive her. This view, we saw, has considerable explanatory force, but if it is taken seriously how can it be consistent with a politics of withdrawal, with a refusal to participate in any of the practices that, by MacIntyre's own analysis, make the modern world what it is? To this question there can be two types of response consistent with MacIntyre's premises, but both are problematical. First, he could deny that the activities that make up the modern world are practices in his sense and claim that the point of his prescriptions is to begin the no doubt difficult task of recreating them. Practices are defined in terms of the pursuit of internal goods—those things necessary to excel within the *telos* of a given practice—but the instrumentalism characteristic of emotivist culture means that we are all constantly preoccupied with the pursuit of external goods, that we are not really engaging in practices at all.[52] One difficulty with this is that it is logical nonsense to say that all goods are external to all practices in a culture, for to be a good something must be internal to some practice by definition. In its most extreme formulation such an assertion must be rejected.[53]

52. See MacIntyre (1984: 190–203).
53. In this regard, although there are serious difficulties about line drawing and definition of goods within Walzer's spheres of justice (see chapter 3, sections II(i) and II(ii)), his recognition that most basic political arguments will be about the line drawing and the definitions is an advance on MacIntyre's analysis here.

MacIntyre should be bound by his argument that the practices in which he finds himself, and the tradition they embody, must to some extent be accepted as given, so that he can "confirm or disconfirm over time this initial view of his or her relationship to this particular tradition of enquiry by engaging, to whatever degree is appropriate, both in the ongoing arguments within that tradition and in the argumentative debates and conflicts of that tradition of enquiry with one or more of its rivals" (MacIntyre 1988: 93, 394). A politics of wholesale dismissal, withdrawal from reality, and the appeal to the creation of an imaginary future that will recreate an ill-specified past may well reflect MacIntyre's understandable anguish and frustration at the difficulties of achieving meaningful political change in the contemporary world. Yet it is not enough to point to one contending tradition with its particular conceptions of justice and rationality; some attempt must be made to show how that tradition would be applied to the moral disagreements that evidently drive his entire project and to how conflicting interpretations of those traditional commitments, as applied, would be resolved. Were MacIntyre to take his own account of the rootedness of morality in social practices seriously, he would be bound to see that his prescriptions are as unwise and unworkable as they are utopian. Ironically, his prescriptions imply a commitment to a kind of voluntarist ethics according to which we just invent the values we want to hold if we dislike those around us that is central to the emotivism that he so detests.

MacIntyre's alternate response would be to argue that the practices of contemporary politics must be eschewed because they are inimical to the overarching Aristotelian *telos* of a unified human life, that our lives cannot become coherent narratives, good stories, through them. This raises large questions about what it makes sense to expect from politics and political theory and about how we distinguish problems endemic to the human condition from those that are the contingent results of alterable social practices, matters that concern me in the final chapters of this book. Note for now that there are at least two serious difficulties with this claim in MacIntyre's formulation. First, his characterization of what is necessary for unified human lives is so rudimentary, general, and schematic that it is not clear what characteristics a practice should have to promote this end or precisely what is lacking in the practices of contemporary politics from his point of view.[54] Why are "civility and the intellectual and moral life" key to the existence of practices? Why, if they are, are these denied by all

54. For discussion of the weaknesses in MacIntyre's conception of the unity of human lives, see section II(i) of this chapter.

participation in and opposition to contemporary politics, and why would they, in any case, be better preserved by "local forms of community" (MacIntyre 1984: 263)? Second, MacIntyre offers no evidence that in the ancient and medieval worlds people's lives were unified narrative wholes in a sense that contemporary lives are not, which must be the premise behind the claim that we should try to recreate what we imagine those premodern communities to have been. The mind boggles at what would be involved in trying to establish it. Then, as now, one suspects that some lived comparatively integrated lives while others did not, that some had the capacities and resources to integrate their activities while others did not, and that some integrated their lives at the expense of others' fragmented ones.

III. Conclusion

The strengths of MacIntyre's analysis derive from the structure of his neo-Aristotelian account of morality, aspects of his discussion of human social practices, and his discussion of Marxism. Because his helpful discussion of these subjects is embedded in a great deal that we have found it necessary to reject, I will end by summarizing those strengths.

MacIntyre's most powerfully defended theoretical claim is that the structure of moral reasoning is irreducibly teleological, and although I argued that the appeal to Aristotle is not necessary to establish it, it is nonetheless useful for at least one reason. Aristotle's case for the unavoidability of teleological moral reasoning, grounded in his purposive theory of human existence, is one of the most compelling versions that has ever been formulated; in reviving it and injecting it into contemporary moral debate, MacIntyre is confronting those who would reject teleological views with a serious protagonist. This is particularly helpful when a generation of political theorists, following Rawls, has tended to regard classical utilitarianism as a paradigm-case teleological argument, easily trashed, and thus revealing the alleged superiority of deontological forms of moral reasoning. The belief in a fundamental conceptual divide between deontological and teleological moral arguments is one of the most enduring myths in the academy today. Whenever one believes that it has been decisively laid to rest, it emerges in a subtly different guise.[55] A great merit of

55. Thus we now have Ronald Dworkin (1985) distinguishing questions of principle from those of policy, holding that the former have to do with rights and the latter with consequences and that judges should think exclusively in terms of the former while the latter belong more properly to the legislative and executive branches. His particular version of this distinction has already drawn heavy critical fire. See, for instance, the reviews by Brian Barry in the *Times Literary Supple-*

MacIntyre's neo-Aristotelian view is that it has no place for this mislead-ing opposition with its concomitant tendency to direct moral argument away from first-order questions about which people genuinely disagree and toward ever more abstract wild-goose chasing after theories of "the right" that do not presuppose theories of "the good." Although much of his discussion of how the teleological element in moral theory came to be rejected may turn out on close inspection to be misleadingly simplistic, MacIntyre is surely right that this truncated and incoherent view holds considerable sway among contemporary moral and political theorists.

My examination of MacIntyre's argument has also shown how little this establishes. To show that morality is irreducibly teleological is not to establish the desirability or viability in today's world of any particular con-ception of the human *telos;* it does not even show that there is such a conception to be discovered. There is no a priori reason for preferring Ar-istotle's substantive conception, and there are large components of it that most of us would want to reject. We have no assurance that any particular *telos* can be realized for all members of a community at the same time or for communities that overlap one with another, as all communities invar-iably do. The neo-Aristotelian view of the structure of moral reasoning helps set the terms of moral debate but no more. Although MacIntyre recognizes that conceptions of both right and good are indispensable to all moral and political argument, his almost exclusive focus on the good in his substantive discussion, as well as his claim that we have lost *the con-cept* of virtue (rather than arguing that our implicit notions of the good have changed), makes him vulnerable to the charge of Gill (1985: 10) and others that he is not taking sufficient account of the implications of his own claim.[56]

MacIntyre's discussion of the rootedness of normative political argu-ment in what he calls practices is also illuminatingly useful. We saw that there are some parallels between his practices and Walzer's spheres and between his distinction between internal and external goods and Walzer's

---

ment, October 25, 1985, and Bernard Williams in the *London Review of Books,* April 17, 1986, pp. 7–8. Just as it should be obvious to Dworkin that there is something conceptually amiss when the value of rights is demonstrated by appeal-ing to the allegedly awful *consequences* of utilitarianism (Dworkin 1985: 81–89)—making evident nonsense of the claim that rights are not concerned with consequences—it should be plain that the more general distinction obscures more than it reveals. All normative claims about politics involve reference to considera-tions of both principle and consequence, however deeply implicit some of these might be. For an extended discussion of this question, see Shapiro (1989a: 51–76).

56. See also Gutmann (1985: 308–22).

"art of separation." Although Walzer's view is superior in that it seriously engages in first-order debate about the nature and distribution of the goods germane to different spheres, about the difficulties of line-drawing, and embeds these issues in a theory of power and ideology (however rudimentary and problematical), there is one respect in which MacIntyre's view is an advance: he offers the beginnings of a systematic account of why we should, to a degree, accept the rules that govern a particular practice. It has been a standard critique of Walzer that he offers no account of this sort, and we saw in chapter 3 that once we move from what I referred to as the tactical to the normative interpretation of his claim, serious difficulties arise concerning why prevailing conceptions of value are to be endorsed. MacIntyre adduces two arguments, one structural and one psychological. The structural argument is that the nature of practices gives us no choice. Because the rules that govern practices typically exist before we enter them and long survive our departure, we accept them willy-nilly, to a degree, and all moral argument is necessarily immanent at some level. Again, it is worth noting that to say this is not to say a great deal: all the questions that arose in our discussion of Rorty's communities and Walzer's spheres concerning which the relevant practices are, how conflicting characterizations of them by participants are to be resolved, how membership and exclusion are to be dealt with, how to cope with the complexities of overlapping and cross-cutting practices, and how to define and regulate even internal goods so that they do not benefit different participants differently and some at the expense of others—all these difficulties are untouched by MacIntyre's discussion. These are among the most obvious difficulties that any communitarian view must confront, and we have yet to discover satisfactory answers to them.

A second aspect of MacIntyre's discussion of practices that is an advance on Walzer's spheres derives from his neo-Aristotelian account of human psychology. Again, it is not obvious that the appeal to Aristotle is essential here, and indeed it leaves MacIntyre with the problem of either being lumped with a lot of metaphysical baggage or seeming arbitrarily to appropriate bits and pieces of Aristotle's view, a serious difficulty given that he wants to cash so many philosophical chips with the claim that there is something in this tradition that our cultural history has rendered us all but incapable of grasping. Yet MacIntyre's account does offer an enduring contribution. We saw in our discussion of Walzer that questions of psychology must become central to any political theory that is based on feelings of community membership. But this was deeply implicit in Walzer's discussion of connected criticism, and he did not come to terms with its implications. MacIntyre, by contrast, makes this both explicit and central.

His antiutilitarian theory of value makes explicit why our conceptions of success and well-being are irreducibly dependent on the judgments of others; that we seek not only to get our way and influence others to our advantage but to be thought well of by those whom we seek to influence. In chapter 8 I build on this account, arguing that it is superior to an alternative orthodoxy that dominates much contemporary political theory, and in chapter 9 I discuss its implications for politics and political theory.

It should be noted in conclusion that for all the weaknesses we have discerned in MacIntyre's analysis of the Aristotelian tradition, the main dilemma that led him to turn to it is real and remains unresolved: the problematical character of Marxist humanism. For those who find the exploitative and dehumanizing aspects of liberal capitalism morally unacceptable, who are unimpressed by its utilitarian and libertarian justifying philosophies, but who are also deeply disillusioned with Marxism—both as a predictive science of a better world shortly to usher itself into existence and as a justifying ideology for totalitarian governments that call themselves socialist—the dilemma remains a major problem of politics. If MacIntyre's turn to the Aristotelian tradition has not resolved this dilemma, the mere fact of his intellectual biography is eloquent testimony to its centrality and importance.

6 History as a Source
of Republican Alternatives

A different historical departure from Enlightenment modes of political argument has been to search for alternatives not in the tradition of which we might self-consciously understand ourselves to be either students or products but for alternatives that are part of our actual history and practices. In this view it is the tyranny of the liberal tradition that is often conceived of as the problem. The stranglehold that Daniel Bell's end-of-ideology thesis and Louis Hartz's all-encompassing reading of *The Liberal Tradition in America* have had over the human sciences in recent decades is said to obscure rich alternative traditions of political thought and action, rooted in our past and potentially still available to us. "There is a conventional wisdom," J. G. A. Pocock tells us, "to the effect that political theory became 'liberal'—whatever that means, and whether or not for more or less Marxist reasons—about the time of Hobbes and Locke, and has in America remained so ever since" (Pocock 1981b: 364).[1] Recent attempts to displace this orthodoxy have led to the discovery, or rediscovery, of alternative pragmatist and socialist traditions in the American past.[2] But the most sustained and influential one has centered on the rediscovery of republicanism in the Anglo-American political heritage.

The revival of interest in republicanism has had a remarkable impact on several academic disciplines since the 1960s. For political theorists its central point of reference is *The Machiavellian Moment*. In this book and a series of subsequent essays Pocock has traced a civic humanist paradigm of political thought and action from the Renaissance revival of Aristo-

---

1. See also Pocock (1981a: 57; 1981b: 354; 1985: 60).

2. On pragmatism, see Kloppenberg (1986), Kaufman-Osborn (1984: 1142–65; 1985: 827–49), and Damico (1978; 1981: 654–66). On America's socialist past, see Weinstein (1984).

166

telianism through seventeenth- and eighteenth-century England to the American revolutionary period and beyond.

Most students of civic republicanism, including Pocock, have reacted not against neo-Kantian political theory but rather against the Hartzian vision of American political thought and the readings of early modern European thought made popular by Leo Strauss and C. B. Macpherson. Yet the revival of interest in republicanism spawned by their work has increasingly been picked up on by theorists and social commentators as an alternative to neo-Kantian liberalism.[3] One reason for this is that people perceive a connection between the individualist logic and agnosticism about theories of the good at the core of the Hartzian arguments and the similar individualism and agnosticism that, perhaps mistakenly, they identify as integral to the neo-Kantian approach to political theory.[4] This "my enemy's enemy is my friend" impetus is reinforced by the civic republican paradigm being taken by many to be one of the most powerful and politically effective communitarian visions available in our actual political culture. Because anti-Kantian theorists are typically hostile to tabula rasa theorizing for methodological reasons, it is not surprising that they gravitate toward this tradition in search of conceptual and political resources. It seems to hold out the possibility of a communitarian vision that is not vulnerable to the charges of utopian unrealism afflicting MacIntyre's account.

I. Pocock's View: Exposition

The sheer breadth and comprehensiveness of Pocock's argument has made it an inevitable center of attention in the new historiographical debate. His critical project is to overturn the "individualist paradigm" wherein all significant developments in the history of ideas after about the time of Machiavelli are read as somehow contributing to the growth of modern liberalism. In its terms, the "paradox of liberty and authority" is the central problem of politics, and the individual is seen as "a private being,

3. See especially Sandel (1984a: 81–96; 1984b: 1–11). *See also* Bellah (1985: 75–80), Michelman (1986: 4–77), Lasch (1990), and the symposium on the civic republican tradition that appeared in *The Yale Law Journal 97*, no. 8 (July 1988), particularly the contributions by Michelman, Sunstein, Brest, Epstein, Kerber, Macey, and Powell.

4. As we saw in chapter 1, many have argued that none of the claims concerning agnosticism or neutrality about conflicting conceptions of the good advanced by the neo-Kantians can be sustained. Protestations to the contrary notwithstanding, every such argument privileges some conceptions of the good and disprivileges others.

pursuing goals and safeguarding freedoms which are his own and looking to government mainly to preserve and protect his individual activity." It is thus identified by writers from a wide array of ideological camps, from followers of Macpherson, Wolin, McWilliams, and Lowi on the one hand to the "classical conservative" followers of Strauss, Arendt, and Oakeshott on the other (Pocock 1985: 59–60). As an alternative to this view, Pocock's constructive project is to describe the civic humanist view of politics, centered on fundamentally different problems, that is best traced to the early Italian Renaissance.

(i) The Renaissance Revival of Greek and Roman Conceptions of Morality and Politics

The defining problem of republican theory, on Pocock's telling, has always been the instability of political institutions. Polybius, a Greek exile in the second century B.C., developed what during the Renaissance came to be seen as a classic of republican theory in the course of trying to explain the unusual internal stability of imperial Rome. His analysis of stability and instability in cities was a modification of Aristotle's sixfold classification of regimes (monarchy, tyranny, aristocracy, oligarchy, democracy, and ochlocracy), transposed into a developmental sequence. Every regime, he declared, must pass through each of the Aristotelian forms (in the order just stated) "and from anarchy must return to monarchy and begin the cycle again." The cycle was a "*physis*, a natural cycle of birth, growth, and death through which republics were bound to pass." A special case of the rotation of Fortune's wheel, this cycle could be escaped only in a regime resembling Aristotle's polity, made up of mutually counterbalancing elements of monarchy, aristocracy, and democracy (Pocock 1975a: 77–78).

In its Roman usage *fortuna* had meant luck, and luck was highly unstable because circumstances could be neither predicted nor controlled. *Virtus* and *fortuna*, virtue and fortune, had commonly been paired as opposites, "and the heroic fortitude that withstood ill fortune passed into the active capacity that remolded circumstances to the actor's advantage and thence into the charismatic *felicitas* that mysteriously commanded good fortune." Yet when the Italian humanists revived these ideas in the fifteenth century, it was in the intellectual context created by an historical awareness of secular time. Central to the Florentine conception of republican government was the tension between universal aspiration and the inescapable particularity of historical self-consciousness; in the battle to achieve permanency in the face of the degenerative effects of the passage of time, the idea of virtue inevitably became politicized. For the republic was now conceived of in the particular, a human and artificial construct "composed of interacting persons rather than of universal norms and traditional institutions." The *vivere civile*, "a way of life given over to civic concerns and the (ultimately political) activity of citizenship," displaced the *vita contemplativa* as the ultimate philosophical ideal (ibid.: 37, 75–76).

(ii) The Humanist Debate on Stability: Prudence and the Theory of Internal Balance

Italian humanists incorporated Aristotle's theory of internal balance via the myth that Venice had exemplified the Aristotelian-Polybian mixture. Before the collapse of Medicean rule in Florence and the advent of the 1494 constitution, most Florentines had thought of Venice as a conventional aristocracy. Now history was rewritten: Venice was heralded as a "uniquely stable blend of democracy, aristocracy and monarchy," and the Florentine constitution was legitimated by comparison (ibid.: 102, 103).

Although strongly elitist in many respects, from the beginning Italian humanism contained the seeds of a populist component. Thus although a writer like Guicciardini had an explicit bias in favor of a political elite, this bias never amounted to support for a formally closed oligarchy. The *ottimati*, the inner circle of powerful Florentine families who thought of themselves as the few in the Aristotelian scheme, saw their characteristic virtue as leadership. This could not be developed or exercised without the presence of "a participant non-elite or many for them to lead," which gave the masses an indispensable—if limited—role in the maintenance of an Aristotelian balance (ibid.: 118–19, 127).

Survival in a dangerous and hostile environment required a prudent realism based on an understanding of the art of governing. Florence could never exert dominant military strength and so must exist "by diplomatic subtlety in a world of princes and *condottieri*" (ibid.: 240).[5] In Guicciardini's world, "the city is disarmed and requires the rule of prudent men." Indeed, "the conduct of external relations in a world not determined by Florentine power is the most important single activity of government" (ibid.: 219, *see also* 225, 238).

The central problem of constitutional design in these circumstances is how to give full rein to the political expertise of the few, explains Bernardo del Nero, the protagonist who argues Guicciardini's view in his *Dialogo del Reggimento di Firenze*. It is essential to take "important decisions away from those incompetent to make them" while being careful not to

---

5. By comparison, Guicciardini argued that if the Romans had employed mercenaries and "had had to live 'as unarmed cities do,' by means of wit rather than arms, their form of government would have ruined them" quickly (ibid.: 240).

"alter the substance of popular government, which is liberty"; one has to take care "that in curing the stomach one does not injure the head."[6] In his attempt to resolve this problem, Guicciardini articulates the two core terms of modern ideas of mixed government. The first results from detaching the idea of *virtù* from that of a citizen militia and historicizing it. Florentine reality exhibits an "acquired second nature," and the physician of politics is limited by it in his prescription for medicines. This second nature consists of the "tissue of accidents built up through experience, use and tradition," knowledge of which is essential to prudent government—though it can only be acquired empirically. Bernardo thus consents to "erect a scheme of government based on civic *virtù* because it is prudent to acknowledge the facts of Florentine nature," of which *virtù* is one. The other predominant values are *equalità, libertà,* and *onore.* As values they are "less intrinsic than given," "which Florentines cannot afford (being what they are) not to acknowledge." This has implications for the few and the many. The *ottimati* must accept that "*ambizione* and the thirst for *onore* are part of their temporal natures, that they require to be satisfied but at the same time to be kept in check." Yet the exercise of prudence, which "may be the highest form of the display of *virtù,*" entails a governmental scheme in which the pursuit of *onore* is limited by the power of others. This was argued to imply a competitive meritocracy within the elite, to make prudence identical with the free pursuit of excellence, "which is the essence of *libertà* and *virtù.*" But it was also seen to imply a popular element, for the few "exist only in the many's sight" (ibid.: 251, 252, 253).

This conclusion dovetailed neatly, Pocock argues, with Bernardo's second argument that the dangers of *libertà* in the many justify a complex polity of "mixed government," a clearly recognizable grandparent of our conception of representative government. For Bernardo, one must balance *libertà* against prudence, the stomach against the head. The nature of *libertà* makes it essential that "the popular assembly be prevented from trying to exercise itself those virtues and functions whose exercise it oversees and guarantees in the few," just as the few must be prevented "from setting up an oligarchy, that is from monopolizing those virtues and functions within a rigidly closed *governo stretto.*" The many are "not themselves capable of magistracy" but "can recognize this capacity in others; though not themselves capable of framing or even debating a law, they are competent judges of the draft proposals of others" (ibid.: 253, 129, 254–55, 128–35).

6. Translated in Pocock (1975a: 252).

(iii) The Humanist Debate on Stability: Revival of the Civic Militia Tradition

Machiavelli's approach to the problem of instability is at once more radical, more audacious, and more idealistic, placing him at the other pole of civic humanist debate from Guicciardini. For Machiavelli, the key to survival is not prudent negotiation in hostile waters but imaginative innovation to control and subdue them. Where Guicciardini's elevation of prudence as a practical ideal rests on a forerunner of modern doctrines of negative liberty, Machiavelli's conception is decidedly positive. Faced with the choice between audacity and prudence, he opts for an armed popular state, redefining *virtù* as "the dynamic spirit of the armed many" (ibid.: 232). Machiavelli departs from conventional humanist interpretations of Polybian theory by taking Rome instead of Greece as his model. Rome impressed Machiavelli because stability was achieved there as nearly as possible in the world of imperfect constitutions "by the disorderly and chance-governed actions of particular men in the dimension of contingency and fortune." Thus Machiavelli rejected the conventional argument that Rome was inherently disorderly, managing to survive for so long only by good fortune and extraordinary military power. He equated civic virtue with disciplined military action and went so far as to suggest that stability is not the only value because a republic may pursue military expansion and empire (in opting for this populist route) at the price of its own longevity (ibid.: 190, 195, 197). The real dilemma is generated by external threat:

> All cities have enemies and live in the domain of fortune, and it must be considered whether a defensive posture does not expose one more to unexpected change than a bold attempt to control it; the antithesis between prudence and audacity is at work again. But the crucial association is that between external policy and the distribution of internal power. Sparta and Venice, for as long as they were able to avoid the pursuit of empire and to adopt the posture of the prudent man who waits upon events, did not need to arm the people or to concede them political authority; consequently they were able to enjoy stability and internal peace. Rome resolved upon empire, upon a daring attempt to dominate the environment, and consequently upon innovation and upon a *virtù* which would enable her to control the disorder which her own actions had helped to cause. (Ibid.: 198, footnotes omitted)

Only a republic that was both perfect in its internal balance and completely insulated from its neighbors might "limit her arms and live in aristocratic stability for ever." But this is impossible; even Sparta and Venice could not escape trying—albeit in the end unsuccessfully—to defend their independence from the external encroachments of fortune. In these circumstances to reject expansion is "to expose oneself to fortune without seeking to dominate her" (ibid.: 198, 199).

Given the inevitable reliance on the military, Machiavelli's core concern becomes the relationship between military discipline and civic virtue. Because the characteristic virtue of the citizen as soldier is his capacity to preserve *libertà*, the military has to be organized so that this virtue will not become corrupted. Mercenaries and professional soldiers are too dangerous, and both are incompatible with Machiavelli's Aristotelian conception of citizenship. Just as a man who devotes all his energy to the *arte della lana* and none to participation in public affairs is "less than a citizen and a source of weakness to his fellows," so the full-time practitioner of the *arte della guerra* is likewise deficient, though vastly more dangerous. Consequently this *arte* must be a public monopoly; "only citizens may practice it, only magistrates may lead in it, and only under public authority and at the public command may it be exercised at all." The militarization of citizenship makes the *Discorsi* more "morally subversive" than *Il Principe*. For the prince existed "in a *vivere* so disordered that only if he aimed as high as Moses or Lycurgus did he undertake any commitment to maintaining civic virtue in others." Yet the republic can be virtuous "only if it is lion and fox, man and beast, in its relation with other peoples" (ibid.: 200, 213). Although Machiavelli had independent reasons for being mistrustful of Christianity (it taught men to value ends other than the republic's health),[7] the militarization of virtue made the clash between Christian and civic virtues inevitable, for "humility and the forgiveness of injuries could have no place in the relations between republics, where a prime imperative was to defend one's city and beat down her enemies." Civic virtue flourishes best where there is no mercy to enemies whose defeat means death or enslavement (ibid.: 213, 214, 216).

In Pocock's view, the Florentine debate transformed the civic republican tradition fundamentally. The core idea of a *vivere civile* had implications that were "pagan, secular, and time-bound." The dimension of grace was lost, and the republic and its virtue became finite. In historical time and space "there were many republics and the virtue of each abutted upon the virtue of others" (ibid.: 214, 215).

7. See (ibid.: 202).

(iv) Anglicization of the Problem

How could the language of civic virtue apply to England's hierarchical feudal structure of rights and obligations, rooted in its island past since at least the time of the Norman Conquest? Pocock rejects conventional explanations of the rise of English humanism as relying on stereotypically misleading conceptions of traditional society that blind their exponents to the dynamic side of English traditionalism.[8] Just as custom supplied the basis for Guicciardini's account of the Florentine "acquired second nature," so the English conception of an "historical and immemorial sovereignty over themselves" dovetailed with an historical understanding of their unique political circumstances (ibid.: 341). The parallel did not end there; in the emerging ideologies of the parliamentary gentry, the House of Commons held a special place in the preservation of liberty—now understood as rooted in immemorial custom and traceable to an ancient constitution, lost in the mists of time.[9] "All English law was common law, common law was custom, custom rested on the presumption of immemoriality; property, social structure, and government existed as defined by the law and were therefore presumed to be immemorial" (ibid.: 340–41, footnote omitted).

The legal humanists invoked some of the vocabulary of civic humanism but kept it within the hierarchical context of a feudal political structure. "This is not wholly incompatible with a classical vision of citizenship," Pocock argues, for "it is possible within limits to say that the Few and the Many are estates which must stay in their due places and practice their proper virtues, and to that extent the republic and hierarchy are one." Yet, as Pocock concedes, there is a fundamental difference between ranked elements "in a descending chain and elements balanced against one another." The former lacks the "kinetic" quality whereby the balance is maintained "by the counterpressures, the countervailing activities, of the elements" that "must practice a relationship among themselves as well as each remaining fixed to its prescribed nature" (ibid.: 349).

Ironically it was the Royalists who took the first step in declaring England to be a mixed government. In June 1642, two months before the civil war, Viscount Falkland and Sir John Colepeper persuaded Charles I to issue *His Majesty's Answer to the Nineteen Propositions of Both Houses of Parliament*. Its immediate aim was to secure the support of the Lords against the Commons, but to do so it rejected the theory of condescending monarchy for the modern idea of mixed government. To the dismay of his

---

8. See (ibid.: 335–36).
9. For a full account, see Pocock (1957: chapters 2–3).

supporters and the surprised pleasure of his adversaries, the king was presented "as a part of his own realm, one of three 'estates' between which there must be balance and (it followed) proportionate equality" (ibid.: 361–62). This political dynamite was immediately latched onto by anti-Royalists of various stripes. For once political authority was no longer depicted as a "direct emanation of divinely or rationally enjoined authority," it became "a contrivance of human prudence, blending together three modes of government." The basic political problem was no longer "one of adjusting descending to ascending authority, but one of sharing specifiable powers" (ibid.: 362). Still cast in the language of monarchy and order, the ideas of mixed government and constitutional balance quickly gained currency in English political argument and were read back into England's past.[10]

Neither the rhetoric nor the content of republican theory had won over the competing idioms of politics (most notably the Hobbesian argument that power is absolute and indivisible), but its seeds had been sown in English thinking about the political order. It was via the other wing of humanist theory, participation of the many, that republican rhetoric was indelibly stamped into English political argument. Harrington's *Oceana*, written to justify the military republic in England as a *popolo armato*, was the vehicle.

The terms of Pocock's analysis of Harrington are set by his critique of Macpherson's "possessive individualist" model, which was utilized to advance the thesis that from the mid-seventeenth century on a bourgeois ideology—characterized by the primacy of economic over political man and a favorable attitude toward unlimited accumulation of wealth—took increasing hold of English political thinking.[11] Pocock argues, by contrast, that there are at least two major traditions of argument about property and legitimacy, both with ancient and with modern manifestations and both involving theories of the relationship between economics and politics. It is in the confrontations between them in the late seventeenth century that the origins of modern conceptions of property are to be sought.

First there is the jurisprudential tradition, which goes back to the Roman civilians, is present in the language of Aquinas to some extent, and is carried on by a succession of natural law theorists into the late seventeenth century. In its terms property is that "to which you have a right" rather than that "which makes you what you are." In this tradition property, that

10. See Pocock (1975a: 366, 375–76, 381–83).
11. For Macpherson's account of his possessive market model, see Macpherson (1962: 53–61), and for his analysis of Harrington by reference to it (ibid.: 160–93).

which one owns, and propriety, that which is proper for a person or situation, become synonymous. Property relations thus consist of

> a system of legally defined relations between persons and things, or between persons through things. Since the law defined justice in terms of *suum cuique*, it was possible to define the good life in terms of property relations, or of human relations as the notion of property served to define them. . . . Because jurisprudence and the jurist's conception of justice were concerned with men and things, they were less concerned with the immediate relations between men as political actors or with the individual's consciousness of himself as living the good life. (Pocock 1985: 104)

Then there is Pocock's Aristotelian tradition "in which property appears as a moral and political phenomenon." It is a prerequisite for the good life, which is "essentially civic."

> In the form of the Greek *oikos*, a household productive unit inhabited by women, minors and slaves, it provided the individual with power, leisure and independence, and the opportunity to lead a life in which he . . . could become what he ought to be. Property was both an extension and a prerequisite of personality. . . . The citizen possessed property in order to be autonomous and autonomy was necessary for him to develop virtue or goodness as an actor within the political, social and natural realm or order. He did not possess it in order to engage in trade, exchange or profit; indeed, these activities were hardly compatible with the activity of citizenship. (Ibid.: 103)

We tend to associate the critique of market relations with Marxism, but Pocock is keen to establish that this tradition "displays an astonishing unity and solidarity in the uneasiness and mistrust it evinces towards money as the medium of exchange." In every one of its major phases, "there is a conception of virtue—Aristotelian, Thomist, neo-Machiavellian or Marxian—to which the spread of exchange relations is seen as presenting a threat." Because so many components of life can be had for money, "we are under a constant temptation to mistake money for the *summum bonum*, and an individual drawn wholly into the life of monetarised exchange relationships would be living in a commodified parody of the natural or divine order" (ibid.: 103–4).

Pocock argues against Macpherson that Harrington falls squarely into the second tradition. He took over the Machiavellian argument that possession of arms is essential to political personality, but whereas Machiavelli had simply stressed that if a man bore arms for others rather than himself he would be incapable of citizenship, Harrington developed this reasoning into an extended critique of feudalism. The key conceptual move (which he believed Machiavelli had missed) was that in a system of feudal tenures the bearing of arms was critically dependent on the possession of property.

> The crucial distinction was that between vassalage and freehold; it determined whether a man's sword was his lord's or his own and the commonwealth's; and the function of free proprietorship became the liberation of arms, and consequently of the personality, for free public action and civic virtue. The politicization of the human person had now attained full expression in the language of English political thought; God's Englishman was now *zōon politikon* in virtue of his sword and his freehold. (Pocock 1975a: 386)

For Harrington as for Machiavelli, then, "the bearing of arms is the essential medium through which the individual asserts both his social power and his participation in politics as a responsible moral being; but the possession of land in nondependent tenure is now the material basis for the bearing of arms." Harrington insisted that transmissible and hereditary property in land was essential to the independence necessary for participation in the commonwealth. Although servants were no part of this scheme, what Pocock sums up as the "economic autonomy of citizenship" did extend to wage laborers as long as they inhabited cottages of their own (ibid.: 390).

Pocock rejects conventional accounts of Harrington's economics as emergently bourgeois, arguing that they were backward looking and based on the Greek view of the relations between *oikos* and *polis*. Although Harrington saw his arguments as applying to mobile property, the key to his conception was freehold land. "When land was acquired, it was in order to bequeath it: to found families or *oikoi* based on a security of inheritance, which set the sons free to bear arms and cast ballots in the muster of the commonwealth. As with Aristotle, the end of land is not profit, but leisure: the opportunity to act in the public realm or assembly, to display virtue." It was in these terms that the later seventeenth-century gentry and freeholders who composed the Country party could see themselves as a classical *populus*, "a community of virtue," which consisted in their freeholds because "freedom and independence consisted in property" (ibid.: 390, 408, footnotes omitted).

Harrington's arguments for freehold property had been attacked by Sir William Temple and others in the generation following the civil war. But Harrington's arguments were revived in the 1670s when the ideal of propertied independence was invoked against the crown's restored power of parliamentary patronage, which latter was increasingly identified with corruption in Country ideology. Neo-Harringtonian political argument came into its own in opposition to the new monied interests, to which the crown seemed increasingly hostage, and which were effectively institutionalized by the mid-1690s through the system of public credit and the creation of the Bank of England. The debate between landed and monied interests generated a confrontation between "two modes of individualism," out of which modern commercial consciousness was born (Pocock 1985: 107, 109). Opponents of the "monied interest" like Bolingbroke and Swift argued that, with the creation of a system of public credit, the new class of speculators and creditors had created a different kind of property that fundamentally altered the relationship between property and political power. They built on Harrington's argument that although in principle the function of ensuring arms and leisure could be discharged by mobile as well as real property, merchants and craftsmen would find it more difficult to leave their activities to engage in self-defense (Pocock 1975a: 427–32; *see also* 1985: 68–69, 109–10).

It was the speculative, rather than the calculating, side of commercial capitalism that the landed gentry found most threatening, "the hysteria, not the cold rationality, of economic man that dismayed the moralists." It was "not the market, but the stock-market, which precipitated an English awareness, about 1700, that political relations were on the verge of becoming capitalist relations; and this awareness could never have developed as it did without the unspecialized agrarian ideal of the patriot to serve as antithesis." Political relations were increasingly becoming relations between debtors and creditors, "and this was seen as leading not merely to corruption, but to the despotism of speculative fantasy." The Country view was that the specialization that resulted from the division of labor under commercial capitalism was incompatible with the "unity of the moral personality which can only be found in the practice of civic virtue" (Pocock 1985: 113–14, 69, 110, 112–13).

The manner in which opponents of the Country view like Wren, Addison, and Defoe answered those arguments revealed that both sides now shared the intellectual common ground of the Machiavellian problem of stability. The counterargument was that society "could defend itself better against its own professional soldiers by controlling the money that paid them than by sending its citizens to serve in their place." This was partly because the reconstitution and maintenance of a stable system of political authority had inevitably to be a problem for seventeenth-century Englishmen—indeed it was the defining problem of politics. But it was also because their common ground extended to the theory of property itself; both sides in the debate shared "an image of social personality" in which "the political individual needed a material anchor in the form of property no less than he needed a rational soul." The argument, which continued through the Scottish Enlightenment, was over which kinds of property best guaranteed independence and with it stability. The "Machiavellian Moment" of the eighteenth century, "like that of the sixteenth, confronted civic virtue with corruption, and saw the latter in terms of a chaos of appetites, productive of dependence and loss of personal autonomy, flourishing in a world of rapid and irrational change" (ibid.: 111, 53–61; 1975a: 486).

(v) The "Americanization" of Virtue

Pocock's narrative culminates in an account of the role of civic humanist ideas in American political thought. With Bernard Bailyn, Gordon Wood, and other "ideological" theorists of the American Revolution and against older orthodoxy, Pocock argues that classical republican ideology was central—and essential—to the entire revolutionary project. But unlike Wood, for whom the Revolution was the last gasp of a classical politics, Pocock believes that although republican ideology was transformed as it became Americanized, its core organizing antithesis of virtue and corruption has persisted into our own political culture. Americans inherited "rhetorical and conceptual structures" in which "venality in public officials, the growth of a military-industrial complex in government, other-directedness and one-dimensionality in individuals" could all be conceived of "in terms continuous with those used in the classical analysis of corruption." Having made the commitment to the "renovation of virtue," Americans have remained "obsessively concerned by the threat of corruption—with, it must be added, good and increasing reason." Their political drama continues,

> in ways both crude and subtle, to endorse the judgment of Polybius, Guicciardini, Machiavelli, and Montesquieu in identifying corruption as the disease peculiar to republics: one not to be cured by virtue alone. In the melodrama of 1973, the venality of an Agnew makes this point in one way; an Ehrlichman's more complex and disinterested misunderstanding of the relation between the reality and the morality of power makes it in another. (Pocock 1975a: 548)

Americans retained a focus on corruption as the central threat to the stability of republican regimes, but their views of the roles of institutional structure and popular participation in forestalling corruption differed substantially from those of their antecedents across the Atlantic. The doctrine of the king in parliament had occupied a middle ground between classical republican theory and English feudalism, but Americans had no use at all for the classical conception of government based on a mixture of social orders. Even before the Revolution the volatility of colonial American politics had been explained by some observers as resulting from the absence of an equivalent to the House of Lords, which, in the British constitution, had been argued to play the role of the classical few. As long as America was thought of as a colony, this lack presented no problem for republican theory, which had always held that colonies and provinces were not fully incorporated and should be ruled by a dependent oligarchy. Once the colony began to be conceived of as an autonomous republic, however, such an oligarchy must inevitably be corrupting. Yet an independent hereditary aristocracy could not be created under colonial conditions, and an appointed second chamber would inevitably be an oligarchy dependent on whoever appointed it. The conceptual impasse thus created could only be escaped by repudiating the idea of hereditary aristocracy as inherently corrupting. This radical move involved a return to the Harringtonian notion of a natural aristocracy, and in most American colonies a patrician elite stood ready to step into this role. It began to be argued on meritocratic grounds that a true elite would always be recognized by the many. "It was assumed that a supply of such persons was guaranteed by nature, and . . . [that] democracy could discover the aristocracy by using its own modes of discernment, and there was no need to legislate its choice in advance" (ibid.: 513–14, 515).

The American people were clearly an undifferentiated mass rather than the combination of estates of conventional republican theory, but Pocock disputes Wood's contention that this meant an end to classical republican politics. He points out that the people's function of evaluating and electing their governors from the reservoir of talent that the natural aristocracy theory implied was by no means trivial. Pocock's burden of argument becomes heavier here, however, because it soon became widely agreed that a natural aristocracy had not yet emerged and could not realistically be expected to do so. As he concedes, in revolutionary America "the tide had been running strongly in favor of the view that elected representatives were highly corruptible delegates, who must be subject to instruction and recall" (ibid.: 519); the difficulty with the Madisonian claim that they should be chosen from the patrician elites was that not only could they no longer be argued to be the few of classical republican theory but they were obviously a far cry from a natural aristocracy. Yet Pocock notes that the dilemma thus created could be and was dealt with as a problem for republican theory. For the Federalists, the failure of a natural aristocracy to emerge indicated that the people could not be virtuous; that they were already corrupt, so that government became "a Guicciardinian affair of guiding a people who were not virtuous, or helping them guide themselves, along paths as satisfactory as could be hoped for in these circumstances." Thus the prudent management of self-interest took its central place in modern republican theory. If men "no longer enjoyed the conditions thought necessary to make them capable of perceiving the common good, all that each man was capable of perceiving was his own particular interest," so that "interest and faction are the modes in which the decreasingly virtuous people discern and pursue their activities in politics." For Madison, the checks and balances of the separation of powers to be built into the federal structure ensure that interest does not corrupt "so that the full rhetoric of balance and stability can still be invoked in praise of an edifice no longer founded in virtue, and the very fact that it is no longer so founded can easily be masked and forgotten." The federal constitution could absorb a potentially limitless number of conflicting interests and thus stave off—perhaps indefinitely—the instability that attends all republican institutions, through perpetual growth and change. Thus despite important differences between Federalist theory and the court ideology of late-eighteenth-century England,[12] the Revolution did not see the "end of classical politics"; rather they were transposed into a new key (ibid.: 520, 522–23, footnote omitted).

Pocock parts company, second, with Wood's analysis as it deals with the social dimensions of popular participation. The tension between landed and commercial interests that infused the English debate was reconciled in the American debate via the argument that in a continuously expanding economy self-interest could actually displace virtue without becoming corruptive.[13] If the federal structure no longer had to preserve an harmonious balance among estates but could absorb innumerable factional interests and remain stable, the traditional ambivalence toward imperialism in republican theory was dissipated and the expanding western frontier could be a source of republican stability. The new federation could be "both republic and empire, continental in its initial dimensions and capable of fur-

12. The court thesis located sovereignty in parliament, not the people; it rested on a version of history in which there were pragmatic adjustments rather than fundamental principles; and it was traumatically influenced by the new monied interest in ways that did not concern Americans in the 1780s (Pocock 1975a: 525).
    13. See (ibid.: 533–34).

ther expansion by means of simple extensions of the federative principle, greatly surpassing the semimilitary complex of colonies and provinces which had extended the Roman hegemony." Thus could William Vans Murray argue that the virtue of the individual was no longer a prerequisite for free government. Subjecting private to public good had been required in a "rude and precommercial society," but now that the true secret of republican liberty—continuous expansion—was known, this was no longer so (ibid.: 524, 526).

The specialization that had been thought the very enemy of virtue in the English confrontation between landed and commercial property could now be embraced unambiguously. Thus Hamilton—who maintained, against Madison, that if virtue is the principle of classical republics, interest is that of empires—defended a view of America as an expanding mercantile and manufacturing economy, competing with the other powerful trading nations of the world. In Hamilton's mind, then, the passage from virtue to commerce was no

> serene withdrawal into liberal complacency, into a world where separate interests balanced one another. He was opting for dominion and expansion, not for free trade, and emphatically rejected any argument that the interests of trading nations were peacefully complementary. There would be war, and there must be strong government. (Ibid.: 531, *see also* 530)

Hamilton's extremist language and his almost open identification of the republic with strong internal government and imperialism abroad caused many to reject his views as corrupting, but the essential thesis was embraced by those followers of Jefferson who wanted to reconcile Jefferson's commitment to agrarian life as the essential basis for virtue with his acceptance that men are transformed by scientific progress so that the republic could not be based on individual virtue *simpliciter.* Jefferson argued that "commerce—the progress of the arts—corrupts the virtue of agrarian man," but he also agreed with Webster's argument that an agrarian society can absorb commerce and that an expanding agrarian society can absorb expanding commerce.

> America is the world's garden; there is an all but infinite reservoir of free land, and expansion to fill it is the all but infinite expansion of virtue. The rhetoric of Smith's Virgin Land, filling the century after Jefferson and Webster, is the rhetoric of this expansion of arms-bearing and liberty-loving husbandmen. . . . The justification of

> frontier expansion is thus Machiavellian, and in the myth
> of Jackson it is seen to entail a Machiavellian *virtù* which
> will extend virtue without corrupting it—a process pos-
> sible in the fee simple empire. . . . The synthesis of
> virtue and *virtù*, achieved by Polybius and Machiavelli
> in their more sanguine moments, is recreated in the Jef-
> fersonian-Jacksonian tradition at a far higher level of
> sociological complexity and hence of optimism. (Ibid.:
> 538–39)

Now "frontier and industry, land and commerce, are both expansive
forces, [and] they can both be described in terms of passion and dyna-
mism: the patriotic *virtù* of the warrior yeoman for the former, the pas-
sionate and restless pursuit of interest for the latter." Yet Pocock concludes
that a degree of ambivalence was built into utopian variants of American
republicanism. Because the land is finite, the end of utopia must eventually be reached; the land will run out, the expansion of virtue will no
longer keep pace with commerce, and the process of corruption will re-
sume so that "even in America, the republic faces the problem of its
own ultimate finitude, and that of its virtue, in space and time" (ibid.:
540–41).

II. Pocock's View: Three Difficulties

There is no denying the richness of Pocock's portrayal of the unfolding of
civic humanism. But how are we to evaluate it as political theorists? The
burden of the remainder of this chapter is to discuss the implications of
three difficulties attending Pocock's account that must inform any analysis
of its normative political significance. First, although Pocock's analysis reveals important dimensions of our cultural landscape of which insufficient
account is typically taken by both liberal political theorists and their critics, Pocock is hoodwinked by a straw conception of liberalism in setting up
his alternative paradigms thesis. This creates a misleading opposition of
gross concepts, directing attention away from the first-order questions we
should be arguing about and toward second-order debates that by their
nature cannot be resolved. Second, the claim that attention to civic republicanism opens up a way of thinking about property and power relations
that is not dominated by the issues surrounding the rise of bourgeois
modes of thought is found wanting; to a great extent these issues are ines-
capably ours. Third, I argue that insofar as a distinctive politics can be
identified as flowing from civic humanism, in its contemporary manifestations it is neither justifiable nor attractive mainly because of its implau-

sibly benign assumptions about the relationship between private property and independence and its almost exclusive preoccupation with instrumental questions concerning the stability of political institutions. In fairness to Pocock I should note at the outset that he is an expositor rather than an advocate of the tradition he describes. Although I maintain that he describes the civic humanist paradigm in unduly favorable terms, it is primarily to those who appeal to the tradition of civic republicanism for contemporary normative purposes that I direct this last part of my argument.

(i) Misleading Anachronism of the Alternative Paradigm Thesis

Pocock wants first and foremost to establish that republican writers use distinctive terms of political argument.[14] To bring these to the surface, he employs two strategies—one linguistic, one analytical. The linguistic strategy consists in describing his paradigms by example: Pocock points to key terms, clusters of terms or preoccupations that are held to be distinctively liberal or republican. Yet on close inspection every such appeal encounters difficulties.

To begin with, the term *republican* exhibits a great many competing meanings. Even if we restrict ourselves to the uses Pocock explicitly embraces, we find a remarkable diversity of referents ranging from the Greek city-states of the ancient world to modern territorial ones and over polities as different in their socioeconomic systems as slave-based ancient societies and feudal, agrarian, commercial, and modern capitalist ones. At times when Pocock speaks of the republican tradition, he lumps together as its "major phases" ideologies as disparate as Aristotelianism, Thomism (which in other contexts is held to be paradigmatically antirepublican),[15] "neo-Machiavellism," and Marxism and claims they display "an astonishing unity and solidarity" in their mistrust of money as a medium of exchange (Pocock 1985: 103–4). Questions inevitably arise, therefore, of how anachronistic it might be to try to describe these different uses with

14. Pocock's view of the relation between liberal and republican ideas is complex, and he has modified it over time but continues to discuss them as constituting analytically distinct paradigms, not translatable or reducible to one another. Pocock now acknowledges that liberalism's "law-centered paradigm" is "the principal theme of the history of early modern political thought" and concedes that there was a period in the eighteenth century when republican and liberal outlooks were fused by the legal humanists (Pocock 1981b: 361, 366–67). Yet even when he identifies his enterprise as "trying to get . . . [the liberal] paradigm into perspective," he continues to maintain that "readers of Kuhn will know that a covert attack on the paradigm may be entailed" (Pocock 1985: 61).

15. See (ibid.: 104).

the same Arendtian political vocabulary[16] and of what consistent meaning over time the term *republican* can have if it is to apply to them all.[17]

Liberalism is notoriously no less problematical. It, too, denotes a host of quite different political ideologies. Pocock seems to think of it in Hartzian terms as representing a view of the world in which asocial individuals are prevented from destroying one another by legal constraints but otherwise pursue their self-interested goals. Yet liberalism has seldom been like this historically. Today it generally denotes a quasi-statist ideology geared to the promotion of public welfare and the protection, even privileging, of historically disadvantaged groups within the constraints of advanced capitalism. Perhaps the libertarianism of Nozick, with its eschewal of patterned theories of the good and insistence on "rights-as-side-constraints," and the Rawlsian insistence that all teleological commitments ride roughshod over the rights of individuals fit the Pocockian stereotype.[18] But these have no more in common with the major historical variants of liberalism than do they with contemporary political liberalism.[19]

Within the alleged paradigms, Pocock's characterizations of key terms

16. Arendt's influence on the architecture of Pocock's civic republican model becomes explicit in Pocock (1975a: 550).

17. If we think about the term *republic* and its cognates more generally than Pocock, the problem of characterization (let alone definition) becomes even more serious. In the history of ideas we can distinguish Plato's conception in *The Republic* from Machiavelli's neo-Aristotelian formulations from the uses of it made by the French revolutionaries of 1789 and the English Chartists of the 1840s and fail to discern obvious common characteristics. At times it is a generic term, almost synonymous with *regime,* so that even a monarchy can be a kind of republic (as indeed it was in the thought of some of Pocock's [1975a: 401–22] English neo-Harringtonian Machiavellians), yet it also exhibits an explicitly antimonarchical connotation—as it did in France in 1789, 1830, and 1848 and as has always been implied in its American usages (though here an anticolonial element enters as well). The many social formations that have historically been labeled *republican* are comparably diverse. The Greek city-states were republics (though they differed greatly in internal structure and organization); there was republican Rome, the English republic during the seventeenth century, and the various short-lived European republics of the nineteenth. The geography of the contemporary world tells a story of perhaps unparalleled diversity subsumed under the term. The United States is a republic, but we also have the Union of Soviet Socialist Republics, the People's Republic of China, the Fifth Republic in France, the Republic of the Philippines, the Federal Republic of Germany, the German Democratic Republic, and the Republic of South Africa, to name but a few. Of the 170 countries listed in *The Countries of the World and Their Leaders, 1987* (Washington, D.C.: Gale Research Company, 1987), pp. 150–62, 113 contain the term *republic* or one of its cognates in their formal names.

18. Even Nozick's libertarian view rests on conceptions of both human and public good. See Shapiro (1986: 165–78, 289–92).

19. For useful discussions of liberalism that establish this case, see Galston (1983: 621–29), Smith (1985), and Kloppenberg (1987).

and preoccupations run into analogous difficulties. He counterposes the emphasis on rights in liberalism's "law-centered paradigm" with the claim that the civic humanist paradigm revolves around the idea of virtue—that "*homo* is naturally a citizen and most fully himself when living in a *vivere civile*." Because the civic humanist and liberal vocabularies are "discontinuous with one another," and they "premise different values, encounter different problems, and employ different strategies of speech and argument," republicanism's virtue "cannot be satisfactorily reduced to the status of right or assimilated to the vocabulary of jurisprudence." The discontinuity remains even when both vocabularies are used "in the same context and to congruent purposes," as when both republican and juristic modes of argument were simultaneously invoked to vindicate republican independence in the late thirteenth and fourteenth centuries (Pocock 1981b: 365, 355–56, 357, 356).

Yet the entire historiographical debate spawned by Pocock's casting of republicanism as an alternative virtue-based paradigm (even if he equivocates about the periods in which it is held to have been distinct) has shed more noise than light on our understanding of early modern thought.[20] Many commentators have pointed out on the one hand that liberalism has always employed conceptions of virtue and on the other that such writers as Harrington, whom Pocock deemed paradigmatically republican, employed much of the liberal vocabulary of law, right, and value.[21] As with all historiographical fads, the endless contortions engaged in by Pocock's followers to save the thesis dilute its explanatory power. An increasingly diverse collection of theorists is deemed somehow to have been republican, including writers like Adam Smith who explicitly rejected core republican arguments, openly embracing standing armies and the division of labor.[22] Even Locke, who Pocock originally argued had been given too much prominence at the expense of civic humanist writers, now teeters on the verge of incorporation into the new civic humanist rewriting of early modern thought.[23] This is ironic, in light of Pocock's original motivation, his dis-

20. For a recent statement of his view, see Pocock (1985: 37–50). In this and the next several paragraphs I draw on arguments in Shapiro (1989a: 62–65).

21. On liberal treatments of virtue and the good, see Galston (1983: 621–29), Smith (1985: 13–59), and Kloppenberg (1987). On liberal assumptions in the English and Scottish republican traditions, see Isaac (1988) and Burtt (1986), and for a critical assessment of republicanism as an alternative paradigm in America, see Greenstone (1986: 1–49).

22. See Winch (1980). For a good critical analysis, see Harpham (1984: 764–74).

23. Thus although Grant (1985: 15) does not argue that Locke was a civic humanist and is not herself a Pocockian, she does argue that Locke's political doctrine "is perfectly compatible with community in many forms and with strong communal institutions."

satisfaction with what he saw as the tendency of Marxists and Straussians alike to give too much attention to Lockean liberalism and to discover everywhere they looked after about the time of Machiavelli either the rise of bourgeois modes of thought or the decline of Western civilization.[24] My point is not that a more scrupulous depiction of the paradigm would resolve these difficulties but rather that just as liberalism has always entailed notions of the good and of virtue, so republican writers have been concerned with law and legitimacy—even if sometimes implicitly—because any theory of politics has to be concerned with both.[25]

No more successful is Pocock's attempt to distinguish his paradigms by reference to liberalism's typical preoccupation with instrumental questions of distribution in the face of republicanism's teleological commitments. As he is forced to concede, there have always been ideas of legitimate distribution in the republican tradition. "If the citizens were to practice a common good, they must distribute its components among themselves, and must even distribute the various modes of participating in its distribution." Indeed, Aristotelian, Polybian, and Ciceronian analysis had shown "that these modes were highly various and capable of being combined in a diversity of complex patterns; political science in the sense of *politeia* took this as its subject matter." Pocock nonetheless continues to maintain that because the virtues that it was the business of these different distributions of means to realize could not be reduced to those means, "the republican or political conception of virtue exceeded the limits of jurisprudence and therefore of justice as a jurist conceived it" (ibid.: 358). Even this formulation should suggest to Pocock that his dichotomous classification is misleading; it is only because he operates with the assumption that the liberal view reduces politics to an account of law and right that he can entertain the notion of an alternative and discontinuous republican vocabulary that reduces it to an account of the good.

Pocock's analytical strategy is to underpin the dichotomy between republican and liberal paradigms with the dichotomy between negative and positive liberty. Although the value liberty is central to both traditions, in the liberal tradition liberty is typically a negative constraint on the power

24. For an illustration of his ringing denunciations of "the paradigm of liberalism," see Pocock (1985: 59–62).

25. In this connection note that Riesenberg (1969: 237–54) criticized an earlier version of the civic humanist alternative paradigm view, as formulated by Baron (1966), by arguing that citizenship in the Italian republics was mainly defined in jurisprudential terms, not those arising from the humanist vocabulary of *vita activa* and *vivere civile*, so that law, right, and obligation were central to the classical republican view of citizenship. Although Pocock (1975a: 83; 1981: 355) has acknowledged the existence of this critique, he has never responded to it.

of others (principally if not exclusively the state) over the individual. The negative liberty view tends to "lower the level of participation and deny the premise that man is by nature political" and to be narrowly preoccupied "with that which can be distributed, with things and rights." By contrast, classical republican positive liberty elevates participation through the Aristotelian affirmation that we are naturally political animals.[26] The laws of the republic, "the *lois* obeyed by Montesquieu's *vertu politique*— were therefore far less *regulae juris* or modes of conflict resolution than they were *ordini* or 'orders'; they were the formal structure within which political nature developed to its inherent end" (ibid.: 359).

Pocock's confrontation between republican and liberal paradigms and the negative/positive dichotomy with which he underpins it are instances of what I have elsewhere described as mutual oppositions of gross concepts. When protagonists argue in terms of gross concepts, they engage in a double reduction. First, they reduce what are actually complex relational ideas to one or another of the terms in the relation over which they range, dealing with the other terms implicitly while seeming not to deal with them at all. Second, they reduce what are often substantive disagreements about one or another of the terms in a relational argument to disagreements about the meanings of the terms themselves, making a self-fulfilling prophecy out of the "essential contestability" thesis, which posits exactly the kind of discontinuous vocabularies whereby protagonists allegedly speak past one another that Pocock is seeking to establish.[27] As MacCallum (1972: 174–93) showed long ago in relation to the negative/positive liberty debate, any assertion about freedom or liberty minimally involves reference to agents, restraining (or enabling) conditions, and actions. It always makes sense to ask of any use of the term, who is free from what restraint (or because of what enabling condition) to perform which action? Negative libertarians tend explicitly to argue by reference to the first two terms in this triad; positive libertarians, the second and third. Negative libertarians usually discuss the second term in the language of constraints, whereas positive libertarians employ that of enabling

---

26. "The republic or *politeia* solved the problem of authority and liberty by making *quisque* [everyone] participant in the authority by which he was ruled; this entailed relations of equality which made in fact extremely stern demands upon him, but by premising that he was *kata phūsin* [by nature] formed to participate in such a citizenship it could be said that it was his 'nature,' 'essence,' or 'virtue' to do so. But [sic] nature may be developed, but cannot be distributed; you cannot distribute a *telos*, only the means to it; virtue cannot therefore be reduced to matter of right" (Pocock, 1981b: 358, 359).

27. *Essential contestability* is the term first popularized by Bernard Gallie (1955: 167–98).

conditions. MacCallum's argument was, first, that constraints and enabling conditions can invariably be redescribed as one another (so that
there is no politically interesting difference between saying that the prisoner is unfree because of the presence of locked chains, not the lack of a
key) and second, that all three terms in the relation must be integral to
any credible account of freedom. He showed that it does not take much
digging to bring an author's assumptions about each of the three terms to
light and that once this is done we can see that negative and positive libertarians do not have different understandings of the meanings of the
terms *freedom* and *liberty* at all. Rather, they disagree about the content
of the substantive terms in his triad, though this is seldom obvious to
protagonists just because their disagreement appears to them to be about
the meanings of the terms *freedom* and *liberty*. But just as the arguments
of negative and positive libertarians can easily be rearticulated in one another's terms, so it can be shown that theories of the right and the good
mutually require one another and are therefore not basic or paradigmatic
terms of political argument. Pocock's analytic attempt to distinguish liberal from republican paradigms fails as a result.[28]

Certainly some writers have believed themselves to be embracing a republican ideal as an alternative to some other, but we make a serious error
if we take them at their word. The very fact that civic humanist writers
employ so many different and conflicting concepts of virtue,[29] that the idea
of liberty is central to both alleged paradigms, and that those paradigm-
case republicans, the American revolutionaries, were obsessed with questions of law and legitimacy should make us suspicious of this dichotomous
classification. There is no exclusive language of the virtues (or of law).
There are many (often conflicting) assumptions about virtue and about
legitimacy embodied in both jurisprudential and civic republican traditions, some conservative, some radical, and some liberal, as we have seen
on Pocock's own account.[30] The interesting questions are which of these
assumptions merit our endorsement and which our rejection, but they are
obscured by the mindless opposition of gross concepts, liberal *versus* republican. Perhaps Pocock can make a case that his interest is that we recover the terms of debate as the protagonists understood them. Granting
this for now (though I dispute part of it in section II(ii) below), my analysis here reveals the limits of such methods from the standpoint of anyone
interested in analytic clarity or normative argument. If a set of assump-

28. I defend a more general version of this claim in Shapiro (1989a: 51–76).
29. Three have been distinguished in a useful paper by Burtt (1986).
30. Even the neo-Kantian political theories of John Rawls and his followers,
which express explicit agnosticism about intersubjective purposes, implicitly make
these assumptions. See Shapiro (1986: 169, 214–18, 260–62, 285–87).

tions about purposes, or about law, is implicit in an argument—perhaps not even evident to its author—this may be one of the most interesting things about it, and exclusive preoccupation with authorial intention will lead us to miss it.

Whether or not a historian like Pocock can formulate a description of his enterprise that makes these issues exogenous, contemporary communitarians like Sandel, who want to invoke the revival of interest in republicanism as part of the normative basis for an allegedly alternate theory of politics, cannot legitimately avoid it.[31] For the debates on "whether-or-not republic" and "whether-or-not virtue" do not begin to get at the questions of what sorts; it is, consequently, small wonder that appeal to the republican conceptual vocabulary has seemed compatible with every political ideology from far left to far right and with every kind of polity from the pastoral village to the nation-state (and many kinds of the latter, at that).

Thus we should not allow the question to be who is right, liberals or republicans? because both are right about one another. Liberalisms that reduce politics to questions of right will always be vulnerable to republican critiques either because they appear to lack conceptions of the good or because their implicit conceptions of the good are not adequately defended. Conversely, republican alternatives that direct attention to the language of virtue while ignoring questions about its substance, about how it might be implemented, about the distributive consequences and external effects of treating one conception of the public good as authoritative rather than another will rightly seem vulnerable to liberals. Arguing by reference to alternative paradigms perpetuates the process of gross opposition because it directs critical attention to the terminologies in which arguments are expressed, rather than the arguments themselves.

(ii) Failure of the Argument Against
Bourgeois Orthodoxy

A powerful motivation behind *The Machiavellian Moment* is Pocock's conviction that understanding the republican tradition will free us of the illusion that the history of the last four hundred years has been the story of the inevitable if gradual triumph of bourgeois modes of thought. Whether a self-congratulatory affirmation of Lockean liberalism or a searing indictment (from the left of more or less self-conscious rationalizations for capitalism, from the right of the passing of traditional society), defenders and critics alike allow the paradigm of bourgeois liberalism to

31. This linking of communitarianism to republicanism is implicit in the argument of Sandel (1982) and later becomes explicit (Sandel, 1984a: 91–93; 1984b: 7). For additional examples see note 3 of this chapter.

set the terms of their understanding of our past, and this weakness limits
their understanding of our present and its possibilities. Yet how convincing is Pocock's case against Macpherson? How powerful is Pocock's claim
that the political argument that emerged from the civic republican tradition offers an alternative set of self-understandings to the bourgeois
thought of liberal modernity?

No one doubts that Harrington used the vocabulary of classical republicanism in his attack on English feudalism; the debated question is to
what extent this signified commitment to classical conceptions of property
rather than innovative argument. Pocock's claim is questionable on its face
because Harrington's target was the feudal structure of land ownership
and the dependencies he believed it fostered; it must therefore be conceded
that he was concerned with problems fundamentally different from Aristotle's or the scholastic Aristotelians'. What, then, are we to make of his
reliance on republican rhetoric? One thing to note, as Jeffry Isaac has
pointed out in a balanced and judicious assessment, is that Harrington's
rhetoric was many-sided and that his republican commitments coexisted
with the open embracing of values we characteristically think of as liberal.
Thus although Harrington argued in the idiom of harmony and stability,
emphasized the centrality of public virtue to politics, and conceived of the
state as "the repository of political virtue and patriotism, of a collective
elan," this is only a part of the rhetorical story (Isaac 1988: 22–36). There
is also a heavy emphasis on the centrality of the rule of law. Thus although
the soul of a nation or city must be virtue, "for as much as the soul of a
city or nation is the sovereign power, her virtue must be law." Harrington's ultimate goal is to prevent the privatization of political power characteristic of monarchy, so that popular government uniquely "reacheth the
perfection of government." Only under popular government can the rule
of law remain supreme (Harrington 1977: 179; Isaac 1988: 23–26).

As well as this populist affirmation of the rule of law, there is a view of
private property and appropriation underlying it that is fundamentally
bourgeois. As Isaac notes, although Harrington did not develop an analysis of property of the sort that can be found in the fifth chapter of Locke's
Second Treatise, he did express "an individualist view of appropriation
quite parallel to that of liberal rights theory" (Isaac 1988: 32). Thus he
wrote in the opening chapter of *The Art of Lawgiving* that

> the donation of the earth by God unto man cometh unto
> a kind of selling it for industry, a treasure which seemeth
> to purchase of God; from the different kinds of successes
> of this industry, whether in arms or in other exercises of
> mind or body, deriveth the natural equity of dominion of
> property; and from the legal establishment or distribution

of this property (be it more or less approaching towards
the natural equity of the same) deriveth all government.
(Harrington 1977: 604)

For Isaac this passage embodies a petty-bourgeois morality, as do Harrington's accompanying appeals for a distribution of property that promotes industry. Harrington opposes those inequalities he considers to be unproductive, but he is quite prepared to tolerate those that conduce to greater productivity. Indeed, as Macpherson (1962: 186) long ago pointed out, as it relates to unequal distributions of wealth, Harrington's view is one of equality of opportunity, not equality of result and he favored inheritance as well as transmissibility of property. Harrington states explicitly (if not entirely coherently) that substantial inequalities of wealth may be perfectly consistent with an "equal agrarian" and popular state; he argues against only those inequalities that would be so great as to destroy the agrarian state (Harrington 1977: 424–25).[32]

Attention to the intellectual context in which these arguments were developed enables us to endorse Macpherson's and Isaac's claims. Harrington's assumptions about industry and productiveness—both in his critique of the feudal distribution of wealth as unproductive and in his elaboration of his own account of industriousness—fall into the mainstream of much seventeenth-century economic thinking on the nature and origins of wealth. Taking the second of these first, Joyce Appleby's seminal study of seventeenth-century economic ideology has made it clear that one innovative change of this period was the redefinition of wealth as the capacity to produce for exchange. The idea of wealth as inhering in a productive capacity is at the core of the labor theories of value embraced by Petty, Hobbes, Locke, Cary, and many others that reflected the growing belief that human work could produce more than nature (Appleby 1978: 156, 135–41).[33] Harrington did not even try to develop a political economy in the way that Petty or Locke did, but he clearly fell into the mainstream of the new seventeenth-century identification of labor and industry with wealth. This is reflected not merely in the continual references to industry as the basis of liberty throughout his writings but also in the very terms of his attack on feudal wealth.[34]

Yet Harrington's criticism is not simply that the nobility is corrupted by its wealth but more important that it is unproductive. "The aristocracy is ravenous," he tells us in many different ways, "not the people" (ibid.:

32. For additional textual evidence, see Harrington (1977: 197, 232, 292–93).
33. For further discussion of the labor theories of Petty, Hobbes, and Locke, see Shapiro (1986: 35–38, 92–96, 303). For more general discussion, see Coleman (1956: 280–95), Wiles (1968: 113–26), and Appleby (1978: 129–57).
34. See Harrington (1977: 202, *see also* 292, 188–98, 239, and 292–94).

292–94). Here again attention to the broader intellectual context reinforces the claim Isaac wishes to advance, for many seventeenth-century economic writers singled out these "unproductive" classes for criticism. As early as 1662 William Petty was forcefully arguing that landlords were parasites on their productive tenants and defending redistributive taxation from the landed to the productive classes. At about the same time William Shepherd defended an excise tax because it taxed extravagance. These writers were embracing the view, later to be articulated by Defoe, that taxation could redistribute from the unproductive to those whose spending would "terminate in the hands of industry and trade." By the later part of the century, Sir Dalby Thomas was arguing that the unproductive included "Gentry, Clergy, Lawyers, Servingmen and Beggars," even though he had no objection to, even embraced, accumulations of wealth and luxury consumption because they promoted productiveness. By this time, Appleby tells us, "the idea that only laboring people could increase wealth had become a truism" embraced by Slingsby Bethel and many others in arguments over taxation policy, immigration, and demography.[35]

Although Appleby does not discuss Harrington, his antipathy for the nobility and its parasitism fits squarely into the tradition she describes. "Your highwaymen are not such as have trades or have been brought up unto industry, but such as whose education hath pretended unto that of gentleman" he tells us in *Oceana*. Lysander, in "bringing in the golden spoils of Athens, irrecoverably ruined that commonwealth," which is a warning that "in giving encouragement unto industry, we also remember that covetousness is the root of all evil." Always there is the example of the Romans, "who through a negligence committed in their agrarian laws, let in the sink of luxury, and forfeited the inestimable treasure of liberty for themselves and posterity" (Harrington 1977: 292, 239, 188).

Harrington never gave an account of the difference between productive and unproductive labor, yet his assumptions about productiveness fell into the mainstream of much seventeenth-century political economy from Petty to Locke in conceiving of it in decidedly bourgeois terms. He embraced inequalities he believed productive and succored industry while rejecting concentrations of wealth among the feudal nobility as corrupt, all in the name of the public good. For, like many of his contemporaries, Harrington did not object to inequality or even to wealth as such but rather to their unproductive and corrupting feudal forms. One cannot help but be reminded of Locke's defense of enclosure, despite his theory of property as

35. For further discussion of these sources, which I draw on here, and a discussion of additional sources, see Appleby (1978: 132–34, 171, 181, and 211).

use rights to the common, through simultaneous appeal to the labor theory of value and a theory of productivity that was essentially a trickle-down theory of wealth.[36] Of course none of this is to say that Harrington was a defender of capitalism (any more than it is to say that Locke was) or that he could have had the slightest idea of what capitalism would be like or even that if he had had any idea of what capitalism would be like that he would have defended it. It is to say, however, that he took for granted the core tenets of the new political economy in his defenses of industriousness and social mobility and in his attacks on the feudal social structure and the absolutist political institutions he thought it had spawned.

Pocock's reading of the neo-Harringtonians confronts analogous difficulties, as Jesse Goodale (1980: 240–57) has shown. By exaggerating the neo-Harringtonians' idealization of the past, Pocock misidentifies a circumscribed and qualified critique of the monied interest as a fundamental rejection of it. Trenchard (the author of *Cato's Letters*), for example, was primarily concerned with political corruption, his central preoccupation with the national debt and the monied interest it benefited and empowered. But he had no particular objection to the emerging property relations; like Harrington he equated the growth of freehold property with the expansion of liberty, yet he did not favor equality in its distribution, only a sufficiently wide distribution to prevent the tyranny of a small, wealthy elite. Although he favored the redistribution of feudal wealth that resulted from the shift in landed property to the gentry and favored the rise of commerce as having expanded liberty, England's political institutions were thought not to have adapted to the changes, and it was to this imbalance that reform had to be addressed.[37]

A brief examination of the terms of Trenchard's diagnosis will reveal his open embrace of commercial institutions. As with Bolingbroke, the primary objection was to stock market speculators and accumulators of the national debt for undermining "honesty and industry" with their "mean and contemptible hands" (Trenchard 1969: I, 6).[38] They have mortgaged the nation's assets, for

> national credit can never be supported by lending money without security, or drawing in other people to do so; by raising stocks and commodities by artifice and fraud, to unnatural and imaginary values; and consequently deliv-

36. On Locke's labor theory of value, see Locke (1963: 330, 331, 337, 338, 341), on his theory of productivity (ibid.: 336).

37. For further discussion, see Goodale (1980: 257), on whom I draw here.

38. In this and subsequent quotations from *Cato's Letters*, the English has been modernized.

> ering up helpless women and orphans, with the ignorant
> and unwary, but industrious subject, to be devoured
> by pick-pockets and stock-jobbers; a sort of vermin that
> are bred and nourished in the corruption of the state.
> (Ibid.: I, 17)

Expanding the national debt "instead of preserving public credit, destroys all Property; turns the stock and wealth of a nation out of its proper Channels." Far from nourishing the body politic, it "produces only ulcers, eruptions, and often epidemical plague-sores: It starves the poor, destroys manufactures, ruins our navigation, and raises insurrections Etc" (ibid.: I, 17). Monopolies or "conspiracies and combinations" of "artful and wealthy merchants" are objected to on the grounds that they are "against general trade" and must eventually "destroy the trade itself." For

> the success and improvements of trade depend wholly
> upon supplying the commodities cheap at market; and
> whoever can afford those of equal goodness at but half per
> cent. cheaper than his neighbors, will command the sale.
> (Ibid.: III, 202)

Not the commercial system or even credit but rather their unproductive abuse for personal gain is at the root of the problem.[39] Corrupt men, who exploit public office for personal gain, are the central source of Cato's fury:

> What can be more invidious, than for a nation, staggering
> under the weight and oppression of its debts, eaten up
> with usury, and exhausted with payments, to have the ad-
> ditional mortification, to see private and worthless men
> . . . grow rich while they grow poor; to see the town
> every day glittering with new and pompous equipages,
> whilst they are mortgaging and selling their estates, with-
> out having spent them. (Ibid.: III, 274)

None of this invective reveals hostility to the emerging commercial system. Compare it with the stock Democratic criticisms of the Reagan administration for corruption and selfish pursuit of the interests of its wealthy constituencies to the detriment of the public good. "Instead of

---

39. Thus, "[a] merchant, or tradesman, is said to be in good credit, when his visible gains appear to be greater than his expenses; when he is industrious, and takes care of his affairs; when he makes punctual payments, and the wares which he sells may be depended upon as to their goodness and value; and when those who deal with him can have a reasonable assurance that he will make a profit by his care from the commodities that they entrust him with. . . . But if a merchant be observed to live in riot and profusion, to leave his estate to the direction of servants, who cheat him, or neglect his business . . . no fair dealer will have anything to do with them" (Trenchard 1969: IV, 13–14).

investing to rebuild America's power as a competitor in a swelling global marketplace," it was complained in the *Democratic Fact Book for 1984*, "the Reagan Republicans are driving the nation—and our international customers—into paralyzing debt. They are wasting financial resources to buy superfluous or gold-plated weapons when what we really need are tools that build. And they are wasting human resources—whose minds and skills must be trained to master the needs of tomorrow." [40] Like much other campaign literature, it was filled with allegations of cronyism and corruption regarding the use of insider information for personal benefit in corporate takeovers, the giving of defense and other contracts to personal friends and business associates without competitive bidding, the cynical refusal to enforce such public interest legislation as antitrust and environmental protection laws, the reduced enforcement of tax compliance, and the staffing of public interest agencies with manifestly incompetent personnel. [41] Yet just as nothing in these Democratic attacks on the Reagan administration's corrupt use of political power should incline us to the view that its authors are rejecting bourgeois values, let alone that they are employing a premodern political language, so it is with the neo-Harringtonians. This is evident not only from the fact that in both cases the problem is diagnosed as an abuse of political power but also because in both cases it is the undermining of market mechanisms rather than their existence that is held to be at fault.

A similar argument can be made against the idea that republicanism presents an alternative to bourgeois modes of thought in early American political argument. Although the ideological theorists of the Revolution never argued that it did, this literature is notable for the paucity of its treatments of matters economic and, most surprising, even of the economic presuppositions of republican ideology; books like Gordon Wood's *The Creation of the American Republic* and Bernard Bailyn's *The Ideological Origins of the American Revolution*, tremendously rich in other respects, are virtually silent on the subject of republican political economy because there was no distinctive republican political economy. [42] Beyond

40. *The Democratic Fact Book 1984* (Washington, D.C., 1984), p. 446.

41. See, for examples, *The Democratic Fact Book 1984* (Washington, D.C., 1984), pp. 423–41, and *The Democratic Fact Book 1986: Democrats for the 1980s* (Washington, D.C., 1986), pp. 98–115.

42. Bailyn (1967) and Wood (1969) de-emphasized capitalism by omission more than by argument, largely as a by-product of their preoccupation with the internal structure of revolutionary republican ideology. Pocock (1975a: 462–552), Banning (1974: 168–77; 1978; 1986: 3–18), McCoy (1974: 633–46; 1980), and others went further, pointing to tensions between republicanism and commercial capitalism and emphasizing, in varying degrees, the pastoral and explicitly anti-modern model of agrarian self-sufficiency that infused much eighteenth-century republican argument. This interpretation has in turn been subject to trenchant

the assertion that great extremes of inequality can be politically dangerous, nothing in republican assumptions about economic relations need be
anticapitalist. On the contrary there was often what with hindsight we
might call a naive embrace of market institutions, particularly private
property, as guarantors of autonomy. This was an understandable result of
the historical preoccupation of many republicans with the rejection of feudal institutions and aristocratic ways.[43] Central to their naïveté was an
overestimation of the importance of land and its differences from movable
property, a failure to see that it was the form rather than the object of
ownership that would shape the social and political relations of the future.
That the land held to guarantee the independence necessary for republican
virtue would be freehold would be far more significant than its being land,
just as the differences between agrarian and commercial capitalism would
turn out to be far less significant than eighteenth-century protagonists
believed.

The ideal of independence as requiring freehold property (which Pocock
locates in the republican tradition long before it reaches America),[44] the
work ethic, and the emphasis on productive expansion as essential for stability (and thus for preventing corruption) all became central to the capitalist world view. The pastoral ideal of the yeoman farmer may not be that
of a nascent capitalist, but from the standpoint of the logic of property law,
they have more in common than does either with a feudal serf or lord.[45]

---

criticism from Appleby (1982a: 833–49; 1982b: 287–309; 1984a; 1986: 20–34),
who has emphasized the commercial aspirations and success of American agrarian
capitalism and the emergence of a new vision from it that was "both democratic
and capitalistic, agrarian and commercial" (Appleby 1982a: 844). This debate is
further complicated by geographical considerations, with Shalhope (1976: 532–33)
and Foshee (1985: 523–50), among others, arguing that the South retained an
antimodern agrarian and pastoral republicanism even into the twentieth century
but that in the North republican ideals were being reconceptualized in ways compatible with commercial capitalism by Jefferson's time. Others, like Marmor
(1967: 377–406), have argued that the story of southern antiindustrialism and
anticommercialism is more ambiguous, and Appleby (1982a: 833–49; 1984a;
1984b: 275–83; 1986: 20–33) continues, in the main persuasively, to resist it entirely. For criticism of her view, see Ashworth (1984: 425–35) and Winch (1985:
287–97).

43. It would be illuminating in this regard to reconstruct the argument of a text
like *Democracy in America* to see where it would lead in the absence of Tocqueville's benign republican assumptions about private property.

44. See Pocock (1975a: 375, 386–88, 390, 408, 440–41) and the discussion in
section I(iv) of this chapter.

45. Even in such strongholds of old world sentiment as the antebellum South
Carolina depicted by Wier (1969: 473–501) and Greenberg (1977: 723–43) and
among the genteel aristocratic Brahmins of early Gilded Age Massachusetts described by Thomson (1982: 163–86), republican commitments were identified
with politically antimodern and antidemocratic instincts that were often aristo-

This is not to deny that some republicans wanted seriously to limit economic inequality or that some saw urban capitalism and its ethic of self-interest as potentially corruptive of the pastoral ideal required by republican theory in its eighteenth-century American variants.[46] Nor is it to say that there are not deep and enduring tensions between the ethic of self-interest fostered by a private property regime and a market society and the dictates of public-spiritedness in politics required by some variants of the republican ethos. This tension is a good deal older than the American nation; it has been shown decisively by Kramnick (1982: 629–64), Burtt (1986), and others to have generated substantial modifications in the republican conception of virtue—to accommodate self-interest and even in some cases to be defined by reference to it—in eighteenth-century England and Scotland.

However the interpretive debates on the changing meaning of virtue are finally resolved, if they are, it is by now clear that republican conceptual vocabulary was not inherently unfriendly to capitalism by the time it reached America, even if a primitive and romantic agrarian capitalism was often the implicit model. Pocock (1975b: 75–76) all but concedes this in a discussion of the Augustan debate when he notes that both sides in the eighteenth-century dispute on commerce shared "the same underlying value-system, in which the only material foundation for civic virtue and moral personality is taken to be independence and real property,"[47] as well as in his discussion of the evolution of American republican thinking (as we have seen).[48] Yet this surely undermines the claim that for too long our view of early modern thought has been driven by the preoccupation with the rise of bourgeois social relations. Indeed, the effectiveness with which republican rhetoric was co-opted—on Pocock's own account—by forces friendly to capitalism is prima facie evidence of their causal significance.

---

cratic in tone, but the case has yet to be made that these sentiments translated into hostility toward capitalism as a socioeconomic system.

46. We are beginning to see a body of scholarship on this subject by historians of political economy, although most of it is focused on the nineteenth century. See, for example, Sabel and Zeitlin (1985: 133–76).

47. Earlier he says more fully, "all Augustan analysts of political economy accept the interdependence of land, trade and credit; and furthermore . . . all agree that land is an important foundation of virtue, stockjobbing a pernicious means to corruption, and money and trade vital components of national wealth and power. The apologists for land make much of the importance of trade, and claim that stockjobbing is ruinous to the value of both; the apologists for war and credit stress that trade is necessary to the value of land, and deny that stockjobbing alters this relationship; and there are, on the face of it, no apologists for stockjobbing at all" (Pocock 1975b: 75).

48. See section I(v) of this chapter.

(iii) Political Unattractiveness of the
Civic Republican Argument

As Pocock explains it, once the republican ideal was extracted from ancient
(cyclical) conceptions of time (where decay would inevitably be followed
by rebirth) and located in secular time, the problem of preventing entropy
and decline became the central organizing question of civic republican
theory. This preoccupation resulted in an instrumentalist preoccupation
that had been absent from the classical Greek conception.[49]

For a political theorist there are two central difficulties deriving from
this instrumentalism. The first has to do with a host of related issues concerning membership, the treatment of outsiders, and external relations
generally in republican theory. If the republic is thought of as comparatively weak, coping with the idiosyncrasies of fortune in a hostile and
uncontrollable world, the republican prudence of Guicciardini might seem
the only sensible option. But this view, if generalized, fails to account for
major differences among the powers and kinds of republics or the fact that
many people will effectively be excluded from all republics. Any moral
claims or dilemmas generated by these facts remain conveniently off the
agenda from the standpoint of this inward-looking political theory. It is
inherent in taking the political community as given and treating its stability as the core problem of politics to be indifferent toward outsiders (or at
most instrumentally interested in them), whether these be individuals or
other communities. As MacIntyre notes in *Whose Justice? Which Rationality?*, the Aristotelian tradition has been criticized for just this reason for
centuries.[50] In Pocock's civic republican tradition, even when outsiders
cease to be declared explicitly to be barbarians, they continue to be treated
purely instrumentally, relevant only to the extent that they affect the stability of the republic. In this light it can scarcely be surprising that there
are powerful links between republicanism and nationalism in the contemporary world, for although republican and communitarian arguments are
typically defended by appeal to the benefits of membership for the
included, they are equally mechanisms of exclusion. Indeed the mere
existence of republics as valued communities requires the existence of
outsiders who are devalued. Despite the heroic attempts of Anderson
(1983: 129–40) and others to distinguish patriotic from racist national-
isms on the grounds that the former need not dehumanize outsiders, a

49. See Pocock (1975a: 53–54, 75, 76–78, 84, 112–13, 136, 208–9, 333, 395–
96).
50. MacIntyre's view is that republican theory could only be brought to bear
on the moral dimensions of external relations through the addition of an independent theological component. See MacIntyre (1988: 121, 146–47).

persuasive case has yet to be made for this view. Certainly the civic republicans never took it. Like Bloom and Rorty, they saw civic commitment as necessarily involving parochial prejudice, but—as Pocock points out—they were much less squeamish about acknowledging its implications, often openly maintaining that war was a normal condition among republics.

Republican prudence might arguably be defensible as a way to deal with the vicissitudes of fortune if we believed ourselves to be playing a game with the gods that we cannot control and are bound eventually to lose. But we have no reason to believe this in our dealings with other political communities. It is, further, scarcely defensible to legitimate the external actions of the world's most powerful nation-state in Guicciardinian terms because the pragmatic justification (there is no other way to survive in a world of hostile and more powerful states) is unavailable.

This leaves the Machiavellian argument that all potentially hostile threats should simply be dominated, which issued, we saw, in Machiavelli's defense of imperial expansion. If we accept Pocock's account of how this argument was eventually modified in America into the notion of a fee simple empire, it becomes instrumentally more effective than even Machiavelli believed it to be. Although stability may still be being bought at the price of longevity of the republic, the day of eventual reckoning is pushed into the distant future, perhaps never to arrive. Moreover, continuous expansion is no longer threatening to the internal social structure of the republic because this latter is no longer believed to be dependent on balancing various estates for its survival.[51] Assuming, for the sake of argument, that the neo-Machiavellian argument is causally true, it is morally unattractive for the same reasons that the Guicciardinian argument is, only more so. Domination of outsiders, rather than mere indifference to them, is assumed to be justified on purely instrumentalist grounds, leaving all questions about political membership and the moral claims of outsiders unasked if not unaskable.

Republican theory may not always have been so morally vulnerable. For the Greek city-states or the republics of Renaissance Europe, the world was an enormous place, its limits unexplored by Europeans and even unknown to them. In such circumstances antipathy toward outsiders must have appeared quite different than in the postcolonial world we live in, with its unprecedented economic and geopolitical interdependence and destructive technological capacities. In our circumstances, where the public policies and economic practices in any major nation have massive effects

51. On Machiavelli's account, see section I(iii) of this chapter, and on its Americanization, section I(v).

on outsiders, a political theory that by its terms denies these latter any moral claim—or even a moral identity—seems intuitively less than fully satisfactory. Why this is so is taken up in chapter 9.

The second morally unattractive aspect of republican instrumentalism concerns its inevitable abandoning of its classical roots once people tried to put it into practice in the modern world. Eighteenth-century republicans had to cope with the centralizing and nationalizing tendencies of the modern state; they had to ask themselves how a model of participatory politics derived from the small self-governing Greek polis (itself something of a romantic idealization) could apply in this quite different social and political context.[52] The federalist-antifederalist debate on how to order institutions to prevent corruption and decay in the new mass republic revolved partly around this question. Yet it was never resolved; it was left hanging as classical republican politics went into decline in the late eighteenth century.[53] By then many of the staunchest republicans had conceded that it was not possible to foster and preserve republican virtue in political life, that the management and control of self-centered factions and interest groups was the most that institutional designers could reasonably try to achieve. These problems came to seem increasingly intractable as the factional model of interest group politics became dominant in the mid-1780s, but they predated this development; they were built into the logic of the new national republic.[54] Even if we grant Pocock's contention that these conclusions were sometimes arrived at in a republican idiom, this was clearly achieved at the price of abandoning the central commitments of Aristotelian republicanism.

That nothing approaching the classical republican ideal was implemented in eighteenth-century America implies that when contemporary American political theorists, activists, and politicians appeal to the republican tradition, they are being doubly romantic. They are not appealing to a pure classical past that existed at some point in American history that has been corrupted or lost and needs to be recreated. To the extent that they are appealing to anything in American culture and history, *they are appealing to an appeal* to a classical politics, to an unfulfilled eighteenth-century agenda in which the tensions between Greek and Roman variants of republican theory had never been resolved.[55] Given that part of what

52. See Ketcham (1984: 69–85, 167–87).

53. This decline is usefully described by Wood (1969: 471–615).

54. See Wood (1969: 606–7, 393–564) and Ketcham (1984: 167–87) on the debate.

55. As Wood usefully puts it: "The sacrifice of individual interests to the greater good of the whole formed the essence of republicanism and comprehended for Americans the idealistic goal of their Revolution. From this goal flowed all of

makes civic republicanism attractive to those disillusioned with the artificiality of neo-Kantian ideal theory is the proposition that it has an actual basis in American history, this is a serious defect. Pocock may be persuasive that the myths surrounding the American republican vision are "not inherently more absurd than those entertained in other cultures" (Pocock 1975a: 543), but this is notably less than an argument for their acceptance or even plausibility. Like all romantic doctrines, their emotional appeal is likely to be exploited for ulterior purposes behind the smoke screens of their unattainable goals.

III. Conclusion

In a different context, John Dunn (1979: 26) has argued that modern democratic theory oscillates between two variants, "one dismally ideological and the other fairly blatantly utopian." The oscillations he had in mind were between the Schumpeterian identification of democracy with the prevailing practices of advanced capitalism and the Rousseauist vision of a self-governing community. The logic of Dunn's observation may be borrowed and broadened for our purposes because republican ideology exhibits an analogous, almost schizoid, form. Given their common origins in Aristotle, there is remarkably little common ground between MacIntyre's rendition of the Greek version of republican theory and what it became when overlaid with neo-Roman preoccupations by the Italian humanists. Not only do MacIntyre and Pocock appear entirely unaware of—or at least uninterested in—one another's arguments, but the Aristotelian ideal of a teleological human nature realized through the living of integrated lives is almost nowhere to be found in the civic humanists' science of political stability. In the tradition Pocock describes, an instrumentalist preoccupation is built into the conception of politics as staving off decay and decline, but it has two more parochial sources as well. First, many of the humanist writings were advice books for princes, and this preoccupation gave the

---

the Americans' exhortatory literature and all that made their ideology truly revolutionary. This republican ideology both presumed and helped shape the Americans' conception of the way their society and politics should be structured and operated—a vision so divorced from the realities of American society so contrary to the previous century of American experience that it alone was enough to make the Revolution one of the great utopian movements of American history. By 1776 the Revolution came to represent a final attempt, perhaps—given the nature of American society—even a desperate attempt, by many Americans to realize the traditional Commonwealth ideal of a corporate society, in which the common good would be the only objective of government" (Wood 1969: 53–54, *see also* 57–58, 59–65, 606–15).

maintenance of political stability central importance. The other historically parochial source is Harrington's materialism: the argument—picked
up and adapted by his successors—that to endure, political institutions
must reflect and embody the distribution of wealth, particularly that of
property. Whether in neo-Machiavellian or neo-Harringtonian form, the
preoccupation with stability generates a conservative relativism whereby
the political system preserves itself by adapting to socioeconomic conditions, and even virtue—that core term of the classical republican
scheme—is eventually redefined to that end.

That such a politics could seem benign to republican theorists since
Harrington, I argued, turned partly on their lack of a plausible political
economy. In marked contrast to their advanced understanding of the dynamics of organized institutions, they greatly underestimated the consequences of linking liberty to freehold property, and this wedded many of
them—some consciously, others not—to a recognizably bourgeois ethos.
To be sure, Jefferson and others were uncomfortable with many of the
political implications of this ethos, but they lacked an alternative political
economy to the emerging market system, and republican ideology did not
begin to dictate that they find one. Like their English predecessors, American republicans generally assumed that, in the main, market relations
were compatible with republican political institutions, indeed often that
they required them.

To sum up, although Pocock and the republican revisionists have en-
riched our understanding of the dynamics of bourgeois culture and its internal tensions, they have not delivered on the promise to provide an alternative. Indeed, we saw that the opposition to liberalism of a republican
paradigm is conceptually and historically misleading: it can appear plausible only when the contrast is to a reductionist version of liberalism, incoherent in its own terms, that equates it with a libertarian ideology of
right. Preoccupation with these second-order issues has served to divert
attention from the moral dimensions of the civic republican political commitment, and when these are laid bare they are revealed to be unattractive.
The methodological commitment to understanding human values within
the changing limits of the possible is a great contribution of the civic humanist tradition, but this tradition has failed to supply us with defensible
substantive values—or indeed even with critical standards for making
substantive choices—within the limits of what is possible.

We saw in chapter 5 that MacIntyre paints a picture of an in many ways
attractive classical republican ideal, but neither he nor its other advocates
grapple with the problems of implementing it in the actual world. Pocock,
by contrast, describes the evolution of civic republicanism as a political

ideology, geared increasingly—with time—to questions revolving around the maintenance of political stability. As such it is emptied of virtually everything that made the Aristotelian ideal attractive to begin with and shot through with morally unattractive forms of political instrumentalism. So we can usefully conclude by paraphrasing Dunn's point: the analysis of this chapter and the last has revealed that at least two major competing views of politics have grown out of the Aristotelian tradition, one hopelessly utopian and the other dismally instrumental. In the final two chapters of this book I take up the challenge of describing and defending a third view—also traceable to Aristotle—that is both credible and attractive as political theory. But let us first take stock of where we stand.

Part Four

Anti-Kantian Foundations

7 Anti-Kantian Complaints Revisited

This inquiry began with a catalog of complaints commonly adduced against neo-Kantian enterprise in political theory concerning its aspirations toward moral neutralism, its treatment of political community, its deontological aspirations, and its naive assumptions about the ideological dimensions of political theory and argument. Now it is time to reassess these complaints in light of the arguments discussed in the last five chapters to see how effectively the alternative views we have been considering respond to the initial complaints. This reassessment is a prelude to my outlining an alternative view of political theory, termed *critical naturalism*, and discussing its central moral and political implications.

I. The Rejection of Moral Neutralism

A major motivation behind the turn to context and history has been the conviction that the neo-Kantian aspiration toward moral neutrality is misplaced. The claim that neutralist projects invariably fail has been around for some time,[1] but most of the authors we have been discussing want to argue in addition that these projects are pernicious. For Bloom and MacIntyre, although the aspiration toward neutralism is philosophically bankrupt, there is an anthropological sense in which it has triumphed, generating an "emotivist" or "subjectivist" culture in which no moral position can be defended because every position is presumed to be equally (in)valid. For MacIntyre, the triumph of neutralism has meant the victory of alienation through the destruction of communitarian practice, whereas for Bloom it has brought the supremacy of a mindless egalitari-

1. For my account, see Shapiro (1986: 200, 214, 240, 249–51, 256, 282–84, 291–301).

anism in terms of which morality cannot even be talked about because every moral view is equally discredited. Pocock's construction of a republican alternative also rests on a view of "the paradigm of liberalism" that is at best agnostic about purposes, narrowly preoccupied as it is "with what can be distributed, with things and rights." Indeed, it is just because liberalism's negative libertarian language appears to reduce politics to matters of law and right that "the republican or political conception of virtue exceeded the limits of [liberal] jurisprudence" (Pocock 1981b: 359, 357–58). Walzer's impatience with a moral philosophy like Thomas Nagel's, explicitly conducted from "no particular point of view" (Walzer 1987: 5), and his defense of a method that through its "connectedness" is explicitly partial and parochial reflect an analogous antipathy for the neutralist aspiration.

Such attacks on neutralism are often closely connected to the claim that the underlying philosophical defect of the neo-Kantian arguments is that they are foundational theories of a particular sort. For it is not just that we have been alienated from our substantive moral commitments by the doctrine of neutrality. Since the seventeenth century our expectation that all our commitments must be justified from first principles places the neutralist aspiration in a paradoxical position. On the one hand neutrality is defended on the grounds that there are multiple and competing conceptions of the good. On the other, at least since Hobbes, it has been an aspiration in the Western tradition of political theory that a political system that takes account of these differences must be scientifically derived from first principles, shown to operate in our objective interests. Yet all such projects have failed, so the argument goes, and as a result the felt need to justify neutrality from first principles compounds our moral alienation. On this view subjectivist moral theories have triumphed on the back of the relativizing influence of failed modernist expectations, undermining the possibility of the kinds of substantive moral conviction that allegedly prevailed in a premodern past.

If the aspiration toward neutrality is thought to be pernicious because it weakens our faith in all substantive moral values, the quest for apodictic foundations to it has had the arguably more serious consequence of undermining our social and political institutions. Thus Rorty's (1984a: 16) claim that it is failed attempts to defend liberal democracy as the objectively best system that have undermined our faith in it and MacIntyre's argument that the Enlightenment Project of justifying morality necessarily had to fail because once we came to believe that the purposes that gave moral deliberation its point had themselves to be morally justified, the setup for disenchantment with our institutions was inevitable. Bloom's claim, embedded in the subtitle to his book, that it is *democracy* that has been failed by higher education, suggests an analogous view. Although Bloom's precise diagnostic argument is difficult to pin down, he appears to think that there were beliefs and values, embodied in the texts of the tradition, that our predecessors accepted as valid in ways of which we have since become incapable. Pocock's concluding plea, in *The Machiavellian Moment*, for an eschewal of all moral absolutes, also suggests a rejection of the philosophical expectations characteristic of the Enlightenment Project.[2]

Now it is not essential to identify the preoccupation with foundational argument with modernity, and some contextualists—notably Walzer—do not embrace the view that contemporary foundationalism is especially pernicious. But Rorty, MacIntyre, and Bloom are clearly all committed to variants of the claim that there is something distinctively pernicious about the Enlightenment foundationalist project. My analysis revealed that as matters of both history and philosophy this view runs into serious difficulties. For Bloom and MacIntyre, I showed that the different historical stories they tell are misleading in their treatments of both past and present. Their accounts of cultural decline since the Enlightenment rest on pictures of a premodern era in which there was agreement about core purposive values that is today held to be missing, but neither author offers any evidence to support these contentions—relying instead on the blanket notion of traditional society as a residual category, indicative of moral cohesiveness. The concept of traditional society has long been under assault by historians, anthropologists, and sociologists, and it is doubtful that this idealization captures much that is accurate about any actual or historical human society.[3]

My discussion of Bloom revealed that there has never been (nor should we expect) the consensus within the tradition that his account presupposes. Although MacIntyre concedes this (holding it to be a feature of every tradition that there be continual arguments over the meanings of its constituting terms), he fails to see that this undercuts his critique of modernity, which took as its point of departure the prevalence of irresolvable moral disagreement. As well as failing to make the case that there were not pervasive moral disagreements in the ancient and medieval worlds, he fails to explain how the contemporary disagreements that so trouble him—over abortion, affirmative action, distributive justice, and nuclear

2. See Pocock (1975a: 552).

3. For a powerful critique of this notion, see Shils (1981: 19, 287–330), who lays to rest romantic conceptions of traditional society in much sociology and anthropology. See also Rudolph and Rudolph (1967) and Gussfield (1975: 37–39).

war—could be resolved on his neo-Aristotelian view. Not only do these backward-looking critiques of modernity present a false view of a comparatively homogeneous past while overestimating the power of subjectivist views of morality today, but they mislead more seriously through inappropriate comparison. In both cases the basic comparison is between a premodern elite culture (be it aristocratic, religious, or scholastic) and contemporary mass culture. If Bloom was to compare instead the lives of medieval peasants, with all their attendant insecurities of war, economic vulnerability, and predictable early death, with the contemporary mass culture for which he has so much disdain, he might be less quick to discern decline or to be surprised that the contemporary masses do not read the Great Dead. After all, the masses of Renaissance and early modern Europe never read at all. Likewise with MacIntyre, if the condition of the many was compared in both cases, he might be less quick to conclude that the modern occidental masses are alienated in ways in which their predecessors were not. None of this amounts to a defense of contemporary liberal culture, of course, but it does suggest that some basic realism about the terms in which debate about it should be cast is lacking in these arguments. In short, the contentions that neutralism has triumphed in the anthropological sense overestimate the moral homogeneity of the past as well as the fragmentation of the present, generating specious arguments for simplistic linear depictions of modern decline.

Pocock deals with the problem of neutralism in the terminology of negative and positive liberty, assuming throughout that liberalism's core deficiency is its reduction of politics to instrumental questions about right and law and its inability, lacking the language, even to articulate questions about virtue, ends, or the good. Powerful as his account may be as a corrective to neo-Kantian political theory's explicit embracing of neutrality and to a Hartzian stereotype of the hegemony of interest group liberalism from the American beginning, we have seen that Pocock's view seriously misleads. As a philosophical matter it fails to take into account the truth that every theory of politics operates with conceptions of the right and of the good. The interesting questions are about their contents, and these are ignored via the mindless opposition of the gross concepts: liberal *versus* republican. Pocock's republic ranges ahistorically, we saw, over virtually every kind of political system, from ancient communities to modern national states, and over socioeconomic systems as different as ancient, feudal, and capitalist; it cannot be surprising that so little is said about the internal nature of the republic given the generality of this conceptual range.

There is, indeed, an irony to be grappled with by those who would embrace Pocockian republicanism as an alternative to "the paradigm of liberalism" in virtue of the latter's chimerical aspiration toward a scientifically justified moral neutralism. For the central preoccupation with stability as the core organizing concern of republican theory in post-Renaissance humanist thought militates against moral argument and critical reflection about many political ends. In the history of republican theory after Machiavelli, on Pocock's telling, the basic problem of politics is irreducibly instrumental: to deal with the inevitable entropy of republics in a world of secular time by searching for sources of institutional stability. We saw how the virtues were continually redefined for this purpose and, indeed, that from the days of the Florentine debate at least, the question of what best conduces to republican stability occupied central attention. Whether it was Guicciardini's claim that aristocratic prudence was the best means of survival in an uncontrollable and hostile world or Machiavelli's argument that fortune should be subdued through decisive action and imperial expansion, the goal of staving off entropy, corruption, and decay remained supreme. This is why it was so important for Machiavelli to establish that imperial expansion did not necessarily invite instability, as had been the conventional republican wisdom. In its English variants, too, we saw that Harrington and his successors were centrally concerned to ensure stability by bringing political institutions into conformity with the social distribution of wealth. In America similar preoccupations were present from the start; much of the Federalist/anti-Federalist debate revolved around questions of what best conduces to institutional stability. Yet stability is an instrumental good: its value depends on what kind of society is being preserved or undermined, and in the usages Pocock describes it takes much for granted that we would find morally controversial. The treatments of outsiders and the elitist view of the role of the many, we saw, left much to be desired just because of the supremacy ascribed to internal stability. This instrumental treatment of substantive values is not a new form of moral neutralism, but it exhibits analogous defects. By keeping many substantive questions off the political agenda entirely or dealing with them only in instrumental terms, the outlook remains indifferent to these questions as moral questions. Whether political participation is inherently desirable, whether and on what basis exclusion of outsiders or territorial expansion can be justified, and whether a market-based system of production and exchange is desirable independently of its effects on stability are not questions that are addressed, or even presented, from the civic republican standpoint. Even the much-vaunted ideal of independence is defended, ultimately, on the grounds that only an independent citizen can contribute to the preservation of the republic. Indeed, the value of stability is never itself explained. In a postfascist and post-Stalinist age, it is natural to inquire under what conditions stability should be thought to be desirable.

The difficulties involved in making and defending substantive political choices in the absence of a neutral or "god's eye-view" standpoint also infect the arguments of Rorty and Walzer. In Rorty's case we saw that he has no mechanism for dealing with conflicting or overlapping community values, with those people who are systematically excluded from or harmed by prevailing social practices, and he seems wholly innocent of the verity that dominant norms and practices play integral parts in the reproduction of power relations. Although Walzer is sensitive to these issues, he also fails, in the end, to explain how to choose among conflicting values and conflicting interpretations of the same values. Historicizing these choices as MacIntyre attempts to do also turned out not to be a solution because an account of the genesis and empirical particularities of a practice will not, ultimately, answer questions concerning the rules for its best organization or its desirability as a practice to begin with. This last, we saw, has been a difficulty for Aristotelianism from the beginning, yet MacIntyre fails to face up to and confront its implications.

Now, as Walzer argues so forcefully in *Interpretation and Social Criticism*, the defense of the contextualist view is not that it is superior as a philosophical system to the paths of discovery and invention of general normative principles but rather that it is inescapable. The paths of discovery and invention turn out on closer inspection not simply to fail in their own terms but to involve interpretation; like it or not we are judges all in Walzer's metaphorical sense. Yet in the last analysis this becomes a complex restatement of the problem rather than a solution to it, for to say that there are no neutral choices and that social criticism must inevitably be contextually informed is not to say what form it should take or to tell us how to choose among competing interpretations of the norms prevailing in our cultures, traditions, and practices. To take a recent illustration, when Walzer criticizes the Israeli policy of beating Palestinians on the West Bank and the Gaza strip in January 1988, arguing that negotiations should be attempted instead, partly on the grounds that this is "the democratic, humane, *and, indeed Jewish* way,"[4] he is invoking an interpretation of Jewish values that many Jews would themselves reject on unim-

---

4. Letter to the editor of the *New York Times* from Irving Howe, Arthur Hertzberg, Henry Rosovsky, and Michael Walzer, Tuesday, January 26, 1988, p. A24, italics added. I am not suggesting that these are the only arguments these authors make against Israel's iron fist policy; several independent (and powerful) arguments are adduced.

peachable biblical authority.[5] Engaging in connected criticism, in short, does not tell the critic what to say.

A great contribution of the interpretivist view is its insistence that, as moral dilemmas arise in the situations of everyday life, they cannot be detached from those situations to be argued over from a neutral standpoint. The sheer complexity of social life, as Aristotle noted long ago, makes reference to the specific context essential to all practical moral argument.[6] However, we cannot assume, as the old legal realists did and as Rorty and Walzer seem to suppose in different ways that we can, that close-to-the-ground analyses of political options will naturally reveal the one best course for all concerned. We know too much today about how little undisputed knowledge there can be in the human sciences to accept this sanguine pragmatism and contextual ethics, and we must take seriously the possibility that where people's natures and interests differ sufficiently, and alternative courses of action are open in a given situation, there may be no best or optimal solution.[7] Understanding moral dilemmas in all their contextual complexity may often recast them for us in ways that we could not possibly have foreseen in the abstract, may reveal courses of action to have probable consequences that we might not have anticipated, and may unmask possibilities that we might not otherwise have considered, but we cannot assume that it will make moral and political choices for us. Although an understanding of contextual complexity is essential to good moral argument, it can never be all there is to moral argument. In the absence of neutral principles for choosing among alternative courses of action, some alternative that does more theoretical work than mere reference to contextual meaning has to be supplied.

II. The Appeal to Community

The idea of community has been invoked against the neo-Kantians for reasons of both substance and method. Methodologically the objection is to their atomistic individualism, which generally takes one of two forms. In the first formulation it is argued that their use of the contractarian

5. To take one of hundreds of possible illustrations, see 1 Samuel, chapter 15, where the story is told of Saul's falling out of God's favor by failing to carry out his directive to destroy the Amalekites who had been Israel's enemies, "man, and woman, infant and suckling, ox and sheep, camel and ass." Because he had shown some compassion, sparing Agag and some of the animals, God sent Samuel to remove his kingship "because I feared the people, and obeyed their voice" (1 Sam. 15: 3–24).

6. See Aristotle (1977: 199–200).

7. For a useful critical discussion of the "situation sense" of the legal realists, see Ackerman (1983: 27, 73, 93–110).

tactic of imagining what institutions prepolitical people could, would, or should create wrongly assumes that the whole is not more than the sum of its parts. The resolutive-compositive method inaugurated into modern political theory by Hobbes, and appealed to in different ways by Rawls, Nozick, Buchanan and Tullock, Wolff, and others, treats all social relationships as incidental to the achievement of individual goals; indeed in this tradition the need for a state at all is frequently taken to arise only because of specific problems of "market failure." The other form of the methodological complaint (often coupled with the first) is that because there is no natural or precontractural person, the neo-Kantians import into their construals of him characteristics of the societies in which they live, treating those characteristics as if they were natural.[8] This complaint often generates pejorative charges of atomistic individualism from a different source. Critics of contemporary society who regard its foundation on market values as alienating, for instance, frequently criticize theorists who appeal to contractarian devices as mechanisms for respecting Kantian autonomy on the grounds that they attribute these values to human beings generally.[9]

The substantive objections flow out of the methodological ones. Some critics of the neo-Kantians, such as Bloom (1975a: 648–62), take them at their word when they claim either to have no conception of the good or to be indifferent among competing rational conceptions and object to that.[10] Most, however, go the route of Sandel in discerning that the Rawlsian-style thin theories may be thicker than their proponents admit but in not liking the particular density they discern. For Sandel, liberalism's commitment to the primacy of justice, and to the priority of right this brings with it, makes it fundamentally unsatisfying. Divorcing public from private lives, it recognizes only in the latter the constituting roles of our cultural attachments. The deontological liberal holds that "while we may be thickly-constituted selves in private, we must be wholly unencumbered in public. It is there that the primacy of justice prevails," and we become "submerged in a circumstance that ceases to be ours." By placing the cul-

---

8. This complaint, as old as the hills, is traceable—in its modern form at least—to Montesquieu's critique of Hobbes on the grounds that "is it not obvious that he attributes to mankind before the establishment of society what can happen but in consequence of this establishment?" (Montesquieu 1949: 4). *See also* Rousseau's attack on Hobbes for attributing to natural man "a multitude of passions which are the product of society" (Rousseau 1964: 129).

9. For my account regarding Rawls and Nozick, see Shapiro (1986: 151–305), regarding Posner, see Shapiro (1987: 999–1047), and regarding Buchanan and Tullock and Wolff, see Shapiro (1989b).

10. The discussion of the remainder of this section partly draws on, partly elaborates on, Shapiro (1989a: 60–66).

tural self beyond the reach of politics, liberalism "makes human agency an article of faith rather than an object of continuing attention and concern, a premise of politics rather than its precarious achievement" (Sandel 1982: 11–14, 183). Thus Sandel claims that extending the intimacies of our cultural commitments into an explicit theory of the political good would provide a more satisfying public community than the impoverished deontological vision.

Sandel's view—that justice belongs characteristically to the world of strangers reified in the deontological vision he rejects—both misdescribes the private communities we live in and rests on expectations for politics that cannot withstand analysis. First, it is false that the idea of justice does not operate in our private communal lives. In the family—that paradigm of the private community, held together in the ideal by bonds of intimacy and affection—justice and the sense of it play indispensable roles. The pertinent currency of family life is not voting rights or economic well-being but caring and affection. Although these are not properly distributed on the basis of merit, desert, efficiency, or Rawls's difference principle, they have their own systems of equities that, when violated, generate powerfully felt injustice and sometimes conflict. The child who knows herself to be loved or respected less than her siblings or the wife who has been abused will certainly bring to bear notions of injustice because they will feel the pertinent economy of love and affection has been violated. The idea that existing private communities provide a yardstick for a kind of postpolitical politics assumes a benign view of those communities that is not defended by Sandel or by any of the advocates of community discussed earlier in this book. Just as there are some happy and stable families blessed by abundance, good health, and fortune, many are not this lucky, and the language of justice comes into play whenever there is scarcity of, and conflict over, the goods internal to the relevant community.

What Sandel understands to be the limits of justice are actually limits to the politicization of communities. By declaring a community to be beyond politics, part of the private sphere, we are rendering it immune from political criticism. So when Nozick (1974: 32) implies, for instance, that sexual leering may use women in ways that violate the categorical imperative but that this is not a political form of using, he is assuming a comparatively narrow definition of politics.[11] Yet the accepted boundaries of politics are constantly shifting as the result of political struggles. When the law changes from denying the possibility of marital rape by conclusive presumption to creating such a crime by statute, a significant movement

---

11. On leering as a form of harassment, see di Leonardo (1981: 51–57).

of this kind has occurred. The public/private dichotomy in this and other prevalent formulations misses such poignant complexities.[12] Those who invoke the idea of justice in traditionally private communities like the family are generally those on the short end of power or distributive relationships. The general rule (to which there are doubtless exceptions) is that the dominated try to politicize to delegitimize, whereas the dominators try to depoliticize to legitimize.[13] It is mere romanticism to suppose that the relations of scarcity, power, and domination that render battles over politicization necessary either do not exist in the private sphere of the present or would not exist if we could return to some idyllic public sphere in our collective past.

This is not to imply, with Foucault, that just because all social structures—historical, actual, and possible—involve relations of power, domination, and scarcity that they are all alike. Some may be preferred to others on various grounds, and arguments about those grounds should be among our central concerns. But such arguments cannot even be engaged in, there is no linguistic space for them, as long as the terms of debate are allowed to be a variant of "whether-or-not-community." Thus we have seen that moral appeals to the primacy of community and republic are consistent with every politics from far left to far right, from rural to urban, from ancient to feudal to modern capitalist and socialist, and from city-state to continental nation. Yet the communitarian appeal is not only vacuous, it is pernicious; it creates the misimpression that a second-order appeal to community will actually resolve moral dilemmas when it will not. This is so not simply because communities differ so much from one another but because, as we saw in our discussions of Rorty, Walzer, and MacIntyre, pervasive disagreements over the interpretations of norms within communities leave most politically interesting disputes unresolved. Even when there is consensus, we saw, there may be circumstances where this is more troubling than its absence. In short, the second-order appeal to community is no more plausible as a basis for critical standards

12. On the changing law of marital rape, see note, "To Have and to Hold: The Marital Rape Exemption and the Fourteenth Amendment," *Harvard Law Review* 99 (1986): 1255–73. Problems relating to changing conceptions of the limits of politics are usefully taken up in Connolly (1981: 63–89).

13. The great exception to this might be argued to be fascist and totalitarian regimes, which often depend on highly politicized ideologies and the continuous mobilization of populations in their legitimating myths. See Friedrich and Brzezinski (1956: 17–27, 85–115). But I would argue that if such regimes endure for any length of time, they invariably try to depoliticize and thus normalize political life. One recent, if anecdotal, illustration is the decision in the Soviet Union to dismantle the huge political slogans that are among the best-known features of the skylines of its cities. See the *New York Times*, May 21, 1988, pp. 1, 4.

than is the second-order appeal to autonomy, which latter is characteristic of the neo-Kantian arguments that the communitarians reject.[14]

More romantic still is the attempt by other communitarians to base the postpolitical community not on some existing or allegedly historical community but on a community yet to be created. In these formulations the necessity for a system of justice can be abolished only when the causes of present conflict and scarcity go with it. This was Marx's view: that a communist society would differ from all its predecessors in that a superabundance of wealth would obviate the conflict generated by scarcity. Goods would be distributed on the basis of need, and government displaced by mere administration. It is often thought that such a view could be persuasive if a theory of needs could be developed that distinguished them from wants; wants may be infinite, as the bourgeois economists argued, and scarcity with respect to them therefore inevitable, but needs are not. A well-developed theory of needs could provide an archimedean point for limiting the induced wants of the market, making an economy of needs not subject to the limitations of scarcity at least a possibility. Yet these formulations assume a static and unrealistic view of human needs.[15] Such lifesaving technologies as dialysis machines and artificial hearts satisfy

14. For elaboration, see Shapiro (1986: 273–305).

15. At times Marx embraced a more dynamic view of needs, as in the argument in *Capital* that what counts as subsistence is socially and historically conditioned. See Marx (1974, I: 164–72). But he never came to terms with the difficulties this raised for his account of communism as a permanent state of superabundance. One contemporary Marxist, G. A. Cohen, indicates awareness of the problem when he says that Marxists' confrontation with liberalism "is avoidable only as long as Marxists continue to maintain that abundance will ensure complete compatibility among the interests of differently endowed people, and abundance on the required scale now seems unattainable. A lesser abundance, which enables resolutions of conflicts of interests without coercion, may well be possible" (Cohen 1986: 117). But he offers no account of how this might be done, and in his more recent work advocating equalization of "access to advantage" he supplies no account of how and by whom different disadvantages are to be weighted in the event (presumably often unavoidable once endemic scarcity is conceded) that equalizing access along some dimension diminishes it along a different one. See Cohen (1989a, 1989b). On these issues, see Rae et al. (1986: 104–29). Even advocates of needs as instruments of social policy-making like David Braybrooke concede that the concept breaks down in the face of demands for medical resources (among other areas), although the difficulty is more serious for his theory than Braybrooke imagines. Braybrooke (1987: 295) perceives conflicts between the need for medical care and other needs and notes that in such circumstances choices will have to be made that bring to bear considerations other than those of meeting needs. But he fails to notice that even within the realm of medical care needs must invariably outstrip resources, so that the problem is not only one of deciding how different goods should be ranked, but of deciding how to allocate particular goods to competing claimants whose conflict with respect to the relevant good is zero-sum.

needs, not wants, on just about any credible definition, yet the potential for such innovation is limitless. Once technological change is taken into account, human needs are infinite, scarcity and concomitant conflict inevitable, and the languages of politics and distributive justice inescapable. It is sheer fancy to suppose that there are any possible conditions of human association in which the need for a system of justice will evaporate, given these facts about the human condition. The limits of justice have nothing to do with liberalism, contra the implication of the title of Sandel's book and the assumptions of many Marxists, for political conflict is endemic to all human social interaction.[16]

In sum, to say that all morality is teleological does not begin to establish that there may not be different and conflicting goods for different persons in the same, different, and overlapping communities, as we saw in our discussions of Rorty and Walzer. For MacIntyre, too, once Aristotle's assumptions about natural harmony are jettisoned, there is no reason to believe that the imperatives of different subordinate practices can be subsumed under the *telos* of a unified human life for an individual, let alone for an entire society or world. Although we can empathize with MacIntyre's disillusionment with contemporary liberalism and Marxism and perhaps even with the quest to re-create ancient communities that it prompted, he has not begun to indicate why they would be superior forms of political communities, let alone how they might be realized in today's world.

The treatment of community in Pocock's analysis raises different difficulties. In addition to the instrumental preoccupation with stability, our examination of the history of republican argument revealed the lack of an adequate account of boundaries or membership, which is a serious defect because communities are always mechanisms of exclusion as well as mechanisms of inclusion. Inherent in all these views, then, is a benign, if not outright romantic, view of communities and the values they reproduce, whether this be of communities that prevail in the contemporary world, those that are imagined to have existed in some premodern past, or those that are to be created in some transformative future.[17] There is often a troubling indifference to the impact of the community on other communities and individuals except to the extent that such impact becomes instrumental to its stability and an almost studied blindness to the ways

16. Many contemporary Marxists have eschewed the utopian ambitions of Marx's politics. See, for example, Sirianni (1981: 33–82), Laclau and Mouffe (1985), and Isaac (1987a: chapter 6). The question for these authors has to be whether there is anything distinctively Marxist about their politics once the classical Marxian *telos* is abandoned.

17. Walzer is an exception to this last charge. His account of dominance is discussed further in section IV of this chapter.

in which the values dominant in a community are instrumental in the reproduction of relations of domination and control.[18]

III. The Rejection of Deontological Aspirations

A third dimension of disaffection with the neo-Kantians derives from skepticism toward the attempts of Rawls and his successors to defend principles of political and economic organization while bracketing considerations Kant dubbed *anthropological*. Rawls's philosophical project can be made sense of only in terms of his contrast between deontological and teleological theory, the point of which was to distinguish purposive views of ethics that depend on particular conceptions of the good from theories that claim agnosticism about them. If a theory of justice could be shown not to rely on any particular conception of the good but to be neutral among competing rational conceptions, the procedure of defending it without reference to consequentialist considerations, indeed without reference to causal matters of any kind, might appear plausible. Thus in teleological theories "the good is defined independently from the right, and the right is then defined as that which maximizes the good." By contrast, a deontological argument like Rawls's "either does not specify the good independently from the right, or does not interpret the right as maximizing the good" (Rawls 1971: 24, 30). Deontological arguments are attractive to neo-Kantians because they appear uniquely consistent with the preservation of individual autonomy, and teleological reasoning in political theory threatens them because it appears to undermine that autonomy. Doctrines like Sidgwick's utilitarianism permit sacrificing the interests of some individual to maximize the general good on consequentialist grounds, a result Rawls is determined to avoid.[19] Likewise with Nozick's rejection of patterned or end-state consequentialist principles of justice in favor of procedural or historical ones, the central claim is that there cannot be genuine liberty in society unless it is liberty to undermine, through voluntary transaction, whatever distributive patterns happen to prevail.[20] Analogous in spirit is Dworkin's attempt categorially to distinguish questions of principle from those of policy, even allocating these to different branches of government.[21] This aspiration toward working out principles of justice in anticonsequentialist terms in the realm of "ideal theory" and

18. For one useful discussion of how dominant conceptions of virtue in revolutionary America functioned to repress women, see Bloch (1987: 37–58). On the generally hierarchical and often repressive character of early American Puritan communities, see Haskins (1960: 9–93).
19. See Rawls (1971: 22–33, 179–92).
20. See Nozick (1971: 161–64).
21. See Dworkin (1985: 81–89).

then applying them to particular situations to see how they measure up gives the neo-Kantian enterprise its deductivist and transcendental whiff, even though its proponents have never actually adduced transcendental arguments in support of their views. The aspiration is revealingly summed up by Rawls (1971: 121) when he remarks that the eventual goal (that he does not yet claim to have attained) is to develop a political theory that is "strictly deductive," a kind of "moral geometry." [22]

Skepticism toward ideal theory of this sort is as old as political philosophy, figuring centrally, for example, in Aristotle's insistence that human social life is too complex and unpredictable for us ever to suppose that principles of justice might adequately be legislated for all circumstances. [23] For this reason he introduced the concept of equity in terms of which the law must be modified as applied to unforeseen circumstances and problems, a little like modern notions of common law reasoning. But where for Aristotle equity was limited either to effectuating what would have been a legislator's intent under changed conditions or to bringing the law into conformity with the requirements of "absolute justice" (dictated in turn by the requirements of the prevailing regime in its uncorrupted form), for most contemporary anti-Kantians all critical argument is exclusively immanent. [24] There is no architectonic structure of ideal justice; all we have is the system of norms and categories that make up our contemporary reality. Thus Rorty invokes Wittgenstein's notion of a language game to argue against all metanarratives. Without explicitly appealing to linguistic behaviorism, Walzer and MacIntyre both argue in different ways for the inevitability of immanent criticism. For Walzer it is not simply his desire to remain "in the cave, on the ground" to develop connected criticism that can have some possibility of influencing those to whom it is directed—its very terms must be derived from the values accepted in a culture. Distributions of goods can thus be just or unjust only "relative to the social meanings of the goods at stake" (Walzer 1983: 9). Prevailing

22. For further discussion, see Shapiro (1986: 151–305; 1989a: 53–55).

23. "Our account of this science [politics] will be adequate if it achieves such clarity as the subject-matter allows; for the same degree of precision is not to be expected in all discussions, any more than in all the products of handicraft" (Aristotle 1977: 64–65). On Aristotle's hostility to abstract moral argument, see (ibid.: 69, 93, 96, 103, 111, 189–90, 199).

24. The discussion of equity and its relation to absolute justice can be found in Book Five, sections vii and x of the *Nicomachean Ethics* (Aristotle 1977: 189–90, 199–200), and that of the reform of regimes in Book Three, chapters 6, 9, 11, and 12 of *The Politics* (Aristotle 1984: 94–95, 97–104). I concede that there are other credible interpretations of Aristotle's understanding of absolute justice (linking it to a higher law theory), but I do not take up the burden of defending my interpretation against these here because the point made in the text is consistent with these stronger interpretations as well as with mine.

usage defines both descriptive meaning and normative ideal. For Mac-Intyre, too, practices are ongoing, rule-governed activities, typically out-living any given generation of participants; it is just because we want to excel in terms of these ongoing practices that we inevitably accept their constituting rules, even if we modify them as we employ them.

Although Bloom would be the last person explicitly to embrace contextual criticism, we saw that the critical standards he invokes rest on no more than an act of faith (however implausible) that there is consensus in the tradition on the ultimate questions of political morality. The irony is that his moral absolutism rests, ultimately, on no more than an appeal to an idealized description of an intellectual context. In the republican tradition as portrayed by Pocock, too, we have long since departed the ideal republic; the realm of prudence is one of cautious adjustment to a dangerous and often unfathomable world, and even projects of Machiavellian mastery must eventually succumb to the corrosive effects of time. There are no moral absolutes, and genuine freedom lies in acceptance of this fact. "There is a freedom to decline moral absolutes," as Pocock sums up a moral of his study, "even those of the polis and history, even that of freedom when proposed as an absolute" (Pocock 1975: 552).

For many of these authors, then, the critique of transcendentalism, like that of neutrality, flows from a basic disaffection with the foundational argument characteristic of the Enlightenment.[25] This may take a linguistic form, as it does explicitly for Rorty and implicitly for Walzer and Mac-Intyre, so that we are locked, in Frederick Jameson's phrase, in "the prison house of language." Or it can be an historical argument, as part of Rorty's and MacIntyre's arguments are and as Pocock's is exclusively. In either case the abandonment of Kantian aspirations turns into that of all foundational argument, and we must now sort out the conflation of arguments that brings about this metamorphosis. For although the critiques of both transcendentalism and deontology are well taken, no good argument has ever been made against foundational argument as such.

Let us begin with the assault on transcendentalism. In most formulations considered in this book, it is not implausible as a theoretical argument but is a red herring because none of the authors commonly dubbed *neo-Kantian* relies on transcendental arguments. Yet by reacting against the transcendentalist whiff of the neo-Kantian arguments rather than what is actually wrong with them, the new contextualists replicate some

25. Bloom is clearly an exception here. Although there is the irony just alluded to deriving from his embracing of the tradition as a source of critical standards, he would disassociate himself from the rejection of foundationalism in any of its forms—even if he has failed to indicate even in broadest outline what a good foundational argument would be.

of their most serious defects. The central weakness of the neo-Kantian arguments is not to be found in the attempt to reason about principles without reference to ordinary usage. As Rawls, Dworkin, Ackerman, and their defenders never tire of reminding their critics, prevailing beliefs and practices are integral to the procedures of justification they employ. To be sure, there are legitimate questions that I and others have raised concerning whether Rawls's argument from the original position can be persuasive without assuming the truth of the Kantian interpretation of his principles, whether Dworkin's recent move toward contextual justification in *Law's Empire* is consistent with his steadfast rejection of it in earlier writings, and whether Ackerman's dialogic method actually plays any philosophical role in the derivation of his principles of social justice. There are further questions about why, if writers like Rawls and Walzer are both claiming to derive their principles from beliefs prevailing in American culture, they reach such different conclusions. But the point to notice here is that the move toward contextual justification need not, and typically does not, dictate a move away from deontological theory in the Rawlsian sense of being justifiable or unjustifiable independently of consequentialist considerations.

I do not mean to suggest that the anti-Kantians do not employ reasoning that Rawls would describe as teleological; they do. They openly commit to the supremacy of conceptions of the good in their accounts of right and justice. But we must not be diverted by a second red herring that lurks in the deontological/teleological dichotomy itself. At the heart of what is implausible in the neo-Kantian arguments is the inability of their authors to see that the distinction between deontological and teleological theory cannot be sustained. Their failure to see, or to concede, that consequentialist considerations invariably enter political theory give their arguments a quality of preaching to the converted. Only readers persuaded in advance of the truth or desirability of their particular assumptions about human nature, about what is good and bad for human beings, and about the causal structure of human interaction will be impressed by their claims that their theories, if implemented, would generate just societies that preserve Kantian autonomy. In effect this means that they rely on undefended and submerged assumptions about human nature and causal theories of how the world works to justify their principles, either naively believing or cynically pretending that these theories were not deeply contested and ideologically charged.[26] Consequentialist argument was en-

26. Here are a few examples: Rawls assumed general laws of psychology and economics to be the neoclassical assumptions about risk aversion and economic rationality and a host of Keynesian macroeconomic assumptions to render his ac-

gaged in, as it inevitably must be in arguments over the design of political institutions, but little serious attention was given to making it plausible. Rather than dealing with these issues by assumption and methodological sleight of hand, theorists who want to persuade anyone other than those with whom they already agree should get their hands dirty in empirical controversy and argue for the particular assumptions about individuals and society that they seek to advance.[27]

What is so frustrating about much of the turn away from neo-Kantian theory is that for all the appeal to historical specificity by which it is often motivated, there has been little serious grappling with empirical complexity and causal argument. In many of the accounts we examined, the neo-Kantians' second-order commitment to an abstraction called *autonomy* was simply displaced by a second-order commitment to an abstraction called *community*. Both in diagnosis of our circumstances and in prescriptive argument, we discovered that in different ways Rorty, MacIntyre, and Bloom all pay scant attention to the empirical credibility of large parts of their arguments. Their causal diagnoses rest on undefended, and prima facie quite implausible, historical arguments about how a few philosophical texts created the problems of modernity, indeed created modernity itself, arguments that can only be stated through tacit reliance on undefended and outmoded notions of traditional society. This causal idealism creates the dangerous misimpression, most explicit in Rorty's account, that the problems they identify could be wished away by undoing the intellectual mistakes embodied in those texts. In their explicit normative claims the arguments of Bloom, MacIntyre, and Sandel were all seen to rest on undefended, and again less than plausible, counterfactuals about cohesive social and political communities that either once existed or would exist but for liberalism's alienating tyranny. Virtually nothing was said about the nature of these communities, about how they did or could work, about how conflicts over core values within them would be resolved (when it was conceded that such conflict could occur), or about what economic and political institutions, forms of ownership, and systems of obligation would prevail. The republican tradition described by Pocock doffs a genuflecting cap to the importance of a "sociology of liberty," but we saw that

count of chain connection (and hence his difference principle) plausible. Nozick assumed without argument that market-based appropriation works to the benefit of all and that the only natural monopoly is the coercive force exercised by his minimal state. These and related issues are taken up at length in Shapiro (1986: 151–270, 289–92).

27. For elaboration, see Shapiro (1986: 241–42, 289–92).

the way in which this tradition evolved, on his telling, made this sociology both undetermined and naive—undetermined in that its core terms were easily appropriated by all sides in the great debates of the past several centuries over the structure of economic and political institutions and naive in that there was generally insufficient awareness that, far from ensuring the republican ideal of independence, a regime of private property and market institutions could and would be deeply threatening to it.

Walzer alone among the communitarians has tried to lay out the substance of a theory of the good and give illustrations of how it would operate in practice and of how different goods would be allocated in different realms of social life. Even in his case, however, we found no answers to the questions of how conflicting interpretations of shared meanings would be settled, of how a market system could be accepted while its globalizing internal dynamic could be "walled in," and of what basic changes in the underlying political economy might actually reduce dominance rather than merely redistribute its incidence.

Why do so many authors who have rejected the neo-Kantian enterprise pay so little attention to contextual complexity and causal practicality, given the terms of their critiques? A large part of the answer is that by casting the turn away from neo-Kantian theory as a rejection of foundationalism as such, many of the contextualists wrongly think that they need no longer articulate, let alone argue for, their foundational commitments. We should instantly be suspicious of the claim that "contextualism" is a meaningful alternative to "foundationalism" when we find one of its most lucid defenders arguing that he wants to "clear the ground" to defend the antifoundationalist view.[28] Just as our inability to generate one type of physical foundation that will support every kind of building on every possible terrain does not mean that builders and architects can henceforth build without foundations, just as the absence of a single skeletal structure common to all mammals does not mean that we could suddenly decide to do without skeletons, so not finding a secure basis for all knowledge in deductive introspection does not mean that henceforth we could—even if we chose to—ignore foundational questions in political theory and philosophy. The failure of that peculiar amalgam of transcendental ambitions and deductive arguments that preoccupied the central figures of the Enlightenment may well by now be undeniable, but to think that in discarding it we can now get on with political theory without foundations is simply false. Yet it is the belief that we can, more or less articulated in different cases, that enables many of the authors we have been

28. See Herzog (1985: 27).

examining to believe that mere appeal to a postulated consensus is sufficient to justify core political commitments.

This endorsing of consensus generates a curious convergence between those who embrace and those who reject the neo-Kantian enterprise in political theory. Labels to the contrary notwithstanding, where the likes of Rawls and Nozick argue that their principles of justice are legitimate because they would be freely chosen by people like us under certain specified conditions, so theorists like Rorty, Walzer, MacIntyre, and Sandel all seem to think that the values they defend, and the institutions that allegedly flow from them, command, commanded, or would—under the right conditions—command agreement. Writers like MacIntyre and Walzer, who are aware that requiring this kind of agreement is a tall order and explicitly disclaim it, end up appealing, we saw, to variants of just this claim in their positive contentions. In no case is evidence for the assumed consensus on the interpretation of prevailing values actually adduced, and we saw that there are good reasons to doubt that it does or could exist. Yet the various appeals to consensus that grow out of the critique of foundationalism appear to render plausible the practice of not defending particular foundational commitments with either argument or evidence. This plausibility comes at the price of the lost interest of those who do not agree with the conclusions in advance. For, as by now should be obvious, the view that foundational questions can be ignored is in fact a variant of the claim that they can be settled.

We can agree with the pragmatist critique of foundationalism if we interpret it to mean that there is no isolated or isolable discipline of epistemology that, once the philosophical specialists have gotten it all straight, so to speak, will generate secure foundations of knowledge for all time. But where we are bound to part company with Rorty, though not with Dewey or Quine, is in recognizing that this does not entail that foundational questions can ever be ignored, abandoned, or otherwise regarded as settled. Indeed the mere statement of the thesis that metanarratives should be abandoned indicates that people like Rorty and Jean François Lyotard (1984: 31–41) are co-opted by the thesis they are attacking; it implies that first- and second-order questions can be neatly distinguished into separate classes, that we can specify what we are going to abandon. It is quite contrary to the spirit of pragmatism to assume this or even to assume that our most basic commitments are epistemological. It makes more sense to begin with the intuition that everything is connected to everything else and that epistemological or any other questions may well be central to many first-order debates about morals, politics, or anything else, though this is not necessarily so, of course, because nothing is necessarily so. Dewey did not advocate abandoning philosophy as Rorty does; rather he took this different and more subtle view: "Better it is for philosophy to err in active participation in the living struggles and issues of its own age and times than to maintain an immune monastic impeccability" (Dewey 1929: I, iii). In this view we should think of philosophy, politics, and life as parts of an interconnected whole, and arguments, no matter where they start, must follow the connections wherever they lead. An argument that begins about whether or not a particular agent is unaware of her interests in a given situation might well become an argument about what it means to know what an interest is and then an argument about what knowledge is. There is no reason, in principle, why this should not be so; often, though not always, it will be exactly what is required. Rorty's resistance to this logic and its implications, we saw, is at the heart of his political and philosophical complacency.

I have sought to show in the last five chapters that in political theory arguments invariably lead protagonists to certain commitments about human nature and social interaction. Every view of politics rests on a conception of human psychology and a set of assumptions about the pertinent causal structure of the social world and about how that structure may facilitate and limit human purposes. The pragmatist tradition of Dewey and Quine offers perhaps the most viable third way between the neo-Kantians and their contextualist critics, but I argued in chapter 2 that it must rest ultimately on a thesis about human survival, not on linguistic consensus. More generally I argued that the only defensible reformulations of the anti-Kantian arguments makes a realist foundational commitment inevitable, that Rorty's Quinean account of how we adapt beliefs to changing circumstances requires exactly the philosophical realism that he claims to reject. Walzer makes us see that a credible analysis of contextually based critical standards must rest on a prior account of how they function in the reproduction of power relations. If he does not himself supply a developed account, he makes clear the imperative for causal argument that strives at least partly to escape, as it explains, the hermeneutic process. My analysis of MacIntyre's neo-Aristotelian account of human practices revealed a comparable need for a causal account of how they interact with one another. MacIntyre's account is also useful because his discussion of the irreducible narrative structure of human experience provides the beginnings of a psychology for political theory that is richer and more plausible than the utilitarian assumptions that inform most liberal and much Marxist political theory. MacIntyre, we saw, also provides one of the few powerful modern defenses of the view that moral argument is inevitably teleological, which in turn implies that any plausible political theory is bound to articulate and defend a theory of the human good.[29] Yet my discussions of the historical arguments of Bloom and MacIntyre revealed that the appeal to history does not obviate the need to defend one's assumptions about human nature and social causation; displacing internalist contextualist argument with internalist historical argument turns into exchanging one idealist demon for another. If our examination of Pocock's civic republican tradition generated the conclusion, contra Rawlsian and Hartzian conventional wisdoms, that every political theory embodies a conception of the human good, it also revealed that no political theory can be better than its causal account of the conditions for that good's realization.

IV. The Ideological Dimensions of Political Theory

The neo-Kantians have been subjected to a barrage of criticism concerning the ideological dimensions of their arguments—either for innocence concerning the ideological uses to which these arguments can be put or for more or less self-consciously dressing up ideologically motivated claims in spurious philosophical garb. Although appeals to context and history are frequently among the best tools for debunking ideologically loaded philosophical arguments, the harvest of the last five chapters in this regard has been notably poor. With the exception of Walzer not only do these authors fail to speak to the ideological dimensions of their own arguments, but they replicate much of the ideological innocence that we hoped to be leaving behind when we rejected the neo-Kantian enterprise.

Pocock's analysis of the republican tradition is disappointing from the

---

29. Two different senses of the term *teleological* must be distinguished for present purposes. In contemporary political theory teleological arguments are contrasted by Rawls and others with deontological arguments, as already discussed in this section, the point being to distinguish purposive theories of ethics, which depend on particular conceptions of the good, from theories that claim agnosticism about particular purposes. Thus in teleological theories "the good is defined independently from the right, and the right is then defined as that which maximizes the good." By contrast, a deontological argument "either does not specify the good independently from the right, or does not interpret the right as maximizing the good" (Rawls 1971: 24, 30). This may be called the analytical sense of teleological. The historical sense of teleological assumes considerably more, paradigm cases being Hegel's teleological view of history and, on my interpretation, Marx's historical materialism. On these views there are purposes immanent in social processes that give history a direction and suggest that it will eventually reach its goal and come to an end. Historical teleologists are usually (perhaps even necessarily) analytical teleologists, but the converse does not hold. Thus, although I have argued that commitment to analytical teleology is inescapable, it will be clear from the argument in the next two chapters that I regard the historical teleological view as untenable.

standpoint of comprehending the relationship between ideology and political theory for reasons of both substance and method. Methodologically his analysis flowed out of the claims of the new Cambridge historians to be rereading the history of ideas as the history of ideologies, but in practice this turned out to be mere internal description of evolving republican arguments as subjectively comprehended by participants without reference to the roles played by these arguments in the changing socioeconomic practices that they were used to undermine, transform, or legitimate. The result is a history that, although an illuminating description in its own terms, tells us virtually nothing about the actual operation of republican ideology and lacks critical edge for its evaluation. Substantively, Pocock's much-trumpeted promise to supply us with a history of our intellectual culture that is not dominated by the problematic of "the rise of bourgeois modes of thought" turned out to be much ado about remarkably little, partly because his straw conception of the liberal paradigm generates a misleading opposition of republicanism to liberalism and partly because— protestations to the contrary notwithstanding—much of his account of the evolution of the republican argument turned out to be the story of its accommodation with capitalist practices and bourgeois social life.

Rorty's argument more than any other exemplifies the innocence involved in an internalist preoccupation with language. By uncritically endorsing the values he takes to be enshrined in our culture, he becomes inexorably wedded to a parochial conservatism, however genial. Of course immanent criticism need not necessarily be ideologically conservative.[30] Because of the tensions and contradictions internal to all ideologies, the practices they legitimate will frequently be open to criticism in their own terms. Yet it is notable that Rorty fails to engage in arguments of this kind, explicitly taking the view that philosophical argument has nothing to contribute to political debate and that philosophical positions are generally without political significance.[31] Yet we saw that his philosophical

---

30. We saw this in our discussion of Walzer in chapter 2. For a more general defense of the view that hermeneutics need not be conservative, see Warnke (1987: 73–141). Although I agree with Warnke's argument that immanent criticism need not necessarily be conservative or reinforce the status quo (as it does for Rorty), I cannot make the leap of faith to the view she appears to share with Gadamer, that over time it should be expected to foster "practical reason or an increased capacity to discriminate" (ibid.: 174). That seems to me to be only one of the possible outcomes.

31. Thus although Rorty recently declared himself to be a fan of poststructuralism (where this is understood to involve the denial of all forms of objectivism and the recognition that culture is irreducibly rooted in language), he maintains that this has no political implications and that he is a "political democrat who doesn't think philosophy does much for the wretched of the earth" *Chronicle of Higher Education*, November 25, 1987, p. A8.

commitments generated a willful blindness to the problems of conflicting and subordinate values in our own culture and an undefended assumption that our political institutions preserve Enlightenment values.

Although Bloom and MacIntyre are, for different reasons, troubled by the institutions of modern liberal democracy and would doubtless be even more troubled by Rorty's suggestion that philosophy has nothing to say about its defects, their own arguments are hopelessly deficient from the standpoint of understanding the relationship between political theory and ideology. The problem is not merely that their idyllic assumptions about a vaguely specified past to which normative appeal is made supplies the basis for their critical judgments about the present but that these assumptions are invariably embedded in implausible causal accounts of Modern Decline. Bloom takes over from Strauss the unargued-for assumptions that the ideas of a few philosophers at the turn of the seventeenth century brought about the first wave of Modern Decline and that the subsequent waves down through the present have been the causal result of intellectual movements within universities. MacIntyre, we saw, literally identifies modernity with changes in the history of philosophy at many points in his argument without ever defending this conflation. Rorty, too, identifies what he takes to be the philosophical mistakes of Descartes, Locke, and Kant as causally shaping the intellectual culture of modernity and undermining "our" faith in our institutions. Not only is this an implausible view of the relationship between ideas and political and cultural change, it militates against serious attention to the actual causal possibilities in the world of contemporary politics. Bloom, we saw, is wholly uninterested in addressing questions about how to alter the modernity against which he is determined to rant. MacIntyre has nothing to say about how his small, self-governing communities are to be created or sustained in the contemporary world, and Rorty's quaint insistence that we can just choose to abandon the Cartesian paradigm—perhaps after a period of therapeutic historical consciousness-raising—ignores the ways in which political and philosophical ideas are woven into the complex processes by which cultural and political relations are reproduced and transformed.

Walzer is the only author we have examined who actively engages the problem of ideology's relation to political theory. His discussions of dominance and monopoly supply a causal account of the dynamics of ideological change, and his conception of connected criticism is intended in part to debunk ideological claims. Yet neither view is without its difficulties. Plausible as Walzer's account of ideological innovation might be, it has a descriptivist quality that undermines his search for a critical edge. If every dominant group becomes imperialistic with respect to the good that it best controls, although it might be predicted that some excluded group will beat back this dominance if it can and eventually impose a new dominant good, it is not obvious why, from Walzer's standpoint, this is desirable. Although he wants to avoid Foucault's position, which reduces all social relationships equally to mechanisms of domination and control, he has made the case neither that some dominant goods are superior to others as dominant goods nor that there could be a society in which no good is dominant. We saw that although his view is complicated by the claim that in a liberal culture opposition to dominance as such is part of the dominant culture in terms of which immanent critical argument is conducted, in the end this resolves neither of the difficulties just mentioned. Because Walzer explicitly refrains from making the claim that our culture is morally superior to others, while embracing the view that moral arguments are never settled definitively, opposition to dominance and the affirmance of a pluralist conception of the good become no more than weapons in this ongoing battle. They may be among the weapons that we are bound to use in our political struggles, but they do not accurately describe any culture nor could they.

More serious are the difficulties attending Walzer's account of connected criticism. We saw that although there is sometimes a good deal of tactical sense behind his argument that only connected criticism can be expected to influence the behavior of those at whom it is directed, this is not always so. In addition, the world of overlapping memberships and conflicting identifications makes the problem of not denying one's emotional bonds a good deal more complex than Walzer's discussion of Sartre and Camus implies. But, more important, we have repeatedly seen that the critic's connectedness (or lack of it) does not begin to tell her what to say. As a consequence, the idea of connected criticism fails as a bridging device between Walzer's descriptive account of the dynamics of ideological change and his own normative arguments. Thus although Walzer's argument is the most powerful of the new contextualists' because he alone among them has both developed a substantive account of the good community (rather than simply invoking the abstract value of community) and grappled seriously with the problem of articulating critical standards from within a contextualist view, much remains to be done. To grapple is not to triumph, and the seriousness and tenacity with which someone of Walzer's sophistication has struggled with this problem without resolving it should hint to us that the limits to mere context as a source of critical standards have by now been fully exhibited.

8   Critical Naturalism
and Political Theory

Contemporary political theorists are locked in an unwinnable battle between foundationalist and contextualist orthodoxies. Yet the preceding analysis has indicated the possibility of a third way and supplied many of the implements with which to begin opening it up. Now it is time to confront this task more systematically. My account of a third way is rooted in the pragmatist philosophical tradition I rescued from Rorty, and it takes full account of the interpretive dimensions of human experience that Walzer emphasizes. Yet it also calls for incorporation of the modes of thought that Walzer characterizes with the terms *invention* and *discovery* as indispensable to a plausible picture of human nature. I suggest that this can be achieved by embracing a version of Aristotle's view of the human condition, but it has to be modified more radically than neo-Aristotelians like MacIntyre are prepared to accept: we have to face up to and accept the full implications of relativizing Aristotle's account of the virtues, recognizing inescapable tensions internal to the human psyche and abandoning the natural harmony thesis.

Like Pocock's civic humanists who wrote of man's "acquired second nature," I maintain that the changing and partly conventional character of human needs and values does not prevent their being objects of scientific study, and (against postmodern orthodoxy) I argue that human beings can reasonably aspire to discover the truth about themselves and their circumstances. Indeed, because human beings are critically reliant on their cognitive capacities to survive and thrive they have an interest, ceteris paribus, in knowing and acting on the truth, in acting—as I put it without intending a reference to Heidegger—authentically. This interest may reasonably be thought of as having an evolutionary basis, but on my account it is not reducible to a biological imperative. The interest in authentic action is better thought of as growing out of our biological imperatives in the inevitably complicating contexts of conventional and self-conscious life; human beings are emergent from nature. Although I hold that it is reasonable for human beings to aspire to know and act on the truth, I resist the Bloomian reification of the capacity to know the truth as the preserve of any elite. Indeed, I argue that where human interaction is concerned all claims about the existence or possession of esoteric knowledge are rightly regarded as suspect. The preceding are the main elements of the view of moral and political theory that I describe as *critical naturalism*, and my final goals here are to explain it, render it plausible, and discuss its central implications for politics and political argument.

My agenda in this chapter and the next has five main parts. I begin with a brief account of the foundational commitments my view requires, which I characterize with the term *pragmatic realism*. After sketching the main elements of a realist conception of knowledge and explaining how that conception contrasts with positivist, interpretivist, and skepticist views, I argue that it is compatible with the most plausible understanding of the pragmatist tradition. I follow with a discussion of the pragmatic realist's ontology as it relates to the human sciences, where I defend a radically antireductionist view of human beings and of their evolving circumstances. Second, I discuss the implications of this view for political theory, showing how it reveals a number of standard contending views to be partly defensible but in the end vulnerable reductionisms. Third, I argue that a version of Aristotle's understanding of the human condition, modified to take account of pragmatic realist considerations, is not vulnerable in the ways that the main alternatives to it are and that it supplies a useful basis for thinking about the appropriate tasks and limitations of political theory. Fourth, at the start of chapter 9, I defend my claim that there is a human interest in authentic action, show how it flows out of my modified Aristotelian view, and discuss its political ramifications. Given my accounts of the limits to social scientific knowledge, the variety and sources of human values, and the endemic presence of domination in social life, I contend that the interest in authentic action is likely to be best served by the prevalence of a democratic political ethos of a particular sort. Fifth, I conclude by arguing that a commitment to this ethos can usefully condition an account of the most appropriate political institutions for human beings, as well as inform the way in which we should conceive of the goals and aspirations of political theory.

I. The Pragmatist Tradition and Philosophical Realism

The pragmatist tradition is often thought to be antithetical to philosophical realism, but as I argued in chapter 2 this view is mistaken. The field analogy at the heart of Quine's analysis of knowledge requires a realist commitment, as we saw, and attempts by people like Rorty to find versions of the pragmatist claim that do not require some such commitment fail.[1] Yet the argument of chapter 2 on this point was cast in negative terms. I want now to make the positive case for a view of science in terms of which empirical knowledge of the social world is available in principle and often attainable in practice. This is so despite there being good reasons for skepticism toward the possibility of a general social and political theory, be it explanatory or normative.

(i) Pragmatic Realism: Epistemological Considerations

The philosophical realist resists both the positivist view of science and the hermeneutic critique of it that has gained currency in recent decades. She holds that the hermeneutic critics of positivism threw the baby out with the bathwater by focusing their attacks on the possibility of objective empirical knowledge on an implausible account of its nature for which Hume was mainly responsible. Hume's basic goal made sense: he sought to dislodge subjective certainty of essences as the hallmark of genuine knowledge, the core epistemological commitment that the early empiricists had embraced.[2] In its place he defended a view of empirical knowledge that allowed that it could be corrigible but nonetheless genuine.[3] On this view science advances, when it does, not by making knowledge more certain but by producing more knowledge. Hume's redefinition of the nature of knowledge left room for a philosophical conception of empirical knowledge that could make sense of what natural scientists had evidently been doing with success for some time. But as contemporary realist philosophers of science like Roy Bhaskar have made clear, Hume and the positivists he influenced misdescribed the scientific enterprise in ways that made the attacks of Kuhn and his successors seem more devastating than they should have done.

The positivist conception of empirical knowledge made it critically dependent on the sense-data theory of perception, the correspondence theory of truth, and the idea that scientists come up with causal explana-

---

1. See chapter 2, sections I(ii) and II(i).

2. For a discussion of pre-Humean empiricist views of science, see Shapiro (1986: 43–48, 74, 87–88, 103–4, 110–19, 143–44, 146, 280–81).

3. Empiricists from Hume to Ayer continued to hold that analytic propositions could be known with certainty because they followed as a matter of definition, a view that modern pragmatists, who reject the analytic/synthetic distinction, deny. See the discussion of Quine in chapter 2, section I(ii). We need not settle this issue here; what matters is that a large class of knowledge claims were recognized by empiricists after Hume as being genuine without being held to be incontrovertible.

tions by observing constant conjunctions of events, positing causal models that can be validated by predicting future such conjunctions and trying to fit their explanations together in ever more general covering-law explanatory models. These positivist assumptions made the empiricist view of science seem vulnerable, as correspondence between language and the extralinguistic world as a criterion for truth was assaulted by ordinary language and pragmatist orthodoxies in the middle third of this century, and it became increasingly evident that the covering-law model of explanation and the positivist conception of constant conjunctions both had little to do with the conduct of science and faced serious problems of justification within their own terms.[4]

Yet rather than take the hermeneuticist's tack of abandoning the possibility of empirical knowledge under the sway of the discovery that all observation is theory laden, contemporary realists point out that it is possible to rescue a sound conception of empirical knowledge without embracing any of the standard tenets of positivism. At the core of the realist view is the recognition that all scientists assume, as a condition of the possibility of what they do, that there are causal mechanisms that operate in nature independently of our ability to comprehend or even perceive them. The conduct of science assumes that we have some possibility of grasping what these mechanisms are, but to discover their natures, scientists do not typically engage either in observation of constant conjunctions or in the building of covering-law predictive models. They try to produce events under the conditions of closed experiments on the basis of assumptions and hypotheses about the nature of the causal mechanisms involved.[5] The main differences among the sciences are methodological rather than ontological on this view, and it is generally in those sciences whose objects of study lend themselves to the conduct of closed experiments that the most progress has been made.

4. For discussion of realism and positivism in the natural sciences, see Harré (1970), Bhaskar (1978), Boyd (1984: 41–82), Churchland and Hooker (1985: 3–242), and Miller (1987). On realist attempts to embrace causal theories of reference without endorsing positivist conceptions of correspondence, see Devitt and Sterelny (1987: 15–111, 161–71, 189–98). On realism and the human sciences, see Keat and Urry (1975), Bhaskar (1979: 153–204; 1986: 224–308), and Benton (1981). For a summary of some of these and other realist arguments, which I draw on here and in the next several paragraphs, see Shapiro (1982: 563–78).

5. Some realist writers, notably Benton (1981), have questioned Bhaskar's exclusive identification of prediction with experimental closure, arguing that this is only one of a number of possible bases of prediction in the natural sciences. Although Bhaskar concedes that prediction is possible in astronomy where closure is not, there are other natural sciences, such as meteorology and geology, where prediction in open systems is typical and others still, such as biology, where if not typical at least common.

The realist concedes that the human sciences differ importantly from the natural sciences in that a large part of their subject matter is human beliefs, but this is not considered a sufficient reason to make scientific study of the human realm impossible. Beliefs can be parts of causal processes and in principle studied as such, even if it is acknowledged as the idealist insists—and no one seriously denies—that "there can be no observational evidence which is not to some degree shaped by our concepts and thus by the vocabulary we use to express them" (Skinner 1988: 250). Beliefs, like many other entities, may be part and parcel of the causal processes that produce and reproduce the social world, and beliefs may be influenced by many things that may be more or less evident to agents in different circumstances.[6]

Despite disagreements among realist writers over the analyses of human belief and action,[7] they unite in rejecting the central assumption common to the hermeneuticists, the conviction that the concept-dependent nature of the social world rules out the possibility of understanding it in causal terms. This antinaturalist view of action, most notoriously associated with the name of Peter Winch,[8] is rejected for a variety of reasons, the most important centering on its linguistic reductionism. In Roy Bhaskar's terminology, people like Peter Winch wrongly construe the partial ontological dependence of actions on agents' beliefs as total.[9] This is why the attempts by social theorists and historians of ideas to employ the methods of ordinary language philosophy and hermeneutics have been argued by realists to involve misleading reductions: they focus exclusive attention on social agents' conceptions of what they are doing and why: the only interesting methodological issues for these writers concern whether this can be discovered and, if so, how.[10] The realist does not coun-

6. See the discussions of Rorty and Walzer in chapter 2, section II(ii), and chapter 3, section I(ii).

7. For a summary account of some of the main differences, see Shapiro (1982: 569–70).

8. See Winch (1958). The Winchean view has been embraced in more recent years by people like Rorty and Skinner, as we have seen. On Rorty, see chapter 2, section I, and on Skinner, chapter 4, section II(ii), and footnote 10 of this chapter.

9. Thus Winch regards the fact that reference to "beliefs and other conceptual matter will in general be necessary for an adequate social explanation" as entailing that such reference "will generally be sufficient" (Bhaskar 1979: 173–74).

10. For my realist critique of Skinner, Pocock, and Dunn along these lines, see Shapiro (1982: 535–78). For Skinner's reply to me and other critics who make similar arguments, see Skinner (1988: 213–88). The core issue between me and Skinner is not whether or not observational evidence is "to some degree shaped by our concepts and thus by the vocabulary we use to express them" (Skinner 1988: 250) but whether or not the beliefs and actions of an agent can be explained purely by an internal analysis of the kind proposed by Austin in his analysis of speech acts. I argued that one cannot credibly claim to be studying the history of ideas as

terpose some alternative reductionist interpretation to the linguistic one. She starts from the assumption that our beliefs and linguistic constructions are parts of the complex social processes through which the social world is reproduced and transformed, and she recognizes that the causal functions of beliefs are often many-sided and may well be opaque to social agents. From this it follows that any rich and plausible account of human action must comprehend it externally as well as internally, understand us as parts of causal processes as well as centers of autonomous action. Whether and to what degree external understanding of this sort is possible for the realist is a subject for scientific investigation, not an a priori argument.

---

the history of ideologies, which Skinner announced with much flourish that he was doing, and still proceed in these terms, eschewing causal analysis. Among other things I pointed out that we have to look at the opaque relations between language and social reality, and the fact that people often perform actions other than, or in addition to, the ones they think they do. For this I coined the term *real act* as a supplement to Austinian analysis to indicate that difficult though it may be, the student of ideologies must try to capture the extralinguistic dimensions of linguistic actions. The complaint that this is jargon (Skinner 1988: 277) is a little rich coming from someone who needed the entire Austinian vocabulary of locutionary, illocutionary, and perlocutionary acts to say that a historian of ideas should try to understand what his subjects were trying to do. Substantively, Skinner is less than accurate when he says that I gave no examples other than redoubling in bridge to show that his equation of the description of an agent's action with his intention is problematic (ibid.: 265). Apart from the fact that that was not my example, I supplied a number of much less trivial ones. I discussed unconscious, mistaken, and distorted intentions, all of which are ruled out of court by a linguistic reductionism that limits explanatory reference to the speaker's avowal or his overt linguistic behavior (Shapiro 1982: 548, 562n74). I gave the examples of inadvertent reproduction of the nuclear family and of wage-labor relationships. I noted that acts of overlooking and neglecting are often pregnant with ideological significance, giving the example of what the Pareto system neglects in its definition of voluntary exchanges and referring Skinner to the political science literature on power since Bachrach and Baratz, which revolves centrally around the study of how what is not said and not perceived by agents can be central to the exercise of political power (ibid.: 554, 542–43). Just in case it might be supposed that these points are without importance for the conduct of historical scholarship, I also noted that Skinner's preoccupation, in his *Foundations of Modern Political Thought*, with internal analysis enabled him to offer an account of the genesis of modern conceptions of rights in which "he never mentions the structural transformations then occurring in European society, or that the development of a generalized right to resist contributed importantly to the growth of an ideology that could justify the transition to a market-based society," giving illustrations from his discussion of the Huguenot revolution (ibid.: 568–69). My point in all this was to show that while Austin's schema may work tolerably well as a theory of meaning in communication (although it confronts difficulties that are serious and well-known), to try to extend it into a theory of ideology commits one to a linguistic reductionism that is little short of absurd. How and why we should try to avoid reductionist traps of this sort is taken up in section I(ii) below.

The human sciences differ most from the natural sciences in that—for reasons partly moral and political and partly technological—in the former, closed experiments are not typically feasible. This may well limit what can be known in them and make many of the conclusions social scientists reach more tentative and vulnerable than in many of the natural sciences and may make prediction all but impossible. But this is not a reason to rule out the growth of knowledge in the human sciences; it might occur, but there is no necessary reason either that it will or that it will not.

Although the realist will often be skeptical of particular arguments and proposals, realism is not a variant of philosophical skepticism. On the contrary, skeptical arguments that a realist will consider embracing often depend for their veracity on knowledge claims that can be argued to be plausible. Skepticism, for instance, toward blueprints for permanently liberating social transformation derives not only from suspicions that their proponents cannot know what they claim to know but also from evidence as various as the historical records of Stalinism and fascism and the academic research of people like Michel Foucault. These and other kinds of evidence can plausibly be argued to create a heavy burden of proof on those who expect people to sign up with the next revolutionary movement that promises final liberation. Likewise, as my debunking discussion of utopian communitarianism in chapter 7 revealed, it is not philosophical skepticism that leads us to reject the possibility of a world without political conflict over scarce resources but commitment to a particular empirical thesis about the dynamic and evolving character of human needs and human capacities for technological innovation.[11] In short, skepticism toward particular theoretical proposals, even skepticism toward the possibility of architectonic systems of political and social theory, in no way implies skepticism about the possibility of reliable knowledge. On the contrary, for the realist, when well-founded, such skepticism presupposes it.

The realist view is compatible with the pragmatist model of adaptive beliefs discussed earlier, once the positivist account of the nature of empirical knowledge is abandoned.[12] We need no longer believe in the sense-

---

11. See chapter 7, section II.

12. Bhaskar does not try to argue, and perhaps would not agree with, the claim I defend here, that the core insights of pragmatism can be rearticulated from within a realist epistemology. We also differ in the substantive political values we seek to defend; Bhaskar (1986) argues for a version of the Enlightenment ideal of human emancipation from realist premises. For reasons that I lack the space to go into here but hope to take up at length in the future, I think Bhaskar fails to establish his case. For this reason, although we share much in the way of substantive commitments and methods of analysis, Bhaskar's critical naturalism differs from mine in major ways.

data theory of perception, the theory of correspondence as a criterion for truth, constant conjunctions of events, or the possibility of a general and predictive social theory to hold that there can be viable, if corrigible, empirical knowledge of the social world. Although we have no a priori reason to reject the possibility of a general social and political theory out of hand, we are bound to recognize that the major systems of social and political theory of the past several centuries, liberalisms and Marxisms both classical and neoclassical, face well-known difficulties. We are in an era of paradigmatic exhaustion in the sense that, despite no shortage of pretenders to the throne, none of the recent succession of fads and "isms" on either side of the Atlantic is credible as a new general explanatory or normative system, and perhaps there will never be one.[13] This may say something about the kinds and generality of knowledge to which we can reasonably aspire but not that things cannot be known.

In the first instance, then, we may be thrown back onto the pragmatist tradition for want of faith in anything better. But I have sought to defend the Quinean view of what knowledge is and of how it develops in positive terms, arguing that it rests on a particular causal thesis about how human beings adapt to and try to comprehend their circumstances that is more plausible than the leading alternative contenders.[14] Now we see that it is possible to articulate a realist view of our foundational commitments that does not undermine the pragmatist thesis, for the link between pragmatism and the interpretivist worldview that Rorty sought to establish has been revealed to be spurious. The Quinean model, we saw, assumes a realist commitment, as does any causal theory of knowledge. Far from being an oxymoron, then, a commitment to pragmatic realism grows naturally out of the present circumstances in which the human sciences find themselves, it makes good epistemological sense, and it seems to offer the best way forward for thinking about the nature of moral and political arrangements.

(ii) Pragmatic Realism: Ontological Considerations

Human beings are tremendously complex animals, and any attempt to capture their nature through a single essence or defining characteristic will founder on the many things it fails to explain. At a quite primitive level human life is biologically based and exists in a universe filled with other forms of biologically based life competing for the scarce resources needed for survival, as well as a host of inanimate forces indifferent—but often

13. For useful summary discussions of many of these pretenders, see Skinner (1985).

14. See chapter 2, section I(ii), and chapter 3, section II(i).

not causally irrelevant—to the fortunes of any particular life-form. It can scarcely be surprising, then, that the life-forms that do persist generate powerful motivations to survive and thrive, as well as capacities to adapt to and otherwise come to terms with changing circumstances. To say that human life is at a primitive level driven by biological imperatives to survive and thrive is to say neither that this is the *most* primitive level at which human life can be described (clearly it is not) nor that more complex aspects of human social existence can be reduced to biological imperatives. Yet it is to insist that the imperatives to survive and thrive are not irrelevant to more complex forms of human behavior.

How, then, are they related? A useful way to think about this is with the concept of emergence. Human beings are natural beings, but they are also, as Bhaskar (1986: 104) points out, emergent from nature. Likewise, social phenomena are conditioned by and in nontrivial ways dependent on natural phenomena, but they are not causally or ontologically reducible to them. Michael Polanyi has helpfully described relations of emergence more generally by pointing out that almost all forms of knowledge, action, and existence consist of multiple entities that stand in tacit emergent relationships to one another. Speech, for instance, consists of at least five interrelated levels, namely, "the production (1) of voice, (2) of words, (3) of sentences, (4) of style, and (5) of literary composition." Each of these levels is subject to its own laws, the first to those of phonetics, the second to those of lexicography, the third to those of grammar, the fourth to those of stylistics, and the fifth to those of literary criticism. These levels form "a hierarchy of comprehensive entities, for the principles of each level operate under the control of the next higher level." So one's voice "is shaped into words by a vocabulary; a given vocabulary is shaped into sentences in accordance with grammar; and sentences can be made to fit into a style, which in turn is made to convey the ideas of a literary composition." Each level, then, is subject to dual control: "first, by the laws that apply to its elements in themselves, and, second, by the laws that control the comprehensive entity formed by them." This in turn suggests an approach to the explanation of complex entities and their behavior that is radically antireductionist:

> The operations of a higher level cannot be accounted for by the laws governing its particulars forming the higher level. You cannot derive a vocabulary from phonetics; you cannot derive the grammar of a language from its vocabulary; a correct use of grammar does not account for good style; and a good style does not provide the content of a piece of prose. We may conclude quite generally . . . that

> it is impossible to represent the organizing principles of
> the laws governing a higher level by the laws governing
> its isolated particulars. (Polanyi 1966: 35–36)

Human activity and cognition should be understood in these antireductionist terms but so too should forms of existence, animate and inanimate. Just as the full nature of a machine cannot be grasped from separate
analyses of each of its constituent parts, so too with human beings. Biol-
ogists are thus quite wrong, Polanyi notes, to try to reduce all manifestations of life to the laws governing inanimate matter. Life-forms everywhere are made up of groups of emergent relations that condition, limit,
and shape one another without ever being reducible to their component
parts:

> The most primitive form of life is represented by the
> growth of the typical human shape, through the process
> of morphogenesis studied by embryology. Next we have
> the vegetative functioning of the organism, studied by
> physiology; and above it there is sentience, rising to per-
> ception and a centrally controlled motoric activity, both of
> which still belong to the subject of physiology. We rise
> beyond this at the level of conscious behavior and intellec-
> tual action, studied by ethology and psychology; and, up-
> permost, we meet with man's moral sense, guided by the
> firmament of his standards. (Ibid.: 36–37)

It is because these levels of existence stand in emergent relations to one
another that, although our explanations at more complex levels must take
account of those at simpler ones, we should never expect the latter to be
reducible to the former. We should try to take account of how the different
levels shape, condition, and emerge from one another, but we should resist
the temptation to turn this view into a new and opposite reductionism—
trying to reduce simpler levels to the more complex ones in which they
participate, as is sometimes thought to be implied by extravagant versions
of the doctrine of "emergent holism." As we saw in our discussion of
Rorty, the assertion of the primacy of language in much contemporary
philosophy and social theory commits just this error.[15] Our social explanations must not lose sight of Polanyi's discussion of dual controls. In
trying to understand the systems of rules of action and existence that interest us, we need to be aware that they are only partly independent of the
more primitive levels on which they are causally dependent. These sys-

15. See chapter 2, section II(ii). For a more general discussion of these issues,
see Manicas (1983: 331–54).

tems are also parts of more complex levels that depend on them at the same time and that may to some extent react back on and exert causal influences on them. Every emergent dimension of an entity will be relatively autonomous of those from which it emerges; once it comes into existence it generates imperatives and rules of its own as a complex system. But these rules and imperatives can only develop and persist in ways that either continue to fit into or reshape the levels on which they depend and those depending on them. The ways in which human beings use their powers of creative innovation in the production of what they need to survive, for example, has effects on the ecosystem that may ultimately have causal consequences on human biology itself. This does not mean that we are unconstrained by biological imperatives, but it does mean that the constraints are always subject not only to their own internal logics but to the ways in which those of other levels of existence affect them. When cultures become more complex, no doubt, so do the causal relations among the multilayered systems that compose them, as the example of the effects of human action on the ecosystem suggests. In short, the ways in which different levels interact with one another may often be as important in understanding a particular dimension of action or existence as the rules germane to that dimension considered alone.

Polanyi's analysis of emergent relations usefully captures and pins down the intuition that complex entities are in a significant sense more than the sum of their constituent parts. Commitment to this view rules out a number of common approaches to moral and political theory. Hobbes's resolutive-compositive method in which the way to understand a complex mechanism like a commonwealth is to take it to pieces and examine the component parts will have to be eschewed, for example.[16] More generally, we should reject the standard identifications of methodological individualism with theoretical rigor, so commonly used to justify contractarian arguments and many other individualist reductionisms.[17] Also likely to fall from serious consideration are social and political theories

16. For a discussion of Hobbes's method, see Shapiro (1986: 50).
17. Note Rawls's (1971: 264–65) remarks in defense of his conception of justice as fairness: "For reasons of clarity among others, we do not want to . . . suppose that society is an organic whole with a life of its own distinct from and superior to that of all its members in their relations with one another. Thus the contractual conception of the original position is worked out first. It is reasonably simple and the problem of rational choice it poses is relatively precise. From this conception, however individualistic it may seem, we must eventually explain the value of community." There are also utilitarian conceptions of the social contract like Buchanan's and Tullock's (1962: 11–15) that rely on similar arguments in defense of their individualist reductionism, as does much, though not all, public choice and game theory.

that try to explain human action and behavior and prescribe for it by reference to a single explanatory dimension or realm. This will be true of biological reductions, as Polanyi notes, but also of every other reductionism. The classical utilitarian claim that all human action is explicable in terms of pleasure seeking and pain avoidance, Marx's reduction of all social and political life to the material realm, and Freud's, to the psychoanalytic; these are not likely to be true in any ultimate sense as social theory. This is not to say that Darwin, Bentham, Marx, and Freud did not make dramatic discoveries that illuminated some hitherto obscure dimension of human life and action; they did. But their insights must be rearticulated within an antireductionist conception of social explanation in a way that will make them necessarily partial as accounts of the human condition.

II. Antireductionist Thinking about Human Nature

It is easier to catalog what an antireductionist view rules out than to explain what it rules in or to spell out how this relates to my search for a third way in moral and political theory. Yet it is the latter that must be our central goal. To advance toward it, I want now to argue that from the standpoint of the pragmatic realist view of knowledge and antireductionist ontology outlined so far in this chapter, we are in a position to see why each path to understanding and critical argument that Walzer describes as invention, discovery, and interpretation captures significant elements of the human condition but why none alone is adequate as a basis for critical argument in politics.[18] Each involves an illicit attempt to reduce human beings to one of their constituent dimensions, and as general social and political theory it goes off the rails as a result. Seeing this also opens the way to rearticulating what is desirable in each of these views as part of a plausible alternative account.

(i) Major Reductionist Views:
Their Insights and Limitations

What Walzer describes as the path of invention is rooted in three plausible assumptions about the human situation: that we be capable of self-

18. Walzer never claimed that these were the only actual or possible paths of moral argument and nor do I, but they certainly are the principal ones, capturing what have been treated as the available possibilities in moral and political theory for some centuries. Nor should I be thought to be attributing to Walzer the view that there is nothing worthwhile to the paths of invention and discovery; even though he ultimately rejects both as inferior bases for critical argument to the path of interpretation that he favors, he explicitly rejects this view. See Walzer (1987: 3–32).

consciously planned behavior, that human social and political institutions are both nontrivially the products of human action and critically reliant on consent (or at least acquiescence or submission), and that human beings have powerful aspirations to free themselves from preexisting and artificial constraints, to try to become masters of their own destinies. Thus understood, it is natural for human beings to strive self-consciously to design and control social institutions and make them subservient to human wills. This aspiration behind the path of invention has been central to the social contract tradition since Hobbes and Locke, both of whom sought to understand society as a human artifact, the creature of human beings because it is their creation.

Among contemporary writers the aspiration is well illustrated by Robert Paul Wolff when he distinguishes the natural world that is "irreducibly *other*," standing "against [man], independent of his will and indifferent to his desires," from a social world that is "nothing in itself, and consists merely of the totality of habits, expectations, beliefs and behavior patterns" of the people who constitute it. Because of this difference, Wolff argues, "it ought to be in principle possible for a society of rational men of good will to eliminate the domination of society. . . . It *must* be possible for them to create a form of association which accomplishes that end."[19] The same assumptions about human innovative power informed George Bush's first speech to Congress as president when he poured scorn on the "voices who say . . . we are bound by constraints, threatened by problems. . . . Let all Americans remember that no problem of human making is too great to be overcome by human ingenuity, human energy and the untiring hope of the human spirit."[20] On the left, Roberto Unger's trenchant attempt to "drive to the hilt" the idea of unconstrained human action builds on the same aspiration. His goal is to take to the extreme the Enlightenment view that human beings make their own circumstances, and through their circumstances themselves, and to work out a comprehensive political and social theory based on that ideal. Thus although Unger sees modern Western democracies as definite advances on systems of explicit and implicit privilege, they represent "no more than a partial move toward the denaturization of society." It is possible to imagine "more complete realizations of the ideal of empowerment through denaturization," and the program of social reconstruction he offers is intended to do just that, to realize the idea of empowerment as "context-smashing" and thus create genuinely free human beings.[21]

19. See Wolff (1970: 72, 76–78, Wolff's italics).
20. *New York Times*, February 10, 1989, p. A9.
21. See Unger (1987: I, 86, 18, 20, 22, 160, II, 79, 95, 126, 341, 361).

Whether in liberal, conservative, or radical formulations, projects of invention comprehend the individual's relationship with society in these basic terms: human freedom is essential to our true nature and can only be achieved to the extent that society can be denatured in Unger's sense and subjected to conscious human design and control. Society is our workmanship in just the same way as we are God's workmanship, as Locke formulated this view, and as such society is our creature just as we are God's creatures.[22] Because of the intuitive power—descriptive and normative—of the ideal of freedom behind this view, whatever difficulties attend theories based on it, they reappear continually in the history of political theory.

The path of discovery also begins with a valid intuition about the human condition: that we are internally complex parts of a complex universe whose operations appear to be law governed but mainly beyond our ken, and that we have a powerful impetus to try to understand ourselves and our circumstances, to find some underlying logic and rationale in the evolving flux around us that can both explain our lives and supply them with meaning and point. The aspiration to discover informs not only the natural law systems of ancient and medieval European political thought but much of the scientific ethos of the Enlightenment as well. At the core of the different materialist ambitions of Hobbes and Marx, of classical utilitarianism, of psychoanalysis, and of modern behavioral social science is a search for the causal principle, the underlying spring of human action, that will make us finally understand our natures, circumstances, and purposes. If the inventor thinks we can only be our true selves by unloading the burdens we were born with or acquired along the way, the discoverer thinks we can be ourselves only when we understand the nature of those burdens and accept them. We cannot deny what we are, and whatever human fulfillment might be thought to consist in, its attainment will require understanding the mechanisms that drive us in our universes, both physical and social.

Walzer's path of interpretation also appeals to a valid insight about the human condition: that human consciousness and action exhibit an irreducible performative character. Our learned linguistic capacities shape our reality, and the significance of many—if not all—human actions and norms cannot be understood apart from the systems of rules that govern their linguistic use. This is one reason why human language is at least relatively autonomous: it cannot be read off from other dimensions, or

22. On Locke's view, see Locke (1963: 215–16, 231, 311, 347, 348) and Tully (1980: 35–50).

combinations of dimensions, of reality to which it allegedly reduces, nor does language in any simple sense correspond to a reality external to it, as the positivists believed. In Austin's famous example when I say "I promise to x" in the relevant circumstances, I am not describing an action that I have performed in some other way; I am performing the action in uttering the words, thereby becoming obligated.[23] The performative insight at the core of Austin's and Wittgenstein's work on ordinary language philosophy is at the heart of the interpretivist ethos and the contemporary interest in hermeneutics: because the linguistic realm essential to human life "constitutes" it, to use the buzzword, understanding and critical argument in politics must work with the rules of conventional usage if it is to speak to the characteristically human situation. *I learn language, therefore I am.* We are traditional and conventional linguistic creatures, and the structure of our conventional usages must be interpreted to supply the basis for any viable political theory.

If what Walzer describes as the paths of invention, discovery, and interpretation draw on aspects of human reality that are intuitively plausible, notice that each of them appears vulnerable from the standpoints of the other two. For instance, an argument like Unger's, which drives the Enlightenment view of freedom and with it the inventor's enterprise "to the hilt," lacks plausibility when serious attention is paid to the traditional and conventional character of human action and the limits of what it is possible to understand and change. From the discoverer's standpoint, Unger's superliberalism exhibits a quixotic character, collapsing into yet another variant of romantic idealism. The idea that all social practices, contexts, traditions, and structures must perpetually be overthrown if we are to avoid the routinized behavior that undermines our capacity to convert "plasticity into power" will be so much tilting at windmills if it is undertaken in ignorance of what we cannot change, of the mechanisms we cannot control. Just as we admire Picasso's abstract paintings because they rest on a massive understanding and control of representational drawing and are unimpressed by the splashings of would-be creative abstractionists who know nothing else, so the social theorist who tells us always to change everything everywhere will provoke more mirth than serious attention.[24] Furthermore, no simple distinction like Wolff's between an unknowable and uncontrollable natural world and a knowable and sub-

---

23. See Austin (1962: 7–108, 121–64).

24. As, indeed, Unger's argument already has. See, for instance, Stephen Holmes, "The Professor of Smashing," *New Republic*, October 19, 1987, pp. 30–38. For a more sober and extensive treatment, see Smith (1988). For my own discussion, which I draw on here, see Shapiro (1989c).

servient social one will withstand much analysis from the discoverer's standpoint. On the one hand, many aspects of our natural environments are susceptible to human influence if not control, from the temperature of our bathwater to aspects of the genetic structures of our beings; on the other, many external effects of human actions are uncontrollable even when they are understood, which is often not the case (think of the endemic controversies over the causes of systemic unemployment or continuous inflation).[25]

From the interpretivist standpoint the notion that perpetual context smashing is the key to human liberation appears will-o'-the-wispish for different reasons. As a philosophical matter it assumes a naive Cartesianism, a voluntaristic control over everything we think and believe. Rorty will be the first to remind us that we can question some of our beliefs only by accepting others, that the tabula rasa approach to theoretical argument is absurd. As a psychological matter it is difficult to imagine what Unger's argument would mean in practice; anyone who has reared children must find it mind-boggling. To raise a child on the principle that she could only be free if taught perpetually to reject every form of structure and limitation, assuming this was possible, would issue in such a miserable and conflicted adult that it is doubtful that she could survive in any society. We may all want our children to think for themselves and to develop critical minds, but a far more nuanced and experimental mixture of freedom and structure is needed, from the standpoint of an interpretivist understanding of human agency, to have any hope of bringing this about.

Exclusive attention to the path of discovery confronts analogous difficulties. From the standpoint of the path of invention, projects of discovery are both implausible on their face and morally bleak. Searches for *deep structures* and *deep logics*, as Unger names them, that underlie and allegedly explain all human action and aspiration deny all efficacy to human agency and creativity. On the surface it is something of a curiosity that the determinist aspirations of modern science and the Enlightenment view of freedom flowed from the same pens (think of Hobbes, Locke, Hegel, and Marx), for these two values seem deeply antithetical to one another. Indeed the Enlightenment view of freedom could only survive the Enlightenment view of science if the process of a scientific understanding of human society and history could be completed; genuine freedom from causal process could only be achieved once causal process was conquered by understanding, both literally and metaphorically. But the fact remains that there are deep and enduring tensions between Hobbes's determinist

25. For my view of these controversies, see Shapiro and Kane (1983: 5–39).

psychology and his view of morality as being critically dependent on free acts of the will, between Locke's simultaneous commitments to linking moral obligations to acts of an autonomous will and to the view that the moral truths of natural law could be known with certainty, and between the materialist conception of history and the urgency of Marx's arguments for consciousness-raising and innovative political action by the working class.[26] Hegel avoided a similar clash only through his less than over-whelmingly plausible contention that the determinist process of world history had reached its terminus at the moment when he set out to de-scribe it in the *Phenomenology,* freeing him to account for it as a complete totality.

For the interpretivist the project of discovery is also implausible on its face. The discoverer's reductionist aspirations seem to fail to take account of the conditioned and conventional character of all human action, and she will scarcely be surprised that searches for deep structures and deep logics in human society and language have so conspicuously failed. The expec-tation that motivates discoverers—that there exists an underlying order to things waiting out there to be excavated—will never be fulfilled. As a result, their attempts to reduce human action to its causal determinants misses the performative dimension, which can never be fully captured in causal language. It can only be interpreted or elucidated from within the system of hermeneutic self-understandings that makes it possible.

This is why discoverers' projects seem not only reductionist but ab-surdly reductionist to those who walk the path of interpretation. What appear to a discoverer to be minor irrelevancies of contextual complexity, to be abstracted from in the search for penetrating explanations that will get at the underlying reality of things, appear to the interpretivist as the central objects of sophisticated analysis. Where the discoverer thinks the interpretivist is skating on the surface of things without penetrating to what matters, the interpretivist sees the discoverer's quest as quixotic at best because it misses the ways in which human beings constitute them-selves and their social relations through their conventional behavior. More likely, as Rousseau argued in his critique of Hobbes, the discoverer will delude himself and those who take him seriously. He will reify parochial

---

26. In Hobbes's case the tension was resolved (some, more accurately in my view, say evaded) by relegating ethics and psychology to different levels in his explanatory schema. Hence the so-called Taylor thesis, positing a schizophrenia between Hobbes's deontological ethics and his egoistic psychology. See Taylor (1965: 35–55). For a discussion of the tensions between Locke's voluntarist ethics and his theory of natural law, see Riley (1982: 63–91), and for an illustration of the tensions between Marx's determinism and his injunctions for action, see Mannheim's (1968: 49–171) struggles with Marx's theory of ideology.

aspects of his society while supposing that he is abstracting from the contingent to get at the essential springs of human action, when in truth there are no essential springs to be discovered in this way.[27]

Yet interpretation appears no less problematical from the standpoint of each of the other two paths. For the inventionist the interpretivist's equation of meaning with use introduces its own reductive determinisms. It seems to defy human capacities for creative innovation and aspirations for autonomy and thereby to miss what is compelling in the inventionist view. It has thus long been a standard critique of interpretivist views that their proponents are committed to a kind of relativistic determinism whereby if all human action is rule governed, yet also conventional and learned, everything we think and do is arbitrary. We are nothing more than the sum total of conventional behaviors that we have been taught; we might have learned different rules in different contexts and so might have been other beings with other values and purposes. This is why views like Wittgenstein's sometimes get labeled and attacked as variants of linguistic behaviorism.[28]

Those committed to the path of discovery will be quick to argue that interpretivist projects fail within their own terms for the reasons summed up in chapter 7 of this book: conventional meanings admit of so many conflicting interpretations that a political theory that has only them for a mooring will drift, if not everywhere, certainly too much to enable us to settle many, if any, of the core disputes of political argument and social theory.[29] From the standpoint of discovery the intrepretivist's eschewal of causal analysis involves an abdication of the scientific aspiration so complete that it appears to prevent its proponents from saying anything at all. It will often not even be evident to the discoverer what the point of interpretivist analysis is supposed to be, as evidenced by the mixture of bemusement and contempt with which many practicing social scientists and philosophers greet advocates of the turn to hermeneutics.

In short, the paths of invention, discovery, and interpretation all capture dimensions of the human condition so compelling that each can reveal the others to involve misleading reductions when developed into full-scale social and political theories. This should not surprise us much because if human beings are emergent from nature in the Polanyi-Bhaskar sense, we should expect considerations from each of Walzer's three paths to bear on human nature and action. We need a conception of politics that takes full account of what is plausible and attractive in each view while

27. See Rousseau (1964: 129–30).
28. See, for example, Chihara and Fodor (1966: 384–419).
29. See chapter 7, sections II and IV.

avoiding the reductionist trap inherent in committing ourselves to any. Put into the terms of analysis of chapter 7, if the neo-Kantians and new contextualists offer arguments that reduce, ultimately, to the paths of invention and interpretation, respectively, in rejecting both we must not appeal to the third reduction of discovery that will be vulnerable for all the reasons that lead people to take the paths of invention and interpretation to begin with. Rather we must find a view that incorporates the insights behind invention and interpretation while taking full account of what motivates the discoverer's enterprise.

(ii) The Aristotelian Ideal of an Integrated Life, Suitably Modified by Pragmatic Realist Considerations

The naturalist tradition traceable to Aristotle offers conceptual resources for this task that are superior to both the neo-Kantian and the contextualist outlooks discussed earlier in this book. Aristotle offers us a view of human nature and of social interaction that has elective affinities with the antireductionist social theory I have been defending, although I have no particular philosophical stake in declaring myself to be an Aristotelian and, as will quickly become clear, I think large parts of Aristotle's system are hopeless and have to be abandoned. Unlike MacIntyre, I do not believe that there is a gratifying geist lurking in the Aristotelian tradition that the history of modernity has rendered us all but incapable of grasping. Nonetheless I do contend with MacIntyre that Aristotle's *Nicomachean Ethics* generates both a philosophical psychology that is more plausible than the conventional liberal alternative and a regulative ideal of integrated living that political theorists can put to good critical use as long as they do not expect too much from it. After sketching this view in general terms, I explain why it stands in need of modification in three basic ways and then show how it takes full account of what is plausible and attractive in the paths of invention, discovery, and interpretation.

At the heart of Aristotle's ethics is the ideal of an entire human life. The Aristotelian *telos* of *eudaimonia* is usually translated as "happiness," but as Bernard Williams (1985: 34) points out, Aristotle was trying to refer to "the shape of one's whole life," not the transient psychic states that this utilitarian word has since come to connote. Thus Aristotle explicated the term by saying that it refers to the greatest good because it was "self-sufficient," which "by itself makes life desirable," and this in turn he explained to mean "not what is sufficient for oneself alone living a solitary life but for something that includes parents, wife and children, friends and fellow citizens" and extends over one's entire lifetime (Aristotle 1977: 73–74, 76). Williams suggests the term *well-being* instead, which is certainly closer to the core ideal of human thriving that Aristotle had in mind. I will talk of human thriving as involving the search for the possibility of integration not because I think that Williams is wrong here but because this captures more of the substance of what Aristotle took well-being to be about.[30]

The three main components of the ideal of a human life are those of practice, reciprocal interaction, and integration, all of which we encountered in our discussion of MacIntyre in chapter 5. As a first approximation we can say that practices are rule-governed, cooperative activities that structure human social interaction. They persist through time, typically preceding and surviving participants in them, although they are seldom left entirely unmarked or unaltered by those who interact through them. From the standpoint of any participant, practices are therefore irreducibly complex. They are inherently other regarding and normative in the sense that participation in a practice can be undertaken more or less well. They reflect our teleological natures in that we derive meaning and purpose in life by participating in practices and by being thought by other participants to excel in terms of the goods and values internal to particular practices.[31] They differ from Wittgenstein's language games in that their basic constitution may or may not be linguistic, and they are more than merely rule governed. The dimension of excellence in terms of which we perform more or less well implies that there is a purposive dimension to all action as realized through practices.

The term *reciprocal interaction* captures the notion that the practices we engage in are many, that their existence and perpetuation affect one another, and that the different practices in which we engage may make different and conflicting demands on us. Thus to excel in a profession governed by meritocratic competition may require a high degree of single-mindedness and indifference to the wants and needs of others, whereas to excel as a parent may require habits of mind and conduct, such as a developed capacity for empathy, that are antithetical to these. Because it is the same individual who participates in these various activities, we need to attend to the third component of the Aristotelian ideal, that of integration. *Unity* is the term often used by Aristotelians, which I resist for reasons that will shortly be clear. The goods that govern different practices are not reducible to one another via a single index, and there is not a form of The Good exemplifying that quality that all good things share in common.

30. See Williams (1985: 34–36).
31. For the argument that fulfillment is inherently other regarding because of man's inherently social nature, see Aristotle (1977: 74).

Yet if the different goods embodied in Aristotle's table of virtues and vices are not reducible to one another,[32] neither are they mutually irrelevant, as we have just seen. To explain how they are related, Aristotle makes a further distinction between two dimensions of goods: *intrinsic* (desirable in their own right) and *instrumental* (desirable because productive of some different good).[33] Most goods have both instrumental and intrinsic dimensions. Intelligence, sight, some pleasures and honors, for example, "are things which, even if we do pursue them on account of something else, nevertheless might be classed as good in themselves" (Aristotle 1977: 71). It is less than entirely clear whether a good could be exclusively instrumental for Aristotle. Although he never explicitly rules this out, neither does he discuss any such goods, and he seems to have in mind the idea that every purposive activity must at some level be desirable in its own right if it involves a good at all.[34] There can, however, in principle be goods that are only intrinsic, and these are "more final" than instrumental goods. The only truly final good is happiness, understood in the full-blown sense mentioned at the outset of this section. Although we pursue honor, pleasure, intelligence, and other good qualities generally, we choose them

> partly for themselves (because we should choose each one of them irrespectively of any consequences); but we choose them also for the sake of our happiness, in the belief that they will be instrumental in promoting it. On the other hand nobody chooses happiness for *their* sake, or in general for any other reason. (Ibid.: 73–74)

Happiness in this overarching sense is the most desirable good, "not reckoned as one item among many; if it were so reckoned, happiness would obviously be more desirable by the addition of even the least good." It is "something perfect and self-sufficient, being the end to which our actions are directed" (ibid.: 74).

The different and often mutually conflicting demands that different practices generate force on us a holistic logic as we try to cope with their competing imperatives. On an Aristotelian view the ways we organize family life, for instance, should be expected to have many consequences

32. See Aristotle (1977: 104–6).
33. In Aristotle's words, some things are good "in their own right, and others as means to secure these" (ibid.: 71, *see also* 73–74, 75).
34. Certainly purely instrumental goods would be ruled out if MacIntyre's account of internal and external goods is an accurate rendition of Aristotle's meaning because on MacIntyre's reading a practice can only be defined by reference to an internal good. See chapter 5, section I(iv).

for other dimensions of public and private life and vice versa. Adapting
Aristotle's argument to the categories of pragmatic realism, we might
think of all the practices that make up a life as parts of the underdetermined system that is embodied in Quine's field analogy discussed in chapter 2.[35] Aristotle's view is holist in a more full-blooded sense, which is
taken up and rejected shortly; note for now that it is a premise of his view
that a human life achieves meaning and coherence as a life only to the
extent that the various practices of which it is composed can be integrated
into a larger whole. The contrary tendency—toward fragmentation—is
incompatible with our basic teleological natures.[36] This is not to say that a
certain amount of compartmentalization among practices may not be desirable; it may be essential to their existence and integrity as independent
practices. It is to say, however, that attention to the logics of different practices and to the competing demands they place on individuals, where they
do, will be essential to the processes of mutual adjustment needed to approach the living of an integrated life. The richness of a life may depend
on the number and kinds of different practices at which one is able to
excel, but unless their demands can be met in mutually reinforcing ways,
the satisfaction that comes from them will be without larger point and will
to that extent tend to be neurotic rather than fulfilling.

(a) *Rethinking Practices and Their Integration.* Yet the ideal of an integrated life as Aristotle understood it stands in need of three kinds of
modification. First, practices are to be thought of more generally than
either Aristotle or MacIntyre conceives of them. We are bound to reject
Aristotle's particular list of the virtues and vices, which turns out to be
culture- and class-specific, as do the lists of latter-day Aristotelians like
MacIntyre. Thus MacIntyre is uncomfortable with aspects of Aristotle's
view about the appropriateness of hierarchy, his treatment of the structure
of the family, and the roles of women and slaves. Yet MacIntyre wants
simply to replace Aristotle's class- and culture-specific list with his own,
as we saw. Although he begins by defining a practice generally to include
"any coherent and complex form of socially established cooperative human activity through which goods internal to that activity are realized"
(MacIntyre 1984: 187), he rules out many activities that meet his general
definition. He says that bricklaying is not a practice whereas architecture
is, for reasons that escape me entirely, and, less trivially (although the
preceding example would seem outrageous to many a self-respecting
bricklayer), that ancient politics consisted of practices but that modern

35. See chapter 2, section I(ii).
36. On the teleological structure of human psychology, see Aristotle (1977: 63,
203, 204, 205–6, 210).

politics do not.[37] This kind of neo-Aristotelian view is hopelessly vulnerable; any particular list of virtues and vices will quickly be unmasked by opponents as idiosyncratic and arbitrary.

I want to preserve the *structure* of Aristotle's account of human psychology, not its particular content; I therefore define a practice quite generally as a learned, rule-regulated, and satisfying cooperative activity, governed by norms internal to it. We cannot come up with philosophical criteria for ruling out some list of activities that meet this definition; neither is it possible to say with Aristotle and MacIntyre that certain practices are inherently undesirable or bad in themselves for philosophical reasons.[38] Any attempt to do this will ultimately be revealed to be arbitrary, reflective of the idiosyncratic values of the theorist or of some subculture, usually but not always an elite one, within the society. Even Aristotle's regulative ideal of moderation can be defended, to the extent that it can, not on the grounds that there is anything inherently desirable about moderation but because lackluster or excessive pursuit of the goods internal to a given practice generally has deleterious effects on the rest of one's life. Beyond this the doctrine of the mean must be abandoned.[39]

The foregoing does not imply that every practice is desirable. What makes a practice desirable or undesirable for an individual depends partly on whether and to what extent it is compatible with the living of an integrated life. The argumentative burden confronted by the would-be critic of a particular practice is to demonstrate why and in what ways it undermines this possibility; that of its would-be defender is to establish the contrary case. This is not the only constraint in the evaluation of practices; we will see shortly that other-regarding considerations inevitably enter as well and in chapter 9 that in general there are good reasons for opposing hierarchical practices. Practices are not morally neutral, but their moral value or lack of it, although partly dependent on meeting internal criteria for the integrity of a practice, can only be fully evaluated by reference to the ideal of integration that they either foster and promote or weaken and undermine. If a woman who is a conventional wife and mother in our society embarks on a career, for example, the additional and competing demands placed on her will necessitate a redefinition of family roles and therefore of critical argument about those roles with the other participants. This will be a double argument about the intrinsic desirability of new modes of doing things versus the old and about the instrumental desirability of it for the overall lives of the relevant participants. If such

37. See chapter 5, section II(i).
38. See Aristotle (1977: 102–3) and chapter 5, section II(i).
39. Here I agree with Williams (1985: 36).

a change in practices starts to be entertained on a large scale, conventional expectations about the norms governing family life will doubtless begin to shift; this is the stuff of everyday moral and political argument.

An implication of this view is that moral argument about the desirability or otherwise of particular practices will have a large empirical component: it will concern the feasibility of alternatives, the causal implications of some practices for others that we may or may not value, whether and to what extent particular practices might be self-defeating, and what distributive and other material conditions they might require to exist as practices. These factors will vary with time and circumstance, placing substantial limits on what can be said about the desirability of particular practices as a matter of philosophy.

Having rejected Aristotle's a priori list of the virtues and vices and the doctrine of the mean, we must confront the possibility MacIntyre evaded: that so much becomes loaded onto the notion of integration that it is in danger of collapsing. Bernard Williams is now free to ask, for instance, what if an integrated life is possible that is perfectly disgusting? Any theoretical account that links the ethical to psychological health through the idea of integration, he points out, potentially confronts this problem. Its defender is bound to contend with the figure,

> rarer perhaps than Callicles supposed, but real, who is horrible enough and not miserable at all but, by any ethological standard of the bright eye and the gleaming coat, dangerously flourishing. For those who want to ground the ethical life in psychological health, it is something of a problem that there can be such people at all. (Williams 1985: 47, 46)

If the idea of an integrated life is the bridging concept between psychology and moral philosophy, how do we cope with the possibility that "the best way of integrating some people would be to make them more ruthless" (ibid.: 47)?[40]

Any naturalist account has to live with this possibility, but it is only one of several possibilities. Naturalists who are squeamish about it often

---

40. Williams also makes a different objection to the idea of integration, treating it as a mechanism for reducing conflict and asking whether conflict might not under certain circumstances be desirable (Williams 1985: 45–47). This seems to me to rest on a mistaken conflation. One could entertain an Aristotelian argument to the effect that a degree of conflict is necessary for an integrated life, perhaps for the very reason that Williams supplies, yet still insist that a life that consisted of *nothing but* conflict would be less than optimal. A full defense of my critical naturalist view will have to take up this and related questions at length.

try to get around it by assumption. Their arguments usually involve holding variants of the claim that the life of an Eichmann or a Stalin could not have been an integrated one, that they must at some deep level have been miserable. Likewise, it is often said that people who demean others must somehow be projecting their own unconscious self-hatred, or that the working classes are shortsighted, prejudice-ridden, and boorish because they are alienated from their true natures by alterable social conditions. Any general theoretical argument of this kind must fail. There may be situations in which particular claims of the sort just adduced turn out to be true, but to hold as a theoretical matter that this must be so amounts to reintroducing a priori assumptions about the benevolent unity of the virtues that there is no good reason to believe warranted. Whether and to what extent utterly ruthless behavior, to pursue Williams's example, is conducive to an individual's or group's thriving is an open question, and the evidence from evolutionary biology on this point is mixed.[41]

Yet there are reasons for doubting that utterly ruthless, hawkish behavior is conducive to human thriving, deriving from my earlier discussion of the values enshrined in practices. Despite what Williams says about the egocentric character of Aristotle's ethics,[42] my discussion of practices in chapter 5 revealed one of the advantages of the Aristotelian view to be its recognition of man's inherent sociality, which renders the Aristotelian view of human psychology more plausible than the standard liberal alternative. At a deep level our actions should be understood as other referential on this view because part of what it means to excel within a practice is to be thought well of by others who engage in it. This dimension of human action cannot be captured by the typical Enlightenment reductionisms that treat people as one-dimensional maximizers, whether of power (Hobbes), pleasure (Bentham), preferences (contemporary neoclassicists), or primary goods (Rawls). We are not Whiggish enough to have the rational life plans of Rawlsian theory or the ranked preference orderings of utilitarianism. One reason that enterprises that presume the contrary seem both artificial and unattractive is that almost no one is a one-dimensional maximizer of this sort, and those who do come close to fitting the model are often among the narrowest, most egocentric, and unenviable people we know. That we want to do well in terms valued by others whom we value makes the theory of human psychology behind the notion of individual maximization inherently suspect. We do not know what we want without reference to others, and then set about trying to achieve it

41. As Williams (1985: 44, 209n13) notes.
42. Ibid.: 35–36.

by putting to work the canons of instrumental rationality. More typically, we do not know what we want until we know what others want whose approbation we seek and whose disapprobation we fear and how they perceive us. And they are in positions comparable to ours. This is one reason Hegel's story about the master/slave dialectic has been so enduring.[43] It is not the suggestion that relations of bondage will be unstable because they are oppressive from the slave's standpoint that we find illuminating. It is the claim that the master will find the relations unsatisfactory that seems pregnant with psychological insight; he needs recognition from those he values.[44]

One can concede that people want recognition from those they value and therefore regard as moral equals, at least, and still fail to come to terms with Williams's objection. A gang of disgusting rogues might well respect and afford recognition to one another without ceasing to be a gang of disgusting rogues. Although possible in principle, there are good reasons for suspecting that this is something of a philosopher's example, for it seems doubtful that a gang of true rogues would be able to maintain the degree of mutual trust necessary for the maintenance of even minimal cooperation.[45] Bloom and MacIntyre, we saw, invoked cousins of the rogue argument on a societywide—tending toward worldwide—basis, arguing that people have become incapable of moral life on so massive a scale that they are no longer able even to grasp that these are their circumstances.[46] Likewise, some members of the Frankfurt school were famous for the view that the social alienation wrought by late capitalism was so all-embracing that people could no longer comprehend what was wrong, that their interests could not be appealed to in the classical Marxist sense because of the extent to which they had been seduced by the consumerist and atomizing culture of modernity.[47] Less apocalyptically, people who were appalled by

43. See Hegel (1977: 111–19).

44. The Hegelian argument about recognition is sometimes thought of as the naturalist's answer to the Eichmann problem, but this claim is dubious at best because the recognition Eichmann sought was not from the Jews whom he brutalized but from peers and superiors whom he was trying to impress with his zeal and efficiency. I argue in chapter 9, however, that we do have a different and more general response to the Eichmann problem; it turns on divorcing the Aristotelian notion of a practice from assumptions about the legitimacy of hierarchy with which it has traditionally been associated. See chapter 9, section II(i)(a).

45. I am indebted to Christopher Lasch on this point.

46. See chapter 4, section I(ii), and chapter 5, section I(iii).

47. Habermas's early work makes arguments of this sort, although they are buttressed by claims that the classical contradictions Marx had identified in nineteenth-century capitalism were failing to work themselves out because technology has now become an independent source of surplus value. See Habermas (1973: 195–252, especially 221–32).

the Don't Worry! Be Happy! ideology of the Reagan years often had comparable arguments and assumptions in mind.

A difficulty with all such claims is that if we assume them to be true, it is difficult to comprehend the source of the moral outrage they generate. If people have, by hypothesis, found ways to live integrated lives on a mass scale, it is difficult to justify the view that this is objectionable merely on the grounds that we find the particular forms of integration they have discovered displeasing. There must be some additional argument, however implicit, concerning the self-defeating character of their striving, or its external effects on third parties, before such arguments can have any plausible critical bite.[48]

Yet, Williams's objection to the naturalist commitment to the modified Aristotelian view begins to look less worrisome when we consider the main alternatives to it.[49] On the one hand, deontological theorists who aspire to deduce an entire ethics from the idea of an autonomous will typically wind up with subjectivist conceptions of individual preferences that are by definition immune to paternalistic criticism, as Sidgwick's critique of Kant long ago made clear.[50] Contextualists, on the other hand, confront even more serious difficulties in this regard than deontologists or modern naturalists. The deontologist can at least appeal to the idea of universalizability, and through it respect for the autonomy of others, as a normative ideal that places some limits on what can be construed as an acceptable action (even if the problems of institutionalizing it turn out to be insurmountable).[51] The naturalist I have been describing has the regulative ideal of an integrated life and its prudential and moral imperatives to which to appeal (even if it is conceded that the content of these imperatives

48. My discussions of Bloom and MacIntyre also revealed that when the empirical claims that drive such massive cultural generalizations are subjected to serious scrutiny, they seldom survive long. See chapter 4, section II(i), and chapter 5, section II(ii).

49. I do not claim to have given due consideration here to the rich texture of Williams's positive antifoundational thesis, which activity would take me too far afield. I hope to take it up in detail in the future.

50. It remains a core problem in much contemporary deontological theory. For discussion of Sidgwick's objection to Kant, see Rawls (1971: 254–55). For a more general critique of Kant's ethics, see Williams (1985: 54–70). For examples of the obsession with avoiding paternalistic judgments and its consequences in the work of Nozick and Rawls, see Shapiro (1986: 157–64, 206–18, 273–305), in that of Wolff, see Shapiro (1989a: 55–56), in that of Buchanan and Tullock and other contemporary public choice theorists, see Shapiro (1989b). In moral philosophy the difficulties of coping with the need to avoid all paternalistic judgments are well-illustrated by Hare's wranglings with his "fanatics." See Hare (1963: 106, 110, 112, 153, 159–85, 192–200, 219–22).

51. For discussion of why, see Shapiro (1986: 273–305).

may vary with time and circumstance). But the contextualist has nothing at all, and Williams's objection thus becomes all the more devastating for her.

In short, the evidence for objectionable values as necessary or even adequate to integrated lives is mixed, the need for valued recognition from others appears to be a powerful drive in human beings that may be argued to generate constraints on individual action both prudential and moral, and the treatment of objectionable values in the major alternative traditions appears even more problematical than that in my modified Aristotelian account. As a result, this view seems at least worth taking seriously and exploring further as a basis for critical argument in politics.

(b) The Ambiguous Character of Human Teleology. A second necessary modification of Aristotle's argument has to do with its implicit theory of human psychology. My analysis in chapter 5 concluded that MacIntyre had made a persuasive case that human beings are basically narrative and teleological creatures. In our brute psychological perhaps even physiological structures, virtually everything we do has a purposive quality, and action lacking such a quality appears to be without moral or point. "The originative cause" of every action, as Aristotle put it, "is the purpose for which it is done." In every human endeavor "there is a sort of target," and it is with his eyes on it that a person "stretches or relaxes his string." No process "is set going by mere thought—only by purposive and practical thought," and everyone who makes anything "makes it for some purpose, and the product is not an end in itself but only a relative or particular end" (Aristotle 1977: 210, 203, 205–6).[52]

Yet there are paradoxical tensions in our natures deriving from the human capacities for conscious innovation and critical self-reflection that mean we are teleological creatures of a quite unusual sort. Although human beings are bound to live and comprehend their lives in essentially narrative form, to try to live well by making their lives into good stories, it is in the nature of a narrative that it cannot be what it is until it is complete. We cannot strictly say that someone has lived a well-integrated life until it is over.[53] This means that as we live our lives they inevitably

52. See also Aristotle (1977: 62, 97–98, 204, 210). There can, no doubt, be nonteleological actions like daydreaming and doodling (though even these might turn out to serve some purposive function of resting or distracting the mind), but the trivial nature of such examples indicates how little human action can seriously be thought of as lacking a purposive character.

53. Aristotle (1977: 76, 82–85) himself made this point, arguing that his doctrine of happiness or well-being could only apply to a person over an entire lifetime. Because of his assumptions about the invariance of the virtues, Aristotle did not draw the same implications from this fact as I do below.

have an open-ended and underdetermined quality that is partly—though only partly—dependent on how we live them. To the extent that narrative unity is essential to pointful existence, then, whether and what point there is to our lives will always be something of an open question.[54] This is true of every narrative creature at some level, but human beings have to come to terms with knowing it and, indeed, with the creative dimension of our natures being such that we would not likely want it to be otherwise.

This suggests that we should not be surprised to discover tendencies in ourselves that are at odds with our teleological natures. A dog is a paradigm-case teleological creature in that it has absolute affinity with its purposes; when they are frustrated it suffers, when they are not it thrives. One cannot think of a healthy dog whose needs are being properly met as dissatisfied. Yet the fact that you would not expect your child to be like your dog in this respect indicates our deep ambivalence toward our teleological natures. In short, we have capacities for critical self-reflection that are at odds with our basic teleological psychologies, and the tensions this generates mean, among other things, that we may develop expectations from social life that we can never satisfy.[55]

Aristotle managed to avoid these issues by treating his account of the virtues as complete and invariant. This made possible his claim that we do not deliberate about ends but only about the means for their attainment, for "nobody deliberates about things that are invariable" (Aristotle 1977: 209).[56] MacIntyre manages to avoid confronting the tensions endemic to human teleology by arguing throughout as if whatever alienation people feel from their purposes is a parochial product of modernity, that human beings could in principle live happy lives in Aristotle's sense even if this

54. See Kermode (1967) and Erikson (1969) on the significance of the sense of an ending to narrative understanding.

55. Mill seems to have had this in mind when he remarked: "It is indisputable that the being whose capacities of enjoyment are low has the greatest chance of having them fully satisfied; and a highly endowed being will always feel that any happiness which he can look for, as the world is constituted, is imperfect. But he can learn to bear its imperfections, if they are at all bearable; and they will not make him envy the being who is indeed unconscious of the imperfections, but only because he feels not at all the good which those imperfections qualify. It is better to be a human being dissatisfied than a pig satisfied; better to be Socrates dissatisfied than a fool satisfied. And if the fool, or the pig, are of a different opinion, it is because they only know their own side of the question. The other party to the comparison knows both sides" (Mill 1971: 19–20).

56. Thus, "A doctor does not deliberate whether to cure his patient, nor a speaker whether to persuade his audience, nor a statesman whether to produce law and order; nor does anyone else deliberate about the end at which he is aiming. They first set some end before themselves, and then proceed to consider how and by what means it can be attained" (Aristotle 1977: 119, *see also* 118, 204).

means coming to terms with their tragic dimensions (of which Aristotle had failed, in MacIntyre's view, to take adequate account). MacIntyre thus regards it as a distinctive feature of modernity that conflict and disagreement are merely managed because we have come to lack the "shared moral first principles" (MacIntyre 1984: 253) to resolve them.[57] Having rejected these views, we are forced to live with the fact that our teleological natures have the built-in potential to seem profoundly problematical to all human beings, as do the institutions through which they seek to realize them.

(c) Rejecting Natural Harmony. The third way in which the Aristotelian view stands in need of modification concerns the interactive logic among and within natural and social systems. Specifically, not only must Aristotle's assumptions about the natural harmony of the universe be rejected but so must latter-day versions of the natural harmony thesis as, for example, most famously in Adam Smith's "invisible hand" theory of markets. Voltaire's dictum that all is for the best in the best of all possible worlds can have meaning, at best, as an ironic expression of fatalism (which he arguably intended it to be) not as an affirmation of the Enlightenment's faith in a logic of harmonious progress somehow embedded in the nature of things. As a theoretical matter we are bound to concede that invisible hands can as well be malevolent as benign.[58] There is no a priori reason to believe in Wolff's Whiggish faith that there must be a rational way to organize social interaction to the mutual benefit of all, and the weight of accumulated historical evidence leaves those who would defend this view with a heavy burden of argument. No system of human organization or political economy has yet been discovered that operates to the mutual benefit of all, that does not have deleterious external effects, or that can regulate itself, and there is no theoretical reason to believe that such a system could be invented or discovered. The story of war, starvation, exploitation, and destruction on an unprecedented scale that is the history of the twentieth century makes it scarcely even thinkable that there is a natural tendency toward harmony in human events or that human history exhibits a teleology of progress that will at some future time make harmony possible. We are only justified in assuming the existence of harmony in the longest of runs and the trivialest of senses, when, as Keynes quipped, we will all be dead. As we saw in chapter 7, zero-sum

57. See chapter 5, sections I(iv) and II(i).

58. In the case of markets we know enough about their self-destructive tendencies—toward insufficient demand, structural unemployment, and monopoly pricing—as well as about their devastating external effects (human and environmental) to see that the price paid for their innovative productive power and efficiency is substantial.

conflict is endemic to much human interaction: only an act of faith that flies in the face of the evidence of human history and psychology makes it possible to deny this.[59]

For those of us unwilling or unable to make such a commitment of faith, the absence of assumptions about natural tendencies toward harmonious equilibrium or progress has far-reaching implications for the moral ideal of an integrated life for both the individual and society. Whether and to what extent a person can achieve an integrated life is an empirical question, depending on her evolved needs and modes of satisfying them and on how the practices individuals engage in affect one another and the nonhuman environment, which is itself evolving as they interact with it. We are evolutionary creatures whose actions partly shape our evolving natures, though in ways that we can seldom fully comprehend (let alone control or even predict), and we have no reason to believe this evolution conforms to a preestablished script and every reason to doubt that it does. For these reasons we may generate mutually incompatible needs as individuals (where the practices we engage in to satisfy one need lead to the frustration of another) or zero-sum needs as groups (where the practices engaged in by A in order to satisfy his needs limit or make it impossible for B to satisfy her needs). We may be lethal mutations of nature or, at least, we have to live with the possibility that however successfully we have evolved in the past, we might become lethal mutations in the future. For once we jettison Aristotle's assumptions about natural harmony as well as their rationalist Enlightenment reincarnations, we are constrained to deal with the external effects of the actions of others and their impacts on our evolving capacities to live more or less integrated lives.

(iii) The Ideal of an Integrated Life and
Antireductionist Political Theory

Now we are in a position to see that the modified Aristotelian account just sketched is fully consistent with the antireductionist view laid out earlier in this chapter.[60] The simplest way to do so is to notice how my view takes full account of what is plausible in each of Walzer's three paths of moral philosophy—invention, discovery, and interpretation—yet is reducible to none of them. Neither is it vulnerable to the standard criticisms that each generates.

The modified ideal of an integrated life takes into account, to begin, that human beings are natural entities, which typically drives projects of

59. See chapter 7, section II.
60. See sections I(ii) and II(i) above.

discovery. Like all biologically based life we are subject to natural imperatives to survive and thrive. But for creatures with our cognitive capacities,
this generates an impetus to try to understand what kinds of creatures we
are as well as the environments, natural and social, in which our strivings
must take place. Thus although we are subject to natural imperatives, we
are not reducible to those imperatives; we are emergent from nature in
the Polanyi-Bhaskar sense. This suggests that although attempts to understand our natural imperatives play an essential part in moral deliberation and argument about the organization of social and political life, no
political theory can be read off from an understanding of those natural
imperatives, no matter how extensive and profound that understanding
might be. It also means that the naturalist commitment does not require
us to stay either with the strand of natural law theory appealed to by
Bloom, which holds by assumption that there are timeless universals in
nature that are pregnant with moral and political significance, or with any
of the architectonic systems of social science, whether Hobbes's, Bentham's, or Marx's.

I am committed to the view that biologically based life is bound to seek
to survive and thrive and the argument that the characteristically human
form this takes involves the self-conscious search for the possibility of
integrated lives. But by itself this regulative ideal generates few conclusions about how social and political life ought to be structured. It might
help us rule out certain practices and ways of engaging in them if they can
be shown to be self-defeating or incompatible with other activities conducive to the living of integrated lives, but it will likely be heavily underdetermined with respect to positive action in many circumstances.[61] Beyond this it will often not be obvious what the best course of action is—if
there is one—for an individual or a society. As I argued in chapter 3, pragmatic adaptive creatures like us get through life as often as not by avoiding
what fails, shying away from the manifestly dangerous, and repeating and
relying on things that appear to have worked in the past.[62] For although I
have just used the term *seek* to describe human attempts at thriving, I
mean it only in the evolutionary biologist's heuristic sense of the term,
which is compatible with the notion that our strivings are critically affected by random events, hit-and-miss maneuvers, and other forms of
negative adaption.

The modified Aristotelian view takes account of the human capacity for
conscious choice and creative innovation, which generally motivates

61. Williams (1985: 44–45) usefully makes this point.
62. See chapter 3, section II(i).

people to choose the path of invention in political theory, in two different ways. First, it treats people as developmental creatures in the conventional Aristotelian sense discussed by MacIntyre.[63] Human beings are conceived of neither as passive mechanisms that respond to external stimuli nor as programmed entities whose future behavior is determined at conception. We do respond to stimuli, and our genetic structure does shape and condition everything we do; however, as creatures who have to learn the skills needed for the characteristically human forms of surviving and thriving, and who can do that learning more and less well, not only does innovative action become an inescapable part of human living but so does a degree of conscious choice as soon as people begin to grasp what learning entails.

Second, the modified Aristotelian view takes account of the innovative dimension through the role it assigns to the capacity for critical self-reflection. Although we are in the psychological sense discussed earlier teleological creatures, we saw that we have the capacity to think critically about our particular purposes and, to a degree, to choose among them. Indeed, I suggested that our critical capacities and partial understandings of our circumstances make it inevitable that we do so. It is a source of our notions of autonomy and responsibility that we take actions that constrain and shape human futures in circumstances where we know that we could have done otherwise. Yet political theory can no more be reduced to a theory about those choices than human beings can be reduced to their innovative dimensions. This is why contractarian arguments in all their forms are in the end unconvincing. As those who walk the path of discovery never tire of pointing out, we are radically constrained in what we can consent to by the powers and resources at our disposal, and no known system has ever come or could come into existence as a result of a contractual agreement. As a result doctrines that reify consent in their foundational myths will tend to be biased toward whatever status quo happens to prevail, hiding this behind the guise of a voluntarist ideology.[64]

From the standpoint of my modified Aristotelian ideal, we can concede the force of these criticisms and endorse them but still maintain that an account of human freedom and how to foster it must be part of any viable political theory. We cannot live characteristically human lives, we cannot be ourselves, without exercising freedom and self-conscious choice, yet this can only be done by seeking to understand what we cannot change

63. See chapter 5, section I(iii).
64. For extended defenses of this view relating to the seventeenth-century and contemporary contractarians, see Shapiro (1986: 273–305), relating to Posner, see Shapiro (1987: 999–1046), and relating to contemporary democratic theory, see Shapiro (1989b).

and accept it. Then we will be better placed to think and argue about what we can choose to change in our lives and whether or not we should.

Finally, although the modified Aristotelian ideal requires accepting that we are in a significant sense conventional creatures, the conventionalist aspect of my account is tacitly dependent, in Polanyi's sense, on other dimensions that limit and condition the forms that conventional behavior can take. Theories like Rorty's that try to reduce all political life (indeed all life) to the conventional dimension are rightly criticized by discoverers for their failure to take account of the extralinguistic and, more generally, the extraconventional dimensions that condition the conventional and linguistic dimensions. Inventors also rightly point out that, while living through conventional systems and practices, we will confront choices that will not be fully determined by conventional meanings. But my view is vulnerable to neither charge. It is conventionalist in treating people as inherently social and other regarding and in conceding the learned and performative character of much human action. But it also takes into account that we have the capacity, even the need, to think critically about conventional behavior, even if never from a tabula rasa point of view. My account rests on the pragmatic realist view that critical thinking about conventional practices requires grasping more than conventional meanings. It has to reach outward and comprehend as fully as possible the dimensions external to the conventional realm that shape it, even as the conventional realm shapes them.

9 Principled Criticism and the Democratic Political Ethos

It might appear that few consequences for politics can follow from the argument of the last chapter. A claim that there is a human interest in surviving and thriving might plausibly be argued to rule out certain kinds of self-destructive political arrangements, but it is difficult—as Williams says—to see how it could generate much beyond this. The substance of my modified Aristotelian account seems, if anything, to place even more formidable obstacles in the path of any general constructive account. I recognized that the goods governing human practices vary with time and circumstance, that people have capacities critically to question their purposes and even to shape them to a degree, and that there is no rational or naturally best way of ordering human practices, internally or as they relate to one another. If these claims are true, it would appear that our expectations in the matter of constructive conclusions cannot reasonably be great, for it seems unlikely that much positive can be said in general terms about the political organization of society.

My goal in this final chapter is to establish that—contrary to these appearances—illuminating conclusions for politics and political argument do follow from the account here developed. I begin by arguing that there is a basic human interest in knowing and acting on the truth, in acting *authentically*, and I show how this claim flows out of the argument of the previous chapter. To say that people have an interest in knowing and acting on the truth is not to say that they always have an impetus so to act; for reasons having to do with inertia, ignorance, and ideology (among others), people often neither know nor act on the truth in specific situations, and sometimes they even actively cause the truth to be obscured. There is thus a certain looseness to the link between authentic action and human adaptive behavior, and there may be circumstances in which inauthentic action will be adaptively effective. Nonetheless, I contend that

265

the human interest in knowing and acting on the truth cannot reasonably be dispensed with and that people generally do not want to dispense with it. Indeed, I suggest that the gaps between the lived realities of everyday practices and the requirements of authentic action often motivate the critical enterprise and supply it with normative bite.

Next, I take up the political implications of the human interest in authentic action. Given my accounts of the limits to social scientific knowledge, the variety and sources of human values, and the ineradicable presence of conflict and domination in social life, I argue that the human interest in authentic action is likely to be best served by a commitment to a democratic ethos of a particular sort. I sketch a view of politics that makes it ever-present in human interaction and argue that it is democracy's principled hostility to hierarchy and to claims of political expertise that makes it uniquely attractive as a system of political organization, despite major difficulties that have been discovered in recent years in the logic of democracy as a representative or participatory system of government. Democracy as I describe it is better thought of as an ethic of opposition than a system of government.

Finally, I turn to the implications of my account for the conduct of political theory. I portray the theorist's task as twofold: describing and justifying the most appropriate system of basic institutional arrangements and engaging in principled criticism of the social practices carried on within them. Principled criticism as I describe it is itself a social practice, geared toward the promotion of authentic action. Its characteristic mode of operation is to find out and articulate the truth about the power dimensions of social practices, usually by placing commonsense understandings in a wider causal context.

I. The Impulse Toward Critical Reflection and the Human Interest in Knowing and Acting on the Truth

Critical thinking is to a degree inescapable for human beings because we adapt and evolve as forms of life partly by using our cognitive faculties to achieve, reorder, and in some cases construct our goals. Yet there are more concrete reasons why critical thinking about the fundamentals of social and political arrangements is all but inescapable for human beings, as can be seen by reference to my three modifications to Aristotle's view discussed in chapter 8.

First, in rejecting the idea that any particular list of virtues is inherently desirable, I took the view that many questions about how we ought to live can never be settled even in principle. Aristotelians like MacIntyre evade these implications, arguing that endemic disagreement stemming from incommensurable premises is a parochial (and, by implication, alterable) fact about modernity, but we saw that this is not a plausible claim, historical or theoretical.[1] That people often engage in forms of rational moral argument while failing to resolve their differences is not so paradoxical as MacIntyre supposes. It indicates in some instances that people may be committed to particular views for ideological reasons that they seek to legitimate with the forms of rationalist defense; in some instances that they may be skeptical of other protagonists' motives for holding *their* views, which are thus challenged on reasoned grounds; in some instances that people have genuine disagreements that they are seeking to delineate as best they can; and in some instances that they do not know what their views on such subjects are or should be—they are struggling to come to grips with an issue and reconcile it with their other commitments. Anyone who watches the CNN current affairs program "Crossfire" will have seen each of these logics at work, sometimes simultaneously, in arguments that protagonists obviously do not expect to resolve. Once we abandon the notion that there once were right answers to the political problems that throw themselves up in social life, right answers that we could discover if only we had not been ruined by the emotivism of modernity, that people might have to struggle endlessly with and argue over the moral and political problems that throw themselves up in daily life can scarcely be surprising.

Second, in modifying Aristotle's account of human psychology to include the capacity to reflect on our purposive natures and so introducing into it the likelihood of enduring ambivalences about human purposes and modes of satisfying them, I suggested the likelihood of a degree of inevitable chafing about existing political arrangements. Aristotle seems to have thought that critical reflection of the highest form—theoretical reason—could be circumscribed into the realm of philosophy, and indeed there are readings of both Plato and Aristotle that suggest that failure to wall it off from civic concerns (which latter are governed by practical reason in Aristotle's scheme) will both have catastrophic effects on the stability of civic institutions and undermine the activity of theoretical reflection itself.[2] Aristotle thought of practical reason as geared toward maintaining the stability of civic institutions through moral education and habituation. But such a view wrongly assumes that there is nothing problematical

1. See chapter 5, section II(i).
2. See the discussion of Bloom in chapter 4, section I(i). As Rogers Smith reminds me, there are alternative readings of Aristotle on this point.

about what people should be taught in the civic realm, that they will not rightly come to believe that much of what they have been weaned on can and should be questioned.[3] Once we abandon the suggestion that what practical reason should teach is self-evident (stemming either from the ordered nature of things or from some idiosyncratic interpretation of conventions or traditions), we are bound to see that what political arrangements should prevail will invariably be subject to controversy. We no longer have any reason to believe that the fundamentals of social and political organization ever were or could be set straight in the way that Aristotle assumed that they could be or as contemporary commentators like Bloom and MacIntyre take it for granted in their different ways that they can. We have to accept that everything is up for grabs even if not simultaneously.

Third, the impetus toward critical reflection is reinforced by the fact that we have no particular reason to believe in the existence of harmonies, whether natural or constructed, in the social and physical worlds with which we are intertwined.[4] We saw in chapter 8 that naturalism is not to be confused with natural law theory where this is understood to imply a belief in the existence of timeless universals that drive or regulate the world "from behind the scenes."[5] Nor does the naturalist commitment imply a belief in a precultural human essence that does or can or should govern actual behavior. Human beings are naturally conventional creatures; any theory of their nature has to account for the centrality of culturally acquired characteristics. Human beings are also naturally evolving animals; many aspects of their circumstances, themselves, and their options and interests change. Naturalists have generally shied away from these facts or seen them as obstacles to be avoided somehow with fancy methodological devices, but they must be basic to any credible view of the human condition. The philosophical psychology sketched in the last chapter tries to get at the relatively enduring characteristics of the structure of human nature that constrain and condition innovative action, but they cannot be declared to be beyond the contingencies of human culture and evolution because nothing in the end is beyond them. It is possible that the structure of human psychology itself evolves over time.[6]

Whether and how we survive in the evolving universe of structures

---

3. Williams (1985: 35–38) and others have pointed this out. For my discussion of this view as it relates to Bloom's argument, see chapter 4, sections II(ii) and (iv).

4. See chapter 8, section II(ii)(c).

5. See chapter 8, section II(iii).

6. See chapter 8, section I(ii).

that we partly shape as they shape us is a question of our future histories, not of a priori theory. Many of the causal processes in which we are caught up are opaque to us; parts of them, most likely, always will be. Yet we have seen that we do have the resources to understand aspects of them, and the hope that we can expand that understanding in various ways supplies a basic motivation for reasoned reflection. On my critical naturalist view we embrace that part of the Enlightenment ethos that commits us to the possibility of scientific knowledge of ourselves and our circumstances, but we remain skeptical of the optimism in which the Enlightenment view of science was shrouded. We should be modernists in embracing the critical scientific stance toward the world, but this commitment should make us skeptical of the mindless faith in progress that has informed so much Enlightenment thought—liberal and antiliberal—over the past several centuries.[7] There is no reason to expect that a complete or architectonic understanding of the world and our place in it will ever be achieved or that the growth of knowledge will bring with it greater human freedom. Knowledge may be power, as Bacon said, but it is a more many-sided and ambiguous kind of power than he could possibly have realized. We have an impetus to attain knowledge to survive and thrive, but knowledge can as easily be a master as a servant and may well in the end cause us to unleash forces that will lead to our own destruction.

Yet we must be mindful that our rejection of the Enlightenment's optimism and faith in progress does not lump us with an equally unfounded pessimism and mindless conservatism, issuing in a wholesale rejection of what critical reflection and the expansion of knowledge can be expected to do for us. Although there is no reason to believe in a natural harmony that would be well functioning if we could somehow not interfere with it, we can scarcely avoid the quest to make our innovative action be better informed by critical understanding. We are finite creatures of limited powers, struggling to survive and thrive as best we can in a world of secular processes on which we can have some limited influence. These processes may be benign or malevolent from our point of view, and we have to be ever ready to adapt to the ways in which they change and the ways in which we change them and change because of them. An analogy to corks bobbing on the ocean would overstate our impotence; finite as our powers are we can often use them to good advantage. But we have to keep our wits about us, we have to be street smart and nimble of foot to deal with and put to good use whatever might come along next. This need reinforces the

---

7. For an exhaustive critical discussion of the idea of progress and its history, see Lasch (1990).

impetus to think critically in yet another way, for the most effective uses of our powers require that we understand what we can and cannot achieve. "A man," as Clint Eastwood reminds us in *Magnum Force*, "has got to know his limitations."

A skeptic might grant these arguments yet still remain less than fully persuaded that in general people have an interest in knowing and acting on the truth. If one conceived of human nature as utterly instrumental, for example, one might say that as soon as it has been conceded that there is plenty of zero-sum conflict in the world, the beneficiaries of that conflict may well generate motives to obscure the truth by use of ideological argument or at least avoid articulating it. If I am an exploiter rather than an exploitee, I have no particular reason to care about the truth on this view. On the contrary, I should be afraid of it if it can be used to undermine my ideological claims and rationalizations. The difficulty with such arguments is that they rest on too mechanical a conception of the relations between interests and ideologies. They might be argued to be consistent, for instance, with crude versions of Marxism that maintain that because the truth is decisively on the side of the working class, the bourgeoisie cannot simultaneously pursue its interests and be committed to the truth; its position in the structure of things necessitates that its members engage in continual obfuscation of the nature and purposes of their actions.[8] Such claims take too little account of the extent to which, willy-nilly, we all become implicated in one another's activities.

We are implicated in one another's activities in the first instance because we are to a degree cooperatively involved with others in the production and consumption of resources that are inherently scarce. It is true that there is no way of organizing social life that is neutral in its allocation of benefits and burdens, yet it is also true that most forms of organizing society fall notably short of slavery in their exploitative dimensions. Indeed even slave systems are notoriously legitimated on the grounds that they allegedly serve the genuine interests of slaves. Really to come up with an example of social interaction based exclusively on oppression, we have to conjure up an image of the galley slave crouched over his oar, threatened with the whip the instant he utters a sound or deviates from the prescribed pace.[9] As soon as slavery becomes a social system, ideolo-

---

8. It is worth noting parenthetically that even this claim rests on a commitment to the value of acting on the truth: it is by appeal to this value that bourgeois ideology is criticized and in virtue of which history is argued to be on the side of the working class to begin with. The proletariat can and should triumph because only it is committed to the genuine interests of mankind.

9. I am indebted to Peter Evans for this example.

gies of legitimation begin to be generated and with them arguments about whose interests are being served by the system, whose not, and how and why.[10]

Of course, the exploitative dimensions of most social systems are considerably more complex than those of slave systems. As a result, although it will be more and less evident in different circumstances who is being exploited and how, in most situations there will not be self-evident interests in the power struggle such that exploiters can press on regardless of evolving realities and the actions of others. People are often unsure of how best to advance their interests or even of what those interests are. They exploit one another, and are exploited, as by-products of unintended externality as often as by design, and they are frequently unable either to understand or to predict a great deal about the world and the actions of others. In this light, the suggestion that people can dispense with the aspiration to the truth is unrealistic. Life has more imagination than we do, and if ignored, reality will invariably begin to reassert itself, undermining our rationalizations and ideological claims and by that token reinforcing the human impetus to understand that reality. Assuming people to be motivated only by prudent self-interest, the claim that attention to the truth can be dispensed with in human affairs in favor of ideological rationalization is at best deeply suspect.

Prudent self-interest is not, in any case, the only source of human motivation. Not only do people seek recognition from one another, as I have argued,[11] they need a degree of authenticity to their lives that militates against self-deception in their dealings with themselves and against its cousin, ideological argument, in their dealings with others. No one wants to be thought to be a fraud, and few can accept inauthentic behavior in themselves indefinitely. Each year when I teach Bentham in my introductory political theory course, I ask the hundred or so undergraduates whether they would be prepared to have their brains connected to electrodes that would make them believe they were experiencing every pleasure they liked as intensely as they liked for the rest of their lives, while actually floating in vats. I never get any takers, even when the example is modified so that the pleasures might be varied and some pains introduced for contrast effects so that one would believe that one was freely choosing them and rendered incapable of knowing that the experiences were not genuine. The reasons given for resisting the example sometimes have to do with fearing loss of autonomy (and people like Nozick, from whom I

10. See Genovese (1971; 1972: 1–284).
11. See chapter 8, section II(ii)(a).

borrowed this experiment, have used it to argue for the importance of autonomy),[12] but far more often the reason given is that the experience would be unreal, fake, fraudulent, or inauthentic. Although the responses of a few hundred students queried in this way is not, of course, definitive evidence, they do indicate that we have reasons for being skeptical of conceptions of rationality that take no account of the human desire for authenticity.[13]

In many aspects of our dealings with others, the desire to act authentically plays an indispensable role. For instance, allegations that one's actions are based on misunderstandings or misrepresentations of reality frequently operate as catalysts to critical analysis whereby both protagonists in an argument try to establish that the truth is on their side. Consider the debate sparked by the advent of dependency theory in the 1970s. Critics of neoclassical trade theory argued that the capitalist system of international trade, defended by neoclassical theorists on the grounds that it worked to the mutual benefit of all, functioned to the systematic disadvantage of Third World economies. The price, argued the *dependistas*, of continuous development in the industrial economies at the center of the world system is perpetual stagnation at the periphery. Apologists for the existing order did not respond that they were uninterested in this thesis, that the critics were free to believe whatever they liked, or that they would continue to hold their own views regardless. Rather the battle was pitched over the question of whether or not the dependency thesis is true. The neoclassicists challenged the logic behind it and the evidence adduced in its defense while simultaneously modifying their own theoretical arguments in ways designed to salvage them from the proffered critique. The *dependistas* responded in kind, conceding eventually that some Third World development was possible but arguing that it would be stunted and

12. See Nozick (1974: 42–45).

13. Indeed, there is an emerging body of evidence from social psychology that buttresses these suspicions. Swann and others have conducted a number of studies that suggest that what people most want from their relationships with others is to confirm what they take to be their honest evaluations of themselves and that they avoid or leave relationships that fail to do this. Even when their self-evaluations are deeply negative (as in instances where people have little self-esteem), the evidence suggests that people tend to seek out relationships that verify or reinforce what they take their true selves to be and avoid those that do not. Thus relationships that might well make people happier or improve their self-esteem are typically eschewed in favor of those that enable them to feel more like themselves. For a description of this research, see Swann (1979). Swann goes on to argue on the basis of this and other evidence that a model of human motivation based on the search for predictability and control—to which wanting to know the truth is integral—makes better sense than a model that suggests that people simply want to feel better about themselves, to enhance their self-esteem.

socially authoritarian in ways the neoclassicists had taken insufficient account of and that the evidence still supported the claim that in much of the Third World development would not occur under the existing order. At the time some argued that the two groups were "speaking past one another," that they were operating from "different paradigms," partly no doubt because Kuhn was then at the height of fashion. But the entire history of the debate—in the media, the United Nations, various international economic organizations, and in the academy—belies this claim, as one useful study made clear.[14] The battle was over whose side the truth was on, and the intensity of energy and effort it generated on both sides underlines how important it is to people to be seen to be acting on the truth.

To take another example, think about why Charles Murray's attack on the welfare state in *Losing Ground* attracted so much attention.[15] Conservative attacks on the welfare state were scarcely unheard of before its publication in 1985, but what made Murray's argument a lightning rod and center of political controversy was that he mounted his attack not on the liberal welfarist worldview that is typically used to justify the welfare state but on a thesis about its nature. In a nutshell his claim was that the welfare state is self-destructive, that it is bound to make the problems to which it is addressed worse because it fosters dependency among those it allegedly seeks to help. This claim was far more threatening to defenders of the welfare state than any general indictment of their worldview, and critics of Murray's position like Christopher Jencks took issue not with his worldview but with his claim to be speaking the truth.[16] The battle was waged over the reliability of Murray's statistics and the veracity of his interpretations of them, and alternative evidence was offered that tended to undermine his thesis and establish its contrary to be true. Murray could not respond that he did not care about whether or not their critiques were valid; the logic of his position required that he and his defenders undermine his detractors' claims that they were appealing to the truth to justify their preferred policies. Once again the conflict took the form of debate over which side could most plausibly claim to be acting on the truth in defending its claims, and the intensity with which the debate focused on this as the core issue is indicative of how important it is to people to have the truth on their side and to be seen to be allied with it. Although engaging in reasoned argument generates no guarantee that "the truth will

14. Biersteker (1978). On the dependency debate generally, see Cardoso and Faletto (1977) and Evans (1979).

15. See Murray (1985).

16. See Jencks's (1985: 41–48) discussion of Murray's analysis.

out," its implicit commitment to the truth makes it an indispensable tool of moral and political argument. Reasoned claims to be speaking the truth are virtually impossible to ignore.

Critical theorists like Habermas argue that reference to the truth is essential to debunking ideological claims on the grounds that these latter typically present themselves as the truth.[17] Credible as this instrumental point is, its very plausibility assumes that there is a powerful human interest in authentic action in my sense. This is surely part of the reason that ideologies present themselves as the truth to begin with. People sense that they need to know the truth about what concerns them, that although they can often get by without reference to it in specific instances, they cannot generally count on ignoring it and getting by. It also seems clear, as noted earlier, that people have strong positive desires to act authentically. These desires may have an evolutionary basis for creatures that are decisively dependent on their cognitive faculties for survival, although they are probably more accurately thought about by reference to the discussion of emergent relations in chapter 8 as being conditioned by evolutionary requirements without being reducible to them.[18]

Whatever its ultimate basis, it is to the human interest in knowing and acting on the truth that the project of science appeals. We might even go so far as to say that this interest supplies all science with its impetus and rationale. Science holds out the hope that we can get beyond the welter of conflicting opinions and ideological claims to the truth of a matter, that we can come to hold a set of beliefs about an entity, event, or action that is most reasonable under the circumstances. As we saw in chapter 8, although this is often difficult in practice, there is no reason to rule it out in principle. Beyond this, little can be said in general terms. Scientific inquiry works itself out differently in different realms of human action and inquiry partly because the ways in which the truth is pertinent to them vary and partly because different methods are appropriate and available in those different realms.[19]

17. For a useful summary discussion, see Geuss (1981: 26–44).

18. See chapter 8, section I(ii).

19. In presupposing a unified view of the sciences here and in the discussion in chapter 8, section I(i), I am implicitly taking a view different than Habermas's account in *Knowledge and Human Interests* and elsewhere, where the different sciences and critical theory are linked to irreducibly different human interests. See Habermas (1968, especially 301–17). Habermas's views on this subject are complex and have changed over time, and I do not claim to have done justice to them here. However, as my discussion of Unger in chapter 8 made clear, I do not believe that a credible case can be made for a basic human interest in emancipation, which drives Habermas's view of critical theory and—on some formulations—of the human sciences. For reasons that it would take us too far afield to explore here (but

II. The Nature of Politics and the Tasks of Political Theory

Politics is centrally about the power dimensions of human interaction. It revolves around what people want from one another and how their actions affect the actions and lives of others. This means that although politics concerns institutional arrangements, it also concerns considerably more. Indeed, I propose to characterize politics as ranging over all human relationships in which power is or has the potential to become a significant factor. On so broad a conception every form of human interaction, every practice, has political dimensions.

In contrast to this broad conception, it is sometimes argued that politics is concerned only with the public sphere, but attempts to distinguish public from private spheres invariably turn out to be vulnerable to counterexample. Because the boundaries to the private sphere are themselves politically constituted and change over time, it is doubtful that any such distinction can ultimately be sustained.[20] No social practice can be declared to be beyond politics and therefore in principle beyond political regulation. Indeed, the term *regulation* is often pregnantly misleading because it implies that the absence of visible action by government is an indicator of the absence of collective political action, but such views invariably rest on indefensible assumptions about the naturalness of the private sphere. Were it possible somehow for society to not undertake collective action, as libertarian writers about its alleged irrationality often assume, such a view might in principle be defended, but it is not possible. The creation and maintenance of a system of legal rights and rules that makes possible what libertarians think of as unregulated private action is itself a collective act, partly financed by implicit taxes on those who would prefer some alternative system. Once this is conceded, the question must inevitably become not whether collective action but rather what sort.[21]

Human practices revolve around the creation and distribution of goods that are inherently scarce, and the possibility of politics within or among practices is ever-present, parasitic on the exercise, or the possibility of the exercise, of power. This means that all human practices are political at some level, although whether they are *politicized*—seen to involve

---

which I plan to discuss at length in the future), I also think that Habermas's typology of the different sciences appeared credible only because he conceded too much ground to the positivist account of the natural sciences.

20. The classic attempt is Mill (1974).

21. The illicit preference for noncollective action in much public choice literature is discussed in Shapiro (1989b), which I draw on here.

power relationships by the relevant participants—is another matter. As we saw in chapter 7, choosing or declining to describe a practice as political often has a great deal to do with the exercise of power within the relevant practice.[22] It is also true that on the causally interrelated view of social practices I took in chapter 8, many of the activities usually thought of as private will have ramifications for what is conventionally thought of as the public sphere and vice versa.[23] For these reasons there is no single or isolated domain of politics; defining the political is itself a political act, and as a result a political theorist who takes its definition for granted will likely be missing major dimensions of politics in her society.

On the broad view of politics just sketched, the tasks of political theory are of two main kinds: describing and justifying the most appropriate political institutions for human beings and engaging in principled criticism of the everyday social practices engaged in within those institutions. The two tasks are related but distinct; they have implications for one another, and there will be circumstances in which they flow into one another as a result of the reciprocal interactions between practices and institutional structures. Both tasks, I argue, are best informed by a commitment to a democratic ethos.

(i) Critical Naturalism and the Commitment to Democratic Institutions

Appeals to democracy generally revolve around conceptions of representation and participation, both of which turn out on close inspection to be profoundly problematical. Indeed, the idea that democracy is a workable system of government has always been suspect. Sometimes the problem is said to be one of scale, that democracy may not be attainable in the national states of the modern world as once it was, say, in the ancient city-states. But we saw in chapter 5 that such claims depend on views of ancient politics that cannot withstand serious scrutiny. Not only did the ancient Greek polities rest on slave economies, but they were internally hierarchical, manifestly oppressive of women, and in many other respects elitist. No doubt the problems of achieving participatory government are greatly worsened by problems of scale and by the realities of power and inequality in the modern world, as Schumpeter argued so forcefully in 1942, but it is doubtful that anything approaching the classical ideal has ever been implemented.

To these considerations we must now add the potentially devastating discoveries of analytical theoreticians of collective choice since Condorcet.

22. See chapter 7, section II.
23. See chapter 8, section II(ii).

Their work demonstrates that even in small committees voting procedures are easily manipulated, that even when not manipulated their results are often arbitrary, that the order of voting and control of the voting agenda may have more to do with outcomes than the wishes of voters, and that intense minorities and interest groups often exert decisive influences on outcomes through lobbies, vote trading, and logrolling. As a result the governments of so-called democratic systems cannot with much confidence be said to represent the wills of their citizens or even the wills of the (often small number of) voting citizens, and there remain serious and enduring questions concerning whether a system could be devised that avoids these results even in principle. There may be little general agreement among collective choice theorists about how to interpret their findings or about what to do about them, but it is undeniable that they have discovered genuine problems in the logic of democracy as a representative or participatory system of government.

Yet it is my contention that a political commitment to a democratic ethos is desirable independently of whether the ideas of representation or participation can be institutionalized or even rendered coherent. On this account democracy is better thought of as an ethic of opposition than a system of government.[24] At the heart of what makes it attractive is the antipathy it generates for all systems of entrenched hierarchy and its principled amateurism, its intrinsic hostility to the idea of political expertise. Let me explain why.

(a) The Rejection of Hierarchy. Aristotelian views of politics have usually been friendly to hierarchical conceptions of the social order, but a wedge must be driven between the two. Neo-Aristotelians like MacIntyre often concede that Aristotle's particular hierarchical conception was in practice an ideology of irrational domination of women and slaves, yet they resist the wholesale rejection of hierarchy as such. "The hierarchy of the best kind of *polis*," MacIntyre insists, "is one of teaching and learning, not of irrational domination" (MacIntyre 1988: 105, 106).

Yet my modifications of Aristotle's account in chapter 8 suggest that such a distinction between irrational domination and rational hierarchy cannot in the end be sustained. Once we abandon the notion that there has been or could be a harmonious ordering of practices in the world, accept that the virtues governing practices will be contentious and will change over time, and recognize that the human capacity for self-reflection will inevitably throw the legitimacy of prevailing practices into ques-

---

24. This view of democracy is more fully discussed in Shapiro (1988: 284–90 and 1989b).

tion, we also have to abandon the idea that there is any way of ordering social reality that can be read off from human nature or the nature of things as rational. The learned character of the values internal to practices does suggest that a degree of hierarchy is invariably present in them, and some practices—child rearing is a paradigm instance—are inevitably hierarchical in a more full-blown sense. But unless the hierarchical dimensions of a practice are in principle self-liquidating, as when the pupil becomes a peer or the child an adult, they cannot plausibly be defended. Thus although most organized religions (including the Catholicism MacIntyre embraces) are hierarchies that involve teaching and learning, they are not self-liquidating hierarchies in my sense because positions of authority and influence are not in principle open to all participants: no woman can aspire to be pope, and therefore no woman can ever hope to escape subordination in the hierarchy of the Catholic church.

Whatever hierarchical orderings happen to prevail at a given time will most likely be the arbitrary result of coercion and historical accident; they will benefit some and harm others and sometimes benefit some at the price of harming others. Yet hierarchical practices are to be resisted not merely because they are arbitrary but because their operation may generally be expected to be at odds with the human interest in authentic action. Hierarchical practices tend to be held hostage by the imperatives for their own maintenance, which typically involve the creation and propagation of fictions about either the nature or the arbitrariness of the hierarchical practice in question. Those who derive particular benefits from a given hierarchical practice will invariably try—more or less consciously—either in some way to obscure its hierarchical character through ideological argument or illicitly to present the particular hierarchical arrangement as rational. An example of the former—brilliantly exposed in Marx's passage on the fetishism of commodities—is the standard defense of market systems on the grounds that they preserve the freedom of all to engage in voluntary transactions. An example of the latter would be a defense of the patriarchal family on the grounds that it is preordained either by God or by alleged genetic differences between the sexes. A more extreme example would be appeals to the alleged natural superiority of the Aryan race to justify the social order of the Third Reich. My critical naturalist view supplies us with conceptual tools to grapple with the Eichmann problem discussed in chapter 8 just because it generates principled opposition to social hierarchy in all its manifestations.[25] That the social structure that the Nazis were striving to create was shot through with practices of hier-

25. See chapter 8, section II(ii)(a).

archy, which they had every intention of entrenching as much as possible, would have rendered this system morally indefensible even had the holocaust not occurred or taken the form that it did.

For reasons analogous to those militating against defensible hierarchy within practices, every attempt to defend a fixed ordering of relations *among* social practices can expect to run into intractable difficulties. Hierarchical social arrangements may be ineradicable parts of the social landscape, but we have seen that every such arrangement can be argued to be morally arbitrary. As a result no matter what forms hierarchies among practices take, defense of them will be vulnerable in the same ways that defenses of hierarchy within particular practices are vulnerable. Attempts to justify their existence will tend to misdescribe them either by obscuring their hierarchical character or by alleging it to be a rational reflection of the nature of things. It is democracy's hostility to all such rationalizations that makes it attractive from my critical naturalist standpoint; it can potentially be pressed into the service of the human interest in authentic action.

The claim that a commitment to democracy implies resistance to hierarchical social orderings is not a claim that putatively democratic systems are not hierarchical in their parts or sum or that there could in principle be a nonhierarchical organization of society. On the contrary, as I have just noted, there is every reason to doubt the tuth of both these propositions. But the democratic ethos as I describe it is unique in two respects that bear on the question of how we deal with the endemic presence of hierarchy and domination in social life. First, it turns into a political principle the idea that although hierarchy and domination may be endemic to human organization, they can never be legitimate, and, second, it takes seriously the political implications of nothing in social life being unconditional. Let me elaborate.

It is sometimes argued that to conceive of legitimacy in such a way that no political system can be legitimate is to empty the concept of all useful content,[26] but there are at least two good reasons for resisting this conclusion. The first is that the admission that a degree of illegitimacy attaches to all our collective actions and institutions undermines self-righteous and categorical action in politics. An extreme example makes this point. Writing in the *New York Times*, Meir Kahane makes the argument that Israel not only should not negotiate with the PLO or any other Arabs about the occupied territories on the West Bank and Gaza but should forthwith annex them and disenfranchise, if not forcibly expel, all Arabs. He con-

---

26. Bob Dahl has forcibly argued this to me in another context.

demns out of hand what he sees as the self-destructive guilt of liberal Jews who have allowed themselves to be defined by Arab perceptions as conquerors and the lands they live on as stolen. On Kahane's view there is no Palestine and never has been. God gave the land of Israel to the Jewish people, and for Jews "the moral imperative is to live and guarantee a home for a Jewish people." To anyone who disagrees his response is simple: "who cares what you think?"[27]

Extreme as Kahane's view is, the example is not so antithetical to conventional assumptions about legitimacy as it might at first appear. As we saw in chapter 6, every political community is as much a mechanism of exclusion as of inclusion; every nation-state reserves by definition the right to exclude and behave without reference to those it deems nonmembers. Kahane's view seems extreme to us because he supplies a religious basis for legitimacy and because the disenfranchised have been excluded sufficiently recently—and are in such close physical proximity—that their plight and their demands are difficult to ignore. In fact Kahane is applying the standard notion of the unconditional legitimacy of sovereign communities to the logic of his circumstances. This is why people find him so threatening: his distasteful conclusions follow from a logic that they generally embrace. Conceptions of citizenship that appeal to things other than God-given rights might appear less arbitrary on the surface, but they are not. Every assignment of citizenship rights is in the end arbitrary and based on coercion; we saw that this is what makes the indifference to outsiders characteristic of the republican political vision morally unattractive.[28] On the view I am advocating, the fact that the very definition of sovereign communities generates hierarchies of entitlements between members and nonmembers undermines their legitimacy to a degree and leaves open the possibility of a reasoned response to Kahane. Israel is not special in the limits to its legitimacy as an exclusionary state; every state's legitimacy is limited, and its exclusionary pretentions may thus legitimately be resisted. It is not that the Palestinians have an unconditional right to national self-determination that rivals Israel's claim of right over the disputed territory; it is that there are no unconditional rights to national self-determination because every such assertion of right involves a potentially coercive hierarchy and is therefore less than fully legitimate.

27. As he elaborates, "The terrible ghosts of Jewish guilt gnaw away at the tortured Jewish liberal soul with the thought that perhaps the Jews are indeed 'occupiers' and colonialists. This Jewish secular liberal agonizes with himself daily because, along with his guilt, he lacks the courage to give up his kibbutz to the oppressed Arab. He wallows in a corrosive guilt that rapidly becomes self-hate." Meir Kahane, *New York Times*, April 7, 1989.

28. See chapter 6, section II(iii).

We may indeed live in a world in which nation-states are ineradicable or in which the alternatives to them are, for a variety of reasons, likely to be worse than a nation-state system; I will assume for the sake of argument that this is so. But the hostility to hierarchy that is integral to the democratic impulse tells us that the inevitability of a system of coercive states does not justify their coercion. On the contrary, it generates an impetus to argue that sovereign rights must be of limited validity, that the claims of the coerced and excluded may not simply be ignored, and that other ways of speaking to them have to be sought after. Far from rendering the concept of legitimacy vacuous, then, the notion that no political system is entirely legitimate can both provide the impetus for critical analysis and function as a useful critical tool in it.

The second source of value in recognizing inherent limits to the legitimacy of all collective action and institutions, no matter how inevitable these might be, is that it directs attention toward more realistic questions about degrees of illegitimacy and injustice and the obstacles to dealing with them rather than toward binary conceptions, which treat the world as made up of just institutions and unjust ones, good guys and bad guys, legitimate states and evil empires. Such conceptions of the world have deeply corrosive effects on those who hold them, both in the smug complacency of those who are sure that they are on the side of the angels— dramatically illustrated in Kahane's case—and in the equally destructive guilt that consumes those who come to believe that they are the devils, as many an émigré white South African will testify. More important, such binary conceptions frequently turn attention from genuine to pseudo-political questions because the agenda behind them is often to legitimate, perhaps implicitly, some coercive relationship by diverting attention to the allegedly evil actions of others. The most pressing and pertinent questions about domination in the Soviet Union do not, for example, concern which particular freedoms exist in the United States that do not exist there. Rather they concern the ways in which domination can be undermined in the Soviet Union, given the peculiarities of Soviet history and circumstances and the available political options. This is not to say that comparisons will never be useful in diminishing domination, but it is to say that comparisons whose underlying purpose or motivation is to vindicate a binary view of the world are unlikely to advance toward that goal.

It is often also thought to be a weakness of the democratic ethos that it involves embracing the view that nothing in politics is unconditional, but I want to suggest that this is actually a strength. It has long been conventional to argue that democratic procedures can undermine systems of rights or entitlements; indeed democratic ideologies were attractive to the dispossessed classes during the nineteenth century precisely because they could be used to redistribute what were seen as the ill-gotten gains of entrenched elites. Yet the twentieth-century experience of democracy has revealed that it is not always the rights of the wealthy and powerful that are ignored or undermined in democratic systems; it can also be those of dispossessed and voiceless minorities. Add to this the discovery that democratic systems are unstable; no matter what the status quo, democratic procedures will always be able to undermine it in ways that are basically arbitrary. In the paradigm-case example from the collective choice literature, in a three-person society that has a dollar to divide among its members, no matter what division is agreed on, there will always be a majority coalition to redistribute it.

These and related considerations have been used to bolster the view that majoritarian processes are inherently suspect and that if some conception of democracy is to be salvaged, it must involve limiting their pernicious effects. The standard arguments are two: either requiring substantially more than simple majorities—in some circumstances perhaps even unanimity—before certain rights can legitimately be abridged or embracing a liberal constitutionalism that ascribes greater responsibility to courts in protecting rights from majoritarian process run amok. But both these strategies of argument run into major difficulties. They make illicit assumptions about the defensibility of alternative decision procedures—whether about unanimity rule or about procedures employed in reviewing courts—and they fail to take into account that the rights they would protect from majoritarian process can themselves be shown to be morally arbitrary.[29] This is not to say that majority rule is always and everywhere desirable. It is to say, however, that once we decline to ascribe any particular moral authority to the distribution of entitlements that happens to be embodied in the status quo, a political system that makes entitlements perpetually vulnerable has some attractive features that might be argued to be preferable to many of the going alternatives.[30] The institutional challenge is to take advantage of these features without allowing them to become self-destructively rampant; democracy as I plan to describe it more fully in the future should be thought of as that system of structured instabilities that best prevents the ossification of arbitrary entitlements and undermines entrenched power without collapsing into anarchical chaos.

29. These claims are defended at length in Shapiro (1989b).
30. Indeed, a case can be made that, under conditions of uncertainty about our future preferences, majority rule or something very like it is best chosen from the standpoint of individual rationality. See Rae (1969: 40–56) and Schofield (1972: 60–80).

(b) The Rejection of Political Expertise. Technical expertise is relevant to politics in many different ways, but we have good and enduring reasons for resisting the idea that there is political expertise in the same sense that there are many other forms of scientific and technical expertise. We can reasonably believe Einstein's theory of relativity to be probably true even if we do not understand it and are incapable of relating our everyday experience to it, and in certain (though not all) circumstances we can reasonably act on the advice of an airplane pilot, an auto mechanic, an architect, or a physician without understanding its rationale or even being interested in it. But the idea that there is analogous political expertise reasonably prompts instant suspicion.

Most minimally, the suggestion that there is political expertise is suspect because there are few reasons to believe that there is much of it. What is typically billed as knowledge about the world of politics seems so meager and so regularly undermined by events that people who set themselves up as political experts often give off the whiff of snake oil. On its own this argument suggests only that political expertise may be quite primitive; after all as medical science advances, quacks and charlatans are gradually displaced from the business of healing. Commentators who argue for the introduction of scientific modes of analysis into politics have often thought in precisely these terms; consider Dewey's lament in 1929 that the then current way of treating such social problems as crime was still "reminiscent of the way in which diseases were once thought of and dealt with" when they were believed to have moral causes. Just as the possibility of "effective treatment" began when diseases came to be seen as having "an intrinsic origin in interactions of the organism and its natural environment," so we should now be looking for comparable solutions to other social and political ills.

> We are only just beginning to think of criminality as an equally intrinsic manifestation [as with disease] of interactions between an individual and the social environment. With respect to it, and with respect to many other evils, we persist in thinking and acting in prescientific "moral" terms. This prescientific conception of "evil" is probably the greatest barrier that exists to that real reform. (Dewey 1962 [1929]: 164)

But here we must part company with Dewey, for his view takes too little account of the enduring power dimensions of much social and political action. Despite his rejection of the epistemological project of the Enlightenment, Dewey took for granted a gradual victory of the scientific ethos that smacks of Enlightenment faith in a perhaps gradual and uneven but nonetheless inexorable triumph of reason in history. He harbored a goal of gradually turning social and political problems into technical ones that is in the end no less fanciful than liberal claims that political institutions can be morally neutral or Marx's view that with socialism's triumph, politics will be displaced by administration. In this respect, although Dewey abandoned the practice of architectonic social theory, he continued to harbor extravagant expectations about progress in human affairs that had driven the major social theorists of the eighteenth and nineteenth centuries. Dewey's shift, in the passage just quoted, from treating the body to treating the body politic is wholly insensitive to the fact that distributive conflict is endemic to all political organization and reform. To pursue his comparison, the likely side effects of a medicine for a particular ailment on other organs of the body can reasonably be thought about in cost-benefit terms to decide whether, on balance, it is desirable for the person to take the particular cure, but the social analogy does not hold. For the person bearing the externality of another's benefit will be unimpressed by the claim that the benefit exceeds the harm and that society is, on balance, better off as a result, even if the cost-benefit calculation is conceded to be accurate.[31]

In the mainstream of the Western tradition of political theory the problem of endemic distributive conflict has been finessed by appealing either to some variant of the claim that it can be neutrally managed or to a version of the growth thesis, the idea that a big enough pie, or a pie that expands at a sufficiently rapid rate, will cause distributive conflict somehow to go away. It is by now undeniable that both strategies fail. With respect to neutrality, no system of ownership and distribution allocates benefits and burdens impartially, and attempts to deny this can quickly be shown to rest on arbitrary assumptions about initial endowments of rights and about what is socially desirable.[32] Appeals to abundance as a source of obviating distributive conflict also fail, whether in their liberal variants as trickle-down theories or in their Marxist variants as claims that true socialism will make possible a permanent state of superabundance.[33] This is not to say that distributive conflict is inevitably zero-sum (though some of it is), only that there is no way either of preventing it or of managing it neutrally.

31. Economic efficiency, however, is sometimes defined in precisely these terms. See Posner (1981: 13–227).

32. This is sometimes argued to generate an argument for minimizing collective action of all kinds, but I have shown elsewhere that such claims are ultimately arbitrary in their allocations of benefits and burdens. See Shapiro (1989b).

33. On the liberal theories, see Shapiro (1986: 151–305; 1987: 999–1047; 1989b). On the weaknesses of Marx's assumptions about superabundance, see chapter 7, section III.

Despite assertions by some communitarians and latter-day civic republicans to the contrary, we saw in earlier chapters that turning to the Aristotelian tradition also fails to banish distributive conflict from politics. The Pocockian claim that entering the republican paradigm leaves distributive questions behind was revealed to be false, and we saw that embracing the more complex view of human psychology embodied in the Aristotelian concept of a practice does not justify abandoning the axiom of endemic scarcity, so that distributive conflict remains inescapable. In addition, our well-justified suspicion of assumptions about harmony in human events makes it all but inevitable that practices will not fit together neatly; they will bump into one another, they will fail to work out as planned even for participants, and people will feel themselves to be short-changed within practices, by being excluded from practices and by the externalities of others' practices on theirs. This is why Dewey's reference to treatment in the social and political realms seems frighteningly Orwellian; the suggestion that any particular form of social treatment will not operate in the interests of some and to the detriment of others is not credible. The experts always turn out to be on somebody's side, not necessarily ours.

(ii) The Democratic Political Ethos Within and Among
Social Practices: Political Theory as Principled Criticism

Much of what has been said about the basic structure of politics is also relevant to the internal dynamics of social practices and to the relations among them. No social practice, we saw, can be declared beyond politics, and any categorial attempt to separate the structure of political institutions from the practices they contain will be artificial to a degree as a result. But the analysis of particular practices will present distinctive problems in different contexts, calling for a variety of analytical tools and methods of critical argument.

With the analysis of particular social practices, the political theorist again starts from the assumption that people have an interest in knowing and acting on the truth. It is when practices start to atrophy into systems of domination that the theorist begins to have something to say; a practice is authentic to the degree that its participants genuinely live up to the values internal to it. The authenticity of practices is under constant threat from a variety of sources already discussed: the endemic scarcity of goods essential to human thriving, the complexity and unpredictability of human interaction, the fact that people are simultaneously involved in many practices that make competing and sometimes mutually incompatible demands on them, the externalities of practices on other practices and the differential benefits within them, the fact that practices are often exclusionary in controversial ways, thus presenting difficulties analogous to those that arose in our discussion of legitimacy, and the fact that the ways in which people try to integrate their practices into comparatively unified wholes can be zero-sum—one life sometimes becomes more rather than less integrated at the price of another life's becoming less rather than more integrated. These, and no doubt other, characteristics of human interaction cause practices to atrophy into relations of hierarchy and domination, and it is the job of the political theorist to delineate and bring into the open the forms this process takes, to expose the genuine character of practices to their participants.

Yet just because the idea of political expertise is no less suspect than the idea of hierarchy, the political theorist cannot set himself up as a bird's-eye view interpreter of the correct or best ways of going about the conduct of practices or interpreting the norms internal to them. Indeed we saw earlier that part of what makes the norms internal to practices *internal* to them is that they are learned from other participants, and it is the judgments of those others that are often, for a given individual, decisive for the meaning and satisfaction derived from a given practice. The very definition of a practice revolves around the idea of learned activities at which people try to excel and which can therefore be performed more or less well according to their own lights. Although a given practice may or may not initially have been entered into voluntarily, being committed to a practice involves accepting, to a degree, the norms governing it and trying to excel in their terms, even as, perhaps, one seeks to criticize and alter them. An author will want to be valued by a critic whose capacities she has come to value; small nuances to every activity from child rearing to cabinetmaking can be fully appreciated only by others who have learned to excel at those same practices. These considerations seem to make practices inherently resistant to external criticism even if they are—paradoxically—in perpetual need of it.

The attempt to resolve this apparent paradox supplied at least part of the motivation for Walzer's claim that social criticism must be connected criticism. But if the political theorist has something to say qua theorist, this must mean either that he is not a participant in the relevant practice or, if he is a participant, that he is able to divorce himself to a significant extent from his participatory role, to see the practice in some illuminatingly different way. Otherwise the suggestion that the theorist has something distinctive to say turns out to be empty. We seem, in short, to be caught on the horns of a dilemma: on the one hand, if the theorist has a distinctive contribution to make she must be something other than, or something in addition to, a participant in the practices she discusses; on the other, any claim that the theorist has a particular expertise is immediately and with good reason suspect.

This dilemma is best dealt with by adopting a view of political theory as principled criticism. What makes principled criticism principled is a basic commitment to finding out and articulating the truth. Principled criticism shares a skepticism toward abstract and universalist moral theorizing with Walzer's idea of connected criticism, but the alternative to this is construed in terms other than Walzer's. For Walzer's rejection of abstract moral argument conflates two quite different dimensions of the critical enterprise: the universalist/particularist dimension, which concerns the content of moral argument, and the disembodied/connected dimension, which concerns matters strategic. Like Walzer, I am a particularist. I think there is every reason to doubt that ideal theory can generate conclusions that are useful in actual moral and political argument because what appears to be ideal theory turns out invariably to be driven by deeply controversial particular commitments that are either hidden from view or declared by definitional fiat to be uncontroversial, to command universal agreement. The price of engaging in political argument with the methods of ideal theory is thus typically that we confirm the support of those who were predisposed to agree with our substantive commitments before we began and ensure the opposition of those who do not.[34] But, unlike Walzer, I contend that nothing of much significance about the content of moral argument turns on how connected or disembodied the critic might be to those whom she criticizes. For these reasons Walzer's maneuverings along the connected/disembodied dimension in recent years in response to objections to his view are not of much help to me.[35] The question of how distant or connected a critic should be, I argued, is basically strategic, and there will be some circumstances at least in which refusal to disconnect in Walzer's sense will be self-defeating. This aside, I showed that the particular location of the critic on Walzer's dimension does not tell her what to say. Walzer's commitment to bonds of connection on the critic's behalf appears to get around this problem only at the price of turning social criticism into a disguised autobiography of the critic. In short, a bad argument does not become good in virtue of being lovingly articulated, and the truth spoken by a knave is not thereby rendered false.[36]

The great difficulty with appealing to prevailing norms as the basis for

34. I defend this view at length in Shapiro (1986: 5–6, 206, 281–305).

35. Compare the discussion of Camus in Walzer (1984b: 315–30), where he offers a radical attack on the notion of critical distance, with the softening of that attack in Walzer (1987: 35–66).

36. See chapter 3, sections II(ii) and (iii), and chapter 7, section I.

social criticism, we saw, is that they are many and conflicting; different conventional norms, and competing interpretations of the same norms, serve the interests of different groups differently. Even when a set of norms or an interpretation of prevailing norms is widely shared, it will often operate to the systematic disadvantage of some, as we saw in chapter 2.[37] The decisive symptom of how hopeless appeals to context are as a source of critical standards is that in the last few years contextualist arguments have been used to generate New Right critiques of establishment liberalism, social democratic arguments like Walzer's, and leftist arguments of the sort informing *Habits of the Heart*. What happens in the end with all such arguments is that the contextualist theorist discovers a reading of conventional values congenial to him, but again, convinces only the constituency that was already on his side. The fact that the various contextualist commentators claim to be appealing to prevailing American values yet read them so differently should alert us to the truth that the *consensus* of the contextualists is no more viable than the *consent* of the neo-Kantians as a basis for critical argument in politics. It also makes clear why the concessions that neo-Kantians like Rawls and Dworkin have made to their contextualist critics in recent years are on this matter beside the point; these concessions fail to reach and grapple with the fact that although we start with prevailing beliefs and practices, we have to devise ways of subjecting those beliefs to critical scrutiny.

Now it is one thing to say that human beings have an interest in knowing and acting on the truth and another to explain how this interest can operate as a source of critical standards in everyday political argument. I do not claim that there is a true, privileged, or best interpretation of prevailing norms that can somehow be said to trump competing interpretations of the norms prevailing in a culture; competing interpretations, as we saw, are both endemic and inevitably loaded politically.[38] Neither do I claim that there is some list of "true values" that the theorist can pull out of a hat and give people in the manner of Moses returning from the mountain with his tablets, which people could then go off and apply to their moral and political disputes and conundrums to get the right answers. There are three insurmountable obstacles to any such view. The first has to do with the limits of our knowledge. I argued in chapter 8 that we no longer have any good reason to believe—and many good reasons to doubt—that any theorist can have or even reasonably aspire to have the requisite knowledge to deliver prescriptive judgments in this way. The sec-

---

37. See chapter 2, section II(ii).
38. This tack of looking for a best or trumping interpretation of conventional practices informs Dworkin's (1986) project in *Law's Empire*.

ond obstacle concerns the nature and sources of human values. We have seen that what is valuable for human beings varies with time and circumstance and is often a function of their interactions with—and evaluations of—one another and that for self-conscious beings capable of some creative innovation, human values are to a degree self-chosen.[39]

The third obstacle to the idea of the political theorist qua secular priest derives from the fact that it is part of the notion of authentic action that one does not do things merely because someone else tells one to do them. Another reason Dewey's comparison between medical treatment and social and political problems is so troubling is that there is more to authentic action than the mindless application of correct principles, as Dewey himself insisted elsewhere.[40] There is a difference between a child who can solve a mathematical problem because he understands the principle involved and one who gets the right answer from a calculator or rote application of a rule; in these latter cases there is a significant sense in which the child is not acting on the truth in that he lacks authentic understanding of what he is doing. This will not reasonably be troubling in every circumstance, but at those points at which power relations are or have the potential to become involved in the conduct of social practices, inauthentic action will rightly make us nervous. Inauthentic action makes practices ripe for atrophy into systems of domination.

These considerations suggest that the relationship between principled criticism and the truth is bound to be complicated. We have just seen that the premise that people have an interest in knowing and acting on the truth militates against the idea that a theorist should even aspire to tell people what to do or even what values to have. A commitment to the practice of principled criticism involves a commitment to telling people the truth about how they live but not to telling them how to live. This does not relegate the theorist to the realm of metaanalysis, for it is impossible neatly to separate first-order from second-order questions in the way that the term *meta* implies.[41] Much principled criticism involves grappling with issues that are first-order on any credible definition, as we are about to see. Nor does my injunction imply that the principled critic be or

39. Concerning the limits to our knowledge, see chapter 8, section I(i). Concerning the nature and sources of human values, chapter 8, sections I(i) and II(ii).

40. See, for example, the discussion of individuality in Dewey (1962: 167–73) and, more generally, Dewey (1954). I skirt the debate—traceable at least to Reinhold Niebuhr's attack on Dewey's faith in social science as the solution to social problems in *Moral Man and Immoral Society*—over how, if at all, Dewey's faith in technical solutions could be reconciled with his commitment to democracy. See Niebuhr (1960: xiii–xxv, 35–38). *See also* Damico (1978: 32–121).

41. See chapter 7, section III.

aspire to be value neutral. The commitment to telling people the truth about how they live and the commitment to refraining from telling them how to live are both moral commitments geared toward influencing human conduct. They rest on the recognition that the manner in which we seek to influence conduct matters. Because the purpose of principled criticism is to promote authentic action, the principled critic is bound to eschew vanguardist aspirations in all their manifestations.

(iii) The Practice of Principled Criticism

To take up principled criticism is to engage in a social practice and, as with any other social practice, involves learning its distinctive norms and modes of proceeding. Principled criticism has just been characterized as telling people the truth about how they live, but what does this mean in concrete terms? Principled criticism of necessity tracks the practices it analyzes; there is therefore no single set of injunctions for its most appropriate conduct. How best to do it depends on the various forms that the atrophy of practices takes. This will vary with time and circumstance but in large part is a function of the nature and evolution of the particular practices to which social criticism is directed. It also depends to some degree on the perceptiveness and inventiveness of the critic both in being able to understand the forms that the atrophy of practices takes and in being able successfully to communicate this understanding to participants. Yet some general considerations about the conduct of principled criticism can nonetheless be sketched.

The first is that *principled criticism cannot be an exclusionary practice.* Given that its existence partly rests on a recognition of the inherent tensions between the human interest in knowing and acting on the truth and claims to political expertise, principled criticism cannot itself be an expert field like linguistics, pure mathematics, or quantum mechanics. Although those who engage best in principled criticism may often be those with much accumulated experience in the critical analysis of social practices (experience that tends to bring with it useful insights about the characteristic forms their atrophy takes), by its terms principled criticism cannot be an esoteric activity open only to initiates. To say that no one may legitimately be excluded from the practice of principled criticism, however, is not to say that everyone can excel at it, that it is easy, or that it lacks in requirements of rigor. On the contrary, it is exceedingly difficult to do well; the risk of failure is always high, the returns on investments never guaranteed. Because the world of social practices is dense and in many ways causally interconnected, the theorist who starts with the critical analysis of one practice will often have to come to grips with many others.

Someone who begins critically to study the nature and dynamics of family life will be driven to attend to many other economic, social, and political practices with which it interacts and will have no guarantees that her mushrooming search will yield definitive conclusions, let alone that any conclusions reached will increase authentic action in the conduct of family life. Engaging in principled criticism at all takes for granted the possibility that it may promote authentic action, but this is no more than a possibility. The principled critic has no reason to make transcendental assumptions about ideal speech situations of the sort Habermas has been urging on us in recent years. Whether, to what extent, and under what conditions uncoerced communication is possible is a subject for scientific investigation on the critical naturalist view, not for a priori argument.[42]

If a theorist is to have any hope of doing principled criticism well, she must be ever ready to take an interdisciplinary approach to the problems that throw themselves up in and among social practices; to muck into controversy about causal argument, evidence, and its relevance; to refuse to take things on trust from self-styled or publicly proclaimed experts; to debunk bunk, clarify complexity, undermine misleading simplification, ask awkward questions, and generally be difficult. The principled critic is a kind of interdisciplinary ombudsman for the truth. Inevitably concerned with subjects that properly occupy political scientists, historians, economists, anthropologists, academic lawyers, and others, practitioners in these fields are among her natural teachers. But the political theorist always maintains a distinctive standpoint as a professional amateur whose goal is to expand normative clarification in the service of authentic action.

A second, related, consideration is that *principled criticism must begin and end in an idiom common to the participants in the practices it analyzes.* Between beginning and ending it may well depart from these commonsense understandings; it may be bound to do so if it is genuinely to illuminate. But unless the argument the principled critic makes is intelligible to those to whom it is ultimately addressed within their own terms of reference, it cannot be efficacious as principled criticism. To say this is not to say that principled criticism must be connected criticism in Walzer's sense. Attacking an ideological rationalization as hypocritical or dishonest or revealing someone to be lying or obscuring relevant facts can be done— perhaps must be done—in a commonsense idiom and be effective without granting legitimacy, let alone emotional warmth, to the object of one's criticism. Connected criticism is one variety of criticism carried on in the

42. See Habermas (1976, 1984). Some will resist this interpretation of Habermas. I certainly do not claim to have done full justice to Habermas's arguments here.

commonsense idiom of a prevailing practice but not the only one, and it is the requirement of a commonsense idiom that matters, not Walzer's particular connected variety of it.[43]

Political theory cannot in the end be thought of as an isolated subdiscipline (whether or not the most fundamental), within political science or philosophy, as a self-contained craft or expertise that feeds exclusively on its own controversies because what drives it, what gives it its raison d'être, is the possibility of having an impact on a world that is external to it, on those social practices to which it is addressed. The mathematician has no aspiration to influence the nature of numbers, or the linguist the nature of language, or the historian the nature of the past; indeed such aspirations would verge on the comic.[44] But the point of principled criticism is precisely to have some impact—albeit complex and indirect—on the objects of its analysis, and it cannot, therefore, sensibly insulate itself from them. A canon of philosophical texts or a series of analytical speculations about the logic of collective action may be argued to be pertinent to principled criticism in a variety of ways, but they are mere tools for talking about the problems characteristic of various practices and about ways in which these problems have been or might be handled. Political theorists who develop all-consuming interests in such tools for their own sake will tend to corrupt the activity of principled criticism by divorcing it from its purpose. This is why political theory that degenerates into exclusive preoccupation with its own disciplinary controversies is likely increasingly to be driven by spurious problems as it grows, at best, irrelevant to other social practices of everyday life.[45] The burden must always lie with the users of tools that are esoteric—from the standpoint of the practice to which they are applied—to demonstrate their pertinence; principled criticism must begin and end in terms that participants in the criticized practices will recognize and grasp.

But what does the principled critic characteristically do? The simplest answer is that *he places the practices he analyzes in a wider causal context than that typically perceived by participants.*[46] Two related reasons for this have to do with the opacity of practices and one of the forms that their atrophy characteristically takes. What do I mean by the opacity of prac-

43. See chapter 3, section II(iii), for an illustration of this point.
44. Historical analysis can, however, sometimes be implicit social criticism aimed at influencing the present, as can be literary criticism and other kinds of social analysis.
45. This view is argued for and illustrated with reference to many of the controversies that preoccupy contemporary political theorists in Shapiro (1989a: 51–76).
46. For this characterization of the theorist's enterprise, I am indebted to the useful discussion by Horton (1979: 131–71).

tices? As became clear in my discussion of Rorty in chapter 2, human action is multidimensional and often many of its dimensions are not consciously present in the minds of social agents.[47] As a result practices can be understood at one level as the products of the intentional actions of participating agents, but they can be understood at many other levels as well; we all do much more than we realize we are doing much of the time. Social reality is frequently created through the performative qualities of human language and action, but this is as often through by-products of intentional actions as it is the direct or transparent result of those actions. When the president takes his oath of office his wife by virtue of that action becomes first lady, whether or not the president-elect intended that result or even thought about it. When two participants say "I do" at the relevant moments in a marriage ceremony, they may be quite unaware that one of the things they are doing in uttering these words is reproducing the social structure of the nuclear family. When a worker agrees to work for a capitalist for a particular wage she may be quite unconscious of the role this action plays in reproducing the economic structure of capitalism.

It is sometimes argued that the internal dimensions of actions are intentional and should be interpreted, understood in hermeneutic terms, or *elucidated* (to borrow Austin's term) and that the external dimensions of action, having to do with motivations rather than intentions, are more appropriately thought about in the language of causation. This has prompted a massive philosophical debate on the question of whether reasons can plausibly be thought of as causes of actions.[48] I argue elsewhere that any categorial distinction between the realms of causal and interpretive explanation is misleadingly simple; in some but not all circumstances, intentions can plausibly be thought of as causes of actions and motives and intentions can sometimes be redescribed as one another.[49] Yet there is something worth attending to in the distinction between intentional and nonintentional realms that people who want to distinguish hermeneutic from causal explanations want to draw. For present purposes we can get at this by saying that there are often causal dimensions to human practices of which participants in those practices are unaware, whether or not they think of the dimensions of which they are aware in causal terms. These opaque dimensions of social practices can range from the kinds of cultural, psychological, and biological conditioning of intentional actions suggested by the discussion of emergent relations in chapter 8[50] to the unperceived

47. See chapter 2, section II(ii).
48. A seminal discussion is Davidson (1968: 79–94).
49. See Shapiro (1982: 535–78).
50. See chapter 8, section I(ii).

causal effects of intentional actions that economists describe as externalities to instances where intentional understandings of actions are in some way contaminated for reasons having to do with self-deception or ideological distortion.

In all such cases (and no doubt there are others), whether or not an intentional understanding is a causal one or—perhaps more accurately—whether or not it is part of an adequate causal explanation of an action, there are additional causal dimensions to the action that are not present in the consciousness of the relevant agent. When this is so, the opaque causal components of the actions that make up social practices can often be brought to the surface by placing commonsense understandings in a wider causal context and explaining the links between this wider explanatory context and commonsense understandings. The psychological constraints of fear of death appealed to by Hobbes, the requirements of evolution that drove Darwin's arguments, and the stock of cultural symbols to which much contemporary anthropology appeals all involve opaque causal dimensions of human action of the first sort just referred to. Arguments about the counterproductive or unanticipated effects of intentional actions—such as those appealed to by the *dependistas*, in Murray's critique of the welfare state, and in collective action problems like the prisoner's dilemma—involve appeals to a wider causal context of the second sort. Explanatory theories of human action like Freud's and Marx's refer to opaque causal dimensions of the third sort. In all these instances commonsense understandings are placed in some wider context of causal explanation, and a narrative is supplied in commonsense idiom that links the new causal account to prevailing understandings. Marx's discussion of why the apparently voluntary transactions of the market are not in fact voluntary may be thought of as a paradigm case of such an account.[51] If such a narrative can be rendered plausible, the hitherto unnoticed causal dimensions of the actions pointed to are brought to conscious attention, illuminating actions in new ways and by that very token recasting previous commonsense understandings in a more complicated fashion. A test of how effective such arguments are will often be whether and to what extent those who have an interest in resisting them are nonetheless compelled to modify their actions and rationalizations, forced to look for ways of coming to terms with them.

Why should the task of the principled critic be thought to revolve

51. This and the preceding examples illustrate why my differences with Walzer are more than semantic; arguments like Marx's and Freud's are ruled out on his account of connected criticism, but it is my contention that they are among the most effective forms of principled criticism.

around placing commonsense beliefs in a wider causal context? The answer is that one of the commonest ways in which practices atrophy into systems of domination is along causal dimensions that are not present in the conscious understandings of agents. Less often for reasons having to do with grand conspiracies built into the scheme of things than Marxists have sometimes thought but more often for sinister reasons than liberals are usually ready to concede, practices atrophy along their darker dimensions. Sometimes conscious understandings are distorted, sometimes intentional actions generate externalities or other by-products that people would find it difficult to live with were they aware of them, sometimes people are driven by unconscious motivations or their conscious actions are conditioned in other ways of which they are unaware, and sometimes there is interplay among several of these and other causal dimensions of actions. In all such cases, what people do not know about the causal dimensions of their actions operates to prevent or undermine their authenticity and inhibits people's ability to know and act on the truth. Good principled criticism credibly illuminates the darker causal dimensions of social practices, thereby expanding the possibilities for authentic action.

On this view it cannot be surprising that some of the social and political theorists who have had the greatest impacts on commonsense understandings and practices—think of Marx and Freud—engaged in principled criticism in the sense just described. They appealed to the truth, to an aspect of the way things allegedly are, and this brought some hitherto opaque dimension of social practices to conscious attention and credibly shed light on the ways in which those practices tend to atrophy. What made the theoretical argument powerful in both cases was that although the causal mechanism was not obvious in its own terms (it required grasping a complex and esoteric theory), the theorist managed to spell out a narrative that connected it to commonsense understandings in ways that cast new light on them. Even though such theories fail qua total explanations of the human condition as they inevitably must,[52] when they contain significant elements of the truth they enhance our understanding of some dimensions of our practices, and this is what gives them and theories like them their appeal.

Of course it is not any or every opaque dimension of an action or practice that the principled critic will seek to analyze and expose. Many physiological dimensions of our actions, for instance, may both be opaque to us and be of little interest from the standpoint of principled criticism, as may be many trivial by-products of our intentional actions. What cen-

52. See chapter 8, section I(ii) and II.

trally concerns the principled critic is those opaque dimensions of actions that are causally implicated in the atrophy of practices into systems of domination. Critical arguments that expose these particular darker dimensions of actions and practices offer the hope of enhanced knowledge that can illuminate major sources of such atrophy. They therefore hold out to the people to whom they are addressed the continuing possibility of authentic action in their dealings with others.

III. Conclusion: The Contemporary Debate and the Revival of the Naturalist Tradition of Political Theory

My story is almost told. Since the late 1960s the revival of first-order political theory has been dominated by a debate between neo-Kantian and contextualist orthodoxies. In one form or another and in a variety of idioms, this debate has consumed a good deal of energy and ink; both sides have criticized their opponents and made a variety of concessions in their own views to accommodate the objections of the other side. As with all such debates, both sides are to a degree co-opted by the terms of reference of what they attack and the resulting arguments begin to look remarkably like one another, professed differences to the contrary notwithstanding. Neo-Kantians like Rawls and Dworkin have contextualized their views, all but abandoning earlier formulations of them, whereas contextualists have increasingly conceded the necessity for some commitments of principle— even if they cannot agree on which—to give the critical enterprise its critical edge.

I have sought to show that the concessions made by these two camps to each other are to a considerable extent beside the point; both are locked into a series of antinaturalist assumptions about human nature, knowledge, and reality that are at the core of their weaknesses. Even Aristotelians like MacIntyre and other latter-day communitarians and traditionalists who draw on aspects of the naturalist tradition have so heavily overlayed these with idealist assumptions that they have lost sight of the foundational commitments that must drive any naturalist account: a view of human nature and human interests and an argument about the injunctions for action this entails given a plausibly defended account of the pertinent causal structure of the social world. The one exception to this that we discovered was in Pocock's account of the civic republican tradition. Although Pocock's analysis was not advanced as political theory, we saw that it contained a causal sociology notably lacking in the arguments of contemporary communitarians and civic republicans. Yet we also saw that the particular causal sociology in Pocock's civic republican tradition turned out on closer inspection to be misleadingly benign. Indeed, whether or not he intended it thus, Pocock's historical description of republican ideology's journey from ancient polis to fee simple empire might usefully be thought of as exposing a paradigm instance of atrophy in my sense.

Much of the debate about foundationalism in recent years, at least in its Anglo-American idiom, has actually been a debate about neo-Kantian foundational views; a variety of failed attempts to defend an implausible deontological foundationalism has made the suggestion that we can somehow get along without foundations appear credible. My goal has been to change the terms of this debate by arguing that, if we are to say anything at all in political theory, a series of naturalist foundational commitments is inescapable but that they must be spelled out and argued for. In *The Evolution of Rights in Liberal Theory*, I argued that the failure to attempt this meant that the neo-Kantians could convince only those who agreed with them before they began, and in the first three parts of this book we have seen that the same is true of their contextualist and historicist critics. Both camps in the foundationalist/contextualist debate gloss over these difficulties by claiming—or at key points assuming—that there is or was or could be a wide consensus about their various undefended assumptions or interpretations of conventional norms, but such claims were seen not to withstand serious scrutiny. In the rare cases where consensus could be argued to exist, we saw that this still did not mean that prevailing beliefs did not stand in need of critical analysis; one person's consensus can often be argued to be another's hegemony.

The question arises, why are political theorists so resistant to defending their assumptions about human nature and the pertinent causal structure of the social world and to making explicit the connections between these assumptions and their normative arguments? The answer is because it is so difficult to say anything on these subjects that is uncontroversial, which implies that would-be philosophical naturalists are in a much tougher intellectual position today than were their predecessors from Aristotle to Marx. We now know so much about how little can be known in the human sciences and about the ways in which human values vary with time and circumstance that every naturalist project in political theory seems fraught with intellectual pitfalls and political dangers. Yet we have seen here that every first-order project in political theory rests on assumptions about human nature and social reality and that denying this fact, or silently acting either as if it was not true or as if such assumptions were uncontroversial, is fraught with no fewer pitfalls or dangers. Taking either of these views is not only misleading; it makes any particular view of politics that one might want to defend instantly vulnerable in its own terms because critics of the view in question have only to point to the existence or controversiality of the undefended assumptions on which it rests.

I have tried to show that a better course involves confronting this fact head on and that the most viable way of doing this involves reviving, adapting, and modifying the naturalist tradition of political theory to make it take better account of what we know today about the world and our place in it, about the nature and limitations of social-scientific knowledge, and about the variety and sources of human values. I have argued that making this commitment need not render us impotent as theorists, and by way of illustration I have sketched some of the main elements of a critical naturalist view of politics whose core commitment is the idea that there is a basic human interest in knowing and acting on the truth. This, I argued, issues in a commitment to a democratic political ethos that can usefully inform both the conduct of political theory as principled criticism and an account of the most appropriate structure of political institutions for human beings. The commitment to a democratic ethos as I have described it generates no guarantees that the world can be made a better place. But any other commitment seems in the end to supply impetus to those forces that are likely to make it worse.

Works Cited

Ackerman, Bruce A. 1980. *Social Justice in the Liberal State.* New Haven: Yale University Press.

——. 1983. *Reconstructing American Law.* Cambridge: Harvard University Press.

Adorno, Theodor W. 1973. *Negative Dialectics.* Translated by E. B. Ashton. New York: Continuum.

Anderson, Benedict. 1983. *Imagined Communities: Reflections on the Origin and Spread of Nationalism.* London: Verso.

Anscombe, G. E. M. 1969. "Modern Moral Philosophy." In *The Is-Ought Question,* ed. W. D. Hudson, 175–95. London: Macmillan.

Appleby, Joyce O. 1976. "Liberalism and the American Revolution." *The New England Quarterly* 49, no. 1:3–26.

——. 1978. *Economic Thought and Ideology in Seventeenth Century England.* Princeton: Princeton University Press.

——. 1982a. "Commercial Farming and the 'Agrarian Myth' in the Early Republic." *Journal of American History* 68:833–49.

——. 1982b. "What Is Still American in the Political Philosophy of Thomas Jefferson." *William and Mary Quarterly,* 3d series, 39:287–309.

——. 1984a. *Capitalism and a New Social Order: The Republican Vision of the 1790's.* New York: New York University Press.

——. 1984b. "The Radical *Double-Entendre* in the Right to Self-Government." In *The Origins of Anglo-American Radicalism,* ed. M. Jacob and J. Jacob, 275–83. London: George Allen and Unwin.

——. 1986. "Republicanism in Old and New Contexts." *William and Mary Quarterly* 43:20–34.

Arendt, Hannah. 1963. *Eichmann in Jerusalem: A Report on the Banality of Evil.* New York: Penguin.

Aristotle. 1977. *The Nicomachean Ethics.* Translated by J. A. K. Thomson. Buckinghamshire, Eng.: Penguin.

————. 1984. *The Politics.* Translated by Carnes Lord. Chicago: University of Chicago Press.

Ashcraft, Richard. 1978. "Ideology and Class in Hobbes' Political Theory." *Political Theory* 6:27–62.

————. 1980. "Revolutionary Politics and Locke's *Two Treatises of Government:* Radicalism and Lockean Political Theory." *Political Theory* 8, no. 4 (November 1980):429–86.

————. 1987. *Locke's Two Treatises of Government.* London: Allen and Unwin.

Ashworth, J. 1984. "The Jeffersonians: Classical Republicans or Liberal Capitalists?" *Journal of American Studies* 18, no. 3:425–35.

Austin, J. L. 1962. *How to Do Things with Words.* Cambridge: Harvard University Press.

Bachrach, Peter, and Baratz, Morton S. 1962. "Two Faces of Power." *American Political Science Review* 56:947–52.

————. 1963. "Decisions and Nondecisions: An Analytical Framework." *American Political Science Review* 57:632–42.

Bailyn, Bernard. 1967. *The Ideological Origins of the American Revolution.* Cambridge: Harvard University Press.

Bambrough, Renford. 1966. "Universals and Family Resemblances," in *Wittgenstein: The Philosophical Investigations,* ed. George Pitcher. London: Macmillan.

Banning, Lance G. 1974. "Republican Ideology and the Triumph of the Constitution." *William and Mary Quarterly,* 3d series, 31:167–88.

————. 1978. *The Jeffersonian Persuasion: Evolution of a Party Ideology.* Ithaca: Cornell University Press.

————. 1986. "Jeffersonian Ideology Revisited: Liberal and Classical Ideas in the New American Republic." *William and Mary Quarterly,* 3d series, 43:3–18.

Barber, Sartorios A. 1984. *On What the Constitution Means.* Baltimore: Johns Hopkins University Press.

Baron, Hans. 1966. *The Crisis of the Early Italian Renaissance.* 2d ed. Princeton: Princeton University Press.

Beer, Samuel. 1984. "Liberty and Union: Walt Whitman's Idea of the Nation." *Political Theory* 12, no. 3:361–86.

Bell, Daniel. 1960. *The End of Ideology.* Cambridge: Harvard University Press.

Bellah, Robert N.; Madsen, Richard; Sullivan, William M.; Swidler, Ann; and Tipton, Steven. 1985. *Habits of the Heart: Individualism and Commitment in American Life.* New York: Harper & Row.

Benhabib, Seyla. 1987. *Critique, Norm and Utopia: A Study on the Foundations of Critical Theory.* New York: Columbia University Press.

Benton, Ted. 1981. "Realism and Social Science: Some Comments on Roy Bhaskar's *The Possibility of Naturalism.*" *Radical Philosophy* 27 (Spring 1981):13–21.

Bernstein, Richard J. 1987. "One Step Forward, Two Steps Backward: Richard Rorty on Liberal Democracy and Philosophy." *Political Theory* 15, no. 4:538–63.

Bhaskar, Roy. 1978. *A Realist Theory of Science*. Sussex: Harvester and Humanities.

———. 1979. *The Possibility of Naturalism*. Sussex: Harvester and Humanities.

———. 1986. *Scientific Realism and Human Emancipation*. London: Verso.

Biersteker, Thomas J. 1978. *Distortion or Development? Contending Perspectives on the Multinational Corporation*. Cambridge: MIT Press.

Blaug, Mark. 1978. *Economic Theory in Retrospect*. 3d ed. Cambridge: Cambridge University Press.

Bloch, Ruth H. 1987. "The Gendered Meanings of Virtue in Revolutionary America." *Signs* 13, no. 1:37–58.

Bloom, Allan. 1968. *The Republic of Plato*. New York: Basic Books.

———. 1969. Editor's introduction to *Introduction to the Reading of Hegel: Lectures on the "Phenomenology of Spirit,"* by Alexander Kojève. New York: Basic Books.

———. 1974a. "Leo Strauss." *Political Theory* 2, no. 4:372–92.

———. 1974b. "The Failure of the University." *Daedalus* 103, no. 4: 58–66.

———. 1975a. "Justice: John Rawls vs. the Tradition of Political Philosophy." *American Political Science Review* 69, no. 2:648–62.

———. 1975b. Review of *The Social Thought of Rousseau and Burke*, by D. Cameron. *Canadian Journal of Political Science* 8, no. 4:573–76.

———. 1980. "The Study of Texts." In *Political Theory and Political Education*, ed. M. Richter. Princeton: Princeton University Press.

———. 1987. *The Closing of the American Mind: How Higher Education Has Failed Democracy and Impoverished the Souls of Today's Students*. New York: Simon and Schuster.

Bloom, Allan, with Jaffa, Harry V. 1964. *Shakespeare's Politics*. New York: Basic Books.

Bloor, David. 1983. *Wittgenstein: A Social Theory of Knowledge*. New York: Columbia University Press.

Boyd, Richard N. 1984. "The Current Status of Scientific Realism." In *Scientific Realism*, ed. Jarrett Leplin. Berkeley: University of California Press, 41–82.

Braybrooke, David. 1987. *Meeting Needs*. Princeton: Princeton University Press.

Buchanan, James, and Tullock, Gordon. 1962. *The Calculus of Consent: Logical Foundations of Constitutional Democracy*. Ann Arbor: Ann Arbor Paperbacks.

Burnyeat, Myles F. 1985. "Sphinx Without a Secret." *New York Review of Books*, May 30, 1985, 30–36.

Burtt, Shelly. 1986. "Private Interest, Public Passion and Patriot Virtue: Comments on a Classical Republican Ideal in English Political Thought." Paper presented at the Folger Institute of Renaissance and Eighteenth-Century Studies, October 23–24, 1986. Mimeo.

Campbell, Blair. 1987. "Paradigms Lost: Classical Athenian Politics in Modern Myth." Paper presented at the 1987 Annual Meeting of the American Political Science Association, Chicago, Illinois.

Cardoso, F. H., and Faletto, E. 1977. *Dependency and Development in Latin America.* Berkeley: University of California Press.

Charvet, John. 1981. *A Critique of Freedom and Equality.* Cambridge: Cambridge University Press.

Chessler, P. 1972. *Women and Madness.* New York: Doubleday.

Chihara, Charles S., and Fodor, J. A. 1966. "Operationalism and Ordinary Language: A Critique of Wittgenstein." In *Wittgenstein: The Philosophical Investigations,* ed. George Pitcher, 384–419. London: Macmillan.

Churchland, Paul M. and Hooker, Clifford A., eds. 1985. *Images of Science.* Chicago: University of Chicago Press.

Cohen, G. A. 1978. "Robert Nozick and Wilt Chamberlain: How Patterns Preserve Liberty." In *Justice and Economic Distribution,* ed. John Arthur and William H. Shaw, 246–62. Englewood Cliffs, N.J.: Prentice-Hall.

———. 1986. "Self-Ownership, World-Ownership, and Equality: Part I." In *Justice and Equality Here and Now,* ed. Frank Lucash, 108–35. Ithaca, N.Y.: Cornell University Press.

———. 1989a. "On the Currency of Egalitarian Justice." *Ethics 99,* 4:906–44.

———. 1989b. "Equality of What? On Welfare, Goods and Capabilities." Mimeo.

Coleman, D. C. 1956. "Labour in the English Economy in the Seventeenth Century." *Economic History Review,* 2d series, 8, no. 3:280–95.

Connolly, William E. 1981. *Appearance and Reality in Politics.* Cambridge: Cambridge University Press.

———. 1983. "The Mirror of America." *Raritan* (Summer 1983): 124–34.

———. 1987. *Politics and Ambiguity.* Madison: University of Wisconsin Press.

Damico, Alfonso J. 1978. *Individual and Community: The Social and Political Thought of John Dewey.* Gainesville: University of Florida Press.

———. 1981. "Dewey and Marx: On Partisanship and the Reconstruction of Society." *American Political Science Review* 75, 3:654–66.

———, ed. 1986. *Liberals on Liberalism.* Totowa: Rowman and Littlefield.

Daniels, Norman, ed. 1975. *Reading Rawls: Critical Studies of A Theory of Justice.* Oxford: Blackwell.

Davidson, Donald. 1968. "Actions, Reasons and Causes." In *The Philosophy of Action*, ed. A. R. White, 79–94. Oxford: Oxford University Press.

Defoe, Daniel. 1690. *Taxes no Charge.*

de Ste. Croix, G. E. M. 1981. *The Class Struggle in the Ancient World, from the Archaic Age to the Arab Conquests.* London: Duckworth.

Devitt, Michael, and Sterelny, Kim. 1987. *Language and Reality.* Cambridge: MIT Press.

Dewey, J. 1929. *Characters and Events: Popular Essays in Social and Political Philosophy*, ed. Joseph Ratner. 2 vols. New York: Henry Holt.

———. 1939. *Freedom and Culture.* New York: Paragon.

———. 1954. *The Public and Its Problems.* Athens: Ohio University Press.

———. 1962. *Individualism Old and New.* New York: Capricorn Books (originally published in 1929).

Dickenson, H. T. 1976. "The Eighteenth-Century Debate on the 'Glorious Revolution.'" *History* 61, no. 201:28–45.

Di Leonardo, Micaela. 1981. "Political Economy of Street Harassment." *Aegis* (Summer 1981):51–57.

DiQuattro, A. 1983. "Rawls and Left Criticism." *Political Theory* 11, no. 1:53–78.

Drury, S. B. 1985. "The Esoteric Philosophy of Leo Strauss." *Political Theory* 13, no. 3:315–37.

Dunn, John. 1969. *The Political Thought of John Locke.* Cambridge: Cambridge University Press.

———. 1979. *Western Political Theory in the Face of the Future.* Cambridge: Cambridge University Press.

Dworetz, Steven M. 1988. *The "Unvarnished Doctrine": Locke, Liberalism and the American Revolution.* Durham: Duke University Press.

Dworkin, Ronald. 1981a. "What is Equality? Part I: Equality of Welfare." *Philosophy and Public Affairs* 10, 3:185–246.

———. 1981b. "What is Equality? Part II: Equality of Resources." *Philosophy and Public Affairs* 10, 4:283–345.

———. 1985. *A Matter of Principle.* Cambridge: Harvard University Press.

———. 1986. *Law's Empire.* Cambridge: Harvard University Press.

Eagleton, Terry. 1985. "Capitalism, Modernism and Postmodernism." *New Left Review* 152 (July/August 1985):60–73.

Edelman, Murray. 1977. *Political Language: Words that Succeed and Policies that Fail.* New York: Academic Press.

———. 1985. "Political Language and Political Reality." *P.S.* 18, no. 1:10–19.

Elshtain, Jean-Bethke. 1981. *Public Man, Private Woman: Women in Social and Political Thought.* Princeton: Princeton University Press.

———. 1985. "The Relationship Between Political Language and Political Reality." *P.S.* 18, no. 1:20–26.

Erikson, Kai. 1989. "Obituary for Big Daddy: A Sociological Parable. Mimeo, Yale University.

Evans, Peter. 1979. *Dependent Development: The Alliance of Multinational, State and Local Capital in Brazil.* Princeton: Princeton University Press.

Feinberg, Joel. 1973. *Social Philosophy.* Englewood Cliffs, N.J.: Prentice-Hall.

Fink, Z. S. 1962. *The Classical Republicans: An Essay in the Recovery of a Pattern of Thought in Seventeenth-Century England.* 2d ed. Evanston: Northwestern University Press.

Finley, M. I. 1973. *The Ancient Economy.* Berkeley: University of California Press.

———. 1983. *Economy and Society in Ancient Greece.* Middlesex: Penguin.

———. 1985. *Democracy Ancient and Modern.* London: Hogarth Press.

Finnis, John. 1980. *Natural Law and Natural Rights.* Oxford: Oxford University Press.

Fishkin, James S. 1979. *Tyranny and Legitimacy: A Critique of Political Theories.* Baltimore: Johns Hopkins University Press.

———. 1982. *The Limits of Obligation.* New Haven: Yale University Press.

Flathman, Richard. 1976. *The Practice of Rights.* Cambridge: Cambridge University Press.

———. 1980. *The Practice of Political Authority.* Chicago: University of Chicago Press.

Foshee, A. W. 1985. "Jeffersonian Political Economy and the Classical Republican Tradition: Jefferson, Taylor, and the Agrarian Republic." *History of Political Economy* 17, no. 4:523–50.

Foucault, Michel. 1980. *Power/Knowledge: Selected Interviews and Other Writings, 1972–1977.* New York: Pantheon.

Friedrich, Carl J., and Brzezinski, Zbigniew K. 1956. *Totalitarian Dictatorship and Autocracy.* New York: Praeger.

Frank, J. 1985. "Camus and the Algerian War." *Dissent* (Winter 1985):105–7.

Frankl, Victor. 1959. *Man's Search for Meaning.* New York: Simon and Schuster.

———. 1975. *The Unconscious God.* New York: Simon and Schuster.

———. 1978. *The Unheard Cry for Meaning.* New York: Simon and Schuster.

Furniss, Norman. 1978. "The Political Implications of the Public Choice–

Property Rights School." *American Political Science Review* 72, no. 2:399–410.

Gadamer, H. 1986. *The Idea of the Good in Platonic-Aristotelian Philosophy.* Translated by C. P. Smith. New Haven: Yale University Press.

Gallie, Bernard. 1955. "Essentially Contested Concepts." *Proceedings of the Aristotelian Society* 56:167–98.

———. 1956. "Liberal Morality and Socialist Morality." In *Philosophy, Politics and Society,* ed. Peter Laslett, 116–33. Oxford: Blackwell.

Galston, William A. 1980. *Justice and the Human Good.* Chicago: University of Chicago Press.

———. 1983. "Defending Liberalism." *American Political Science Review* 76, no. 3:621–29.

Genovese, Eugene D. 1971. *The World the Slaveholders Made: Two Essays in Interpretation.* New York: Random House.

———. 1972. *Roll, Jordan Roll: The World the Slaves Made.* New York: Random House.

Geuss, Raymond. 1981. *The Idea of a Critical Theory: Habermas and the Frankfurt School.* Cambridge: Cambridge University Press.

Garvin, Harry R., ed. 1980. *Romanticism, Modernism, Postmodernism.* Lewisburg: Bucknell University Press.

Gewirth, Alan. 1982. *Human Rights: Essays on Justification and Applications.* Chicago: University of Chicago Press.

Giddens, Anthony. 1976. *New Rules of Sociological Method: A Positive Critique of Interpretative Sociologies.* London: Hutchinson.

———. 1981. *A Contemporary Critique of Historical Materialism.* Berkeley: University of California Press.

Gill, Emily R. 1985. "Goods, Virtues and the Constitution of the Self." Paper presented at the annual meeting of the American Political Science Association, New Orleans, August 29–September 1, 1985.

Goodale, Jesse R. 1980. "J. G. A. Pocock's Neo-Harringtonians: A Reconsideration." *History of Political Thought* 1, no. 2:237–59.

Grant, Ruth. 1985. "Locke's Political Anthropology and Lockean Individualism." Paper presented at annual meeting of the American Political Science Association, New Orleans, September 1985.

Greenberg, K. S. 1977. "Representation and the Isolation of South Carolina, 1776–1860." *Journal of American History* 64, no. 3:723–43.

Greenstone, J. David. 1986. "Political Culture and American Political Development: Liberty, Union and the Liberal Bipolarity." In *Studies in American Political Development,* ed. Karen Orren and Stephen Skowronek. New Haven, Conn.: Yale University Press. Vol. 1, 1–49.

Gunnell, John. 1978. "The Myth of The Tradition." *American Political Science Review* 72, no. 1:122–34.

———. 1985. "Political Theory and Politics: The Case of Leo Strauss." *Political Theory* 13, no. 3:339–61.

Gussfield, Joseph R. 1975. *Community: A Critical Response*. Oxford: Blackwell.

Gutmann, Amy. 1985. "Communitarian Critics of Liberalism." *Philosophy and Public Affairs* 14, no. 3:308–22.

Habermas, Jürgen. 1968. *Knowledge and Human Interests*. Boston: Beacon Press.

———. 1973. *Theory and Practice*. Boston: Beacon Press.

———. 1976. *Communication and the Evolution of Society*. Translated by Thomas McCarthy. Boston: Beacon Press.

———. 1984. *The Theory of Communicative Action*, vol. 1, *Reason and the Rationalization of Society*. Translated by Thomas McCarthy. Boston: Beacon Press.

———. 1987. *The Philosophical Discourse of Modernity*. Translated by Frederick Lawrence. Cambridge: MIT Press.

Hare, R. M. 1952. *The Language of Morals*. Oxford: Oxford University Press.

———. 1963. *Freedom and Reason*. Oxford: Oxford University Press.

Harpham, E. J. 1984. "Liberalism, Civic Humanism and the Case of Adam Smith." *American Political Science Review* 78, no. 3:764–74.

Harré, R. 1975. *The Principles of Scientific Thinking*. Chicago: University of Chicago Press.

Harrington, James. 1977. *The Political Works of James Harrington*, ed. J. G. A. Pocock. Cambridge: Cambridge University Press.

Hart, H. L. A. 1961. *The Concept of Law*. Oxford: Oxford University Press.

Hartz, Louis. 1955. *The Liberal Tradition in America: An Interpretation of American Political Thought Since the Revolution*. New York: Harcourt Brace Jovanovich.

Haskins, George L. 1960. *Law and Authority in Early Massachusetts: A Study in Tradition and Design*. New York: University Press of America.

Hayek, Friedrich A. 1976. *Law, Legislation and Liberty*, vol. 2, *The Mirage of Social Justice*. Chicago: University of Chicago Press.

Hegel, G. W. F. 1977. *Hegel's Phenomenology of Spirit*. Translated by A. V. Miller. Oxford: Oxford University Press.

Herzog, Don. 1985. *Without Foundations: Justification in Political Theory*. Ithaca: Cornell University Press.

———. 1986. "Some Questions for Republicans." *Political Theory* 14, no. 3:473–94.

Hirsch, Harry N. 1986. "The Threnody of Liberalism: Constitutional Liberty and the Renewal of Community." *Political Theory* 14, no. 3:423–50.

Hobbes, Thomas. 1968. *Leviathan*. London: Pelican.

Horney, Karen. 1937. *The Collected Works of Karen Horney*. 2 vols. New York: W. W. Norton.

————. 1967. *Feminine Psychology*. New York: W. W. Norton.

Horton, Robin. 1970. "African Traditional Thought and Western Science." In *Rationality*, ed. Bryan R. Wilson, 131–71. New York: Harper & Row.

Isaac, Jeffrey C. 1987a. *Power and Marxist Theory*. Ithaca: Cornell University Press.

————. 1987b. "On the Subject of Political Theory." *Political Theory* 15, no. 4:639–45.

————. 1988. "Republicanism vs. Liberalism: A Reinterpretation." *History of Political Thought*. In press.

Jameson, Fredric. 1984. "Postmodernism, or the Cultural Logic of Capitalism." *New Left Review* 146 (July 1984):53–92.

Jencks, Christopher. 1985. "How Poor are the Poor?" *New York Review of Books*, May 9, 1985, 41–48.

Kamenka, Eugene. 1969. *Marxism and Ethics*. London: Macmillan.

Kane, John. 1982. *Justice and the Good: The Logical Priority of Conceptions of the Good in Arguments of Right and Justice*. Ph.D. diss., London School of Economics.

Kant, Immanuel. 1970. *Kant's Political Writings*. Edited by H. Reiss and translated by H. B. Nisbet. Cambridge: Cambridge University Press.

Kateb, George. 1984. "Democratic Individuality and the Claims of Politics." *Political Theory* 12, no. 3:331–60.

Kaufman-Osborn, Timothy. 1984. "John Dewey and the Science of Community." *The Journal of Politics* 46, no. 4:1142–65.

————. 1985. "Pragmatism, Policy Science and the State." *American Journal of Political Science* 29, no. 4:827–49.

Keat, R., and Urry, J. 1975. *Social Theory as Science*. London: Routledge and Kegan Paul.

Kenyon, J. P., ed. 1966. *The Stuart Constitution, 1603–1688*, Cambridge: Cambridge University Press.

Kermode, Frank. 1967. *The Sense of an Ending: Studies in the Theory of Fiction*. New York: Oxford University Press.

Ketcham, Ralph. 1974. *From Colony to Country: The Revolution in American Thought, 1750–1820*. New York: Macmillan.

————. 1984. *Presidents Above Party: The First American Presidency, 1789–1828*. Chapel Hill: University of North Carolina Press.

Kloppenberg, James. 1986. *Uncertain Victory: Social Democracy and Progressivism in European and American Thought, 1870–1920*. Oxford: Oxford University Press.

————. 1987. "The Virtues of Liberalism." *American Historical Review*. In press.

Klosko, George. 1986. "The 'Straussian' Interpretation of Plato's Republic." *History of Political Thought*, no. 2:275–93.

Kojève, Alexander. 1969. *Introduction to the Reading of Hegel*, ed. A. Bloom. New York: Basic Books.

Kramnick, Isaac. 1968. *Bolingbroke and His Circle: The Politics of Nostalgia in the Age of Walpole*. Cambridge: Harvard University Press.

———. 1982. "Republican Revisionism Revisited." *American Historical Review* 86:629–64.

Kuhn, Thomas S. 1962. *The Structure of Scientific Revolutions*. Chicago: University of Chicago Press.

Kuklick, B. 1984. "Seven Thinkers and How They Grew: Descartes, Spinoza, Leibniz, Locke, Berkeley, Hume, Kant," In *Philosophy in History*, ed. Richard Rorty, J. B. Schneewind, and Quentin Skinner, 125–39. Cambridge: Cambridge University Press.

Laclau, Ernesto, and Mouffe, Chantal. 1985. *Hegemony and Socialist Strategy: Toward a Radical Democratic Politics*. New York: Verso.

Lakatos, I., and Musgrave, A., eds. 1970. *Criticism and the Growth of Knowledge*. Cambridge: Cambridge University Press.

Lasch, Christopher. 1990. *Hope Against Hope: The Idea of Progress and Its Critics*. New York: Norton. Forthcoming.

Lindblom, Charles E. 1977. *Politics and Markets: The World's Political-Economic Systems*. New York: Basic Books.

Locke, John. 1963. *Two Treatises of Government*, ed. Peter Laslett. Cambridge: Cambridge University Press.

Lukes, Steven. 1974. *Power: A Radical View*. London: Macmillan.

Lyotard, Jean-François. 1984. *The Postmodern Condition: A Report on Knowledge*. Translated by Geoff Bennington and Brian Massumi. Minneapolis: University of Minnesota Press.

MacCallum, J. R. 1972. "Negative and Positive Freedom." In *Philosophy, Politics and Society*, ed. Peter Laslett, W. G. Runciman, and Quentin Skinner, 4th series, 174–93. Oxford: Blackwell.

McCoy, Drew. 1974. "Republicanism and American Foreign Policy: James Madison and the Political Economy of Commercial Discrimination, 1789–1794." *William and Mary Quarterly*, 3d series, 31:633–46.

———. 1980. *The Elusive Republic: Political Economy in Jeffersonian America*. Chapel Hill: University of North Carolina Press.

MacIntyre, Alasdair. 1966. *A Short History of Ethics*. London: Routledge and Kegan Paul.

———. 1968. *Marxism and Christianity*. New York: Schocken Books.

———. 1977. "Epistemological Crises, Dramatic Narrative and the Philosophy of Science." *The Monist* 60:453–72.

———. 1984. *After Virtue*. 2d ed. Notre Dame: University of Notre Dame Press.

———. 1988. *Whose Justice? Which Rationality?* Notre Dame: University of Notre Dame Press.

Macpherson, C. B. 1968. *The Political Theory of Possessive Individualism: Hobbes to Locke*. Oxford: Oxford University Press.

Manicas, Peter T. 1983. "Reduction, Epigenesis and Explanation." *Journal for the Theory of Social Behavior* 13, no. 3:331–54.

Mannheim, Karl. 1968. *Ideology and Utopia: An Introduction to the Sociology of Knowledge.* New York: Harcourt, Brace.

Marcuse, Herbert. 1965. "Repressive Tolerance." In *A Critique of Pure Tolerance,* ed. Robert Paul Wolff, Barrington Moore, Jr., and Herbert Marcuse. Boston: Beacon Press.

Marmor, Theodore. 1967. "Anti-Industrialism and the Old South: The Agrarian Perspective of John C. Calhoun." *Comparative Studies in Society and History* 9, no. 4:377–406.

Marx, Karl. 1974. *Capital.* Vol. 1. London: Lawrence and Wishart.

Michelman, Frank I. 1986. "The Supreme Court 1985 Term Foreword: Traces of Self-Government." *Harvard Law Review* 100, no. 1:4–77.

Mill, John Stuart. 1971. *Utilitarianism,* ed. Samuel Gorovitz. Indianapolis: Bobbs Merrill.

———. 1974. *On Liberty.* London: Pelican.

Miller, Richard W. 1987. *Fact and Method: Explanation, Confirmation and Reality in the Natural and the Social Sciences.* Princeton, N.J.: Princeton University Press.

Montesquieu, Baron de. 1949. *The Spirit of the Laws.* Translated by Thomas Nugent. New York: Haffner.

Moore, Michael. 1982. "Moral Reality." *Wisconsin Law Review* 82:1061–1156.

Mueller, Dennis C. 1979. *Public Choice.* Cambridge: Cambridge University Press.

Murray, Charles. 1985. *Losing Ground: American Social Policy, 1950–1980.* New York: Basic Books.

Nelson, John R. 1988. *Liberty and Property: Political Economy and Policymaking in the New Nation, 1789–1812.* Baltimore: Johns Hopkins University Press.

Newell, W. R. 1984. "Heidegger on Freedom and the Community: Some Political Implications of His Early Thought." *American Political Science Review* 78, no. 3:775–84.

Niebuhr, Reinhold. 1960. *Moral Man and Immoral Society.* New York: Charles Scribner's Sons.

Nozick, Robert. 1974. *Anarchy State and Utopia.* Oxford: Blackwell.

Nussbaum, Martha. 1987. "Undemocratic Vistas." *New York Review of Books.* November 5, 1987, 20–26.

Okin, Susan M. 1979. *Women in Western Political Thought.* Princeton: Princeton University Press.

Panitch, Leo. 1977. "The Development of Corporatism in Liberal Democracies." *Comparative Political Studies* (April 1977):61–90.

Parker, R. B. 1979. "The Jurisprudential Uses of John Rawls." In *Constitutionalism,* ed. J. R. Pennock and J. W. Chapman, 269–95. New York: New York University Press.

Phillips, Kevin P. 1982. *Post-Conservative America: People, Politics and Ideology in a Time of Crisis.* New York: Vintage.

Pigou, A. C. 1960. *The Economics of Welfare*. London: Macmillan.

Pitkin, Hanna F. 1972. *Wittgenstein and Justice: On the Significance of Ludwig Wittgenstein for Social and Political Thought*. Berkeley and Los Angeles: University of California Press.

Pocock, J. G. A. 1957. *The Ancient Constitution and the Feudal Law*. Cambridge: Cambridge University Press.

———. 1975a. *The Machiavellian Moment: Florentine Political Thought and the Atlantic Republican Tradition*. Princeton: Princeton University Press.

———. 1975b. "Early Modern Capitalism—the Augustan Perception." In *Feudalism, Capitalism and Beyond*, ed. Eugene Kamenka and R. S. Neale, 63–83. Canberra: Australian National University Press.

———. 1981a. "The Machiavellian Moment Revisited: A Study in History and Ideology." *Journal of Modern History* 53, no. 1:49–72.

———. 1981b. "Virtues, Rights and Manners: A Model for Historians of Political Thought." *Political Theory* 9, no. 3:353–68.

———. 1984. "Verbalizing a Political Act: Towards a Politics of Speech." In *Language and Politics*, ed. M. J. Shapiro, 25–43. Oxford: Blackwell.

———. 1985. *Virtue, Commerce and History*. Cambridge: Cambridge University Press.

Polanyi, Michael. 1966. *The Tacit Dimension*. New York: Doubleday.

Posner, Richard A. 1981. *The Economics of Justice*. Cambridge: Harvard University Press.

Quine, W. V. 1953. "Two Dogmas of Empiricism." In *From a Logical Point of View: Logico-Philosophical Essays*, 20–46. New York: Harper Torchbooks.

Rae, Douglas W. 1969. "Decision-Rules and Individual Values in Constitutional Choice." *American Political Science Review* 63, no. 1:40–56.

———. 1975. "Maximin Justice and an Alternative Principle of General Advantage." *American Political Science Review* 69, no. 2:630–47.

———. 1979. "A Principle of Simple Justice." In *Philosophy, Politics and Society*, ed. Peter Laslett and James Fishkin, 5th series, 134–54. New Haven: Yale University Press.

Rae, D., et al. 1981. *Equalities*. Cambridge: Harvard University Press.

Rapaczynski, Andrzej. 1987. *Nature and Politics: Liberalism in the Philosophies of Hobbes, Locke and Rousseau*. Ithaca: Cornell University Press.

Rawls, John. 1962. "Justice as Fairness." In *Philosophy, Politics and Society*, ed. Peter Laslett and W. G. Runciman, 135–57. Oxford: Blackwell. Reprinted from *Philosophical Review* (1958).

———. 1971. *A Theory of Justice*. Cambridge: Harvard University Press.

———. 1980. "Kantian Constructivism in Moral Theory." *The Journal of Philosophy* 78, no. 9:515–72.

———. 1982. "Social Utility and Primary Goods." In *Utilitarianism and Beyond,* ed. Amartya Sen and Bernard Williams, 159–85. Cambridge: Cambridge University Press.

———. 1985. "Justice as Fairness: Political not Metaphysical." *Philosophy and Public Affairs* 14, no. 3:223–51.

Riesenberg, P. N. 1969. "Civism and Roman Law in Fourteenth-Century Italian Society." *Explorations in Economic History* 7, nos. 1–2:237–54.

Riley, Patrick. 1982. *Will and Political Legitimacy.* Cambridge: Harvard University Press.

Rorty, Richard. 1979. *Philosophy and the Mirror of Nature.* Princeton: Princeton University Press.

———. 1982. *Consequences of Pragmatism, Essays: 1972–80.* Minneapolis: University of Minnesota Press.

———. 1980. "A Reply to Dreyfus and Taylor." *Review of Metaphysics,* no. 34 (September 1980):39–55.

———. 1983. "Postmodernist Bourgeois Liberalism." *The Journal of Philosophy* 80, no. 10:583–89.

———. 1984a. "Solidarity or Objectivity?" *Nanzan Review of American Studies* 6:1–19.

———. 1984b. "Habermas and Lyotard on Postmodernity." *Praxis International* 4, no. 1:32–44.

———. 1984c. "Science as Solidarity." Paper presented at Yale Legal Theory Workshop, November 1984. Mimeo.

———. 1986a. "The Contingency of Language." *London Review of Books,* April 17, 1986, 3–6.

———. 1986b. "The Contingency of Selfhood." *London Review of Books,* May 8, 1986, 11–15.

———. 1986c. "The Contingency of Community." *London Review of Books,* July 24, 1986, 10–14.

———. 1987a. "Thugs and Theorists: A Reply to Bernstein." *Political Theory* 15, no. 4:564–80.

———. 1987b. "Method, Social Science and Social Hope." In *Interpreting Politics,* ed. Michael T. Gibbons, 241–59. New York: New York University Press.

———. 1988. "The Priority of Democracy to Philosophy." In *The Virginia Statute for Religious Freedom,* ed. Merrill Peterson and Robert Vaughan, 257–82. Cambridge: Cambridge University Press.

Rorty, Richard; Schneewind, J. B.; and Skinner, Quentin, eds. 1984. *Philosophy in History.* Cambridge: Cambridge University Press.

Rosenblum, Nancy L. 1984. "Moral Membership in a Postliberal State." *World Politics* 36, no. 4:581–96.

———. 1987. *Another Liberalism: Romanticism and the Reconstruction of Liberal Thought.* Cambridge: Harvard University Press.

Rousseau, Jean-Jacques. 1964. *The First and Second Discourses,* ed. Roger

D. Masters. Translated by Roger D. Masters and Judith R. Masters. New York: St. Martins Press.

Rudolph, Lloyd I., and Rudolph, Susanne H. 1967. *The Modernity of Tradition: Political Development in India.* Chicago: University of Chicago Press.

Russell, Bertrand. 1963. *A History of Western Philosophy.* London: Allen and Unwin.

Sabel, Charles, and Zeitlin, Jonathan. "Historical Alternatives of Mass Production: Politics, Markets and Technology in Nineteenth-Century Industrialization." *Past and Present,* no. 108 (August 1985):133–76.

Sandel, Michael J. 1982. *Liberalism and the Limits of Justice.* Cambridge: Cambridge University Press.

———. 1984a. "The Procedural Republic and the Unencumbered Self." *Political Theory* 12, no. 1:81–96.

———. 1984b. "Introduction." In *Liberalism and its Critics,* ed. Michael Sandel, 1–11. New York: New York University Press.

Saxonhouse, Arlene. 1986. "From Tragedy to Hierarchy and Back Again: Women in Greek Political Thought." *American Political Science Review* 80, no. 2:403–18.

Schofield, Norman. 1972. "Is Majority Rule Special?" In *Probability Models of Collective Decision Making,* ed. Richard G. Niemi and Herbert F. Weisberg, 60–80. Columbus, Ohio: Merrill.

Schumpeter, Joseph A. 1942. *Capitalism, Socialism and Democracy.* New York: Harper.

Shalhope, Robert E. 1976. "Thomas Jefferson's Republicanism and Antebellum Southern Thought." *Journal of Southern History* 42:532–56.

———. 1982. "Republicanism and Early American Historiography." *William and Mary Quarterly* 39:334–56.

Shapiro, Ian. 1981. "Fiscal Crisis of the Polish State: Genesis of the 1980 Strikes." *Theory and Society* 10, no. 4:469–502.

———. 1982. "Realism in the Study of the History of Ideas." *History of Political Thought* 3, no. 3:535–78.

———. 1986. *The Evolution of Rights in Liberal Theory.* New York: Cambridge University Press.

———. 1987. "Richard Posner's Praxis." *Ohio State Law Journal* 48, no. 4:999–1047.

———. 1988. "A Comment on John Harsanyi's 'Democracy, Equality, and Popular Consent.'" In *Power, Inequality, and Democratic Politics: Essays in Honor of Robert Dahl,* ed. Ian Shapiro and Grant Reeher, 284–90. Boulder: Westview Press.

———. 1989a. "Gross Concepts in Political Argument." *Political Theory* 17, no. 1:51–76.

———. 1989b. "Three Fallacies Concerning Majorities, Minorities, and Democratic Politics." In *NOMOS XXXII: Majorities and Minorities,*

Political and Philosophical Perspectives, ed. John Chapman and Alan Wertheimer. New York: New York University Press. Forthcoming.

———. 1989c. "Constructing Politics." *Political Theory* 17, no. 3 (August 1989):475–82.

Shapiro, Ian, and Kane, John. 1983. "Stagflation and the New Right." *Telos,* no. 56:5–39.

Shils, Edward. 1981. *Tradition.* Chicago: University of Chicago Press.

Shklar, Judith. 1987. *Montesquieu.* Oxford: Oxford University Press.

Sikora, R. I., and Barry, Brian, eds. 1978. *Obligations to Future Generations.* Philadelphia: Temple University Press.

Sirianni, C. 1981. "Production and Power in a Classless Society: A Critical Analysis of the Utopian Dimensions of Marxist Theory." *Socialist Review,* no. 59 (September/October 1981):33–82.

Skinner, Quentin. 1969. "Meaning and Understanding in the History of Ideas." *History and Theory,* no. 8:3–53.

———. 1972. "The Context of Hobbes' Theory of Political Obligation." In *Hobbes and Rousseau: A Collection of Critical Essays,* ed. Maurice Cranston and R. S. Peters, 109–142. New York: Doubleday.

———. 1973. "The Empirical Theorists of Democracy and Their Critics: A Plague on Both Their Houses." *Political Theory* 1, no. 3:287–306.

———. 1975. "Hermeneutics and the Role of History." *New Literary History,* no. 7:209–32.

———. 1978. *The Foundations of Modern Political Thought,* vol. 1, *The Renaissance,* vol. 2, *The Age of Reformation.* Cambridge: Cambridge University Press.

———, ed. 1985. *The Return of Grand Theory in the Human Sciences.* Cambridge: Cambridge University Press.

———. 1988. "A Reply to My Critics." In *Meaning and Context: Quentin Skinner and His Critics,* ed. James Tully, 231–88. Princeton: Princeton University Press.

Smith, Rogers M. 1985. *Liberalism and American Constitutional Law.* Cambridge: Harvard University Press.

———. 1988. "After Criticism: An Analysis of the Critical Legal Studies Movement." In *Judging the Constitution,* ed. Michael McCann and Gerald Houseman, 92–124. New York: Little, Brown and Co.

Smith, Steven B. 1987. "Hegel's Idea of a Critical Theory." *Political Theory* 15, no. 1:99–126.

———. 1989. *Hegel's Critique of Liberalism: Rights in Context.* Chicago: University of Chicago Press.

Stepan, Alfred J. 1978. *The State and Society: Peru in Comparative Perspective.* Princeton University Press.

Stevenson, Charles L. 1944. *Ethics and Language.* New Haven: Yale University Press.

Strauss, Leo. 1952. *Persecution and the Art of Writing.* Westport, Conn.: Greenwood Press.

———. 1953. *Natural Right and History.* Chicago: University of Chicago Press.

———. 1959. *What is Political Philosophy?* Westport, Conn.: Greenwood Press.

———. 1964. *The City and Man.* Chicago: University of Chicago Press.

Stourzh, Gerald. 1970. *Alexander Hamilton and the Idea of Republican Government.* Stanford: Stanford University Press.

Swann, William B. 1989. "To Be Adored or to Be Known? The Interplay of Self-Enhancement and Self-Verification." In *Motivation and Cognition,* ed. R. M. Sorrentino and E. T. Higgins. New York: Guilford. In press.

Tarcov, Nathan. 1982. "Quentin Skinner's Method and Machiavelli's Prince." *Ethics* 92:692–709.

———. 1983. "Philosophy and History: Tradition and Interpretation in the Work of Leo Strauss." *Polity* 16, no. 1:5–29.

Taylor, A. E. 1965. "The Ethical Doctrine of Hobbes." In *Hobbes Studies,* ed. K. C. Brown, 35–55. Cambridge: Harvard University Press.

Taylor, Charles. 1979. *Hegel and Modern Society.* Cambridge: Cambridge University Press.

Thigpen, R. B., and Downing, Lyle A. 1983. "Liberalism and the Neutrality Principle." *Political Theory* 11, no. 4:585–600.

Thomson, M. S. 1982. "Ben Butler versus the Brahmins: Patronage and Politics in Early Gilded Age Massachusetts." *The New England Quarterly* 55:163–86.

Timmons, Mark. 1987. "Foundationalism and the Structure of Ethical Justification." *Ethics* 97, no. 3:595–609.

Tocqueville, Alexis de. 1969. *Democracy in America.* New York: Doubleday.

Toulmin, Stephen E. 1953. *An Examination of the Place of Reason in Ethics.* Cambridge: Cambridge University Press.

———. 1970. "Does the Distinction between Normal and Revolutionary Science Hold Water?" In *Criticism and the Growth of Knowledge,* ed. I. Lakatos and A. Musgrave, 39–47. Cambridge: Cambridge University Press.

Trenchard. 1969. *Cato's Letters or, Essays on Liberty, Civil and Religious, and Other Important Subjects.* 4 vols. New York: Russell and Russell.

Tuck, Richard. 1979. *Natural Rights Theories: Their Origin and Development.* Cambridge: Cambridge University Press.

Tully, James. 1980. *A Discourse on Property: John Locke and His Adversaries.* Cambridge: Cambridge University Press.

Turnbull, Colin. 1973. *The Mountain People.* London: Cape.

Unger, Roberto Mangaberia. 1987. *Politics: A Work in Constructive Social Theory,* vol. 1, *Social Theory: Its Situation and Its Task,* vol. 2, *False Necessity: Anti-Necessitarian Social Theory in the Service of Radical Democracy,* vol. 3, *Plasticity into Power: Comparative-Historical Studies of the Institutional Conditions of Economic and Military Success.* New York: Cambridge University Press.

Wallach, J. 1983. Review of *After Virtue,* by Alasdair MacIntyre. *Telos,* no. 57:233–40.

Walzer, Michael. 1983a. *Spheres of Justice: A Defense of Pluralism and Equality.* New York: Basic Books.

———. 1983b. "The Politics of Michel Foucault." *Dissent* (Fall 1983): 481–90.

———. 1984a. "Liberalism and the Art of Separation." *Political Theory* 12, no. 3:315–30.

———. 1984b. "Commitment and Social Criticism: Camus's Algerian War." *Dissent* (Fall 1984):424–32.

———. 1987. *Interpretation and Social Criticism.* Cambridge: Harvard University Press.

———. 1988. *The Company of Critics: Social Criticism and Political Commitment in the Twentieth Century.* New York: Basic Books.

Warnke, Georgia. 1987. *Gadamer: Hermeneutics, Tradition and Reason.* Stanford: Stanford University Press.

Weinreb, Lloyd L. 1987. *Natural Law and Justice.* Cambridge: Harvard University Press.

Weinstein, James. 1967. *The Decline of Socialism in America.* 1st ed. New Brunswick: Rutgers University Press.

Weir, R. M. 1969. "'The Harmony We Were Famous For': An Interpretation of Pre-Revolutionary South Carolina Politics." *William and Mary Quarterly,* 3d series, 26:473–501.

Wellbank, J. H.; Snook, D.; and Mason, T. D., comps. 1982. *John Rawls and His Critics: An Annotated Bibliography.* New York: Garland.

Wiles, R. C. 1968. "The Theory of Wages in Later English Mercantilism." *Economic History Review,* 2d series, no. 21:113–26.

Williams, Bernard. 1980. "Political Philosophy and the Analytical Tradition." In *Political Theory and Political Education,* ed. Melvin Richter, 57–75. Princeton: Princeton University Press.

———. 1985. *Ethics and the Limits of Philosophy.* Cambridge: Harvard University Press.

Winch, Donald. 1980. *Adam Smith's Politics: An Essay in Historiographic Revision.* Cambridge: Cambridge University Press.

———. 1985. "Economic Liberalism as Ideology: The Appleby Version." *Economic History Review* 38, no. 2:287–97.

Winch, Peter. 1958. *The Idea of a Social Science.* London: Routledge and Kegan Paul.

Wittgenstein, Ludwig. 1953. *Philosophical Investigations*. Oxford: Black-well.

Wolff, Robert Paul. 1970. *In Defense of Anarchism*. New York: Harper & Row.

Wood, G. S. 1966. "Rhetoric and Reality in the American Revolution." *William and Mary Quarterly,* 3d series, 23:3–32.

———. 1969. *The Creation of the American Republic*. New York: W. W. Norton.

Yack, Bernard. 1985. "Community and Conflict in Aristotle's Political Philosophy." *The Review of Politics* 47, no. 1:92–112.

Index

Compositor:	Graphic Composition, Inc.
Text:	10/13 Aldus
Display:	Aldus
Printer:	Edwards Brothers, Inc.
Binder:	Edwards Brothers, Inc.